I0889066

PITTSBURGH THEOLOGICAL MONOGRAPH SERIES

General Editor

Dikran Y. Hadidian

18

JESUS CHRIST AND THE FAITH

A Collection of Studies

JESUS CHRIST and the FAITH

A Collection of Studies

by
PHILIPPE H. MENOUD

Translated
by
EUNICE M. PAUL

PICKWICK *Publications* • Eugene, Oregon

Originally published as *Jésus - Christ et la Foi.*
1975, Delachaux et Niestlé.

Pickwick Publications
An imprint of Wipf and Stock Publishers
199 W 8th Ave, Suite 3
Eugene, OR 97401

Jesus Christ and the Faith
A Collection of Studies
By Menoud, Philippe H. and Cullman, Oscar
Copyright©1978 Pickwick
ISBN 13: 978-0-915138-22-7
Publication date 6/7/2015
Previously published by , 1978

CONTENTS

IV. ASPECTS OF NEW TESTAMENT THEOLOGY

PREFACE

Jacques Rigaud in his review of *Jésus Christ et la Foi*[1] expressed the opinion that the clarity of Menoud's language and the soundness of his biblical commentary, the high standard of his scholarship and its technical skill must make his work valuable to any lover of the Scriptures. For one not a biblical scholar to attempt a translation of this work would seem audacious, but if we can succeed in some measure in making Menoud's work available where it would otherwise be unknown it is because of the qualities outlined by Monsieur Rigaud.

The volume is a collection of the works of Philippe Menoud which was prepared for publication by his colleagues after his untimely death. For this reason it has the spontaneity and liveliness of a work which has not been revised too often by its author. But there is the inevitable repetition of ideas and phrases always to be found in a collection of this kind. However, there has been no attempt to edit the works as this would remove the personality of their author from them and would detract considerably from their interest. The volume is a tribute to Philippe Menoud the man as well as to Philippe Menoud the scholar and exegete.

The biblical quotations used throughout the translation do not correspond to any particular version of the Bible. Menoud himself was not specific on this point and we have tried to interpret the French version according to the particular point which Menoud wished to make. Where errors were found in the biblical references, these have been corrected.

Thanks are due to several scholars for their assistance on technical points which were outside my knowledge: Virgil Cruz, Paul K. Jewett, Douglas R. A. Hare, and particularly Dikran Y. Hadidian. I am also grateful to Martin Paul and Timothy Paul who helped to Americanize my English idiom, and particularly to my husband, Robert, not only for his help and advice with the manuscript but also for his patience and understanding during this fascinating but time-consuming task.

Eunice Paul
Austin, Texas
1978

1. *Centre Protestant d'Etudes et de Documentation,* Nouvelle Série, no. 207, Janvier, 1976, p. 58.

FOREWORD

This volume in the series *Bibliothèque théologique* offers to our readers a selection of New Testament studies from the pen of Professor Philippe H. Menoud, who died at Neuchâtel on November 24, 1973.[1]

As an introduction to these essays, which have already appeared in various journals and special collections, we are reprinting (with the kind permission of Professor Jean-Louis Leuba) the lines which he wrote in honor of his colleague and friend in the columns of the *Feuille d'Avis* of Neuchâtel on November 27, 1973. We have asked another of Philippe Menoud's friends and colleagues, Professor Oscar Cullmann to recall him as an exegete and as a historian of early Christianity. We should like to thank Oscar Cullmann and Jean-Louis Leuba for their cooperation.

This work is dedicated to all those who have known, loved, and appreciated the teaching of Philippe Menoud, and also to those who, as they read these pages, will be interested, perhaps fascinated, by his lucidity, his precision and the continual evidence of a profound yet gentle faith.

Les Editions Delachaux et Niestlé

---

[1]Philippe H. Menoud, Professor of New Testament in the Faculty of Theology at Neuchâtel, was one of the founding members of the theological committee for our *Editions*; his name is prominent also in the list of those works which we publish in the field of biblical theology.

We are grateful to the editors who have given us permission to reproduce the studies by Philippe Menoud which appeared in their journals and collections as well as to the management of the *Feuille d'Avis* of Neuchâtel which consented to our reprinting the article by Jean-Louis Leuba.

INTRODUCTIONS

Philippe H. Menoud - the Man and the Friend

With the death of Philippe Menoud we have lost a man of rare quality, of keen sensibility and of intellectual and Christian influence which was all the more powerful as it was unobtrusive and unpretentious. An influence so unobtrusive that sometimes it could be misjudged. A flash of his ruthlessly clear mind would hide the distress he would feel at not being able to refrain from noting stupidity, incompetence, or unworthiness and naming them as such. But in any conversation with him, his most fundamental characteristic would surface, namely kindness and fellow-feeling toward those who are not afraid of frankness and honesty.

Menoud was an exegete well-trained by Maurice Goguel in Paris, then at Union Theological Seminary in New York, where he received his doctorate in 1930, at the early age of 25. Menoud brought to the service of New Testament study philological and historical disciplines as he understood them--his goal being to find out what actually happened and not to fantasize on what might have happened. More remarkable perhaps is the fact that this very scientific approach often enabled him to bring out more clearly than others, who were more preoccupied with "enlightenment" or "relevance", the power of the Gospel to regulate life and provide an ultimate finality more durable than the fleeting ideologies of current gospel trends, political or otherwise. His peers made no mistake about him.

They reserved for him, on the international level, a high place which brings honor to our town and to its University.

This combination of a scientific approach and firm faith can be found in all the writings he left for us on the subject of the life of the infant Church, about its relationship to the Jewish faith, about the work of Luke, about the Johannine literature, and particularly about Saint Paul and that apostle's witness to Christ--a witness which served as inspiration to Menoud himself throughout the whole of his life.

Although he was strongly "conservative" and would never allow himself to be persuaded to give allegiance to the varied movements of the present century (except perhaps the railways, for which he had a weakness--but are the railways so real after all?), and although he never concealed his by no means conventional opinions in a society to which he only "lent" himself, his students loved him. But should we say "although"? Should we not rather say "because"? However that may be, he evoked a significant combination of respect, curiosity, and tenderness in the numerous listeners whom he introduced to the New Testament and, consequently, to the Christian faith, while he was a professor at the Free Faculty of Theology at Lausanne from 1934 until 1945, then at the Faculty of Theology at the University of Neuchâtel from 1945 until his death (teaching at the same time from 1951 to 1963 at the Free Faculty of Theology at Montpellier, which granted him the degree of doctor *honoris causa* on the occasion of his departure). Those who heard him may not have understood him completely but they were convinced that here was a man whose life was based not on one or other of the countless futilities of this world, but on the single, immovable rock of faith in Christ, the manifestation of the plenitude of God. Moreover this confirmed, but not obdurate, celibate had the gift of arousing affection even in his colleagues in other disciplines, whenever the occasion arose (probably not of his own seeking) to come into contact with them in the Faculty room or on some committee or other, when he would combine the wisdom of his opinions with strong, but always courteous, warnings against the laxities and frivolities of the age. It is unnecessary to add that, in such circumstances, it was a joy to have Philippe Menoud as a colleague in the Faculty of Theology.

We could recall many other aspects of this multi-faceted individual: his pastoral ministry for three years in the south of France, of which he had fond memories; his discreet but always loyal and timely presence when misfortunes befell his friends; his attachment to the Community of Grandchamp, where he conducted spiritual retreats for so many years; his kindness towards those on whose service he depended, whether at home, in restaurants, or in stores; and also his delicious and sometimes cutting irony at the expense of all bombast, whether political, academic, journalistic, worldly, or ecclesiastical. A healthy sign, certainly, but also the sign of true faith: a faith which, being able to put everything in its place, can put pretence and triviality in theirs.

But good health, like all things, comes to an end. His health, which had been undermined for a long time, collapsed suddenly. He did not depart without leaving a final testimony of faith to his family and friends during his last days of full consciousness. Sadness according to God, of which Saint Paul speaks, is the only kind of sadness one should feel at his death. Certainly this does not prevent feelings of personal loss but it guards against feelings of rebellion or, worse still, of resigned indifference. In this way Philippe Menoud, so dear to the hearts and minds of those who knew him, continues among us his ministry of a believer and a scholar of the Church.

Jean-Louis Leuba

Philippe H. Menoud - the Exegete and the Historian

More and more often nowadays we find authors putting together one or more volumes of studies which they have previously published in different journals. This kind of publication provides a great service, in spite of the technical problems it produces. In fact, the most original ideas are often to be found in short articles. The present collection of works of the late Professor Philippe H. Menoud has been put together by his colleagues, who feel that these pages set forth some of the principal ideas of his thought. The publication of this volume is all the more essential, as Menoud himself did not reproduce the content of his articles in later works.

Death took Philippe Menoud from New Testament studies[1] before he could complete the great commentary he was planning on the Acts of the Apostles. Instead of bequeathing us large volumes, he has left us a great number of succinct studies full of provocative ideas. This volume should figure among the works on the New Testament which will "endure". In its brevity and its conciseness each of these works is a small masterpiece. Specialists and laymen alike will profit greatly from them. While they may give rise to some differences of opinion, they will certainly stimulate further study.

Individually, these studies might have been forgotten. They are in fact to be found either in large collections or

---

[1]An active member of the scholarly "Studiorum Novi Testamenti Societas", he was one of its first lecturers.

specialist journals, or in publications which are not readily available. Moreover, it can happen that sometimes an excessive interest in novel ideas makes theologians indifferent to the merits and the value of their masters, particularly if their name is not found on a weighty volume.

Menoud himself never made the slightest conscious effort to gain publicity for his always interesting ideas. He sees the real problems, including those which might easily be overlooked, and he knows how to present them. Here are some, chosen at random: Why is the expression "One Church" (μια ἐκκλησια), which is so familiar to us, not found in the New Testament, which is, nevertheless, so concerned with the unity of Christians? Why, in the book of Acts, is the gap in the ranks of the Apostles caused by the departure of the traitor, Judas, filled, while that caused by the death of James, the son of Zebedee, is not? Are the gospel of Luke and the Acts of the Apostles two distinct and separate books? It would be easy to cite more examples.

In other works Menoud attacks the continuing problems and takes part in the great controversies. He attacks them all in his own original way whether it is a question of the Church and its ministers, infant baptism, or Saint Paul's "thorn in the flesh", that well-known exegetical "crux".

The works collected here show that Menoud's researches cover almost all areas of New Testament scientific study, from biblical philology, textual community, to the theological thought of the New Testament. This last element brings unity to all the different articles. All the problems he attacks (even those connected with the history of the text) are, in his opinion, related to the question of New Testament theology. The harmony between history and theology, sometimes missing in current biblical studies, is demonstrated perfectly in his works. We have the feeling that our author has his own synthesis, his own overall view of the problems, even if he has never published it. This underlying synthesis is nowhere more evident than in the areas of systematic or ethical studies or those connected with the Church. These are contemporary problems: I have already mentioned the problem of ministry in the Church; I can think also of studies on the relationship between the Word and the Sacraments, the unity of the Church (ecumenism), the Christian attitude to Judaism, and the Christian meaning of death, a subject which borders on philosophical reflection.

There should be no surprise at the place taken by the theology of Luke in the researches of Menoud. The studies on the book of Acts, gathered together in the present volume, give us an overall view of his thought in this area. They will perhaps provide some consolation for the commentary he had promised us which we did not receive. In our time the fundamental agreement of the Acts of the Apostles with the essence of the New Testament has been questioned and Luke has even been denied a place in the Canon. While recognizing the justification of certain arguments put forward, Menoud has endeavoured to rehabilitate, so to speak, the theology of Luke as authentic New Testament theology.

There are only two Johannine studies in this collection. But Menoud was an exegete who was up-to-date with all the historical, linguistic, and interpretative problems arising from the Johannine Corpus. We only need to recall his well-researched study, "The Gospel of John according to Recent Research", published in 1942, which was very well received by the specialists. The article, "Johannine Studies from Bultmann to Barrett", reprinted in the present volume, is to some extent a continuation of the first work.

Reading the works of Menoud is all the more pleasant as they are written in such a lively style. They keep our interest alive by the problems which they raise and by the force of the argumentation. They also bring us face to face with the personality of their author on every page by resurrecting--and keeping alive--his human qualities. We see him before us with his frankness, his modesty, his good sense, his kindness (but a kindness accompanied by a well-developed critical sense), his pleasant smile, and his unique gentle irony.

The reader will notice at once the great clarity of writing which is characteristic of these works, from the lucid statement of the problem to the conclusion which he never fails to add. This clarity is not merely the result of the writer's literary gifts. It is part of his very nature. Never does he move round and round in a narrow circle of ideas; never does he make use of esoteric and obscure language. Never does he launch himself into interminable hermeneutical discussion. He uses a method which succeeds by its steadiness, maintaining his personal faith while at the same time avoiding anthropocentric subjectivism.

He also makes use of the literary method known today as *Redaktionsgeschichte*, but without insisting on the word itself, and without feeling constrained by this method to draw, in respect to the historicity of facts, negative conclusions which are not necessarily self-evident.

For him, to clarify a problem never means to make it more simple. Intellectual honesty always impels him to view problems in all their complexity. He knows how to deal with objections--those made to him by others, and those he poses for himself. In tackling opinions which seem to contradict each other he does not seek a compromise, but he attacks the accepted ideas which often consider only one side of the problem. This is how he destroys false alternatives and re-establishes the harmony which exists in the New Testament between its different elements (inspiration *and* tradition; word *and* sacrament; in Saint Paul, marriage *and* celibacy). The same intellectual honesty forces him to abandon ideas which he previously defended, when facts force him to do so.

Always ready to learn from others (without allowing himself to be bound within the categories of such-and-such a school of thought or theological current) he has examined all interpretations written in French, German, English, or Italian by Catholics or by Protestants. His critical studies on recent New Testament research are evidence at one and the same time of his great erudition and the sureness of his judgment.

Menoud always kept up-to-date with the latest discoveries and he always left himself open to any new way of presenting problems. But his sense of perspective, his shrewdness, his good sense prevented him from becoming a slave to theological fashions and slogans which pass by so quickly. The evolution of the "secular" world (whose importance he never underestimated) never shook his firm conviction that the Bible could not be given up as the norm for faith. In the wisdom of "the early Church", he writes at the end of one of his articles, "we can find many great and useful lessons for our present situation". This conviction is the basis of his love for biblical research and teaching. For this reason this volume, by its way of posing and handling problems, will not grow old and out of date, in spite of the revisions and refinements which future progress in biblical studies may bring to some of its conclusions. Theologians and laymen alike will be able to place their trust in this guide who dedicated his life to a better understanding of the New Testament.

Oscar Cullmann

I. PROBLEMS IN PAULINE THEOLOGY

Marriage and Celibacy According to Saint Paul[1]

Public opinion maintains that the apostle to the Gentiles was unmarried, was strongly opposed to the emancipation of women, and had very little esteem for the state of matrimony. Certain words written to the Corinthians are quoted as Paul's definitive ideas on the subject: "I wish that all were as I myself am"; "he who marries does well, and he who refrains from marriage will do better"; "to the unmarried and the widows I say that it is well for them to remain single, but it is better to marry than to burn with vain desire". These words lead to the conclusion that in the apostle's judgment marriage is "a concession granted by God to human weakness, a social institution preferable to loose morals",[2] a "necessary evil",[3] or at the very least "inevitable",[4] "lawful concubinage".[5]

Other writers show us a more moderate view of marriage in Saint Paul. "If Paul does not have a high opinion of marriage," writes W. G. Kümmel,[6] "it is not because he considers marital union as evil in itself by virtue of ascetic dualism; it is because the Parousia is at hand and he himself has received the gift of continence." Otto Michel goes a step further;[7] if he excuses Paul "as a celibate from being unable to sing a hymn in praise of marriage",[8] he admits that the apostle's thinking follows closely that of Jesus himself; Paul defends the lawfulness, both of marriage itself and its practice, to the religious leaders in Corinth who thought that they should live an ascetic life.

Moreover, several writers recently have emphasized that Paul sees in celibacy a gift which allows the person who benefits from it a freedom to serve the Lord and not "a state which is more perfect and spiritually more advantageous than marriage". Marriage is, according to the will of God, for those of his creatures who are not called to celibacy and, even if it is a remedy against dissolute living, it is above all the only form of union between a man and a woman which is compatible with their life in Christ. All things considered, marriage is a *positivum* not a *negativum*.[9]

It is in this sense, it seems to us, that we should understand the apostle's thought if we are to render him justice. At the risk of being repetitive we want to emphasize that Paul considers both marriage and celibacy as two states equally lawful for Christ's followers. He is also of the opinion that marriage and celibacy, in their different ways, can both contribute to the realization of salvation; that is, life in Christ.

The apostle Paul never deals with the subjects of marriage or celibacy *ex professo*. In fact he speaks of them quite rarely, always incidental to and in connection with a much wider subject: the vocation or the salvation of the Christian. He never sees in celibacy the means of reaching greater spiritual heights nor does he see marriage as an obstacle in the race to the goal of every Christian.

It is true that Paul does not hide his preference for his own state. "I wish," he writes, "that all were as I myself am" (I Cor. 7.7), that is to say not caught in the bonds of marriage nor set free from them (I Cor. 7.8).[10] But the apostle has hardly made this avowal when he sets limits to it. He himself is endowed with a special grace and each person receives his own grace from God. That is to say his avowal can only be taken *cum grano salis*. Not everyone is called to live alone as he did. Solitary life is a "charisma" and not a vocation for all. The vocation for all is life in Christ, the way forward towards salvation. For those who have not received the charisma granted to Paul "it is better to marry than to burn with vain desire" (I Cor. 7.9), because, unlike dissolute living, marriage is not incompatible with life in Christ. Which means to say that everyone will be like the apostle when everyone lives like him, in all honesty according to the gifts they have received, freed by Christ from the problem of the difference between the sexes, as they are freed from the pride or the shame of being Jew or Greek, free or slave, man or woman.

For the rest, if Paul prefers celibacy, it is for practical and not theological reasons. The celibate has two obvious advantages over the married man. First of all, the celibate is in a more favorable position with regard to what the apostle calls τὴν ἐνεστῶσαν ἀνάγκην (I Cor. 7.26), by which we must understand the contemporary problems of the believers--a small band in the midst of a large corrupt city, doubtless liable to police investigation as members of a religion which was new and therefore not lawful--and not eschatological troubles, "impending disasters".[11] ἐνεστώς always has a here-and-now meaning for Paul. On the other hand, the apostle never sees in the close approach of the Parousia any reason for advocating renouncement of marriage. On the contrary, in I Thessalonians 4 and 5, for instance, where the eschatological expectancy is so great, to live in holiness in the married state is one of the means, along with honesty and hard work, of pleasing God and of honoring the name of

Christian before unbelievers--in short, of taking care not to be caught by surprise on the day of the Lord's coming.

The allegiances of a celibate, then, are undivided (I Cor. 7.32f.). His only aim is to please the Lord, while the married man or woman has to think also of pleasing the partner. But here again we cannot but think that Paul's words should be taken *cum grano salis*; he does not make it a matter of life and death. He does not criticize these marital concerns; they are legitimate, given the married state. The exhortations of the epistles to the Colossians and the Ephesians suggest that the apostle would be more likely to reprove the husband who neglected his wife.[12] Now if husbands must "love their wives" (Col. 3.19) and even "love them as Christ loved the Church" (Eph. 5.25), it is obvious that husbands would devote to their wives part of the time that celibates can give to the Lord. Christ glorified can only be served by those "little ones" (both men and women) who believe in him. Furthermore, if the marriage is a mixed marriage of which Paul speaks in I Corinthians 7.12-16, it is by the expression of marital love that a Christian partner can sanctify, that is bring to Christ in some way, the pagan partner.

In short, in Paul's view, marriage is good but celibacy is better. But it can only be so for those who have received the gift of the ability to live alone. For others marriage is good in opposition to the evil of loose living. Moreover, it is on the practical level and not the theological level that celibacy is the better in relation to marriage. The celibate will be less worried than the married man by the disquieting circumstances of the present time; he will be more free to attend to the Lord's affairs; if he is an apostle, he will be less encumbered on his missionary journeys than those who take their wives with them (I Cor. 9.5) and so he will be able to "work harder than them all" (I Cor. 15. 10). But by making a particular charisma of solitary life the apostle emphasizes its exceptional characteristics. This gift has not been given to all, any more than all have been called to be apostles, prophets, or teachers. Moreover, although Paul recognizes and defends prerogatives which are properly apostolic--he is an apostle because he has seen the Lord (I Cor. 9.1) and, as such, he has wrought miracles which are "the signs of a true apostle" (2 Cor. 12.12)--he does not mention any religious prerogatives for a celibate. He never says, or even suggests, that the celibate can reach a level of communion with Christ which is inaccessible to married Christians.

Nevertheless the apostle Paul allies his personal preference for celibacy with a very positive appreciation for marriage. He speaks of it at length in I Corinthians 7 in reply to questions which had been put to him and in order to refute the false beliefs widespread in Corinth. His teachings in this chapter agree with his exhortations in the epistles to the Thessalonians, the Colossians and the Ephesians, although, in these three epistles, he only touches fleetingly on one aspect of the question.

All the mistaken ideas of the Corinthians, whether it is a question of the unity of the Church, the relationship of men and women, the eucharist or the resurrection, stem from their misunderstanding of the Pauline idea of salvation. According to Paul redemption takes over the whole being completely, body and soul. If "flesh and blood cannot inherit the kingdom of God", the body is not the flesh. It is destined for resurrection; it is from now on the habitation of the Holy Spirit; the believers, who are individually the members of Christ, together form the earthly body of the Lord. That is why it is equally inadmissible to maintain that there is no resurrection of the body, to celebrate the eucharist in an unworthy fashion when this is where the body of Christ comes together, to wish to divide the body of Christ according to personal preferences or finally to claim that the physical life of the believers is not also governed by the Lord's will.

The last point is the only one with which we are concerned here, and in this regard the Corinthians seem to have adopted two attitudes which are in fact contradictory but which both arise from the neglect of the cardinal truth that the whole human being, body and soul, is called to sanctification and salvation. Starting with the erroneous idea that the body has no place in the glorious destiny of the believer, some of the apostle's converts concluded that "everything is permissible" and tended towards licentiousness (I Cor. 6.12-20); others, on the other hand, were inclined to ascetism and the condemnation of marriage (I Cor. 7.1).

Paul's reply had to be most careful. It is very subtle without losing its clarity. On the one hand he had to oppose the two different points of view; he could not allow either licentiousness or contempt for marriage to become established as norms for the Church. On the other hand, he could not establish his doctrine of marriage without admitting the elements of truth contained in each of the two doctrines prevalent in Corinth. In dealing with the ascetics Paul recognizes the value of celibacy for the Lord's service; but he has to remind them that celibacy is a gift and not a general rule, and that marital union is not only lawful but rich in religious value. Thus the apostle seems to be granting some semblance of right to the libertines; he must denounce all the more vehemently their claim to be allowed to engage in all kinds of sexual alliances, on the grounds that marriage is permitted, and point out to them the specific characteristics of Christian marriage.

In Paul's opinion the advantage of marriage is not the merely negative one of being a remedy against misconduct.[13] Above all it has the advantage of contributing to the redemption of the partners. This positive aspect of marriage is evident wherever the apostle speaks of marital union.

First of all Paul makes it quite clear that his idea of the marriage of believers is a real consummated marriage with no idea of sin attached to it. In I Corinthians 7.3-5 where, as Jean Héring says, "Paul dots his 'i's'", "the apostle does not permit ascetism in marriage, he would only allow it as an exception during a time of spiritual retreat. For any exaggeration in the sense of ascetism can only be to do business with Satan, who hovers in the background and who, knowing human nature, holds the threat of licentiousness over the partners in a marital union which is deemed nothing but a spiritual union".[14]

In the apostle's view, taking advantage of their union in marriage will be a means of placing Christian partners out of Satan's reach. If this is so, it is not merely because marital union is a remedy against immoral living, but for a more positive reason connected with the central theme of Pauline thought: the participation of the believer in the body and life of Christ. In fact, according to the apostle, the union of two believers can only have a quite opposite result from that of a union between a Christian and a prostitute. If, by linking himself with a harlot, who is the servant of the devil, a believer enters into communion with the devil (cf. I Cor. 6.15f.), and thus loses communion with Christ whom he has betrayed, then, on the other hand, union in marriage of believers who are members of Christ cannot alienate them from Christ. Bodily union is never unimportant in Paul's opinion. If loose living deprives the believer of his communion with Christ, living in a Christian marriage not only safeguards this communion but helps to secure it and strengthen it.

We should remember at this point that the apostle had already written to the Thessalonians (I, 4.3-5): "It is the will of God that you should be holy." He goes on to explain: "To be holy, is for you to abstain from immorality and for each of you to live with your wife in holiness and honour." The holiness and honor of this married life does not result from its being merely a spiritual union. Paul expresses himself in terms which preclude this meaning. Paul knows and hands on to the churches which he is founding the teachings of Jesus on the subject of marriage, which is conceived as a divine institution, strictly monogamous and indissoluble. The apostle places this divine institution firmly in the perspective of life in Christ. Those joined by God in marriage, if they are believers, take part, by their very union, in the life of Christ. This theme is developed by Paul in I Corinthians 7.10-16 and in Ephesians 5.22-33.

There are two elements in the pericope I Corinthians 7. 10-16: a reminder of the Lord's commandment with regard to the indissolubility of the marriage of two believers (v. 10-11) and instructions regarding the marriage of a believer and an unbeliever (v. 12-16).

The first of these elements should doubtless refute once and for all the disastrous conclusion which might be drawn from the fact that, in the view of the apostle, sexual life in itself is not contrary to life in Christ. It might be concluded that all believers could be quite free among themselves, in this area, from the time when they become members of the body of Christ. Paul must therefore remind his readers that it is only within the bounds of marriage, and marriage as the Lord again defined it, that sexual life is assumed and, so to speak, taken fully in charge by life in Christ.

Next, addressing himself to "the others", that is, to those members of a marriage between a believer and an unbeliever--more precisely a marriage which has taken place before one of the partners has become a believer--the apostle makes his ideas absolutely clear about what such a marriage should be. That Paul here authorizes separation is a quite secondary issue. The main point is his affirmation that the pagan partner is "hallowed" by the Christian partner. Within the framework of marriage a certain bond is produced which has some resemblance to that resulting from the union of a Christian with a harlot. But whereas in the latter case the woman "demonizes" the man who links himself to her, in the case of a mixed marriage the Christian partner "christianizes" or sanctifies the pagan partner, that is to say brings the partner, through their union, into union with Christ.[15]

This opinion of the apostle's is a bold one and, at the same time, calculated. It is daring in that it affirms that marital union itself is a step on the way to redemption. It is guarded because Paul does not say that this attachment to the body of Christ by the attachment to a partner who lives in Christ makes the conversion of the pagan partner unnecessary. He rather implies the contrary, reminding his readers that the "consecration" of the pagan partner does not provide for his or her salvation (v. 16). Nobody can be "saved" by marriage. The fact remains, however, that marriage leads in the direction of salvation and not away from it.

Paul's teaching on the subject of mixed marriages is merely a particular application of the general exhortation given in I Thessalonians 4, where, as we have just seen, the state of matrimony helps to bring about the sanctification God desires for all believers. This same idea finds its highest expression in the well-known passage in Ephesians 5.22-33. Here the apostle is not afraid to compare the union of a husband and wife to the union of Christ and the Church; he writes that husbands should cherish their wives as Christ does the Church, and they should love their wives as Christ has loved the Church, with a love which hallows.

That Paul should have recourse to this image to depict the ultimate reality of Christian marriage is proof that, in his opinion, marriage is by no means merely a modest benefit for the purpose of avoiding the worst of evils. On the contrary the apostle's conception of marriage is the highest man has ever had. Neither monogamy nor the indissolubility of the marriage bond were new ideas in the first century. These were not new ideas introduced by Christianity and Paul. Paul revives Christ's opinion that marriage is a gift by the grace of God to man, and he gives the greatest significance to this divine grace by incorporating it into his christology.

Thus marriage is not merely a legal and social institution as it is in paganism and even in Judaism. It is a religious institution. Christian marriage unites two people on all three levels on which human beings function: physical, mental, and spiritual. A religious institution, marriage is one of the ways through which the grace of God reaches man, and reaches him throughout his whole being.

Two lines of thought emerge from a study of the Pauline texts on marriage and celibacy. On the one hand Paul maintains that celibacy is a gift by the grace of God which has certain advantages; on the other hand he lifts marriage to the highest possible level. If possible we must try to understand this duality. It cannot be explained by a theory such as that of a dual ethic or of two levels of perfection. The advantages which the apostle finds in celibacy are practical ones. A pagan married to a Christian is closer to salvation than an unmarried pagan by virtue of the power of Christian marriage to unite one with Christ.

Neither can this juxtaposition of the two ideas be explained by the theory that celibacy should be reserved for the apostles and marriage for the believers. For Paul, who does not take with him a "sister-wife", is such a notable exception among the apostles that we might conclude, seeing him live alone, that he does not have this apostolic prerogative, and consequently, should not have the title of apostle (cf. I Cor. 9.1-5).

Must we give up any attempt at explanation and say, with Friedrich Buechsel, that Paul has not joined together into a single system the idea, which was already traditional in the Church of his time, that marriage is an order and a gift from God, and his own personal realization that the bonds of matrimony would prevent him from devoting himself completely to the service of his Lord?[16] But when speaking of marriage Paul does not limit himself to recalling the heritage of the infant Church--he places marriage within the perspective of his theology of the body of Christ. The apostle has rethought the Christian theology of marriage and given it definitive expression; he has not accepted it simply as a traditional gift.

The explanation is to be found in the Pauline doctrine of redemption, and, more precisely, in its center, which is life in Christ. The gospel which Paul preaches is the message of redemption by Jesus Christ, who came to die and to rise again for those who believe in Him, who has been lifted to the right hand of God and who will preside at the establishment of the Kingdom of God when the present world comes to an end. Like the work of Christ, the redemption of the believer is on two levels; it is both present and eschatological. The apostle can write without any danger of contradiction: "we have our redemption, the remission of our sins" (Col. 1.14) and "we await our redemption, the deliverance of our bodies" (Rom. 8. 23). This final deliverance and the reclothing of the new bodies will take place at the arrival of the world which is still to come. Only those who, starting now, in this world of ours, live in Christ, that is to say live a new life through the power of His spirit, will take part in this entry into glory.

If the apostle never loses sight of the final state of redemption his insistence is on the present aspect of salvation; he exhorts the readers of all his epistles to live their lives in Christ. Life in Christ is in fact possible for man still living in the flesh. Man needs only to believe, that is to say he needs only to admit that Christ died and rose again on his behalf; he himself does not need to have died already and have risen to be with Christ; benefiting from His righteousness, he is living his life through Him.

"It is no longer I who live," writes the apostle using the "I" collectively to include all believers, "but Christ who lives in me, and I in Christ." This "I" is so all-embracing that it cancels out all the distinctions made by men and even by creation. "All of you who have been baptized into Christ have clothed yourselves with Christ. There cannot be Jew and Greek, slave and free man, male and female; you are all one in Christ Jesus." Elsewhere Saint Paul expresses the same idea when he says that the believers form only one body, of which Christ is the head and they are the members. The apostle's whole theology shows that in his view the body of Christ is a reality and not merely an image.

The only necessity for salvation, then, is to be this new creature incorporated into Christ. If the believer becomes and remains a member of Christ, he is saved, whatever his racial, legal, biological, or civil status may be. What is important is not whether one is Jew or Greek, enslaved or free, man or woman, married or unmarried, it is that one is a new creature, that one is in Christ, even if one is also Jew or Greek, enslaved or free, man or woman, married or unmarried.

This is precisely what Paul declares to the Galatians in two similar verses: "In Christ Jesus neither circumcision nor uncircumcision is of any avail; but only faith working through love" (5.6); "Neither circumcision nor uncircumcision is of any importance, but only a new nature" (6.15).

There is a third verse similar to these in I Corinthians 7.19, "Circumcision is nothing, and uncircumcision is nothing; obedience to God's commands is everything." This text comes in the middle of the pericope 7.17-24 where Paul deals with the relativity of different states of man with regard to salvation, which, through Christ, is for all believers. Moreover, this pericope itself is to be found right in the middle of the chapter where the apostle deals with marriage and celibacy. In the opinion of the commentators, the apostle is writing this passage "in parentheses" or at least he is "enlarging the area of consideration". Perhaps we should go one step further. There is no doubt that Paul brings up this point of debate intentionally to show that marriage and celibacy themselves are human conditions which are relative to salvation.

Paul, it is true, did not write, "Marriage is nothing and celibacy is nothing; what matters is to be a new creature." In one sense he might have written it. For salvation does not depend on the civil status of the believer, in view of the fact that marriage is not a sin and that celibacy does not make entry into Christ any easier than does married life. Celibates and married people are equal when facing salvation. The important point is not the actual state of the celibate or the married man or woman, but the way in which he or she lives in that state. The distinction, as Paul sees it, is not between celibate Christians and married Christians; it is between those who avoid πορνεία and those who fall prey to it--in other words, between those who are indefectibly bound to Christ and those who betray him. What matters is to live in Christ whether one is married or not.

But in another way Paul could not possible say that celibacy is nothing and marriage is nothing for--as we have seen while re-reading the apostle's words--each of these states has its own advantages with regard to salvation, each of them is very definitely something. The unmarried, not having to share themselves, are freer to concern themselves with the Lord's work. Married people work together, by their union in the Lord, for their mutual salvation. Both kinds live according to the gift and the vocation which God has given them or the grace he has bestowed on them.

If Saint Paul therefore can speak positively about both marriage and celibacy, it is because he is confident that God makes use of both of these states to further his work of redemption, just as he calls the Jews to salvation by the ministry of the Twelve and the Gentiles by the ministry of the apostle set apart "from his mother's breast" precisely for this mission. But just as the apostle to the Gentiles and the Twelve preach the same gospel and arouse the same faith (cf. I Cor. 15.11), so also faithful celibates and married believers live the same life in Christ.

Celibacy is not a condition for salvation and marriage is not an obstacle to it. That is why the apostle Paul, who works to save all men, can, without contradicting himself in any way, give thanks to God for his own celibacy, which allows him to be undivided in his service to the Lord, and at the same time make the union of Christ and His Church the image of Christian marriage.

NOTES

1. A paper read at a meeting of the "Société vaudoise de théologie" at Lausanne on January 29, 1951, and published in the *Revue de théologie et de philosophie*, n.s. 38, 1950, p. 21-34.

2. H. Preisker, *Christentum und Ehe in der ersten Jahrhunderten. Eine Studie zur Kulturgeschichte der alten Welt*, Berlin, 1927, p. 127. Cf. "Ehe und Charisma bei Paulus," *Zeitschrift für systematische Theologie*, 1928, p. 91-95.

3. G. Delling, *Paulus Stellung zu Frau und Ehe*, Stuttgart, 1931 (Beiträge zur Wissenschaft vom Alten und Neuen Testament IV, 5), p. 17; E. Stauffer, "Γάμος" in *Theologisches Wörterbuch zum Neuen Testament*, Stuttgart, 1932, I, p. 650; H. Lietzmann in Lietzmann-Kuemmel, *An die Korinther I-II*, 4. Aufl., Tübingen, 1949 (Handbuch zum Neuen Testament 9), p. 29.

4. R. Bultmann, *Theologie des Neuen Testaments*, Tübingen, 1948, p. 199.

5. H. Leenhardt, *Le mariage chrétien*, Neuchâtel-Paris, 1946, p. 22. Yet, when he speaks of Ephesians 5 and not of I Corinthians 7, the same author writes that "the married couple, because of the love-relationship between them, is already of the Church" (p. 30), and this is the idea of marriage which is deemed to be Pauline as it reappears at other places in the body of the work.

6. Lietzmann-Kuemmel, *op. cit.*, p. 176.

7. O. Michel, "Wie spricht Paulus über Frau und Ehe?", *Theologische Studien und Kritiken*, 1933, p. 215-225.

8. O. Michel, *op. cit.*, p. 222.

9. Cf. for example W. Michaelis, "Ehe und Charisma bei Paulus," *Zeitschrift für systematische Theologie*, 1927, p. 426-456; O. A. Piper, *The Christian Interpretation of Sex*, New York, 1941; F. Buechsel, "Die Ehe im Urchristentum," *Theologische Blätter*, 1942, p. 113-128; J. Héring, *La première épitre de saint Paul aux Corinthiens*, Neuchâtel-Paris, 1949 (Commentaire du Nouveau Testament, 7).

10. It is τοῖς ἀγάμοις καὶ ταῖς χήραις whom Paul recommends should remain single like him. The χῆραι are widows. The expression ἄγαμος is more difficult. The word appears again, this time in the feminine, in I Cor. 7.34 where ἡ γυνὴ ἡ ἄγαμος is distinguished from the παρθένος. It is a question then, in contrast to a young girl, of a woman who has been married but is so no longer (cf. I Cor. 7.11-16). The ἄγαμοι may be Christians deserted by their wives who remained unbelievers. But it may be that Paul is following the general custom in Greek, which only uses χήρα in the feminine, except for a few rare exceptions, and designates a widower, like a bachelor, by the word ἄγαμος, which is not used for a widow, who is known as χήρα or ἄνανδρος (cf. Liddell-Scott-Jones, *A Greek-English Lexicon*, New edition, Oxford, 1948).

Returning to I Corinthians 7.8, is Paul a bachelor, a widower, or separated from his wife? The brief indications in the New Testament do not lead to any definite conclusion. It must be emphasized, however, that the common tradition which makes Paul a bachelor is not based on any categorical text. Moreover it is not a unanimous opinion. Clement of Alexandria (*Stromates* III, 6) and Eusebius (*Ecclesiastical History* III, 30) assert that Paul is greeting his wife when he uses the expression Γνήσιε σύζυγε in Philippians 4.3, and E. Renan (*Saint-Paul*, Paris, 1869, p. 148-149) maintains that the lady is Lydia, the seller of purple. On the other hand J. Jeremias upholds the thesis that Paul was a widower ("War Paulus Witwer?", *Zeitschrift für die neutestamentliche Wissenschaft*, 1926, p. 310-312, and "Nochmals: War Paulus Witwer?", *ibid.*, 1929, p. 321-323). This hypothesis has been attacked by E. Fascher, "Zur Witwerschaft des Paulus und der Auslegung von I Kor. 7", *ibid.*, 1929, p. 62-69. On the basis of the sound observations of J. Jeremias, and taking into account Paul's general idea about marriage and certain expressions in the epistles, one might suggest that after his conversion the apostle lived apart from his wife (ἄγαμος), who remained loyal to the Jewish faith.

11. J. Héring, *op. cit.*, p. 56-57.

12. "The apostle knew well enough that there are, alas, many husbands who do not think about pleasing their wives" (J. Héring, *op. cit.*, p. 59). Doubtless the apostle was also well aware that there are many wives, alas, who do not think about pleasing their husbands.

13. It is surprising that so many exegetes, including the best, only see this negative aspect of marriage in Pauline teaching and judge the whole question in the light of I Cor. 7.1-2. Verse 1 is, without doubt, a quotation from the letter of the Corinthians to Paul (cf. "everything is permissible", 6.12). Even if these are the apostle's own words, in view of the verses which follow, and without admitting that Paul was contradicting himself without realizing it, they can hardly be any more than a kind of pious wish or whim (cf. Gal. 5.12) meaning this: life would be easier if there were no differences between the sexes with all their resulting difficulties, or if all believers could exercise sexual abstinence easily. But Paul knows that the problem exists and that a positive solution "in the Lord" is required. In I Cor. 7, verses 10-16 in particular would make no sense if, in the apostle's view, marriage were nothing but a remedy against immoral living. For the rest, even if it were only that, it would already be a positive state since it replaces licentiousness, that is, the devil, with life in Christ.

14. J. Héring, *op. cit.*, p. 51.

15. This declaration must have come as a surprise to the Corinthians. Paul also gives objective proof of the existence of the bond of which he speaks. He adds that children born of mixed marriages are "saints" and not just "blessed", that is to say they are members of the Church, without any shadow of a doubt. This proof based on the "sanctity" of the children ends the debate; it is as definitive as a quotation from the scriptures. It is the clear indication, it seems to us, as F. Godet has already noted (*Commentaire sur la première épître aux Corinthiens*, Neuchâtel, 1886, I, p. 315f.), that the sanctity of the children is itself based on the objective and undeniable fact of their baptism. In the early church nobody can be a "saint" without being baptized.

16. F. Buechsel, *op. cit.*, p. 121-122.

The Thorn in the Flesh and Satan's Angel[1] (2 Cor. 12.7)

In chapters 11 and 12 of the second epistle to the Corinthians, Paul speaks of the high-points and the miseries of his ministry. In chapter 12 verses 1-6, particularly, he recalls the extraordinary revelations which were granted to him and which might have made him proud and boastful. But to avoid succumbing to this temptation, "there was given me," he says, "a thorn in the flesh, Satan's angel to torture me.... Concerning this, three times have I besought the Lord that he might leave me; but He has said to me: My grace is sufficient for you, for power is perfected in weakness" (v. 7-8). Paul continues by enumerating the persecutions he has endured for Christ (12.9-10; cf. 11.23b-33) and his undeniable claims to be granted the rank of apostle, claims which include the sufferings he endures as a minister of Christ (12.11-13; cf. 11. 21-23a).

Since early Christian times there has been speculation about both the nature of the thorn in the flesh and the angel of Satan who tortures the apostle. Several of the explanations put forward over the years have been given up today.[2] In fact, it cannot be a question of the goad of the flesh since the apostle lets it be known that he has received the gift of continence (I Cor. 7.7-9). Neither can one put forward the idea of temptations to unbelief since Paul makes no mention of problems of that kind. The idea, put forward by Osiander,[3] that the angel of Satan reminds the apostle incessantly of the cruelties he heaped upon the believers, is taken up again by A. Schlatter.[4] There are two objections to this theory. First, in other parts of the epistles, the apostle does not hesitate to admit, without mincing words, that he has persecuted the Church (I Cor. 15.9; Gal. 1.23). Secondly--and this argument stands up against all the explanations mentioned so far--Paul says quite definitely that the thorn appeared in his flesh at a specific time; there was a time when he was free from these attacks by Satan. Therefore it was a new phenomenon, coming upon him after he had embarked on his missionary career.

Nowadays most exegetes and historians are of the opinion that Paul is referring to an illness from which he was not able to be cured despite his ardent prayers, and which would be a great handicap to his missionary career.[5]

This explanation is an old one since it is already to be found in Tertullian.[6] It has become so universal that it is commonly held to be "unzweifelhaft".[7] This is forgetting that its basis is very tenuous. Paul never says in so many words that he has suffered an illness. None of the texts quoted in support of the theory is decisive.

In Galatians 4.13-15, the apostle writes that it was "in a state of bodily infirmity" that he first preached the gospel to the Galatians. Almost all modern commentators maintain that Paul fell ill in Galatia. We ourselves have agreed with this explanation elsewhere,[8] but we do not think it can be sustained. It is more logical to think--along with the Fathers and a few modern exegetes[9]--that when Paul arrived in Galatia he was injured or suffering from the wounds and persecutions he had endured as a preacher of the gospel.

Doubtless *astheneia* (with or without *tès sarkos*) is, in one accepted sense, synonymous with *nosos*.[10] But this is not the only possible meaning and, in this particular case, there is no reason to presume it to be the correct one. In the only other passage where Paul uses the expression "bodily infirmity" or "weakness of the flesh" (Romans 6.19), he uses it in the sense of the Latin *imbecillitas*, that is to say incapacity (to hear and understand the Gospel). Moreover, Paul often mentions the physical hardships connected with the exercise of his apostleship[11] but never the state of his health. We might, it is true, find references to the supposedly poor health of the apostle in 2 Corinthians 4.7-12, where he writes: "We have this treasure in fragile earthen pots... always carrying about in our bodies the putting to death of Jesus....Death is at work in us...." But Paul is alluding, seemingly, to the sufferings, hardships, hazards, and even the danger of death which are the lot of missionaries and which gradually wear out their feeble flesh. It is the most obvious meaning, reinforced moreover by the context. Likewise there is no reason for thinking that the apostle was an invalid. His travel plans were never changed or hindered by illness. His route was mapped out by the will of the Lord (I Cor. 4.19; 16.7), by the concern to go where the name of Christ had not yet been heard (Rom. 15.22), by love of the believers (2 Cor. 1.15; 2.4), or by the obstacles placed in his way by Satan (I Thess. 2.18) and not by the state of his health. Paul's missionary career, his exuberant activity, his unceasing travels were not the activities of a man in poor health.

The book of Acts confirms the apostle's own testimony on this point. The accounts put together by the writer to Theophilus about the life of Paul do not mention illness at all, but, like the epistles, recount the hardships and persecutions (Acts 14.19-20; 16.22f.; 17.3f.; 17.13f.; 20.3) and plans which are governed by the will of the Holy Spirit (Acts 16.4) or of God (Acts 18.21).

We must also draw attention to the following fact. If Paul never mentions that he himself is tormented by illness he says that among the believers in Corinth, "there are many who are sick and ailing[12] and a certain number have died" (I Cor. 11.30), because these Christians are guilty of taking the eucharist unworthily; having underestimated the power of life provided by communion with Christ, they are taken over by the forces of destruction, namely illness and death.[13] Now this idea of illness is different from the dominant idea in 2 Cor. 12.7, if this text, as common opinion would have it, envisages the illness of the apostle himself. In I Cor. 11. 30, illness is the punishment inflicted by the Lord on unworthy believers; in 2 Cor. 12.7, illness appears as a means of maintaining humility in the sufferer and showing that the Lord is the source of all power. In other words, it joins the believer more firmly to Christ, while in the other passage, it is the sign of a break between Christ and the believer. We can hardly believe that Paul himself would have these two different conceptions of illness. We must add that, if the apostle were suffering from a chronic ailment, as has been supposed, the argument he uses in I Cor. 11.30 could be turned against him. He would be admitting that he himself was among those who take the eucharist unworthily; by the confession which he lets fall in the second epistle, he would take away any value from the exhortation given in the first. That is inconceivable.

Therefore our conclusion from the preceding arguments would be that ill-health had no place in the life of the apostle Paul.

The remarks about the thorn in the flesh and Satan's angel are to be found in a context of two contrasting ideas. On the one hand we read of the extraordinary revelations granted to Paul (2 Cor. 12.1-6) and the distinctive signs of apostleship which he possesses as much as, if not more than, the "archapostles" at Corinth (v. 11-12). On the other hand we have the "infirmities, insults, distresses, persecutions and grievous difficulties endured for Christ's sake" (v. 10)--that is to say, trials connected with the exercise of his ministry. From all evidence the thorn in the flesh and the angel of Satan are among these trials, and are the most grievous which the apostle had to suffer.

According to earlier exegesis, based on the Greek Fathers, particularly on Chrysostom and Theophylact,[14] Paul is alluding to the different tribulations of his ministry and to the sufferings inflicted on him by his enemies, who are also the enemies of the preaching of the gospel and who are envisaged as being in the service of Satan. Several contemporary commentators are returning to this interpretation. They think, for example, that Paul envisions a satanic majesty, lord of all the enemies he meets on his way,[15] or even that he is speaking of the "presence" beside him of the angel of darkness, who has the power to interfere in his affairs and to thwart his plans, while consigning him to every weakness known to man.[16]

It is highly unlikely that the apostle who lived in Christ would really have felt the presence of Satan personified beside him. Also by speaking of an angel of Satan and not of Satan himself, he does not seem to be referring to such an immediate presence. On the other hand, we should hold on to the idea that Paul means, by the thorn, the setbacks in his ministry and that, behind these setbacks, he is aware of the working of Satan. It is even possible to be more precise about the nature of this impediment.

If the thorn in the flesh and the satanic angel are among the trials connected with the exercise of the total apostolic ministry, they are a particular tribulation which torments only the apostle Paul and which is an added burden for him alone. All missionaries are exposed to dangers and persecutions; only Paul suffers this additional trial, which is the counter-balance--as the context shows--of the particular revelations which he alone received. Now, it seems to us that Paul's greatest suffering was that he could not win the Jews to the gospel.

Paul, in fact, bears in his Jewish heart and his apostle's conscience[17] a wound which causes him great pain and humiliation. Whereas his preaching is so well received by the Gentiles that he can write this report of missionary victories: "Beginning from Jerusalem and the surrounding districts, I have preached without reserve even as far as Illyrium the gospel of Christ" (Rom. 15.19) and that he has to journey to the west to find a new field of endeavour (Rom. 15.22-24), on the other hand his word falls on deaf ears among his brothers in the flesh, the Israelites. That is psychological suffering, because Paul always feels one with his race.[18] It is, even more, theological suffering. For the negative attitude of the Jews is not only a refusal of their own salvation; it is a rejection of the redemption prepared in Israel; it is the denial of the very gospel which Paul preaches to the world and which is to be "to the Jew first and also to the Greek" (Rom. 1.16); it is in itself a counter-mission.

Although he is by definition the apostle to the Gentiles, Paul is perpetually concerned about the salvation of Israel (Rom. 3.1-3; 9-11; I Cor. 9.18-22; 2 Cor. 3.13-16;

Eph. 2.11-18). If he recalls, and sometimes in strong language (I Thess. 2.15-16; 2 Cor. 11.21-22), that the Jews remain outside the faith, it is because their unbelief is the major obstacle in the path of the spreading of the gospel.[19] In fact it is more difficult to show that the promises are fulfilled in Christ, since the recipients chosen by God for those promises remain unbelieving; and urged on by their unbelief, the chosen people throw more and more obstacles in the way of the apostles, especially Paul, the most dangerous in their view, since he preaches that the gospel is the end of the Law (Gal. 5.11; cf. Acts 21.21).

Paul could not help but think how much easier his missionary task would have been if the Jews had accepted the Gospel. In Israel's stubborn disbelief, he could not help but see the work of Satan, that great adversary of the preaching of the Gospel--Satan, who, on one occasion in particular, prevented him from going to Thessalonika (I Thess. 2.18). From the moment when the apostle sees in the crucifixion of the "Lord of glory" the work of evil powers (I Cor. 2.7-8), he would quite naturally think that an angel of Satan was also at work to prevent the Jews from accepting the evidence of a crucified and risen Christ.[20] And Paul's opinion of his missionary vocation was too high for him not to conclude that this interference by the devil was directed against him personally.

Therefore, at the beginning, Paul prayed that the Lord would take away the thorn, that is to say would allow him to reach and convert his own people. Then he stopped praying for that. He understood that his failure with the Jews was part of God's plan. In his inability to convince his own people, he saw God's intention to keep him, of necessity, in a state of humility from which his visions and revelations might have removed him. At the same time, he was assured that if the unbelief of the Jews--and consequently the obstacles they heaped in his path--made his missionary task more difficult, the grace of the Lord would suffice and His power would be all the more manifest as His apostle became weaker. Later God would reveal to Paul this "mystery" that Israel's unbelief is temporary, that it plays a positive role in the history of salvation, in spite of appearances--it allows the Gentiles to enter into the covenant of grace--and that finally Israel would be converted (Rom. 11.25-32). Thus, inherent in the idea which Paul must accept--that he cannot win the Jews to the gospel, that the grace of the Lord must be sufficient for him, and that he must pursue his ministry among the Gentiles in spite of the thorn and the angel of Satan (that is in spite of the resistance and opposition of the Jews)--is a foretaste of the "mystery" which the apostle will know about, when he writes his letter to the Romans.

Taken in this sense the apostle Paul's remarks on the thorn and the angel of Satan find their parallel in a passage in the book of Acts. The puzzling event of the vision of the Lord granted to the apostle in the temple at Jerusalem (Acts 22.17-21) becomes quite clear if it is regarded in the light of 2 Cor. 12.7: "to keep me from being unduly elated by the magnificence of such revelations, I was given a sharp pain in my body which came as Satan's messenger". In the passage in Acts, Paul, telling the story of his conversion, says that the Lord appeared to him in the Temple and bade him leave Jerusalem, warning him that the Jews would not accept his testimony (while the apostle seemed to be objecting that if any man can convince the Jews it is he, since he is known to have been a persecutor of the infant Church) and called him to carry the gospel to the Gentiles.

It is difficult to see Paul's *ipsissima verba* in these verses. When he speaks of his vocation, in the epistles, he does not differentiate, as does the passage in Acts, between his conversion and his call to the ministry. It is with a ministry to the Gentiles in view--not excluding preaching to the Jews, however, as is proved in Rom. 1.16 and I Cor. 9.18-22--that God stopped him on the road to Damascus (Gal. 1.15-16).

But this passage in Acts suggests that Paul's companions remembered that his failure with the Jews had gone very hard with him, but that finally he had understood that this failure was part of God's plan. The equivalent of the vision of the Lord in the Temple is not then either of the christophanies which Paul mentions in his letter (Gal. 1.15-16; I Cor. 9.1; 15.8), but the apostle's declaration about the thorn in the flesh and the grace which is all-sufficient.

NOTES

1. *Studia Paulina in honorem Johannis de Zwaan*, Haarlem, 1953, p. 163-171, reprinted by kind permission of the publishers De Erven Bohn bv Uitgevers, Amsterdam.

2. Cf. G. Heinrici, *Der zweite Brief an die Korinther* (Meyer, VI, 7 Aufl.), Göttingen, 1890, p. 373-375; A. Plummer, *A Critical and Exegetical Commentary on the Second Epistle of St. Paul to the Corinthians* (ICC), Edinburgh, 1915, p. 349-351; E. B. Allo, *Saint Paul, Second Epître aux Corinthiens* (Etudes bibliques), Paris, 1937, p. 311-313.

3. Cf. G. Heinrici, *op. cit.*, p. 373.

4. A. Schlatter, *Paulus, der Bote Jesu. Eine Deutung seiner Briefe an die Korinther*, Stuttgart, 1934, p. 667.

5. Cf. among recent writers R. H. Strachan, *The Second Epistle of Paul to the Corinthians* (MNTC), London, 1935, p. 31; H. D. Wendland, *Die Briefe an die Korinther* (Das N.T. Deutsch), 2. Aufl., Göttingen, 1935, p. 147-148; K. L. Schmidt, *ThWzNT*, III, p. 820-821 and *Ein Gang durch den Galaterbrief* (Theol. Studien, 11-12), Zollikon-Zürich, 1942, p. 51; Lietzmann-Kuemmel, *An die Korinther I-II,* 4. Aufl. (Handbuch z.N.T., 9), Tübingen, 1949, p. 156-157 and 212; J. Klausner, *From Jesus to Paul*, 2 ed., London, 1946; p. 325; M. Goguel, *La naissance du christianisme,* Paris, 1946, p. 233; J. Maritain, *La pensée de saint Paul*, Paris, 1947, p. 70-71; J. Baruzi, *Creation religieuse et pensée contemplative*, Paris, 1951, p. 49; M. Simon, *Les premiers chrétiens*, Paris, 1952, p. 57; W. Bauer, *Wörterbuch z. N. T.*, 4. Aufl., Berlin, 1952, col. 1376.--Opinions differ, however, when it comes to deciding the nature of the apostle's illness. On this point, cf. E. B. Allo, *op. cit.,* p. 314-323.

6. *De Pudicitia* 13, 17 ("a pain in the ear or in the head, as far as we can tell"). The explanation of illness is however not universally accepted by the Fathers. Chrysostom, who knew of it, refuses to admit its validity (cf. E. B. Allo, *op. cit.*, p. 313, n. 3). The *Acta Pauli* make no reference to any illness in Paul, and yet they do not present a very flattering picture of the apostle (chap. 3).

7. Lietzmann-Kuemmel, *op. cit.*, p. 156.

8. Cf. Ph. H. Menoud, *La vie de l'Eglise naissante* (Cahiers théologiques 31), Neuchâtel-Paris, 1952, p. 49; *L'Eglise naissante et le judaïsme* (Etudes théologiques et religieuses), Montpellier, 1952, p. 15.

9. Cf. H. Schlier, *Der Brief an die Galater* (Meyer VIII, 10 Aufl.), Göttingen, 1949, p. 148, n. 5.

10. Cf. Moulton-Milligan, *The Vocabulary of the Greek Testament...* and Liddell-Scott-Jones, *A Greek-English Lexicon...* sub verbo.

11. Cf. I Cor. 15.31-32; 2 Cor. 1.8-11; 7.5-7; I Thess. 2.1-2; 3.2.

12. Πολλοὶ ἀσθενεῖς καὶ ἄρρωστοι. Ἄρρωστος is a *hapax* for Paul; ἀσθενής only appears here with the figurative meaning of "sick". Everywhere else--except I Tim. 5.23, but we take the pastoral epistles to be deuteropauline--under the pen of the apostle the word ἀσθενής--and others with the same root--has the proper meaning of "weak" or the figurative meaning provided by the Latin *imbecillis* or *inconstans*.

13. Cf. O. Cullmann, "La délivrance anticipée du corps humain selon le Nouveau Testament", *Hommage et reconnaissance à Karl Barth*, Neuchâtel-Paris, 1946, p. 38; Ph. H. Menoud, "Wunder und Sakrament im Neuen Testament", *Theologische Zeitschrift*, 1952, p. 182.

14. Cf. the commentaries by Heinrici, Plummer and Allo cited in note 5 above.

15. K. Bornhäuser, "Der Pfahl im Fleisch", *Die Furche*, 1937, p. 387-388.

16. L. Cerfaux, "L'antinomie paulinienne de la vie apostolique", *Mélanges Jules Lebreton I, Recherches de science religieuse*, 1951, p. 229-230.

17. Μου...τῇ σαρκί does not mean that the thorn attacks his physical body. The expression is a *dativus incommodi*, meaning that it is to the fulfillment of one of the apostle's most fervent desires that the unbelief of the Jews is an obstacle (we are indebted to our colleague, professor Ch. Masson of Lausanne for this observation.--The expression has its parallel in Rom. 9.2: τῇ καρδίᾳ μου; cf. also Rom. 9.3: τῶν συγγενῶν μου κατὰ σάρκα.

18. "Paul never felt himself a non-Jew," J. Klausner, *op. cit.*, p. 452.

19. On the subject of antijudaism and love for Israel in Paul, cf. Ph. H. Menoud, *L'Eglise naissante et le judaisme,* p. 11-17.

20. The same idea can be seen even more clearly in John's gospel where Jesus declares to the Jews who reject His testimony: "The father whose sons you are is the Devil" (John 8.44).

Revelation and Tradition

The Influence of Paul's Conversion on His Theology[1]

In the history of the Christian Church three men stand out, qualified beyond others by their genius and experience: Paul, Augustine, and Luther. All three have in common the fact that they attained such Christian faith and practice through a profound and dramatic conversion. In truth, their conversions are often put in parallel; they are even supposed to be identical, as if the same intellectual and mystical adventure had been lived thrice.

In fact the motives of their conversions seem to be of a different kind. Luther experienced failure in the struggle for righteousness and could not find peace with God until a new life had been given to him by faith alone in Jesus Christ. His conversion may be described as the type of a spiritual conversion.

Augustine was troubled by the struggle against sin and the impossibility for him to live in chastity and purity. He was in need of a new ethical way of life, and that is what he found. His conversion may be described as typically moral conversion.

It is the aim of this paper to call attention to the originality of Paul's conversion and its consequences. Saul of Tarsus, compared with both Augustine and Luther, stands apart. He had what may be called an ethical nature, and as a Pharisee had a moral conduct high above the common average. Again, Saul the Pharisee sincerely believed in righteousness by observing the law of Moses; he was at peace with the God of his fathers, and was assured of being saved in the last judgment. To him, his conversion means a new revelation of the God of Israel, a new act of God in Christ, and consequently, a reorganization of his Jewish messianic faith and hope. In one word, his conversion is the model of a theological conversion. The effects of that conversion are not so much a new spiritual or ethical life as a new theological position, at least in the sense that the new spiritual life of Paul the apostle has its source in a new theological truth.

THE NATURE OF PAUL'S CONVERSION

According to his own testimony Paul, when still a Jew, does not seem to have been morally troubled--he was a sincere Pharisee--nor to have been spiritually restless when he was trying to destroy the Church of God--he was a sincere persecutor.

It is true that very often in the past and still sometimes nowadays the apostle's conversion has been explained as the issue of a long conflict, along the one or the other of these ways. But the pictures which have been made of Paul suffering the sting of conscience, belong more to the sphere of romance than to that of historical reality. At least Paul himself never says a word about such a struggle in his own self.

When reporting on his former Jewish life, Paul writes to the Galatians: "I advanced in Judaism beyond many of my own age among my people, so extremely zealous was I for the traditions of my fathers" (1:14). He says still more precisely to the Philippians (3:5f.): "As to the law, a Pharisee, as to zeal a persecutor of the Church, as to righteousness under the law blameless." This passage is of particular weight, as the apostle first gives the testimony that, according to Jewish standards, his life has been without any blame, and, secondly, confesses that even his persecuting activities had been inspired by religious zeal. He was conscious of serving God when pursuing the followers of Jesus as blasphemers.

Now an objection may appear to the mind of some reader. It must be answered before going further.

According to some interpreters, Paul gave a graphic picture of himself at the time before his conversion, when he wrote Romans 7:7-25, saying, among other sentences: "For I delight in the law of God in my inmost self, but I see in my members another law at war with the law of my mind and making me captive to the law of sin which dwells in my members." This would be of the proof that Paul had been aware that his ethical ideal always transcended his practice.

That argument is by no means decisive. Romans 7 is one of the most disputed passages in Paul's Epistles. Now the interpretation just mentioned does not seem to be the most suitable, viewed both from its immediate context and from the general outline of Pauline thought. In Romans 5 to 8 the apostle relates the destiny of humanity condemned by Adam's sin and redeemed by the death and resurrection of Christ. In particular the apostle deals with the part played respectively by the law and by the Cross in the history of salvation. The "I" of Romans 7 is not personal, biographical. It is a collective "I" and denotes mankind as a whole, such as it appears in the light of the Cross. Paul is not alluding to a chapter in his own life, but to an epoch in the history of mankind.

Against the personal application of Romans 7 to the apostle the following argument, taken from among others which could be put forward, must be mentioned. We have no other example of the fact that the law had ever been considered by any Jew as a burden. This is the Christian interpretation of Jewish law. On the contrary, for the Jews, the law is the privilege and the pride of the nation, the very expression of the grace of the God of Abraham, of Isaac, and of Jacob. God has chosen Israel among all the nations of the world; he has given to his people the law as a sign of their election, and by it is sanctifying them and maintaining them apart from the "Gentile sinners" (Gal. 2:15; cf. also Rom. 9:3-5). This last expression used by Paul himself--together with the word of Philippians already quoted, where the apostle says that he was "blameless"--makes it hard to agree that in Romans 7 Paul would be alluding directly to his trouble of conscience as a Pharisee or to his remorse as a persecutor of the Church.

It has already been said that Saul was moved by zeal for God when he was pursuing the believers in Jesus. To him they were nothing but impostors. For Jesus could not be the Messiah. To Saul, as to every Jew, a Messiah crucified was a stumbling-block, a contradiction in terms. The Messiah, according to the common expectation, was to appear suddenly in power and glory to put an end to the present age and to establish the kingdom of God. Well, Jesus had been condemned not only by the highest authorities of Judaism, but even by God himself who had permitted him to suffer the most ignominous death and to fall under this sentence of the law: "Cursed be every one who hangs on a tree" (Deut. 21:23, quoted Gal. 3:13). It is not to be overlooked that the law was considered as the very word of God, given by the angels (cf. Gal. 3:19).

All this shows clearly that no other reason than his Jewish theological loyalty set Saul of Tarsus in opposition to the Christian faith. Consequently, a theological revolution had to happen in order that an apostle be made out of the persecutor. The conversion on the road to Damascus is that providential interference.

When speaking of it, the apostle does not say that profound reflection on the messianic problem, nor meditation on Stephen's death, nor any other proceedings led him to change his mind. Of course the psychologist may always hold that such a slow development occurred in Paul's subconsciousness. As a matter of fact, Paul himself says nothing about this. The important point is that Paul is very conscious of being conquered by a power beyond his own self, a power which it was impossible for him to resist. He has been arrested by God himself, revealing to him that Jesus was in fact what the Christians said he was, that is to say, that Jesus of Nazareth was the Messiah promised to Israel, that he lived at the right hand of God, and at the same time acted powerfully among his believers by the Spirit, and that "the Lord of the glory" (II Cor. 2:8) was to come at the end of this world and preside over the last things. In other words, God gave Paul to know that the Christians were right and that he himself had been wrong, but that he now was called to believe and to "preach the faith he once tried to destroy" (Gal. 1: 23). In fact, when Paul is speaking of his past life, he does not present his conduct as a moral or spiritual failure but as a messianic misconception.

The theological conversion of Paul the apostle had two main consequences. First, as God himself revealed to him his Son, the theology of the apostle appears as a revelation.

"The gospel which was preached by me is not man's gospel, for I did not receive it from man, nor was I taught it, but it came through a revelation of Jesus Christ" (Gal. 1:11f.). The theology of Paul is a God inspired theology.

Second, as the gospel revealed to Paul is in fact the same as the gospel already believed and preached before him, Paul is not called to be the founder of a new religion, but to take his place, as great as it might be, among those "who were apostles before him" (Gal. 1:17). In this second sense the theology of Paul is a theology relying on tradition.

These two main characteristics of Paul's thought--revelation and tradition--are by no means contradictory. Their coordination in the apostle's mind explains itself by the very nature of his conversion. Attention should now be called to each of these two aspects of Paul's theological position.

THE PLACE OF REVELATION IN PAUL'S THEOLOGY

On three points the theology of Paul appears to be more particularly dependent on the revelation received at Damascus. These are: the unity of the divine work in the Old and New Covenant, the redemptive value of the Cross, and the two stages in salvation.

The Unity of the Work of God in the Old and New Covenant

The God who reveals his Son to Paul is the same God that Saul served as a Pharisee, the God of Israel. This looks like some commonplace subject, but it is not. Paul does not, indeed, follow Stephen in throwing over as a complete error the whole of the past development of the Jewish religion. Still less does the apostle announce the distinction made by Marcion between the God of the Jews and the God of Jesus Christ. According to Paul the final word of God to man in the person of Jesus fulfills all that had gone before in the Old Covenant and creates a New Covenant, in continuity with the past. The apostle is so firmly convinced of the unity of the divine work that he gives to the people of Christ the very name of the chosen people in the past, calling the Church "the Israel of God" (Gal. 6:16).

Consequently, the conversion cannot conduct Paul to an entirely new theology. As a Christian he adores the same God he was worshipping as a Jew. Then the apostle has in common with the Pharisee the idea of God as the Creator of earth and heaven, as the God of history revealing himself in factual happenings and acting in the world towards the redemption of the sinful creature. Further, the apostle has in common with the Pharisee the same notion of the world and mankind. In other words, in matter of theology in the limited sense of the word, of cosmology, and of anthropology, Paulinism does not essentially differ from Judaism. Besides, as a believer Paul lives in the same passionate zeal for the glory of God as he did in his recent past.

The new element which creates the difference between the Pharisee and the apostle is that Paul now no longer expects in the future a still unknown Messiah. On the contrary he knows from the revelation given to him by God that the Messiah did come indeed in "Jesus our Lord, who was put to death for our trespasses and raised for our justification" (Rom. 4:25). The central quest of religion is still the same: How can men be saved and be admitted finally into the kingdom of God? But the answer is now different, because a new fact has been revealed. The new fact is the christological faith of the apostle, and its main consequence: salvation is not to be gained by observing the law; it has been brought about by Christ on the cross and it is granted by grace to the believers. This leads us to the second point alluded to above.

The Redemptive Value of the Cross

Saul the Pharisee could not believe in Jesus, because he saw the Cross under the curse spoken of by Deuteronomy. To that Pharisee the conversion is the evidence revealed from God himself that Christ has been glorified, that his death followed by his resurrection, is a part of the divine plan of salvation. It is not so that Paul ceased to attach any importance to the curse of the sentence in the law. His quotation of it, when writing to the Galatians, proves the contrary. For him the Scripture possesses divine authority and cannot be overthrown. He always affirms that he "upholds the law" (Rom. 3:31). Paul had to take into account both the resurrection and glorification of Christ, given to him as facts at his conversion, and the death on the Cross, to which a peculiar curse was attached.

The solution is given in the Epistles of Paul. It may be summed up as follows. The curse is not for Jesus personally. It is an expiatory and substitutive curse. It abolished the curse which Adam's sin had brought upon mankind. Christ is the One greater than Adam, whose obedience and sacrifice alone could suffice to make amends for that offense committed by others than himself. By his death Christ has substituted for the solidarity of sin in Adam a new solidarity of life in him for the believers. Thus, the Cross which was a stumbling-block to Saul, is seen by the apostle as "the power of God and the wisdom of God", "the foolishness of God" wiser than "the wisdom of the wise" (cf. I Cor. 1:18-25).

That is the reason why Paul gives to the Cross a redemptive value and significance and makes of it the very center of the gospel he preaches. The whole of Paul's theology could be quoted here. But that would lead too far. What must be emphasized is this: Paul does not believe in salvation by the Cross because as a Jew he was in doubt regarding salvation by the law. On the contrary it was given to him to admit that the Cross was the means chosen by God to save men. He then understood that salvation is the work of God and not of man, and he consequently as a Christian became more sceptical than he had been as a Pharisee on the possibility for man to live by his own efforts according to the will of God. The cross of Christ gave him a deeper vision of the holiness of God and of the gravity of the offense made to the divine majesty by man's sin. He was in the meantime convinced that in Christ, and in him alone, a new life and a new power over sin was given to believers, as a consequence of the Spirit of Christ imparted to them.

The Two Stages in Salvation

According to Jewish expectation the Messiah had to appear in glory and power at the end of this age and to inaugurate a new order of things.

With his coming in the midst of history, the Christian Messiah accomplishes only in part the traditional hope. He came in humility and his glorification after his death is but an anticipation of his glorious manifestation in the future. He gives by the Spirit a new power to believers in him, but these are not yet entirely saved. Living "in Christ", they are still "in the flesh", and they must die in order to enter the world yet to come by the final resurrection.

Paul expresses this twofold situation of the believer, when he speaks of redemption as at the same time an actual and a future experience. He writes to the Colossians (1:13): "In the Son we have redemption, the forgiveness of sins", and to the Romans (8:23): "We ourselves, who have the first fruits of the Spirit...wait for the redemption of our bodies." There is no contradiction between these two uses of the same word. Redemption is the actual gift of the Spirit which makes out of those who receive it, new creatures. Redemption is also the fulfillment of salvation and refers to the moment when these new creatures shall enjoy the glory of a future order of existence.

Redemption in the first sense has been accomplished by the death and resurrection of Christ. Redemption in the second sense shall be fulfilled by the coming of Christ at the end of this world. Faith in what Christ has already done is the foundation of hope in what Christ shall yet do.

There we have the more original character of Paulinism and Christianity in general compared with Judaism. For the Jews the whole salvation depends on the coming of the Messiah and is therefore expected in the future. In that sense Judaism is an eschatological religion, a religion of hope. Paulinism is a religion of faith and hope, of history and eschatology. A part of the Jewish hope has become historical reality by the coming of Christ Jesus. What is still expected depends on the coming of the same Christ in glory and power.

This new view of the history of salvation with its two main epochs is the final consequence of the christological faith of Paul.

THE PLACE OF TRADITION IN PAUL'S THEOLOGY

By his conversion Paul does not become the founder of a new religion but an apostle of a faith already preached before him. Paul the apostle has, in a very high degree, a sense of historical continuity in God's action. He manifests this sense of tradition in three ways: by communion with the other apostles, by the keeping of apostolic traditions, by the maintenance of the Church's unity.

"Those Who Were Apostles Before Me"

For Paul the identity of the risen Christ and the historical Jesus is obvious. The "Lord of glory" whom he saw is not a purely heavenly being, but Jesus of Nazareth who lived in Galilee and died in Jerusalem. In fact, the apostle has not been witness of the earthly career of Jesus. Yet for Paul the humanity of Christ is of the utmost importance, because it is by his human death on the cross that redemption is worked out. Besides, if the death of Christ has a vicarious significance, it is because Jesus, as a sinless being, did not have to die for his own sins, and consequently was able to expiate the sins of others. Now, Paul who was not among the Twelve, must rely on their testimony as far as the ministry of Jesus is concerned.

As Paul saw the unity of the God of the Old Covenant and of "the Father of our Lord Jesus Christ"--as has already been said--so he understood, with the same feeling of continuity in history, that he received at Damascus the explanation of a divine action which had been experienced by "those who had been apostles before him" (Gal. 1:17). The gospel which is given to him as a revelation from above is at the same time an historical happening which is the object of a tradition.

The apostle would have rejected with an energetic "by no means" all modern explanations which tend to give him the honor of having founded Christianity. On the contrary Paul is conscious of being placed by the Spirit in an historical development whose start is anterior to his own conversion.

Paul never forgets that he was not a witness of Christian origins in the sense in which the Twelve were. That is the reason why he always finds it necessary to live in communion with the apostles of Jerusalem. The most striking example occurs in Galatians 2:1-10, where the apostle says that he came to Jerusalem "lest somehow I should be running or had run in vain". Such would be the case, if his ministry among the Gentiles was not recognized by the "pillars" of the Church. Paul makes this visit to them precisely because he finds it indispensable that the authentic character of his apostleship, and consequently the authentic Christian character of the churches he founded, be established.

In other words it appears to him that he, as an apostle, and the believers gathered by him among the heathen, must be received in the apostolic communion. Moreover, these feelings of Paul were shared by the other apostles. For they gave him "the right hand of fellowship". The collection for the Jerusalem Christians which Paul undertook, is the seal of that communion demanded by Paul and admitted by the Twelve.

"The Traditions"

According to Paul there is no authentic Christianity without communion with Jerusalem. For the mother church possesses the authoritative traditions concerning the origins. Twice the apostle recalls to the mind of the Corinthians that he transmitted to them original traditions on faith. Concerning the Eucharist, he writes: "I received from the Lord what I also delivered to you..." (I Cor. 11:23), that is, "What I passed on to you concerning the origin of the Lord's Supper forms part of the apostolic tradition which goes back through those actually present at the event to the Lord himself."

Later in the same Epistle, speaking on resurrection, Paul says in almost identical terms: "I delivered to you what I also received..." (I Cor. 15:3). It is worth noting that in this passage the apostle first mentions the tradition about the visions of the risen Lord--quoting an old confession of the faith, as most recent interpreters rightly suggest--and only thereafter says that the Lord appeared to him also (I Cor. 15:8). The apostolic tradition goes before his own testimony.

More generally Paul does value at a high price the traditions of the primitive church. He once more writes to the Corinthians: "I commend you because you maintain the traditions even as I have delivered them to you" (I Cor. 11:2). These traditions concern not only the fundamental happenings on which the Church is built, such as the institution of the Eucharist and the resurrection of the Lord--as we just saw--but also the order and uses which must rule the life of the whole Church. There is no other law than the practice of "the churches of God" (I Cor. 11:11) or of "the churches of the saints" (I Cor. 14:34), and Paul means in these verses the churches where the word of God originated (I Cor. 14:36), in other words, "the churches of Christ in Judea" (Gal. 1:22).

If Paul could so firmly remind the Corinthians that the word of God did not originate in the Gentile church, it is because he himself never forgot that neither did the apostolate originate with him.

The Unity of the Church

All that precedes proves that Paul has a very strong idea of the unity of the Church. Once more he is not called to create anew a community of believers. Of course, as a missionary, he always makes it his ambition "to preach the gospel, not where Christ has already been named, lest I build on another man's foundation" (Rom. 15:20). But, as this confession implies, he preaches to the Gentiles the same gospel the other apostles preach to the Jews. The same Lord "who worked through Peter for the mission to the circumcised worked through me also for the Gentiles" (Gal. 2:8). Yet, after quoting the apostolic tradition on the risen Christ to the Corinthians he adds: "Whether then it was I or they"--that is, the apostles of Jerusalem--"so we preach and so you believed" (I Cor. 15:11).

Paul is so much convinced of having joined by his conversion the original tradition, that he makes of Jerusalem the very starting point of his own missionary work. Summing up his activities in the Orient, he writes to the Romans (15:19): "From Jerusalem and as far round as Illyricum I have fully preached the gospel of Christ." One would expect the apostle to the Gentiles to say here "from Damascus" or "from Antioch", rather than from Jerusalem, as either of those cities might at first sight be preferred as the factual starting point of the Pauline mission to the heathen. If, nevertheless, the apostle himself places the origin of his own work at Jerusalem, it is because his mission can not have any other theological beginning than the place where Christ died and rose again, and where the gospel of the risen Lord was preached to the world for the very first time. For there is but one Lord, one gospel, one Church.

CONCLUSION

The conversion of Paul is the example in the history of the Church of a theological conversion. Paul was not converted in order to turn from a worldly man into a religious one, nor from a troubled spirit into a soul in peace with God and his own self. On the contrary God himself stopped him in order to reveal to him that Jesus whom he was persecuting in the form of his believers was in reality the Lord of glory, just as his worshippers said he was.

Consequently the whole of Paul's theological thought and zealous activity for God was re-examined and reorganized. The Lord crucified and raised up again became the very center of his theology, and the apostolic tradition concerning Jesus Christ, which originated at a time when Paul was not yet a believer, was recognized by him as the normal rule of faith and order in the one Church of the one Lord.

That is the deep reason why revelation and tradition are so intimately united in Paul's thought. This fact can never be too strongly emphasized. Paul was the man who could have created his own movement, as so many Christian leaders did in the course of history from the second century onwards. But Paul did not. He understood that the gospel is all both revelation and tradition by the very nature of things. Its profound meaning is revealed by the Spirit of God, but it is built on historical happenings: the holy life, the death, the resurrection and glorification of Christ, which all have happened once for all.

Paul knew consequently that nothing had to be founded again, that he himself was called to join those who, like him and even before him, had experienced the same living power of Christ, and to live in their communion.

The very greatness of Paul the apostle is due to the fact that he was able to unite both revelation and tradition in his thought and work.

NOTE

1. This article appeared in *Interpretation; A Journal of Bible and Theology* 7 (1953), p. 131-141. It is reprinted by kind permission of the publishers.

The Meaning of the Verb Πορθεῖν[1] (Gal. 1:13, 23; Acts 9:21)

There is no doubt that Paul of Tarsus was among those who persecuted the followers of Christ before he was called to preach the Gospel. The apostle's statement of the fact is quite positive and it is confirmed by the book of Acts. One question remains unanswered, however: what kind of attacks did this zealous pharisee wage against the Church of God? The Acts mention physical violence, arrest, imprisonment. Paul mentions nothing of this kind although he makes it clear that his persecution was extremely vigorous and was intended to destroy the Church.

Theoretically it is possible that the apostle does not mention the outrages reported in Acts because he limits himself to recalling his role as a persecutor in just a few words, without taking time to describe it in detail. But there is another possible explanation. We may suppose that Paul attacked the faith of the believers rather than their bodies, that is he sought to bring down the Church from its foundations by showing, through scripture, that Christ crucified could not be the Messiah. In the following pages we shall attempt to show that that is the image of Pauline persecution suggested by the passages from Galatians and that this image can also be seen behind the traditional accounts found in Acts.

Four times in his epistles Paul recalls his persecution of the Church (Gal. 1:13, 23; Phil. 3:6; I Cor. 15.9).[2] In I Corinthians 15:9 and Philippians 3:6 he merely mentions the fact, making use of the verb διώκειν in the literal sense, common in the New Testament, of "to attack", "to persecute".[3] On the other hand, the apostle is more precise in the two verses from Galatians, where he explains διώκειν by the stronger and more expressive verb πορθεῖν. He declares in Galatians 1:13 that he used to persecute the Church in order to destroy it, and in Galatians 1:23, reporting in rumors about him after his conversion: "he is now preaching the faith he once tried to destroy."[4] Therefore it is the exact meaning of the verb πορθεῖν that we must define.[5]

Πορθεῖν has been in use since the time of Homer to describe the destruction of a region and the sacking of a town by an army on the offensive. This primary meaning is found throughout Greek civilization; in Hellenistic and Roman times we find it particularly in Philo and Josephus and in the papyri.[6] War does not spare the inhabitants of the countries where it is waged. That is why πορθεῖν, in classic tragedy, also means the ill-treatment and torture endured by those citizens who fall into the hands of the enemy. Approaching the Christian era we find πορθεῖν used with this meaning, particularly in 4 Maccabees 11:4 in describing the martyrdom of the seven brethren under Antiochus Epiphanes. We find it also in Philo to describe the misfortunes of the Jews handed over by Flaccus to the populace of Alexandria, on the occasion of the troubles in the year 38, as the inhabitants of a vanquished city are handed over at the whim of the conqueror.[7] Already in Euripides the verb πορθεῖν evokes the captives' fate, often worse than death,[8] and Philo suggests, without any shadow of a doubt, that the Jewish population of Alexandria had to endure all manner of ill-treatment and not merely loss of life.

In short πορθεῖν always has a strong meaning. Whether applied to things or to people it always conveys the idea of material assault or even more violent physical or mental destruction. And the precise meaning of the verb is governed by the context. If πορθεῖν is relatively little used, it is because it is more or less synonymous with λυμαίνεσθαι, which has a broader meaning, however--it can have the strong meaning of πορθεῖν but it can also be used in the weaker sense of "to impede", "to hinder". For this reason it is more common, especially from Hellenistic times, among writers, on inscriptions and in papyri. The Septuagint uses only λυμαίνεσθαι. The Acts and Josephus use λυμαίνεσθαι and πορθεῖν with the same meaning. On the other hand Philo does not seem to give as much force to λυμαίνεσθαι as to πορθεῖν. For, while making use of both verbs to describe the persecutions suffered by the Jews in Alexandria under Caligula, he uses, as we have just seen, the verb πορθεῖν when writing of the ravages against the population, and he uses λυμαίνεσθαι to describe the desecration of the holy places.[10] It is in the weak sense of "obstruct", "impede" that λυμαίνεσθαι appears in Claudius' Letter to the Alexandrians.[11]

To return to the accounts in Galatians. Paul doubtless would know the word λυμαίνεσθαι, which was in common use and which he would have read in the Septuagint. However, it is πορθεῖν which he uses to describe his efforts to destroy the Church. We can find two reasons for this preference. First of all πορθεῖν is the opposite of οἰκοδομεῖν and Paul is fond of such verbal contrasts. The opposition which is implicit in 1:13 is quite explicit in 1:23: he who now builds up the Church by preaching the Gospel formerly wanted to destroy it.[12] Secondly, by choosing the stronger of the two possible words, Paul doubtless intends to emphasize the violence of his assaults on the Church. Moreover, he declares that his attacks on the believers resulted from excessive zeal, found rarely in the Jews of his time (1:13f.). This implies that he acted alone, without the active support of his colleagues. This is also suggested by 1:23, reporting that the churches of Judea breathed a sigh of relief when they learned of the conversion of their only persecutor. All this goes to show that, in Paul's view, his persecution was formidable and dealt harshly with the believers.

By what means did Paul strive to destroy the Church? The verb πορθεῖν, which can mean both physical and spiritual destruction, opens the door to two explanations: either the pharisee brought about the ill-treatment and imprisonment of the believers, or, by his knowledge of the scriptures, he demonstrated how their belief in a crucified Messiah was absurd and blasphemous. We must now try to determine the exact nature of Paul's persecution.

If our only evidence were that of the apostle himself, we would not hesitate to admit that his attacks on the Church must have been essentially theological. A pharisee is an exegete; he is neither a policeman nor an executioner. "When Paul mentions the first part of his life...he shows his former attitude as a mistake and not as a crime."[13] It is in the Acts and not in the epistles that we find the image of the persecutor "whose every breath was a threat of destruction for the disciples of the Lord".[14] But this image is unclear. Luke, while taking great care not to give Paul an active role in the murder of Stephen (Acts 8:1; 22:20), connects the Pauline persecution with the execution of the first martyr (Acts 8:1-3), both literally and chronologically. Thus Paul follows in the line of succession of Stephen's murderers; he appears as a formidable persecutor; even more he alone "*is* persecution",[15] although this comes to an end as soon as he is converted (Acts 9:31). But Luke, or at any rate his sources of information, knows very little about this terrible enemy who desires the suppression of all believers[16] without, nevertheless, inflicting the ultimate punishment on them.[17] According to Acts, as also according to the epistles, Paul has no blood on his hands. Moreover, Luke, who records the charges against Stephen, does not tell us what charges Paul leveled at the Christians he was pursuing; we do not know by virtue of what authority the pharisee went into "house after house" and how he identified the homes of Christians. Nor are we told anything of the fate of those unfortunates who were chained and thrown into prison. In short, Luke's descriptions remain up in the air; they are made up of conventional characteristics which could belong just as well to any other persecutions as to that of Paul. Luke knows that Paul attacked the Church, but he does not seem to have a clear, precise idea of the motives, the methods, or the results of the persecutor's activities.

However, we must beware of disparaging the writer of the Acts. Doubtless he had no concrete evidence at his disposal apart from the fact that Paul, at first, had opposed the Church with all his might. And he could not have had any concrete evidence because a devastating, physical persecution of the believers was legally hardly possible in the third decade. Apart from the case of a riot like the one which cost Stephen his life, it is difficult to see how the followers of Jesus, the Messiah, could have been exposed to all the rigors of authority. The only dogma of Judaism is the affirmation that the one and only God was revealed to his people Israel in the Law handed down by Moses. Messianism and eschatology were not rigorously defined doctrines. It was possible to hold very different opinions on these questions quite openly. The Sadducees denied the resurrection of the dead without losing any of their authority over the people. R. Akiba, who, in the second century, had hailed Bar Kokheba as the Messiah, has remained one of the most revered scholars in Israel.[18] Without any doubt, the first Christians, who confessed faith in a Jesus condemned by the Sanhedrin and crucified, must have been a severe irritant to the Jewish authorities. There is no love lost on those who want to reopen a case that has already been decided, and who, by so doing, seem to be attacking the judges and the law itself. But that would not justify a persecution. The only physical measure which Paul the pharisee could take against the followers of Christ was that which he himself had endured five times, according to 2 Corinthians 11:24--the infliction of thirty-nine lashes.[19] In view of the harshness of justice at that time, this punishment was not among the most severe. But then, if Paul had only inflicted on the Christians the cruelty of "forty lashes all but one"--and once again we repeat we can see no legal grounds for a physical persecution--how is it that Paul is traditionally regarded as a formidable persecutor and how can he himself write that he made every effort to destroy the Church? There can be only one answer to this question. We must take the strong verb πορθεῖν in the spiritual sense and not in the physical sense when the apostle is describing his work of persecution. Paul wanted to destroy the Church not by punishing the believers physically but by undermining their faith at its base. In other words, he preached against Christ before he proclaimed the Gospel.

This is the most obvious meaning of the passages in Galatians to which we have referred. As we have seen above, the apostle declares that he is now propagating the faith he formerly sought to destroy. If the contrast between the work of the persecutor and that of the apostle is so easily established, it must be because the methods were the same in each case. Now Paul establishes the Church by preaching that "Christ died for our sins according to the Scriptures...and He rose on the third day in accordance with the Scriptures" (I Cor. 15:3f.); formerly he probably attempted to demolish the faith of the believers and to destroy the Church by proving through the Scriptures that Christ crucified could not be the Messiah.

Paul has always viewed the person and work of Christ in the perspective of the cross.[20] More precisely, he has always seen in Christ crucified the one who is the object of the divine curse, for it is written: "Cursed is everyone who hangs upon a tree" (Deut. 21:23; Gal. 3:13). This part of the Law shaped his life as a pharisee and also his life as an apostle. If he is an apostle, it is because he has understood that the curse which falls upon Christ is a substitutive curse which gains salvation for those who are one with Christ. If formerly he persecuted the Church, it is not only because, in his view, as in the view of all Jews, the crucified one was personally cursed by God,[21] but also because his pharisaic zeal could not tolerate the blasphemous avowal that the one whom God has cursed is the Messiah of Israel. And so Paul went over to the attack. In the synagogues which the followers of Christ still attended he pointed out that faith in the "Messiah" Jesus was condemned by the very word of God. The scriptural knowledge of the man from Tarsus would sweep aside the protests of the believers, few, if any, of whom could conduct a debate on equal terms. In the synagogues where the fiery pharisee had spoken, there would be found not believers suffering in body--and happy to suffer in the name of their Savior--but creatures in great distress whose reason for believing had been snatched from them. In fact Paul's theological persecution was more damaging than any physical persecution. The Christians whom the pharisee left behind him were destroyed spiritually. We can understand why the apostle, when reviewing his previous activities, would choose to describe them with the verb πορθεῖν which brings to mind pillaging and devastation.

This interpretation of the attacks launched by Paul against the Church can be confirmed to some extent by the traditions about the pharisee's persecution which have been maintained in Christianity. Traditionally Paul is portrayed as a formidable adversary of the believers and an adversary who acts alone. As we have seen in Acts, Paul alone "*is* persecution" (E. Haenchen). It is on his own initiative that he asks the high priest for letters of recommendation to the synagogues at Damascus (9:1f.); he is not an agent of the Sanhedrin. Neither does he appear as the mouthpiece of Pharisaism; his extraordinary zeal distinguished him from his colleagues who were perhaps more prone to follow the "wait and see" policy advocated by Gamaliel (5:38f.). All the same, in the pseudo-Clementine literature, Paul appears on the scene as the lone adversary of the Church under the title of *homo inimicus*.[22] Moreover, a campaign undertaken by a pharisee acting alone and armed only, though more than adequately, with his knowledge of the Scriptures, could only be waged on theological grounds. To initiate a physical persecution it is necessary to be a petty king, making use of armed might, like Agrippa. And it is only a theological undertaking which can really destroy the Church. Physical cruelties merely produce martyrs and, according to tradition,

Stephen was the only martyr between the time of the first preaching of Peter and the conversion of Paul.

It is true that tradition seems to have lost sight of the real character of Paul's persecution. But there are two reasons for this. First, in order to understand the central place of the cross of Christ in Paul's thought and consequently his zeal either for or against the crucified Christ, it is essential to know the apostle's doctrine as it is set down in his epistles. Now Luke has not read Paul, and Paul himself avers that his ideas, known only through hearsay, were often misunderstood and distorted. Secondly, between the time of the conversion of Paul and that of the writing of Acts, about the fifth decade, a regime of extreme violence had become established in Jerusalem, carried out by the Zealots and particularly by the most fanatic of them, the Sicarii, who chose as their victims anyone who might be suspected of having any sympathy for the Greeks or the Romans.[23] This zealotry, which was at work also in the diaspora, was exercised particularly against the Church involved in missionary work in pagan countries. This same zealotry was undoubtedly responsible for the persecution of the Christians in Judea, according to Paul's testimony,[24] persecution of which he himself was so often in danger of being a victim.[25]

Now it would seem that the experiences of the Zealot persecutions would have obliterated from Christian tradition the memory of Paul's persecution without losing completely its distinctive characteristics. In fact, at a closer look, Luke's descriptions are not homogeneous, as they should be if he had written them in a straightforward manner; they seem to combine elements from different sources. The scenes of violence seem reminiscent of the activities of the Zealots; it was they, for example, who could track down the Christians in their homes, for from the fifth decade, after the Council of Jerusalem, the enemies of the Church could recognize the houses which gave sanctuary to Christians. On the other hand, Luke makes use of information coming more or less directly from the apostle, because he uses in one instance (9:21) the Pauline verb πορθεῖν. This may be quite a chance occurrence.[26] However, it is more likely that is not the case. Luke, in fact, also says that the pharisee sought out the believers in the synagogues (9:2; 22:19; 26:11); but the only way Paul could find out who they were was by preaching what amounted to an attack on their faith and thereby calling forth a confession. Doubtless that was when he forced them to "blaspheme", that is to recognize their error with regard to the Messiah (26:11). Here we find the pharisee who persecutes the Church theologically.[27]

Paul's choice of the verb πορθεῖν means that his persecution of the infant Church was very strong. If the verb is taken in its literal sense, we would have to conclude that Paul launched a veritable massacre of the Christians. But even his fiercest enemies, both Jews and Judeo-Christians, did not accuse him of murder. It was the convictions of the believers, and not their bodies, which the pharisee attacked with the burning passion of a blinded Zealot which he later renounced. In this way he treated the Church more severely than he would have done with acts of violence, and undoubtedly more effectively. It is because his persectuion was theological that it holds such an important place both in history and in legend.

NOTES

1. *Apophoreta. Festschrift für Ernst Haenchen.* (Beihefte zur Zeitschrift für die neutestamentliche Wissenschaft, 30), Berlin, 1964, p. 178-186, by kind permission of the publishers Walter de Gruyter & Co., Berlin.

2. Cf. I Tim. 1:13.

3. On Paul's use of διώκειν in the figurative sense cf. R. Bultmann, *Theologie des Neuen Testaments*, 1953, p. 221.

4. Must we presume that the use of the imperfect tense ἐπόρθουν (v. 13) and ἐπόρθει (v. 23) indicates the intention (Burton) or the length and continuation of the persecution (Schlier)? This question is not relevant to our thesis. The perpetuation of Pauline persecution by tradition leads us to think that his zeal was no fruitless effort.

5. The variant επολεμουν (1:13), επολεμει (1:23) of F G is of secondary importance. It is merely the case of a common word replacing a more unusual one. Our problem would still exist; πολεμεῖν like πορθεῖν can be interpreted both in a physical sense and a moral sense.

6. Cf. the Liddell-Scott, Bauer and Moulton-Milligan dictionaries.

7. Philo, *In Flacc.* 54: ἐφεὶς [the subject is Flaccus] ὡς ἐν ἁλώσει τοῖς ἐθέλουσι πορθεῖν 'Ιουδαίους; cf. E. Schürer, *Geschichte des judischen Volkes im Zeitalter Jesu Christi*, 4. Aufl., 1901, I, p. 498.

8. Euripides, *Phoen.* 564f.:

ὄψει (δὲ) πολλὰς αἰχμαλωτίδας κόρας
βίᾳ πρὸς ἀνδρῶν πολεμίων πορθουμένας

cf. Aeschylus, Sept. 329-31:

...βοᾷ δ'
ἐκκενουμένα πόλις
λαΐδος ὀλλυμένας μιξοθρόου·

where the scholiast reads πορθουμένας in place of ὀλλυμένας.

9. Acts 8:3; 9:21. Josephus, BJ IV 534 uses the two verbs in the same sentence with the same meaning.

10. Philo, *Leg. ad Caium* 134.

11. P. Lond. 1912, I.85f.--The text is quoted by Lake-Cadbury (*The Beginnings of Christianity I, The Acts of the Apostles IV*, 1933, p. 88) and by H. Conzelmann ("Die Apostelgeschichte", *Handbuch zum Neuen Testament* 7, 1963, p. 52). The Emperor Claudius orders the Alexandrians "not to hinder the traditional ways in which the Jews honor their god and to allow them to follow their usual customs" (translation of Th. Reinach, "L'empereur Claude et les Juifs", *Revue des études juives*, 79, 1924, p. 118f.). The connection between this and Acts 8:3 is purely one of vocabulary.

12. "Hoc plane contrarium *aedificationi* notat" Bengel, *Gnomon Novi Testamenti*, 1855, p. 717.

13. M. Goguel, *Introduction au Nouveau Testament*, IV 1, 1925, p. 205.

14. Acts 8:3; 9:1f., 13f., 21; 22:4, 19f.; 26:9-11.

15. E. Haenchen, *Die Apostelgeschichte*, 13. Aufl., 1961, p. 249.--Those who journey with Paul on the road to Damascus (Acts 9:7; 22:9; 26:13) are traveling companions (Wendt, Lake-Cadbury, Renié, Haenchen in their commentaries) and not a "Begleitkommando" from the Temple guard (Stählin, from Zahn). Deporting Jews from Damascus to Jerusalem was outside the jurisdiction of the high priest, and I Macc. 15:21, which is often quoted in support of the historicity of Acts 9:2 was an exceptional case and did not authorize permanent extradition rights. Cf. Haenchen, p. 268f.; H. Conzelmann, *Die Apostelgeschichte*, 1963, p. 57.

16. Cf. Acts 9:21 (πορθεῖν).

17. In Acts 22:4 which speaks of persecution unto death--cf. also 26:10--we are dealing with a generalization with regard to Stephen (E. Haenchen, p. 555).

18. Cf. M. Simon, *Verus Israël. Etude sur les relations entre Chrêtiens et Juifs dans l'empire romain (135-425)*, 1948, p. 303; M. Goguel, *La naissance du christianisme*, 1946, p. 488.

19. Cf. among others A. Loisy, *L'épître aux Galates*, 1916, p. 73; *Les Actes des apôtres*, 1920, p. 392; A. D. Nock, *Saint Paul*, 1938, p. 33; E. Haenchen, *op. cit.*, p. 249; G. Bornkamm, *RGG*, 3. Aufl., V, 1961, col. 169.--This was the measure taken against the apostles Peter and John, Acts 5:40. J. Klausner (*From Jesus to Paul*, 2nd ed., 1946, p. 292) suggests that, according to the pharisees, Stephen was not liable to any other punishment.

20. Cf. M. Goguel, *Introduction au Nouveau Testament*, IV, 1, 1925, p. 210f.; *La naissance du christianisme*, 1946, p. 99f.; Ph. H. Menoud, "Revelation and Tradition: The Influence of Paul's Conversion on His Theology", *Interpretation*, 7, 1953, p. 131-141, *supra* p. 31-46.

21. Cf. G. Bertram, *ThWbNT*, III, p. 918; M. Dibelius-W. G. Kuemmel, *Paulus*, 1951, p. 106.--The importance of Deut. 21:23 in discussions between Jews and Christians is well-known. See particularly Justin, *Dial.* 32:1; 89:2; 90:1; 96:1. On the same point, cf. A. L. Williams, *Adversus Judaeos. A Bird's-Eye View of Christian Apologiae until the Renaissance*, 1935, p. 39 and 49; M. Simon, *op. cit.*, p. 192f.

22. Rec. I 70. Cf. O. Cullmann, *Le problème littéraire et historique du roman pseudo-clémentin*, 1930, p. 243; H. J. Schoeps, *Theologie und Geschichte des Juden-christentums*, 1949, p. 412.

23. Cf. E. Schürer, *op. cit.*, I, p. 567ff.; F. M. Abel, *Histoire de la Palestine depuis la conquête d'Alexandre jusqu'à l'invasion arabe*, 1952, I, p. 462ff.; B. Reicke, *Studia Paulina*, 1953, p. 182ff.

24. I Thess. 2:14-16.--There is no reason to maintain that this passage, which does not contradict Rom. 9:5ff., has been interpolated; according to the apostle, anti-Judaism and love of Israel are two complementary attitudes and not in any way exclusive one of the other. (Cf. Ph. H. Menoud, "L'Eglise naissante et le judaisme", *Etudes theol. et relig.*, 27, 1952, I, p. 11f. *Infra* p. 436f.).

25. Cf. 2 Cor. 11:23ff.; Gal. 4:29; Rom. 15:31.

26. Cf. among others Wendt and Haenchen in their commentaries; M. Goguel, *Introduction au Nouveau Testament*, III, 1922, p. 115, n. 2; E. Trocmé, *Le livre des Actes et l'his-*

toire, 1957, p. 153, n. 2. In any case, this in itself is not an indication that Luke is acquainted with the epistle to the Galatians (see Loisy, *Les Actes des apôtres*, 1920, p. 416; Ch. Masson, *Theologische Zeitschrift*, 18, 1962, p. 163f.).

27. The idea that Paul's persecution was theological seems to exist even in the pseudo-Clementine story (Rec. I 70): Paul intervenes after James has called the crowd to be baptized and he exhorts the Israelites not to be led astray by the disciples of a magician; it is when James wants to answer him that he stirs up the crowd against the Christians and himself attacks the Lord's brother. It is perhaps also the recollection of the real nature of Paul's persecution which makes Eusebius say (In Esaïam 18:1) that Paul was a Jewish apostle before being a Christian apostle (cf. J. Klausner, *op. cit.*, p. 318).

II. THE GOSPEL ACCORDING TO LUKE-- THE ACTS OF THE APOSTLES

The Western Text and the Theology of Acts[1]

Much learning has been spent in studies upon the two different texts offered by the manuscripts of St. Luke's works. Both the recension of the great Uncials, the so-called Alexandrian text, or may we say briefly the B text, and the recension represented by the Bezan Codex and other so-called Western authorities or the D text, have been more than once minutely investigated. More light has been thrown on the nature, characteristics and probable date and place of birth of both recensions. Yet, despite all the progress that has been made, the problem of the relation between the two texts and between both texts and the primitive text has not been solved. Agreement among scholars is far from having been reached. This problem remains, now as ever, "a thorn in the flesh" for every student of the third gospel or the book of Acts.

As far as Acts is concerned, the explanation presented more than fifty years ago by Friedrich Blass is generally discarded. It seems impossible to admit that two so strikingly different recensions may have both come from the author himself and may be two successive editions of his work. As J. H. Ropes rightly says: "The decisive argument against Blass is that in many passages the conception of the event described, the mental picture of what took place, is different in the two forms of the text."[2]

In the last twenty-five years the views of scholars have been governed by the opposite theories of J. H. Ropes[3] and A.

C. Clark.[4] The former argues in favour of the text of the great Uncials and holds the Western text to be a deliberate expansion of the primitive text, made by a second-century writer. "An entirely opposite estimate of the longer text of D has been proposed by Clark, who found in the Bezan Uncial, not only a text which is the better representative on the whole of the primitive text of both the Gospel and Acts, but a fuller and more circumstantial text of which the Vatican recension represents a shorter edition and a deliberate scholarly abridgement."[5]

Since 1933, scholars either divide themselves into followers of Ropes or Clark,[6] or hesitate to decide in favour of either text as a whole, preferring to pursue what G. D. Kilpatrick calls "an eclectic method, based on criteria independent of any one type of text".[7] That eclecticism seems now, if I am rightly informed, to receive more and more consideration.[8]

In fact, as G. D. Kilpatrick remarked,[9] eclecticism had already raised its head even in the works of Ropes and Clark. Ropes, in his text, admits a few Western readings; Clark likewise has to call in aid the Alexandrian authorities more than once. Similarly B. H. Streeter, who gave a warm welcome to Clark's thesis, does not hesitate to find secondary readings in the Western text.[10] Lake and Cadbury, in their Commentary based on the Alexandrian text, frequently allow that the Western text may be right, and Lake explains in the preface to vol. IV of *The Beginnings of Christianity* (Sept. 1932): "I am glad to have the opportunity of confessing that after fifteen years I am more often doubtful about the true text than I was before."[11] Such balanced judgments could be found in many recent works on the book of Acts.

The eclectic method seems to recommend itself at least for the two following reasons. First, progress in the study of the great Uncial manuscripts and the discovery of Greek papyri such as P^{38} P^{48} and P^{45} have definitely established that the Alexandrian text is itself a revised text which "cannot be traced back beyond the third century".[12] It follows that both the B text and the D text must be regarded as two different recensions of a lost primitive text. Consequently the question is not so much to make a choice between them, as to work back, if possible, to the primitive text with the aid of both recensions. Each of the two has an equal right to be heard.

Second, the text offered by the Western authorities does not seem to be either good or bad as a whole. It is better to say that it presents good and bad readings.[13] Further, its readings may be better in general on certain subjects and worse on some others. For instance, in the matter of geographical data, the Western authorities seem to have preserved more than one precious indication. Let us take but one example. In Acts xix. 29 Gaius and Aristarchus are called Macedonians; but in xx. 4 Gaius is said to be a native of Derbe in Asia Minor. Clark shows that the D reading for Derbaios is Doberios (d: doverius; gig.: doberius) and that twenty-six miles from Philippi there was a town Doberus which is mentioned by Thucydides and sent, centuries later, a bishop to the council of Chalcedon.[14] If the accuracy of the Western text may be so well proved at one point, where external evidence can be produced, there is a strong presumption that on other similar data the D text may be equally right.

But on other matters the Western authorities do not offer such good readings. The D text shows, for instance, a tendency towards reverential amplification of the titles applied to Jesus, in adding the words *Kurios* or *Christos* or both. These words are most probably devotional additions to the primitive text, for it is difficult to admit that any Christian would have suppressed them, had he found them in the text he was copying. In such cases the natural tendency is to add and not to omit.

These examples indicate that each particularity of the Western text--additions, omissions or changes--must be examined and estimated for itself. Accuracy of the writer of D in matters of geography does not prove that he is equally right in readings concerned with religious or theological matters. These readings must be judged for themselves.

It is the purpose of this paper to study the peculiarities of the Western text which have or may have a theological significance. They are but few and at first sight not very important. The most numerous and striking differences between the Western and Alexandrian texts concern the narrative parts of Acts and not the discourses, where the religious thought of the author is to be found rather than in the more historical sections. Yet we are perhaps in a more favourable position to estimate the theological discrepancies between the two texts for the following reason. As far as the history of the growing Church is concerned, Acts is practically our only source of knowledge. The information taken from the Pauline Epistles, precious as it is, is but fragmentary. On the contrary, the theological thought and religious life of the Church in the first century is known to us, apart from Acts, from valuable indications contained in the gospels and the epistles of the New Testament. In a great measure, too, it is possible to know what the Church of the first century did believe and practice from the later developments offered to us in second century writings. In fact we are not without criteria which may be of great assistance and value when comparing Alexandrian and Western readings and trying to decide which text has more exactly preserved the letter and the meaning of the primitive text.

We shall begin with the study of the apostolic decree in Acts xv. In these verses other and more primitive readings are available than those of either the Alexandrian or the Western recension. It is possible to work back in this matter to the original text and therefore to discover in some measure the motives and intentions of the writer of the D text. With that key in our hands we shall then examine other Western readings of a theological or at least a religious nature.

The passage from Acts xv. 20 and 29 concerning the contents of the apostolic decree promulgated at the Jerusalem conference, with the different readings of the Alexandrian and the Bezan texts, and the controversy thereon are well known. In fact, we have four different readings, provided that the texts offered by Tertullian and by P^{45} (Chester Beatty) are taken into account. These supplementary textual testimonies are not insignificant variations from the Uncials, as is sometimes assumed. They have their own value, and they may allow us to take a step behind the great Uncials towards the original text.

The four readings are as follows:

1. B reads in xv. 20: *ton halisgematon ton eidolon kai tes porneias kai pniktou kai tou haimatos.* In xv. 29 we find the same four terms but in a different order and with differences in words but not in sense: *eidolothuton kai haimatos kai pniktou kai porneias.*

2. D, in xv. 20 as in xv. 29, omits *kai pniktou* but adds at the end of the verse what is called the golden rule, in a negative form. The number of four terms is thus maintained.

3. Tertullian, *De pudicitia* xii. 4 and other authorities[15] depart from B in omitting *kai pniktou* and from D in omitting the golden rule. Thus the reading contains three terms instead of four.

4. P[45] reads in xv. 20: *ton hali[sgematon ton eido] lon kai tou pniktou kai tou haimatos,* thus being alone in omitting *tes porneias.* Verse 29 has not been preserved. Here too therefore we find only three terms.

Let us compare these four readings, keeping in mind the good old rule given by Griesbach and Tischendorf, that the reading which explains how all the others came into existence, must be chosen as the original. The first noticeable fact is that there are only two terms common to the four readings: *ton halisgematon ton eidolon* and *tou haimatos.* To these two basic terms P[45] adds *tou pniktou;* Tertullian: *tes porneias* and *tou pniktou,* i.e. the additions of both P[45] and Tertullian; D: *tes porneias* and the golden rule.

It appears from these different additions that there has been a tendency to enlarge the apostolic decree, evidently in order to strengthen its authority, as Hans Lietzmann rightly pointed out.[17] In consequence, the supposition that the omission of *tes porneias* in P[45] is due simply to inadvertence[18] cannot be maintained. If the decree had originally mentioned four terms instead of three or even two, we do not see any reason which will explain the shortening of the text. It was natural to cover as many fields of religious and moral Christian life as possible by apostolic authority. If we consider the history of the growing Church, we see no example of development of thought in the opposite direction. These general considerations point strongly to the view that the more fully developed forms of the apostolic decree must be later and should be regarded as differing elaborations of a shorter primitive text.

This argument gains more weight if we now consider the meaning of the two basic terms as well as the meaning of each of the additional terms.

The only question which the Jerusalem conference had to decide was how to arrange that both Jewish and Gentile Christians could live peaceably in the same community.[19] "The necessary things" of which Acts xv. 28 speaks are in fact but one: that Gentile Christians should observe the Jewish rule of eating only *kosher* meat,[20] that is to say, meat which had not been consecrated to pagan divinities and had been prepared according to the rules of the Mosaic law. In other words it was a question of food, of ritual purity of food, which had to be settled, as was done, and not questions of moral Christian conduct. The practice of idolatry, murder and fornication is not to be expected from Christians. The meeting of a formal council as well as the sending out of an authoritative decree were not necessary to prohibit them. Such immoral conduct is not consistent with Christian life, and the point would have been settled in the first missionary preaching.

Now if we come back to the four readings of Acts xv. 20 (and 29), it appears that the two basic terms suffice to give expression to the solution adopted at Jerusalem. They render it in a concise and lapidary formula, which does not leave place for improvement. "To abstain from what has been sacrificed to idols and from blood" is to observe the smallest possible and yet sufficient prohibition permitting common meals between Gentiles and Jewish Christians and safeguarding the unity of the Church. Thus all was said which it was necessary to say.

In fact the longer formulae of the four known readings do not offer any real improvement in regard to the two basic terms. The additional terms are either purely verbal developments or they bring with them a new meaning to the whole decree and make of it a summary of Christian obligations in place of a unique prohibition commended by historical circumstances. In short, it seems that the primitive text of the decree was limited most probably to the two basic terms and that all four readings offered by our textual testimonies are but differing revised texts.

This will appear more evident if we review these four readings.

1. The text of P^{45} is very near to the original. It relates only to food. The addition of *kai pniktou* seems to have been made in order to include all flesh improperly slaughtered, and is more a verbal than a substantial alteration. If our conjecture about the original text appears to be too hazardous, this text of P^{45} can be regarded as the original.[21] But the quotation of Tertullian without *pniktou,* and the D reading with the same omission, rather support the conjecture proposed here.

2. The text of Tertullian with the addition of *tes porneias* runs to some extent parallel to that of P^{45}. Yet in adding *porneias* where P^{45} adds *pniktou,* the text given by Tertullian goes a little further away from what we consider to be the original text. The addition of the papyrus is purely explanatory, whereas the addition which Tertullian is the first to attest is not simply a precise addition to a prohibition already expressed in another word. It is a new regulation in order to extend the authority of the decree to a matter which had apparently not been under discussion at the Jerusalem conference.

That Tertullian should be held responsible for the introduction of *porneias* (or the change of *pniktou* to *porneias)* is not probable. It is true that he interprets the decree as relating to morals, not to food, when he quotes Acts xv. 29.[22] But this is not sufficient to show that he deliberately omitted *tou pniktou* from the text he was using, in order to have a canonical text more in conformity with his exegesis. Elsewhere[23] he speaks of the actual practice of the Christians in not eating "things strangled", but this is not a proof that he was there acquainted with a text of Acts containing four terms. For in this passage he makes no reference to the text of Acts,[24] and in addition he goes even further than the text of Acts in writing: *suffocatis quoque et morticinis abstinemus* (we abstain from animals strangled and from animals which perished naturally). The addition of *morticinis* to *suffocatis* indicates that he takes his argument from the Christian use of his day and not from the text of Acts.

3. The B text appears as a conflating revision which unites the additions of both Tertullian and P^{45}.

4. The D text has a double character. It is conservative in omitting *tou pniktou*. On the other hand the addition of the golden rule shows that the primitive text has been revised and enlarged to become a summary of Christian ethics. Now we must try to see for what reason the Western reading is so peculiar.

According to common opinion the Western text gives to the apostolic decree an ethical meaning. Thus in its reading the golden rule takes the place of the specifically ritual prohibition "things strangled", to which a moral sense could not be given, as it can be to "the contaminations of idols" and to "blood".

True as this opinion may be, it perhaps requires to be examined and deepened. First, it must be remembered that the omission of "things strangled" and the addition of the golden rule are not necessarily in close relation to each other, nor are they the cause of each other. If "things strangled" is really an old addition to the original decree containing only two terms, as is proposed in this paper, then it is most probable that the author of the Western text knew of the secondary character of "things strangled" and wished to discard it, just as he seems able and willing to return to the original text in the matter of geographical data. Thus the writer of D would have at the same time a conservative and an innovating tendency.

Further, it must be emphasized how strange it is to find here, as an addition, the golden rule instead of some other ethical regulation more or less parallel in style to the other terms of the decree. For the golden rule is not comparable to any other rule. It is a regulation as wide as possible, which summarizes all Christian duty or the Christian attitude as a whole. This inclusive character of the golden rule leads to the conclusion that the writer of D had in mind some other purpose than merely to make an addition to the decree. This point requires some attention.

The meaning of the golden rule is not modified by its negative form in Acts. Its form is in harmony with the context. This negative form is the perfect equivalent of the positive formula given by Jesus and retained by the Gospel tradition.[25] The golden rule is itself an abbreviation of the summary of the law[26] which Jesus presents as the new law, both putting aside and fulfilling the old law. Now in the Gospel tradition both the golden rule and the summary of the law have a polemical character. It is the answer to the Jews accusing the Master and his disciples of violating and abolishing the Mosaic law. The very same attitude is taken by St. Paul. The apostle announces to the world that Christ is the end of the law; yet he does not teach believers to continue in sin that grace may abound, as he is falsely accused of doing; on the contrary, he subjects those who have been called to freedom in Christ to the law of Christ, and he practically identifies this law of Christ with the golden rule.[27] Briefly, if Christianity differs from Judaism in rejecting the law of Moses, it appears nevertheless as the religion of the summary of the law, abridged in its turn in the golden rule. This golden rule becomes a standard of Christian belief and practice, so much so that this rule cannot be practised except in Christ or in the Spirit, and the actual possession of the Spirit is the God-given gift which separates Christianity from Judaism.

The golden rule is often quoted, either in its positive or in its negative form, either alone or in connexion with other commands, by the Fathers.[28] They preserve in it its double character; it is the mark of Christianity as such, and it is its answer to the Jewish accusation of being a religion without any law. On the contrary, the golden rule is scarcely referred to by the Jews.[29] The reason for this loss of credit is certainly the fact that the golden rule has become a Christian asset.

We may now come back to the Western reading in Acts xv. 20 and 29 and see more clearly the motives which gave to that reading its peculiar form.

The primitive decree had a ritual meaning and had been promulgated to meet a historical emergency, namely, to make possible the social intercourse of both Jewish and Gentile Christians in the same community. But mixed communities did not exist everywhere. They were confined most probably to Palestine and Syria. Besides, even in these countries Jewish Christianity did not play any leading rôle after the year 70, and was therefore forced to live apart and later to be absorbed either by the great Church or by Judaism.[30]

The prohibition of "things strangled" and then of fornication, added to the decree, were intended no doubt to maintain its authority in other circumstances and situations than its original occasion, to enlarge the sphere of the Christian life governed by it, and to give it in some measure a more ethical significance. For the four regulations of the text, as it is given in the Alexandrian reading, are capable of more than one shade of meaning and it is not always easy to decide in what sense it is to be understood. The question, ritual or moral?, presents a somewhat hard antithesis. It happens that the same author interprets the decree sometimes along the ritual, and sometimes along the ethical, line. Let us take for instance the two quotations from Tertullian already given. Tertullian gives to the decree a moral sense in *De pudicitia* but he maintains the original ritual meaning in *Apologeticus*, thus showing that the Church of his time was still bound by the Noachian rules. Other testimonies confirm that during the second and third centuries the Christians in Gaul and Northern Africa were ruled by the decree in the matter of food.[31] It is a proof that the decree could retain its ritual meaning. Even the prohibition of fornication was interpreted in that sense, for instance in the Clementine Homilies.[32]

On the contrary the addition of the golden rule is of far greater importance. It stresses the moral obligation and, above all, it makes out of a regulation governed by a time-given situation a timeless principle of Christian conduct. What is now imposed on all Christians by apostolic authority is not only some regulation more or less common to both Jews and Christians alike; it is essentially the new principle of Christian thought and life, practicable only by those who have the guidance of the Spirit. The formal mention of the Spirit at the end of the Western reading in Acts xv. 29 attests the specific Christian value attached to the golden rule.

In other words the writer of this Western reading reveals here his chief intention: to emphasize the newness of the Christian faith as regards Judaism, and to do so both negatively and positively. Negatively in denouncing and condemning the unbelief of the Jews: there is an undeniable anti-Jewish tendency peculiar to many Western readings. Positively, by insisting on the greatness and unity of the Church, and on the authority of the apostles, and also simply by mentioning with predilection the grandeurs which separate Christianity from Judaism, that is to say, the Holy Spirit and Jesus as Christ and Lord.

This purpose of the writer of D must now be followed in a few instances in the book of Acts.

The theological peculiarities of the Western text may be thus divided into the following groups: (a) those relative to anti-Jewish prejudice, (b) those concerning the Church and the apostles, (c) those dealing with the presence and the action of the Spirit, (d) the mere mention of Jesus as Christ and Lord.

(a) JEWS AND CHRISTIANS.

The anti-Jewish tendency is developed along two different lines. First the writer of D emphasizes again and again the responsibility of the Jews not only for the death of Jesus (iii. 17) but also for the persecution directed against the apostles (iv. 9; xiii. 45; xiv. 2-7; xviii. 12-13). It seems that in his judgment there is no excuse for the attitude of the Jews, while the B text--and most probably the primitive text also--minimizes the part taken by the Jews in the crucifixion, arguing that "they acted in ignorance" (iii. 17). The writer of D does not suppress the expression in spite of his own attitude, doubtless owing to respect for the primitive text.[33] But he neutralizes the word in making the addition of *to poneron,* that is to say, in specifying that that action done in ignorance was nevertheless a crime. Once more his work seems to show a mind at once conservative and innovating.

Secondly, he insists on the powerlessness of the Jews in their enterprises against the apostles and the Church (v. 39;

vi. 11). Where B says that the Jews "had nothing to say" in answer to the apostles, D adds, further, "they could do nothing" (iv. 14). More than that, it would be a crime to threaten the life of the apostles (v. 38).

In addition, love for Israel fails in D, a love which, however, is present in writers such as Paul and John, who are as anti-Jewish as the writer of D. Paul accuses the Jews of "opposing all men by hindering us from speaking to the Gentiles that they may be saved" (I Thess. ii. 15f.), and John has against the Jews the hardest word of the New Testament, accusing them to be "of their father the devil" (Jn. viii. 44). Yet Paul declares that he could wish to be "cut off from Christ" for the sake of his brethren (Rom. ix. 3), and John says that "salvation is from the Jews" (Jn. iv. 22). There is neither contradiction nor interpolation of Paul or John in these passages. They just make the necessary distinction between historical Judaism, which fails in its mission because of its unfaithfulness, and the people of God to which a vocation has been addressed by God which is "without repentance". The D writer of Acts seems to be too much dominated by historical circumstances to make that distinction.

(b) THE APOSTLES AND THE CHURCH.

The writer of D is also more universalist than the B reviser.

In Acts ii. 17f. the Western reading represents a series of changes from the LXX, which is quoted more literally by the Alexandrian recension.[34] The main change is this: in the words of the prophet, "all flesh" is put into the plural in order to emphasize that the promise is to all men, not only to the Jews. Consequently the thought in the D text is far more universal than in the B text, thus making Peter the preacher of the Pauline Gospel, giving salvation to all mankind.[35]

Shall we say that the D writer is himself anti-Pauline? One might be tempted at first sight to draw this conclusion from what has just been said and from another verse, xv. 2. According to the B text of this verse, Paul comes from Antioch to Jerusalem by his own will. The D text says, on the other hand: "Those who had come from Jerusalem ordered Paul and Barnabas themselves and some others to go up to the apostles and elders at Jerusalem to be judged before them about this question."

Yet in spite of appearances the Western writer cannot have, either here or in ii. 17, the same point of view as the Clementine Homilies, where Paul appears as the *echthros anthropos*. For there is no trace of an anti-Pauline tendency in the Western readings. On the contrary, D specifies that the proconsul Sergius Paulus was listening to Paul and Barnabas "with great pleasure" (Acts xiii. 8), these words being not mentioned in B. Further, D stresses that Paul is under the guidance of the Spirit (xix. 2; xx. 3). The emphasis in the D reading of Acts xv. 23[6] is not against Paul but in favour of the authority and unity of the Church. D does not reveal any secret prejudice against the apostle of the Gentiles. Its attitude is rather the departing point of the line which leads to the well-known passage in II Peter (iii. 15-16), where Paul, "our beloved brother", has become a recognized grandeur, and a grandeur inserted into the Church and warranted by it.

(c) THE HOLY SPIRIT.

Another feature of the D text is to make more frequent mention of the Spirit and to show a preference for the formal expression, "the Holy Spirit". There is no theology of the Spirit peculiar to the Western writer. For him as for the New

Testament as a whole, the Spirit is confined to the Church,[37] and its main work is the leading of the missionary enterprise. Twice D insists that the Spirit interposes its authority against the plans made by Paul (xix. 2; xx. 3), thus referring to a theme which is treated by both recensions earlier in the career of the apostle (xvi. 6-7).

A special mention must be made of the addition in Acts viii. 39, telling that the Holy Spirit fell on the Ethiopian eunuch after his baptism by Philip. It is possible that this Western reading--not found in fact in the Bezan codex--is original and was omitted in the Alexandrian recension because it is contradictory, first "to the narrative a few verses earlier, which implies that the Spirit came only through the hands of the apostles",[38] and secondly to the general tendency of the Western recension to strengthen the authority of the apostles.

In short, if the Western recension puts some emphasis on the Holy Spirit, what is says is in accordance with the ideas of first-century Christianity and does not justify the hypothesis of a Montanist influence, such as that proposed by J. R. Harris.[39] To the supposed indication of Montanist tendency, J. H. Ropes objects that D is not in favour of women prophets "by the somewhat clearer, though slight, indication of what may fairly be called 'anti-feminist' tendency in the variants of xvii. 12 and of chapter xviii".[40]

It is true that in xvii. 2, D speaks of the "wives of the leading men", where B mentions the "leading women". Again in xvii. 12, D reads "many men and women of those of good position believed", when B mentions the women first. It is true also that in chapter xviii, D generally mentions Aquila first, whereas B generally gives the first rank to his wife Priscilla.[41] But the order of the two people is perhaps without any great importance. Paul himself speaks either of

Aquila and Priscilla (I Cor. xvi. 19) or of Priscilla and Aquila (Rom. xvi. 3; cf. II Tim. iv. 19). Also the anti-feminist tendency of the writer of D seems to be more or less general in the last decades of the first century.[42] In any case it is not one of the major trends in the thought of the Western recension.[43]

(d) THE LORD JESUS CHRIST.

There is not very much to say here, for the alterations offered by the Western readings are neither numerous nor important. Jesus receives more frequently than in the B text the title of Christos[44] or Kurios[45] or both.[46] These additions are commonly considered as devotional in character. Yet is may be observed that these titles were in the meantime most offensive to the Jews, who considered Jesus neither as Christ nor as Lord. Further, in making them, the writer is rather conservative and contents himself with using the more traditional titles; he avoids the more emphatic designations used sometimes by the Apostolic Fathers.[47] This is perhaps an indication that the text of D may be more ancient than the Apostolic Fathers and not contemporary with them, as J.H. Ropes suggested.[48]

More than half a century ago Bernard Weiss concluded his careful review[49] of the Western readings with the negative statement that the D text afforded no essential contribution to our knowledge of the history and ideas of the primitive church gained from the other manuscripts of Acts. As far as capital facts and central dogmas are concerned, this judgment remains true. It could hardly be otherwise, for the Bezan codex does not contain, after all, another work on the beginnings of Christianity than that of Luke, which we have also in the great Uncials. But if we look into the details, the problem is different. Examined on theological matters, the writer of D appears to be both conservative and innovating. He seems not only to have access to the original text, but to be willing to preserve it, as long as his historical sense is consistent with what seems to have been his task: to modernise in many ways the primitive text in order to render it more intelligible and better adapted to the need and taste of his age.

It was no doubt his combination of tradition and innovation that made the writer of D capable of achieving what he considered to be his task, without falling either into the legendary narratives of the apocryphal writings or into the theological weaknesses of the heretics, and finally of remaining even now a valuable source of information on the first age of Christianity.

NOTES

1. Ph. H. Menoud, "The Western Text and the Theology of Acts", *SNTS Bulletin,* 2, 1951, p. 19-32, reprinted by kind permission.

2. J. H. Ropes, *The Text of Acts* (The Beginnings of Christianity, Part I, Vol. III), London, 1926, p. ccxxix--See too Sir Frederic Kenyon, *The Western Text in the Gospels and Acts,* London, 1938 (Proceedings of the British Academy, XXIV).

3. J. H. Ropes, *op. cit.*

4. A. C. Clark, *The Acts of the Apostles.* A critical edition with introduction and notes on selected passages, Oxford, 1933.

5. M. Black, *An Aramaic Approach to the Gospels and Acts,* Oxford, 1946, p. 28.

6. See A. F. J. Klijn, *A Survey of the Researches into the Western Text of the Gospels and Acts,* Utrecht, 1949, p. 81 and note 330.--To the followers of Ropes may be added O. Bauernfeind, *Die Apostelgeschichte,* Leipzig, 1939 (Theologischer Handkommentar zum Neuen Testament, V) and W. Michaelis, *Einleitung in das Neue Testament,* Bern, 1946, p. 134.

7. G. D. Kilpatrick, "Western Text and Original Text in the Gospels and Acts", *Journal of Theological Studies,* 1943, p. 25.

8. See M. J. Lagrange, *Introduction a l'étude du Nouveau Testament, II: Critique textuelle,* 2: *La critique rationelle,* 2. éd., Paris, 1935, p. 413 et passim; W. G. Kuemmel, "Textkritik und Textgeschichte des Neuen Testaments", *Theologische Rundschau,* 1939, p. 97-102; M. Dibelius, "The Text of Acts; An urgent critical task", *Journal of Religion,* 1941, p. 421-431; M. Black, *op. cit.,* p. 30; A. F. J. Klijn, *op. cit.* p. 170-171; K. W. Clark, "The Manuscripts of the Greek New Testament", in M. M. Parvis and A. P. Wikgren, *New Testament Manuscript Studies,* Chicago, 1950, p. 13-24.

9. p. 34.

10. B. H. Streeter, "The Primitive Text of Acts", *J.T.S.*, 1933, p. 232-241.

11. Page ix.--See, too, K. and S. Lake, "The Acts of the Apostles", *Journal of Biblical Literature*, 1934, p. 34-35.

12. G. D. Kilpatrick, *op. cit.*, p. 35.

13. Cf. A. F. J. Klijn, *op. cit.*, p. 168; "We never can speak of a bad text or a good text in general, only a text with many good readings or few good readings".

14. See A. C. Clark, *op. cit.*, p. 374f.

15. See J. H. Ropes, *op. cit.*, p. 265f.

16. Cf. M. J. Lagrange, *op. cit.*, p. 21.

17. H. Lietzmann, "Der Sinn des Aposteldekretes und seine Textwandlung", in *Amicitiae Corolla. A volume of essays presented to J. Rendel Harris*, London,1933, p. 203-211.--It may be of interest to note that the Clementine Homilies go a step further in the same direction. They put on the lips of Peter, when giving instructions to the communities of Tyre and Sidon, the apostolic decree in a far more extended form (Hom. VII, 8 and VIII, 19). See G. Resch, *Das Aposteldekret nach seiner ausserkanonischen Textgestalt* (Texte und Untersuchungen zur Geschichte der altchristlichen Literatur, Neue Folge, XIII, 3), Leipzig, 1905, p. 161-162, and H. J. Schoeps, *Theologie und Geschichte des Judenchristentums*, Tübingen, 1949, p. 303.

18. See O. Bauernfeind, *op. cit.*, p. 197.

19. We adopt the view that Galatians II and Acts XV refer to two different historical occasions.

20. This point has been rightly emphasized by H. Lietzmann in his study already mentioned.

21. See for instance M. J. Lagrange, *op. cit.*, p. 414, and "Le papyrus Beatty des Actes des Apôtres", *Revue biblique*, 1934, p. 168.

22. *De pudicitia* XII, 4.

23. *Apologeticus* IX, 13-14.

24. See J. H. Ropes, *op. cit.*, p. 265, note 1.

25. Mt. VII, 12; Lk. VI, 31.

26. Mk. XII, 28-31 and par.

27. Rom. XIII, 8-10; Gal. V, 14.

28. The texts have been collected by G. Resch, *op. cit.*, p. 135-143.

29. See G. Resch, *op. cit.*, p. 134; Strack-Billerbeck, *Kommentar zum Neuen Testament aus Talmud und Midrash,* I, 1922, p. 459-460.

30. Cf. M. Simon, *Verus Israel. Étude sur les relations entre Chrétiens et Juifs dans l'empire romain* (135-425), Paris, 1948, p. 313.

31. Cf. M. Simon, *op. cit.*, p. 388.

32. See H. J. Schoeps, *op. cit.*, p. 303.

33. The idea that the Jews acted in ignorance is peculiar to Luke. The only parallel to Acts III, 17 is Luke XXIII, 34. Another text alleged by Lake and Cadbury in their Commentary (*The Beginnings of Christianity,* Vol. IV, p. 37)--I Cor. II, 8--is not really a parallel. There, the heavenly powers, not the Jews, have failed to recognize the Lord of glory in the man Jesus.

34. In details the textual problem is in this passage very obscure. See J. H. Ropes, *op. cit.*, p. ccxxxiii; M. J. Lagrange, *op. cit.*, p. 392; Lake and Cadbury, *op. cit.*, IV, p. 21-22.

35. The same universal touch appears elsewhere, for instance in II, 47 and IV, 31.

36. On the textual problem of this passage, see Lake-Cadbury, *op. cit.*, p. 169-170.

37. See P. H. Menoud, *L'Église et les ministères selon le Nouveau Testament,* Neuchâtel-Paris, 1949, p. 11-16. *infra,* p. 363-435.

38. Lake and Cadbury, *op. cit.*, Vol. IV, p. 98.

39. J. R. Harris, *Codex Bezae* (Texts and Studies. Contributions to Biblical and Patristic Literature, II, 1893, p. 148-153). Harris' thesis is discarded by J. H. Ropes, *op. cit.*, p. ccxxxiv; M. J. Lagrange, *op. cit.*, p. 393; Klijn, *op. cit.*, p. 21.

40. J. H. Ropes, *op. cit.*, p. ccxxxiv.

41. The case is as follows: 1. Aquila and Priscilla; Acts XVIII, 8 B and D; XVIII, 26 D. 2. Priscilla and Aquila: Acts XVIII, 18 B and D; XVIII, 26 B.

42. Cf. 1 Tim. II, 11-15; Apoc. II, 20, etc.

43. An embarrassing case is offered by the D reading of Acts I, 14: *sun tais gunaixi kai teknois.* B reads: *gunaixi.* The absence of the article in B is noticeable. Such as it is, that reading may be an abbreviated form of the Attic phrase *meta gunaikon kai teknon* (see Blass, quoted by Lake-Cadbury, *op. cit.*, p. 11) which has an equivalent in XXI, 5 (*sun tais gunaixi kai teknois*). The D reading of I, 14 may have been influenced by that verse, or it may be the original. Now the meaning of the D text is that the apostles had with them their own wives and children, which is not impossible. Paul holds that the Jerusalem apostles were married, and considers his celibacy as such an exception in the apostolic circle, that it might lead to the false conclusion that he was not an apostle with full right (1 Cor. IX, 4f). The later tradition was not always embarrassed to recognize that the apostles had been married (see Eusebius, H.E., III, 30, 1). Sometimes Paul himself was represented as a married man (see P. H. Menoud, "Mariage et célibat selon saint Paul", *Revue de théologie et de philosophie,* 1951, p. 23, note 1). On the contrary, if the primitive text is that of B, the women in question are those mentioned in Luke VIII, 2 and XXIV, 10. It is not easy to decide between the two readings and meanings. It is difficult to find the reason why the wives and children of the apostles should have been afterwards introduced in a text not mentioning them originally; for they do not play any part at all in the primitive Church. The only possible reason would be the "anti-feminist" tendency of the writer of D, in virtue of which he would have been shocked to find women having such a place in the very heart of the growing Church. On the other hand, if the wives of the apostles were mentioned in the original text, they will have been discarded in order to make room for these better known women who had followed Jesus and still perhaps played a greater part than the apostles' wives in the life of the Jerusalem community.

44. Cf. Acts II, 30; IV. 33.

45. Cf. Acts II, 38; VII, 55; XVII, 4 and 5.

46. Cf. Acts VI, 8; XIV, 10; XVI, 4.

47. Cf. for instance Clemens Rom. XXXVI, 2-5; Ignatius, Magn. VIII, 2; Trall. VII, 1; Eph. I, 1; Barnabus XII, 10, etc.

48. *Op. cit.*, p. x and ccxliv.

49. B. Weiss, *Der Codex D in der Apostelgeschichte*, Leipzig, 1897 (Texte und Untersuchungen zur Geschichte der altchristlichen Literatur, Neue Folge, II, 1), p. 105.

The Acts of the Apostles and the Eucharist

None of the specific terms used in early Christian literature to describe the eucharist--κυριακὸν δεῖπνον,[2] θυσία[3] and εὐχαριστία[4]--is to be found in the book of Acts. Nor is there a detailed account of the eucharistic liturgy comparable to that given by Justin Martyr.[5] However, there is no doubt that the communion of the Lord's Supper was celebrated in the Church from the very beginning. St. Justin includes the eucharist in the last meal of Jesus with his disciples and explains its celebration at the Lord's command as in Luke 22. 19: "Do this in remembrance of me."[6] He therefore maintains that communion was one of the original elements of Christian worship. The evangelical tradition would not have preserved the words from Luke quoted by the apologist if the Church of the first century had not celebrated the eucharist. The apostle Paul asserts that the institution of the communion by Jesus, and His command that the believers should repeat it, are part of the tradition given by Paul to the Corinthians which should be maintained until the second coming of the Lord (I Cor. 11. 23-26). There is every reason to believe that the apostle handed on the same tradition to all the churches which he established, in view of its fundamental importance for him; he preaches the same faith everywhere and there is but one Gospel. But the only time he writes about the eucharist is in his letter to the Corinthians, and this is because they were conducting the ceremony in such a disorderly fashion that the vigilant apostle was forced to intervene. If the Corinthians had conducted "The Lord's Supper" in a worthy fashion and if, moreover, they had not been bothered by the problem of idolaters (cf. I Cor. 10. 14-22), it is doubtful if we would have received any instructions from the apostle about the eucharist. For apart from the passages we have just cited, it is never mentioned, not even if we consider the few implicit references like those to be found in the epistle to the Hebrews.[7]

Generally speaking, therefore, it can be said that the Christian writers of the first century had little or nothing to say about the celebration of the communion. We shall return later to the possible reasons for this reticence which nevertheless must be mentioned right away since we must bear it in mind when approaching the question of the eucharist in the book of Acts.

According to the writer of the second book to Theophilus, the Christians at Jerusalem and those in the churches resulting from Paul's mission practise "the breaking of bread." This practice, or ritual, is, from all evidence, connected with the meals taken by Jesus with His disciples in the course of His ministry, during "the night on which He was betrayed" and after His resurrection. For, in the New Testament, leaving aside the book of Acts, the only mention of "the breaking of bread"--ἡ κλάσις τοῦ ἄρτου--and of "to break bread"--κλᾶν ἄρτον--is in those passages in the gospels connected with the multiplying of the loaves,[8] the institution of the eucharist[9]--including the Pauline passages already mentioned--and at the meal of the risen Jesus with his disciples at Emmaus.[10]

Of all the passages in Acts concerned with the "breaking of bread," those connected with the church at Jerusalem have been studied in depth, and all possible explanations have already been advanced. As far as these are concerned it will be enough to give an account of the present situation in research and to point out what seems to be the best solution. On the other hand, other passages have received less attention and their possible contribution to our knowledge of the practice and significance of the eucharist in the first century has not been brought to light. These passages are Acts 20. 7-11 and 27. 33-36. We would also add the verse 16.34 which does not speak of "breaking bread" but of "spreading a table" which can only be, as we shall endeavour to show, "the table of the Lord."

1. *Acts 2. 42,46*

After describing Peter's first public address, the first conversions, and the first baptisms, the author of Acts writes that the believers "were constant in attendance on the teaching of the Apostles, and in fellowship, the breaking of bread and at prayers" (2.42). Of these four characteristics of the life of the Church, or perhaps more precisely, of its worship,[11] the third, the breaking of bread, poses the most problems. Of what does it consist? Theoretically, there are three possible explanations. The author may have in mind ordinary meals, a love-feast, or the eucharist.

It is impossible to sustain the first interpretation. To continue to take ordinary meals, even in common, is not the distinctive mark of the Christian life nor an act of worship; it is a simple necessity of physical existence. Appearing as it does, between the communion and the prayers, the breaking of bread can only designate another act of worship.[12] This expression is a kind of "liturgical formula"[13] whose original meaning has been brought to light by recent researches. In fact the expression is foreign to both classical and Hellenic Greek. Its origin is Jewish. It appears once in the Old Testament (Jer. 16.7) and is common in the rabbinic writings. In Jewish use, it means the rite at the beginning of every meal which consists of breaking the bread into pieces for the guests and pronouncing a blessing. But it never refers to the whole meal, not even in Jeremiah 16.7. Christian usage differs from the Jewish in that the former refers to the whole meal in the words "breaking of bread."[14] How can we explain this change? To say that the words describing the inaugural ceremony have naturally been expanded to mean the whole meal[15] is insufficient, since the expansion of meaning only took place in Christianity and not in Judaism.[16] The only explanation which can be sustained is that the Church gave a new significance to the expression in order to describe a meal which was essentially new, a meal called by the apostle Paul "the Lord's meal."

If the believers retained the Jewish expression while giving it new content, it is more than likely that this was done to avoid publicity for the central act of their worship, as is maintained by Joachim Jeremias, who writes: "The 'breaking of the bread' is a *Deckname*; the non-Christian is not to understand what is happening."[17] The Göttingen professor shows in a convincing way that the testimonies--and the silences--of Christian writers up to the end of the second century (inscription of Aberkios) are obedient to the strict discipline of the arcana, in order to defend the sacred nature of the eucharist and protect it from desecration.[18] It seems to us that we could go one step further and suggest that the hidden words in the book of Acts are two in number. To κλάσις τοῦ ἄρτου we would add τράπεζα, as we shall see in connection with Acts 16.34.

There is one point still to be examined with regard to Acts 2.42-46. Does the breaking of bread mean just the eucharist as such, or, on the contrary, does it also imply a communal meal, a love-feast--and, in this case, does the communion precede or follow the love-feast? Verse 42 and its context make it evident that the eucharist is celebrated as part of a complete meal. This is made clear by the writer, in verse

46, where he repeats that the believers "break bread" and adds that "they take their meals with great happiness and single-heartedness." The easiest way to understand this passage is to apply the words κλῶντες τε κατ 'οἶκον ἄρτον to the eucharist and the words μεταλάμβανον τροφῆς ἐν ἀγαλλιάσει καὶ ἀφελότητι καρδίας to the love-feast. In fact, κλᾶν ἄρτον picks up again the τῇ κλάσει τοῦ ἄρτου of verse 42; by repeating the words, the writer emphasizes that the chief element in the meal of the believers is the eucharistic communion.[19] Moreover, whenever the writer of Acts mentions a meal he seems to take great care with his vocabulary. He never uses the word ἄρτος except in eucharistic expressions (2.42, 46; 20. 7, 11; 27-35). When he describes a meal which is not the eucharist, he simply talks of "eating"[20] or "taking food".[21] He is particularly careful about his choice of words when, as in 2.46, he puts the eucharist in the setting of a meal. This is also the case on the occasion at Troas, where we find the expression κλάσας τὸν ἄρτον καὶ γευσάμενος (ὁ Παῦλος) (20.11); γευσάμενος does not seem to have the eucharistic force reserved for κλάσας τὸν ἄρτον. Similarly, in the story of the meal on the boat (27. 33-38), κλάσας ἄρτον describes the prophetic eucharist[22] celebrated by Paul, and the verbs ἐσθίειν and τροφῆς προσλαμβάνειν are used to describe the meal taken by Paul and his fellow-passengers.

The same precision of language can be found in 2.46. After the eucharist (κλῶντες ἄρτον), the believers take a meal. The word τροφή keeps its neutral meaning here.[23] What distinguishes this meal from an ordinary meal and gives it the nature of a love-feast is that it is linked to the eucharist. It is a meal taken in the eucharistic atmosphere of "great happiness and single-heartedness," that is of joy[24] which remains pure and can give rise to no charge of drunkenness like that thrown at the first believers by the inhabitants of

Jerusalem on the day of Pentecost (Acts 2.15).[25]

In Acts 2.46, the eucharist is mentioned before the love-feast. Perhaps it was in fact celebrated at the beginning of the meal, as is apparently the case at Troas. However, we must avoid being too dogmatic. In the passage 42-47, it is possible that, in verse 46, the writer mentions the eucharist first because of its importance. For the rest, in verse 42, κοινωνία must be taken in a very broad sense, which would include also the *Tischgemeinschaft*. In this case, we would have the primitive order in 2.42 (meal, then eucharist),[26] and the eucharist would be mentioned first, in 2.46 in order to pick up the thought of verse 42 again, after the rather strange interpolation of verses 43-45.[27]

2. *Acts 16. 34*

The writer of Acts recounts how Paul, after he had been freed from prison at Philippi by an earthquake, converted the gaoler and the members of his household and baptised them all (16.32-33). Then the gaoler took Paul and Silas to his house, "spread a table for them, and was filled with joy, with his whole household, that he had found faith in God". (v. 34).

The word τράπεζα only appears in Acts here and in 6.2 where "the serving at tables" implies the communal meal and doubtless also the distribution of the communion.[28] From the fact that, as we have seen, the writer of Acts chooses his expressions very carefully when he mentions meals, we would submit that it is not by chance that he mentions a table here, and that he uses the word τράπεζα, like the expressions κλᾶν ἄρτον and ἡ κλάσις τον ἄρτου, to describe a meal which is not (or not merely) and ordinary meal. In other words, the expression τράπεζα may also be a cryptic word to inform the believers that the meal signifies the eucharist.[29]

We should also point out that the "joy" of the gaoler at

Philippi is expressed by the verb ἀγαλλιᾶσθαι, which corresponds to the noun ἀγαλλίασις used in Acts 2.46 to describe the joy with which the believers took part in the communal meal.[30]

Our interpretation finds support in the use of the word τράπεζα in the remainder of the New Testament. Except in the gospels, where the meaning is neuter, and in quotations from the Old Testament, τράπεζα only appears in St. Paul's warning: "You cannot be partakers both in the table of the Lord and in the table of demons" (I Cor. 10.21) where "partaking in the table of the Lord" means to take part in the meal of the eucharist.[31] It is therefore more than likely that the apostle Paul celebrated the Lord's Supper at Philippi, with the gaoler and his household, immediately after he had converted and baptised them.[32]

3. *Acts 20. 7-11*

The allusion to the eucharist is obvious in the story of the night which Paul spent among the Christians at Troas, on his last journey to Jerusalem. These verses are permeated with the atmosphere of a liturgical festival.

First of all, the day of the ceremony. The church has come together on "the first day of the week" (v. 7). Here we have the earliest evidence of the celebration of Sunday by the Christians, evidence confirmed by I Corinthians 16.2, John 20. 19, and Revelation 1.10. Our text quite clearly hints at the reasons for which this day is set apart. In making use of an expression used also in Luke 24.1 (cf. John 20.1-19) when speaking of the day of first christophanies [appearances of the risen Christ], the writer of Acts points out that Sunday commemorates the resurrection of Jesus. The text makes it clear that this is also the day when the Church celebrates the "breaking of bread", that is to say, the eucharist. In our passage, in fact, the breaking of bread appears as a usual part of Sunday worship[33] rather than as an exceptional occurrence caused by the imminent departure of the apostle.[34] The extraordinary element in this gathering is the fact that Paul's exhortation continued until dawn. We can see here then, if not the first instance, at least the first mention of the practice attested by Justin Martyr of celebrating the eucharist each Sunday.

Our text makes it clear that the Church came together in the evening, at night fall. Does this mean Saturday evening--the night between Saturday and Sunday[35]--or Sunday evening--the night between Sunday and Monday?[36] The first theory is based on the custon of the Jews and the early Christians to count the days as beginning with twilight; in which case the night between Sunday and Monday belongs entirely to the second day of the week. The second theory is based on Roman (and modern) custom; it would use the expression τῇ ἐπαύριον, at the end of verse 7. In fact, according to the Jewish method of counting, Paul, as he left Troas in the morning of this memorable night, would not be leaving on the next day, but on the same day. But we cannot be sure that the writer himself is strictly accurate. The question can be left open.[37] It is, at any rate, a secondary issue.

More importantly, let us emphasize that the service, taking place at night for obvious social and economic reasons--many Christians, particularly the slaves, were occupied during the day[38]--places the eucharist, by the simple coincidence of the time, in close connection with two events which take place at night and both of which give the eucharist its particular significance: First, the final meal of Jesus with His disciples taken "on the night he was betrayed",[39] and second, the resurrection of Christ, the time of which was not fixed in earliest tradition, but which, quite clearly on, was placed "on the night when Sunday rises".[40]

It is, without any doubt, the simultaneous commemoration of the two nights, inseparable from now on, to which believers owed their redemption, which prompted the Christians at Troas to celebrate the eucharist with a great deal of light. There were, in fact, "a good many lights" in that upper room (v. 8).

This circumstance is explained by the commentators in many different ways. It can be said, quite simply, that night had come, so lamps were necessary, and there is no reason to give them a ritual significance;[41] the writer, an eye-witness of the event, mentions them as he remembers them.[42] But it is remarkable that the writer emphasizes this particular detail while he keeps quiet about many other features of this service--features which seem at first glance more important, such as the distribution of the eucharist to the believers and their meal with Paul (v. 11). Some interpreters think that the writer wants to answer the charge that the gatherings of the Christians, held in secret, were a pretext for licentious acts.[43] But this charge does not make its appearance until the second century. Justin Martyr seems to have been the first to recognize it and to repudiate it (*Apol.* 26. 7; cf. 27. 5).[44] Or yet again, the writer wants to refute the reproach that the young Eutychus fell from the third floor because care had not been taken to see that the room was adequately lit.[45] But the young man's fall was due to his sleepiness, not to the darkness. Following the same line of thought, it has been said that the writer wants to explain why Eutychus fell asleep and fell to the ground: the many lamps made the atmosphere warm and stuffy and made the young man fall asleep and then to the ground.[46] But to make it possible for him to fall the shutters must have been open, and, as a result, fresh night air would have been coming in to the room. It has also been suggested that the writer has carried over into Christian worship the Jewish custom of lighting a lamp to mark the beginning of the sabbath.[47] But this connection does not seem valid, as the writer makes it clear that the Church came together on the day following the sabbath. Finally, it has been suggested that the numerous lamps were lit in honor of the Apostle; they express the joy brought to the believers by Paul's presence among them.[48] This explanation is satisfactory in the sense that the profusion of light can only be, in fact, an expression of the joy which dominates the ceremony. But the mere presence of the Apostle is, in itself, inadequate reason for exuberant joy. The abundant light can only be the counterpart, so to speak, of the overwhelming joy of the believers at Jerusalem and Philippi. It makes the eucharist the great festival of the Church, the time and place where already the light of salvation shines through the darkness of this world. It proclaims in advance the dazzling light of the day of the Lord when there will be no more night.[49]

The events at Troas emphasize in yet another way that the eucharist is the feast of light and joy. This is shown in the episode of Eutychus. It matters little whether the young man escaped his fall without injury,[50] or whether he was killed and Paul brought him back to life;[51] the idea is the same. When the eucharist is celebrated, Christ is especially present in His Church and reveals His power to preserve the believers and repel the forces of evil and even of death.

It is strange that the exegetes have not thought to set the episode of Eutychus in relationship to what Paul said concerning the sick and the dead at Corinth, who were struck down for taking the eucharist unworthily.[52] The same motif appears however, in reverse so to speak, in the warnings given by Paul to the Corinthians about the seriousness with which the eucharist should be taken. The believers at

Corinth were inclined to confuse "the Lord's supper" with ordinary meals, when one eats and drinks to satisfy hunger. The apostle declares that, "anyone who eats and drinks without discerning the body of the Lord eats and drinks judgment upon himself", and he adds, "that is why many among you are weak and ill and not a few have died" (I Cor. 11. 29-30). Undoubtedly the apostle would not draw the contrary positive conclusion that a sufficiently worthy participation in the eucharist would enable the believers to escape sickness and death. He does say, however, that by the means of the eucharist the Spirit can imbue the faithful with his revivifying power and curb the effect of evil forces. It is notable that at Troas, in the episode of Eutychus, we have an example of the effects, according to Paul, of the eucharist taken in a worthy fashion.

Our interest is drawn to one last point: at what time, during this night, did the eucharist take place? Did the meal precede it or follow it? The opinion of the exegetes is divided. Some think the reference is to the agape in verse 7 and the eucharist in verse 11.[53] Others are of the opinion that verse 7 announces in advance the ultimate aim of the assembling of the Church--to celebrate the eucharist--and that the communion (κλάσας τὸν ἄρτον), followed by the agape (γευσάμενος), does not take place until after the incident of Eutychus.[54] Finally, others suggest both alternatives, turn and turn about,[55] or maintain that it is impossible to decide.[56]

However, the choice is not difficult if we take into account the care with which the author of the Acts chooses his words. The second meaning must prevail.[57]

Thus, at Troas, the eucharist precedes the agape. This order may be the original one; we have seen it in connection with 2.46. But that is not absolutely certain. The opposite order is usually regarded as the older, because Jesus instituted the communion at the end of His last meal with the disciples[58] and because this order was followed at Corinth and also kept in the *Didache*.[59] It is sometimes suggested that Paul himself at Troas inverted the order followed at Corinth, in order to avoid a repetition of the abuses which happened there.[60] This is not out of the question. Whether the order followed at Troas was the original one or not, it is possible that it was perpetuated in Asia Minor and that an allusion to it is found in Pliny's letter to Trajan concerning the Christians in Bithynia.[61] Pliny reports that the Christians came together first before day-break to sing hymns to Christ and to join together in a *sacramentum*, which would be, according to the apostates he questioned, a vow of good conduct; and then later on the same day, at a time which Pliny does not specify, they came together to take an ordinary meal. Pliny's testimony is vague, probably because his information was incomplete.[62] It seems more likely that the place of the eucharist was in the early-morning worship[63] and not in the second assembly[64] which would be the agape. Thus the eucharist would be separate from the meal, but it would precede it, as at Troas.

However that may be, the doubts surrounding the respective order of the eucharist and the meal of the believers seem to show that customs varied according to the place and the circumstances and that no supreme importance was attached to the order.

4. *Acts 27. 33-36*

One final passage in Acts can be examined from the point of view of the eucharist. This is the story of the meal taken at sea, in the midst of the storm, by Paul and his ship-mates on the way to Italy. When the boat and the lives of all a-board were threatened, Paul urges his companions to take some food "essential for their safety". "Having said this, he took some bread, and after giving thanks to God before them all, he broke it in pieces and began to eat. This raised the spirits of all, and they too took food" (27. 33-36).

B. Reicke has studied this passage very closely recently.[65] Contrary to the opinion of the great majority of exegetes,[66] the Swedish scholar believes, and rightly so, that the resemblances between these verses and the eucharistic texts of the New Testament are close enough for us to conclude that the writer of the Acts was not describing an ordinary meal. Terms characteristic of the eucharist are used to describe this meal. Doubtless Paul did not actually celebrate the eucharist, since the passengers on board were not all Christians. But by the words he pronounced and by his actions, he created between the passengers and himself a bond which, to all appearances, intentionally recalls the Christian communion, evoking a symbolic prediction of the success which the mission of evangelism will have in the West. In short, the apostle makes his companions on the ship partakers in a prefiguration of the eucharist, in order to prepare them for the faith which is destined to be theirs.

There is in fact a resemblance, too marked not to be intentional, between the expressions used by the writer of Acts here and those which he uses to describe the eucharist at Troas. In both cases Paul "breaks bread and eats".[67] That is, he follows a particular ritual and then presides over a communal meal. He is not the only one to eat, either on the boat or at Troas. Moreover there is a basic parallelism between the two accounts. The eucharist at Troas is interrupted by the accidental fall of Eutychus; that is, by an event demonstrating that the eucharist reveals a power of life so strong that it preserves from all evil those who take part in it. On the boat, the food which the passengers take is "for their safety" (v. 34). The word σωτηρία, in this context, seems to have a double meaning. The immediate safety of the travellers is one point. The prisoners were not put to death immediately after the ship-wreck, as the soldiers recommended (v. 42-43), and all the passengers managed to reach land safe and sound (v. 44). The other point is their spiritual salvation, since the writer of Acts puts into Paul's mouth here the words of the eucharist. This eucharist, which might be called prophetic, is a reminder that the occurrence at Troas was not an exception. It shows that the power of life of the Gospel is evident everywhere.

Finally, we should attempt to draw from the preceding analyses some conclusions concerning the practice and significance of the eucharist according to the book of Acts.

First of all, we must make it clear that the references to the eucharist appear in passages based on the oldest and strongest traditions available to the writer of the Acts. The two verses 2.42 and 46 are part of the primitive basis of the first "summary" describing the life of the infant Church, and this is the opinion of exegetes who have studied these passages recently.[68] The three examples of the Pauline eucharist (16. 34; 20. 7-11; 27. 35) appear in a "first-person" context, or very close to it--that is to say in passages which can be traced back, in all probability, to one of Paul's companions. The book of Acts thus adds its testimony to that of tradition on the institution of the eucharist, and to that of the apostle Paul himself, to establish that the Church celebrated the eucharist from the very beginning. The episode at Philippi in particular, if our interpretation is correct, shows that the eucharist, and baptism too, was practised as soon as a group of believers was formed. There is no Church without the eucharist.

The writer of Acts observes that the discipline of the arcana is responsible for the scarcity of references to the ceremony which gives the Church its specific character and which, already at Jerusalem, separated the followers of Christ from the Jews. Luke may be at pains to show that Christianity is true Judaism and should therefore benefit from the privileges granted by the Roman state to the religion of an old ally.[69] But he had to keep quiet about the eucharist, or at least couch it in cryptic terms, as it could not have been taken for the Jewish Passover, since it was celebrated at Jerusalem every week, and perhaps even every day, in the earliest days of the Church.

However, according to the book of Acts, the eucharist appears, as we have seen, in connection with a meal without it being clear, at the beginning, whether the eucharist preceded or followed the meal itself. If, in the first century, the eucharist does not exist as an isolated liturgical ritual, it is probably because of the memory that Jesus had instituted the ritual in the course of His last meal with His disciples.

It is true that, in the passages we have studied, there is no specific reference to this last meal. It would seem that the remembrance of it is missing only because of the fact, supported by all our evidence, that the eucharist is a joyful occasion. It should be particularly emphasized that on Paul's mission field, at Philippi and at Troas, the eucharist does not appear as a melancholy meal. On the contrary, it appears to be the kind of eucharist which, according to Hans Lietzmann's theory, would be like that at Jerusalem, and not what is more generally accepted as Pauline. This fact is all the more worth pointing out since, as we have said, these eucharistic texts belong to the oldest and most stable traditions of the book of Acts and not to its edited elements. This is an indication that the Pauline eucharist itself probably did not have the melancholy character attributed to it if one relies only on the testimony of I Corinthians. Moreover we must not forget that "the Lord's death" which the believers proclaim when they take communion is the death of someone who is now living, since His death is proclaimed "until He comes" (I Cor. 11. 26). Paul never separates, in his mind, the death and the resurrection of Jesus, for His death alone would have no beneficial significance. Paul persecuted the Church as long as he saw only the death of Jesus. After his conversion he always sees this death in the light of the resurrection. If he preaches "Christ crucified" (I Cor. 1. 23), it is because God has raised Christ from the dead and because, without the resurrection, preaching, and the faith it awakens, would be in vain (I Cor. 15. 14). Just as the church at Corinth, with its anarchic and demagogic tendencies, which the apostle strives to restrain and suppress, is not a model of ecclesiastic organization, and just as the church at Philippi, with its bishop and its deacons, probably had a much tighter structure, so it is probable that it was only at Corinth, and because of particularly serious abuses, that Paul wanted to cut short ill-conceived joy and recall the serious nature of the Christian faith. The events at Philippi and Troas lend credence to the view that the eucharist at Corinth was more the exception to, than typical of, the Pauline churches.[70]

If the believers celebrate the eucharist in joy and light, according to the book of Acts, this does not necessarily mean that recollection of the death of Jesus is missing from their worship. But they see this death and, for that matter, the whole life of Jesus *sub specie resurrectionis*. They are all the more likely to do it as the power of life of the risen Christ vitalizes their eucharistic gatherings and reveals itself as capable of preserving the believers from all evil.

Paul too, as we have seen, reminds the Corinthians that miracles can happen when the eucharist is taken worthily (I Cor. 11. 29-30). This accord is an indication that the Lord's Supper is not essentially different, whether we take the testimony of the apostle himself or the traditions about Paul preserved in the book of Acts. If the Church does not exist unless the eucharist is celebrated in it, it is because the eucharist gives to the Church its characteristic of a community of Christ, founded by His redemptive work and living by His grace in the expectation of the glorious fullness of time.

NOTES

1. *Revue d'histoire et de philosophie religieuses,* 33, 1953, p. 21-36, by kind permission of the Faculté de Théologie Protestante at Strasbourg.

2. I Cor. 11. 20.

3. Did. 14. 1,2,3.

4. Ignatius, *Phil.* 4. 1; *Smyr.* 7. 1; 8. 1; Justin Martyr, *Apol.* 66. 1; but not Did. 9. 1,5, where εὐχαριστια keeps the general (and New Testament) meaning of "act of grace". Cf. A. Arnold, *Der Ursprung des christlichen Abendmahls im Lichte der neuesten liturgiegeschichtlichen Forschung* (Freiburger theologische Studien, 45), Freiburg i.B., 1937, p. 28; M. Dibelius, "Die Mahl-Gebete der Didache", *ZNTW,* 1938, p. 33 and 41; J. Jeremias, *Die Abendmahlsworte Jesu,* 2. Aufl., Göttingen, 1949, p. 66, n. 5. These writers are correct on this point in contrast to the opposite opinion put forward by for example, J. Behm, *Theol. Wörterb.,* III, p. 729 and B. Reicke, *Diakonie, Festfreude und Zelos in Verbindung mit der altchristlichen Agapenfeier* (Acta Universitas Upsaliensis, 1951, 5), Upsala-Wiesbaden, 1951, p. 9.

5. *Apol.* 65-67.

6. *Apol.* 66. 3.

7. Cf. C. Spicq, *L'Epître aux Hébreux,* I (Etudes bibliques), Paris, 1952, p. 316-318.

8. Mk. 8. 6-19; Matt. 14. 19; 15. 36. But Luke himself does not use κλᾶν ἄρτον when speaking of the multiplying of the loaves.

9. Mk. 14. 22; Matt. 26. 26; Lk. 22. 19.

10. Lk. 24. 30-35.

11. Several writers agree that we have here a description of the service of worship of the first believers. O. Bauernfeind, *Die Apostelgeschichte* (Theol. Handkomm. z. N. T.,5), Leipzig, 1939, p. 54; O. Cullmann, *Urchristentum und Gottesdienst* (Abh. z. Th. A. N. T., 3), Basel, 1944, p. 7 and *passim;* J. Jeremias, *op. cit.,* p. 25. But here--as also in Justin, *Apol.* 67--the alternative: either Christian life in

general or the life of worship in particular, is of secondary consideration (cf. P.-H. Menoud, *La vie de l'Eglise naissante* (Cah. théol., 31), Neuchâtel-Paris, 1952, p. 9-10 and 38-39).

12. The fact that it is mentioned twice (2.42 and 46) is already an indication that "it must have had a religious significance" (M. Goguel, *L'eucharistie des origines à Justin Martyr*, Paris, 1910, p. 129). Consequently it is difficult to subscribe to the affirmation of K. Lake and H. J. Cadbury: "Breaking of bread merely means an ordinary meal. This gives a reasonable sense in all the passages in Acts" (*The Beginnings of Christianity, Part I, The Acts of the Apostles, IV*, London, 1933, p. 28).

13. E. Jacquier, *Les Actes des apôtres* (Etudes bibliques), Paris, 1926, p. 87.

14. Cf. R. Otto, *Reich Gottes und Menschensohn*, München, 1934, p. 264-266; A. Arnold, *op. cit.*, p. 44-47; E. Lohmeyer, "Vom urchristlichen Abendmahl", *Theologische Rundschau*, 1937, p. 275-276; J. Jeremias, *op. cit.*, p. 64-65.

15. J. Behm, *Theol. Worterb.*, III, p. 729.

16. E. Lohmeyer, *op. cit.*, p. 276

17. *Op. cit.*, p. 65.

18. *Op. cit.*, p. 58-67

19. Bauernfeind's interpretation (p. 58), that in verse 46 it is a question of an ordinary meal, seeing that the eucharist has already been mentioned in 2. 42 and that it is missing from the other "summaries" in the Acts (4. 32f; 5. 12f), does not seem to us to hold water.

20. Φάγειν: Acts 9. 9; 10. 13-14; 11. 7; 23. 12-21; γεύεσθαι: Acts 10. 10; 20. 11; 23. 14; ἐσθίειν: Acts 27. 35.--Δειπνεῖν and δεῖπνον are uncommon.

21. Τροφὴν λαμβάνειν (or the compounds): Acts 2. 46; 9. 19; 14. 17; 27. 33-38.

22. We shall clarify our use of this expression later.

23. On this point we disagree with J. Jeremias (*op. cit.*, p. 65), who tends to see "perhaps also" in τροφή a cryptic word to designate the eucharist.

24. Cf. R. Bultmann, *Theol. Wörterb.*, I. p. 20.

24, Cf. B. Reicke, *op. cit.*, p. 202-205; C. Edlund, *Das Auge der Einfalt. Eine Untersuchung zu Matthaus 6. 22-23 und Lukas 16. 34-35* (Acta Seminar. Neot. Upsal., XIX), Copenhagen-Lund, 1952, p. 83-85.--If the writer of the Acts really wished to forestall the charge of drunkenness by emphasizing the purity with which the believers conducted their meals, this would prove that wine was served and consequently that the eucharist, which was part of the meal, was not a *communio sub una*.

26. In Corinth, the eucharist follows the meal, (I Cor. 11. 25). This is also the order presupposed by the prayers in the *Didache* (9. 1 - 10. 5 suggest the love-feast; 10. 6 is an introductory liturgy to the eucharist, to which 14 refers), as several writers have indicated (A. Arnold, *op. cit.*, p. 26; M. Dibelius, *op. cit.*, 32-41; J. Jeremias, *op. cit.*, p. 66.

27. Cf. P. Benoit, "Remarques sur les 'sommaires' de Actes 2. 42-45," *Aux sources de la tradition chrétienne, Mélanges M. Goguel*, Neuchâtel-Paris, 1950, p. 2-3.

28. R. B. Rackham, *The Acts of the Apostles* (Westminster Commentaries), 14th ed., London, 1951, p. 82.

29. The use of τράπεζα in this sense has its parallel to some extent in the use of το υπερῷον Acts 1. 13), that supreme upper-room, where the eucharist perhaps was first instituted and where christophanies took place.

30. In the Acts, ἀγαλλίασις only appears in 2. 46 and ἀγαλλιᾶσθαι only in 16. 34, except for 2. 26, which is a quotation from Ps. 16. 9.--R. Bultmann, *Theol Wörterb.* I. p. 20, points out that in Acts 16. 34 ἀγαλλιᾶσθαι is used in a liturgical sense.

31. The epistle of Diognetus has perhaps preserved the specific meaning of the word τράπεζα. The author, as he enumerates the distinctive characteristics of the Christian life, writes: τράπεζαν κοινὴν παρατίθενται (5. 7) using the same noun and the same verb as Acts 16. 34.

32. A very few commentators on Acts (Jacquier and Rackham among them) think that the table at Philippi is the Lord's table but they bring no arguments to support their theory. B. Reicke (*op. cit.*, p. 217-218) also admits that it was the eucharist and that the writer does not expressly call it that because he is obeying the discipline of the arcana. He cites

parallel examples in the Acts of Peter (5) and in the Pseudo-Clementine writings (Hom. 14. 1), where baptism is followed immediately by the eucharist and where both ceremonies are dominated by the same joy and gladness. We might mention once again (with Bauernfeind, p. 58) that already in Acts 2. 42 the eucharist follows very closely on baptism (Acts 2. 41).

33. H. H. Wendt, *Die Apostelgeschichte* (Meyer, III, 9. Aufl.), Göttingen, 1913, p. 286.

34. As Bauernfeind suggests, p. 236.

35. According to H. W. Beyer, *Apostelgeschichte* (Das N. T. Deutsch), Göttingen, 2. Aufl., 1935, p. 121; Rackham, p. 377.

36. H. J. Holtzmann, *Die Apostelgeschichte* (Hand-Kommentar z. N.T., I, 2), 3. Aufl., Tübingen u. Leipzig, 1901, p. 126; Th. Zahn, *Die Apostelgeschichte des Lukas* (Kommentar zum N. T., V), Leipzig, 1921, II, p. 705; Lake-Cadbury, p. 255; F. F. Bruce, *The Acts of the Apostles*, London, 1951, p. 372 and 374.

37. According to E. Jacquier, p. 598.

38. Rackham, p. 379; J. Héring, *La première épître de saint Paul aux Corinthiens* (Comment. N. T., VII), Neuchâtel-Paris, 1949, p. 99.

39. I Cor. 11. 23, which repeats the original tradition.

40. Gospel of Peter, 35.

41. F. J. F. Jackson, *The Acts of the Apostles* (The Moffatt N.T. Commentary), New York, 1931, p. 188; Bruce, p. 373; Oepke, *Theol. Wörterb.*, IV, p. 28.

42. R. Knopf, *Die Apostelgeschichte* (Die Schriften des N.T., 3. Aufl.), Göttingen, 1917, III, p. 112; Jacquier, p. 599.

43. E. Preuschen, *Die Apostelgeschichte* (Handbuch z. N.T.), Tübingen, 1912, p. 121; Bauernfeind, p. 239 (with reservations).

44. That is doubtless why he returns to the subject of the eucharist so often and is so careful to give a complete description of it. (J. Jeremias, *op. cit.*, p. 67).

45. Wendt, p. 286; A. Loisy, *Les Actes des apôtres*, Paris, 1920, p. 764.

46. Zahn, p. 707; Lake-Cadbury, p. 256.

47. Rackham, p. 379.

48. Knabenbauer and Felten, quoted by Jacquier, p. 599.

49. In Acta Thomae 26 there is a description of a eucharistic service where numerous lamps were lit. The motif is doubtless taken from the canonical Acts.

50. This is the interpretation particularly of Holtzmann, p. 126; Preuschen, p. 121; Lake-Cadbury, p. 256; Beyer, p. 121.

51. The followers of this theory include Wendt, p. 286; Loisy, p. 765; Jacquier, p. 599; Zahn, p. 707f; Rackham, p. 380; Jackson, p. 186; Bruce, p. 373; R. Morgenthaler, *Die lukanische Geschichtsschreibung als Zeugnis. Gestalt und Gehalt der Kunst des Lukas,* I (Ab. z. Th. A.N.T., 14), Zürich, 1949, p. 129 and 140.

52. Cf. O. Cullmann, "La délivrance anticipée du corps humain selon le Nouveau Testament", *Hommage et reconnaissance à Karl Barth,* Neuchâtel-Paris, 1946, p. 37-38; P.-H. Menoud, "Wunder und Sakrament im Neuen Testament", *Theol. Zeitschrift,* 1952, p. 181-182.

53. For example Zahn, p. 706 and 708.

54. Cf. Jackson, p. 188; Bruce, p. 374.

55. Rackham is among these: agape and eucharist, p. 40 and 377; eucharist and agape, p. 378.

56. Cf. Jacquier, p. 600; Lake-Cadbury, p. 255-256.

57. Cf. *supra.*

58. Ἐσθιόντων αὐτῶν, Matt. 26. 26, Mk. 14. 22; μετὰ τὸ δειπνῆσαι Lk. 22. 20, I Cor. 11. 25.

59. Cf. *supra.*

60. W. L. Knox, *Saint Paul and the Church of Jerusalem,* Cambridge, 1925, p. 385; Rackham, p. 378.

61. *Epist.* X, 96, 7.

62. In Pliny's ignorance there is another argument in favour of the existence of the arcana (cf. J. Jeremias, *op. cit.*, p. 66). It is difficult to agree with P. Batiffol when he writes: "The Christians disclose everything, even the eucharist", *Etudes d'histoire et de théologie positives*, I, 8ème éd., Paris, 1926, p. 17; cf. also p. 299.

63. W. L. Knox, *loc. cit.*; M. Goguel, *L'Eglise primitive*, Paris, 1947, p. 381, and on the subject of the problem posed by Pliny's letter, *L'eucharistie des origines à Justin Martyr*, p. 259-265.

64. P. Batiffol, *loc. cit.*; and J. Jeremias, *loc. cit.*

65. B. Reicke, "Die Mahlzeit mit Paulus auf den Wellen des Mittelmeers", *Theol. Zeitschrift*, 1948, p. 401-410.

66. To the list given by B. Reicke (p. 402, n.3) we could add Rackham, p. 40 and 490, and Bruce, p. 465. Cf. also J. Behm, *Theol. Wörterb.*, p. 729, n. 16. Among the commentators who establish some connection between Acts 27. 35 and the eucharist (p. 401, n.1) we could also mention Jackson, p. 232. --Cf. also M. Goguel, *L'eucharistie des origines à Justin Martyr*, p. 141: "This passage gives us an indication that, originally, there was perhaps not the complete difference between the eucharist and an ordinary meal that existed later."

67. Acts 20. 11: και κλάσας τον ἄρτον και γευσάμενος; Acts 27. 35: και κλάσας ἤρξατο ἐσθίειν.

68. This is the agreed opinion of L. Cerfaux, J. Jeremias and P. Benoit. Cf. P. Benoit, *art. cit.*, p. 2.

69. Cf. P.-H. Menoud, *L'Eglise naissante et le judäisme* (Etudes théologiques et religieuses), Montpellier, 1952, p. 46-47, *Infra*. p. 436-496.

70. On this question, cf. E. Schweizer, "Das Abendmahl, eine Vergegenwärtigung des Todes Jesu oder ein eschatologisches Freudenmahl?", *Theol. Zeitschrift*, 1946, p. 81-101; M. Goguel, *L'Eglise primitive*, p. 360-362.

Observations on the Ascension Narratives in Luke-Acts[1]

The writer to Theophilus, whom we call Luke for the purposes of simplification, is the only New Testament writer who gives an account of the Ascension of the risen Lord and who places the Ascension forty days after the Resurrection. More precisely, Luke mentions the Ascension three times. He alludes to it or actually mentions it, (depending on whether verse 51 is read in the short or the long version) at the end of his gospel (Luke 24. 50-53). According to this passage, Jesus definitely took leave of his disciples on the night after the Resurrection itself. In Acts 1. 2-3, Luke declares that the Ascension was the culmination of a forty-day period during which the risen Lord appeared to His disciples several times. Finally, in Acts 1. 9 Luke describes the Ascension in very restrained terms: Jesus is carried away from His disciples and a cloud hides Him from their sight.

These three passages from Luke pose several questions which have attracted attention for a long time. We do not wish to reconsider the whole problem here. We will limit ourselves to some comments concerning the tradition about the Ascension, the forty days, and the integrity of Luke's work.

I

Believers in the first century gave two successive expressions of their faith in the victory of Christ. In our day, exegetes and historians generally agree in admitting this fact, even if their opinions differ in the explanations they give.

According to earliest tradition, cited by Paul in I Corinthians 15, Christ's Resurrection is at the same time His exaltation. It is from on high that He reveals Himself as the glorified Lord. The apostle shares this view. This is the reason why Paul can hold that the christophany granted to him on the road to Damascus is as factual as the appearances experienced by the other disciples. According to this theory, the Ascension, considered as a theological affirmation, is included in the idea of Resurrection-exaltation. It is not an independent historical event. Theologically speaking, there is no time limit to the christophanies.[3]

Soon the Resurrection of Jesus was regarded as a temporary return to this earthly life, an occasional resumption of communal life with the disciples. It was not long, therefore, before the Ascension appeared as the necessary event to put an end to the life of the Risen Lord on this earth and, consequently, to the christophanies. Finally, the last stage, the length of time between the Resurrection and the Ascension was fixed.

It is important to point out that the tradition concerning the Ascension and the account of the forty days are not conclusive.[4] It is worth noting that in the pericope Acts 1. 1-12, the report about the forty days (v. 3) is not connected with the account of the Ascension (v. 9). The tradition on the Ascension is of long standing, since it appears in the gospel of John (Jn. 20. 17),[5] who, furthermore, does not set a time limit on the appearances. The Fathers, from the second century, make several references to the Ascension, but do not mention the tradition of forty days.[6] We must wait for Tertullian before we find the time period specifically mentioned. Eusebius had no qualms about ignoring the tradition.[7] Moreover we know that the early Church had other sources of information, apart from the Acts, about the length of the appearances and that it extended the time period as far as eighteen months, or even twelve years.[8]

In short, even though the tradition of the Ascension goes back to the first century, the tradition of the forty days appears as a later piece of information which was not very wide-spread--Acts 1.3 excepted. It is surprising that (if it existed) this tradition did not find an earlier echo in the Fathers or even in the book of Acts itself. Luke, who never hesitates to repeat two or three times any facts which seem important to him, and which he wishes to emphasize as such to the reader,[9] could have mentioned the forty days again in 11. 16--where he recalls the Lord's words to His disciples recorded in Acts 1.5--and particularly in 13. 31, where he writes, referring to 1. 3, that "Raised from the dead, for many days he appeared" to the apostles. Now, in these two cases, Luke keeps quiet about the forty days. As O. Bauernfeind writes: "Wenn Lukas die Stelle 1.3 selbst geschrieben hätte, wäre es geradezu auffällig, dass er die Zahl hier wegliesse."[10]

We would therefore ask whether the beginning verses of Acts--and consequently the last verses of the gospel of Luke--really belong to the early work or whether they are not a later addition.

II

For a long time it has been thought that Luke's work has been "touched up." We can rule out the small problem of the presence of μέν standing alone in Acts 1. 1; this is not a real difficulty, as there are other examples in the Acts of the absence of the correlative δέ.[11] But many other problems remain.

First of all, there is the contradiction between Luke 24. 51 and Acts 1. 3 about the time of the Ascension. The current explanation is that when Luke was writing the gospel he had not yet heard of the tradition of the forty days, which reached him later when he was beginning the Acts. But there is no proof that there was a long interval between the two parts of Luke's work. The introduction to the gospel seems rather to announce a single piece of work devoted both to the ministry of Jesus and to the activities of the "ministers of the word" (Lk. 1. 2).

Secondly, there is the textual question: the variations of Luke 24. 51-52 and especially of Acts 1. 2 clearly show that these verses have been corrected and overloaded with additions, to the point where it is impossible to reconstitute the original text.[12] Finally, for reasons indicated above, we must accept Harnack's judgment that the account of the Ascension in Acts 1. 1-12, "ist wohl das jüngste Stück der Apostelgeschichte,"[13] is fully justified. This is the reason why so many scholars do not hesitate to presume that all or part of the account of the Ascension has been rewritten or even added later.[14]

It seems more than probable that the beginning of Acts is a later addition, but it appears less certain that any interpolation would include the whole account of the Ascension. K. Lake and H. Sahlin seem to have put forward the most justifiable opinion, namely that the addition consists of Luke 24. 50-53 and Acts 1. 1-5.[15] Lake emphasizes that the real beginning of Acts is at 1. 6, which picks up the conversation interrupted in Luke 24. 49; Luke 24. 50-53--a summary of Acts 1. 6-12--and Acts 1. 1-5 were added in the second century, when Luke's work was divided into two books. Sahlin is of the same opinion. He rightly considers Acts 1. 1-5 as "ein stilistisches Monstrum",[16] which can only have been put together in stages: verse 1 is a dedication copied from Luke 1. 1-4; verse 4 finds its inspiration in Luke 24. 49: verses 2-3 are there to serve as a bridge;

verse 5 is taken from Acts 11. 16. Likewise the verses in Luke 24. 50-53, also put together in stages, consist of material taken from Acts. 1. 6-16. The interpolation took place at Rome in the second century, in connection with the entry of Luke's work into the canon, when his work was cut into two parts. This separation necessitated the addition of a conclusion to the gospel and an introduction to the Acts. If the addition is removed, Luke's work is restored to its original unity and clarity; the conversation of Jesus with His disciples, interrupted in Luke 24. 49, continues naturally in Acts 1. 6; the Ascension is mentioned only once, in Acts 1. 9, without any reference to the forty-day tradition.

This seems to us a compelling hypothesis, since there are still more arguments in its favor than those we have already presented. Let us examine first of all Luke 24. 50-53. It must be admitted that the verses are poorly connected to the rest of the chapter. It is difficult to tell whether the scene described in verses 50-53 took place the same evening--or rather the same night, since the two disciples left Emmaus at the end of the day (v. 29)--or the next day. The transition from verse 49 ("you, wait patiently in the city") to verse 50 ("he brought them out") is not smooth. As a contrast we should note the great artistry in Acts 1. 6-12 where the hand of a man who knows how to write is obviously at work: we arrive smoothly at the Ascension and it is only at the end of the account that the writer indicates the place where Jesus was taken up from his disciples.

On the other hand, Lake's affirmation: "There is nothing un-Lucan in the language of Luke 24. 50-53" is perhaps too dogmatic. The expression at the end of verse 50: ἐπάρας τὰς χεῖρας αὐτοῦ εὐλόγησεν αὐτούς has no parallel in the New Testament nor in the Apostolic Fathers.[18] Nowhere else does Jesus use for His disciples this gesture which is reminiscent of the blessing given during church worship.[19] It seems clear then that verse 50b is written in the liturgical style of the second century and is not Lucan.

In verse 52, there is no motive for the χαρὰ μεγάλη which excites the disciples—Jesus has just been taken away from them. Such an Ascension would be rather a reason for sadness.[20] On the other hand the reason for the disciples' great joy is clearly shown in Acts 1. 9-11,--the promise of the angels concerning the second coming (v. 11); moreover the cloud which hides Jesus (v. 9) foretells the eschatalogical cloud on which He will return.[21] In short, the note on the Ascension in Luke 24. 50-52 seems to be a summary of the scene described in Acts 1. 9-12, just as Luke 24. 53 is an abridgement of Acts 2. 46-47.

Let us now look at Acts 1. 1-5. We shall not spend time on the points we have already made, namely that verse 2 is so loaded with additions that we despair of unearthing the original text and that, generally speaking, the style of these five verses is the most ponderous and confused of the whole work. Let us restrict ourselves to a few particular points.

In verse 1, the expression ποιεῖν τε καὶ διδάσκειν has a certain elegance of style. It would not be unworthy of Luke. But neither he nor the other writers of the New Testament customarily make use of such terms to describe the mission of Jesus; this manner of expression belongs more to the second century.[22] In verses 3-4, we find four words which are hapax legomena in the New Testament: τεκμήριον, ὀπτάνομαι, συναλίζω, περιμένω.[23] In verse 5, we find the cumbersome expression οὐ μετὰ πολλὰς ταύτας ἡμέρας, which it is agreed contains a Latin idiom. But it must be noted that in parallel passages Luke used the more elegant turn of phrase that places the negative after the preposition.[24] The change from indirect speech to direct speech in verses 4 and 5 is particularly clumsy. Elsewhere, in similar cases, Luke makes the transition more smoothly by inserting a ὅτι (Acts 14. 22) or a φησίν (Acts 25. 5).[25]

As he moves from verses 1-5 to verses 6-12 the reader experiences the same feelings as the mountain climber who after floundering in the melting snow of a glacier, finally sets foot on firm granite. At the beginning of verse 6, the expression μεν οὖν appears, one of the favorite phrases of the writer of Acts to introduce a new development closely connected to what has gone before.[26] Now Acts 1. 1-5 links up better with Luke 24. 49 than with Acts.1.1-5. In Luke 24. 49, Jesus bids His disciples to "sit" in Jerusalem until they are endued with power from on high. The verb καθίζω quite naturally evokes the idea of the Messianic kingdom where Jesus will "sit" on his royal throne (Acts 2. 30; Mk. 10. 37, 40 and par.: Matt. 20, 21, 23; Rev. 3. 21). Consequently Jesus' way of expressing Himself in Luke 24. 49 serves as a good introduction both to the disciples' movement around the risen Lord to receive His supreme revelation (συνελθόντες)[27] and their question: "Is this the time for you to restore the kingdom to Israel?" (Acts 1. 6). On the other hand, in the existing context of the Acts, the disciples' question makes no sense, since it has just been said that for forty days Jesus had been telling them about the Kingdom of God (Acts 1. 3).[28]

Furthermore, verses 1-5 leave the reader in the same place, so to speak, or even lead him backwards--everything has already been said at the beginning, since the Ascension is mentioned at the end of verse 2--while verses 6-12 complete the conversation begun in Luke 24. 44. Continuing logically from there, these verses arrive at the Ascension, after which the gift of the Spirit will be possible, this being the main teaching of Jesus in this passage, obviously in one continuous progression.

Finally it is not superfluous to point out that the language of verses 6-12 is that of Luke. The verb ἀποκαθιστάνω (v. 6) is undoubtedly a hapax legomenon, but we find the noun ἀποκατάστασις in 3. 21; νεφέλη (v. 9) is unique in Acts, but appears five times in Luke; the noun ἐλαιών (v. 12) is to be read in this form--and not in the form ἐλαία--in Luke 19. 29 and 21. 37 also.[29] The only expression which is not found elsewhere in the New Testament is σαββάτου ὁδόν (v. 12). But one single original expression in the account of a unique event is no reason for surprise.

Therefore it seems very probable that neither Luke 24. 50-53 nor Acts 1. 1-5 form part of the original work. In the beginning Acts 1. 6 followed immediately after Luke 24. 49. In other words, at the end of His last appearance to them Jesus was instructing His disciples about the meaning of the Scriptures relative to His death and Resurrection and the necessity for the wise use of the Holy Spirit which would supervene between His earthly ministry and His second coming: then, before their eyes, He was lifted away in a cloud, annunciator of the eschatological cloud on which He was to return.

III

With the later addition removed, Luke's work presents a more coherent testimony to the Ascension. The writer to Theophilus knows the oldest tradition, doubtless from its sources, according to which the Resurrection of Jesus is at one and the same time His exaltation.[30] But he is writing at a time when faith was attempting to make a distinction between the different stages in Christ's victory.[31] There was also a desire to stress that the period of "appearances" was definitely over. This is certainly the motive behind the account of the Resurrection in Acts 1. 9-11. By declaring that the Apostles will see Jesus return in the same manner in which they saw Him disappear, the angels are announcing that it is not part of the divine design to grant new christophanies before the second coming.

The account of the Ascension therefore has the same significance as the words of Jesus in John 20. 29: "Blessed are those who have not seen and yet have believed." These words, addressed to Thomas, are not a veiled reproach. Thomas is in the same position as the other apostles; like them, he has seen and then he has believed. Jesus' words are addressed to the disciples of the future, to the readers of the gospel. They have no right to demand, in order to believe, to be blessed with a personal encounter with Jesus, as Thomas was. They have to defer to those who were eye-witnesses, yet at the same time they are assured, like those who have seen for themselves, of attaining, through the apostolic testimony, the fullness of salvation.[32] In Acts as in John, the context (Luke 24. 47-48; Acts 1. 8) lays emphasis on the universal value of the witness of the apostles.

But it would be going too far to think that the account of the Ascension has an anti-Pauline thrust. The book of Acts is not anti-Pauline. It only stands in a different perspective from the apostle himself in I Cor. 15, in order to make a judgement on Paul's ministry and thereby on the vision of Damascus. According to Acts it was from the very center of heavenly glory, after the Ascension, that the Lord appeared to Paul. The apostle to the Gentiles is not among those who "ate and drank" with the risen Lord (Luke 24. 41-43; Acts 10. 41); he is not a Witness from the beginning (Acts 1. 21-22; 13. 31). However, he is "the chosen instrument" (Acts 9. 15; cf. 22. 21; 26. 16), and the objective of the apostolic mission was realised with his arrival in Rome.

As for the time when the addition of Luke 24. 50-53 and

Acts 1. 1-5 was made, Lake and Sahlin are clearly right to place it in the same period the canon was originally constituted, when the gospel material was separated from the rest of Luke's writings, in order to place it alongside that of the other Evangelists.

Therefore there is every reason for thinking that originally the work of Luke was a unity. In his "Commentary on the Preface of Luke", H. J. Cadbury has shown convincingly that Luke 1. 1-4 provides an introduction to the Acts as well as to his gospel.[33] When the prologue was written Luke had but to note, when the moment came (Luke 24, 47-48; Acts 1. 8), that the personal work of Christ was finished and that all that remained was for His apostles to receive the gift of the Holy Spirit and carry their testimony from Jerusalem to the remotest parts of the earth.

NOTES

1. *Neutestamentliche Studien für Rudolf Bultmann,* Berlin, 1954, p. 148-156, by kind permission of the publishers, Walter de Gruyter & Co., Berlin.

2. We can list among recent writers: M. Goguel, *La foi à la résurrection de Jésus dans le christianisme primitif,* Paris, 1933, p. 352 and *passim*; "Quelques observations sur l'oeuvre de Luc", *Revue d'histoire et de philosophie religieuses,* 1953, p. 42f; E. Hirsch, *Die Auferstehungsgeschichten und der christliche Glaube,* Tübingen, 1939, p. 4-8; P. Althaus, *Die Wahrheit des kirchlichen Osterglaubens. Einspruch gegen E. Hirsch,* Gütersloh, 1940, p. 30-33; A. N. Wilder, "Variant Traditions of the Resurrection in Acts", *Journal of Biblical Literature,* 1943, p. 307-318; W. G. Kümmel, *Theologische Rundschau,* 1948, p. 7f; P. Benoit, "L'Ascension", *Revue biblique,* 1949, p. 161-203;; A. M. Ramsey, "What was the Ascension?" *Studiorum Novi Testamenti Societas,* Bulletin II, 1951, p. 43-50; R. Bultmann, *Theologie des Neuen Testaments,* Tübingen, 1953, p. 46.-- For a different approach, cf. W. Michaelis, *Die Erscheinungen des Auferstandenen,* Basel, 1944, p. 81f.

3. Cf. M. Goguel, *La foi à la résurrection de Jésus,* p. 268, and "Quelques observations sur l'oeuvre de Luc", *Revue d'histoire et de philosophie religieuses,* 1953, p. 42, n.14: "We do not see any indication, in Pauline christology, that after a certain time no further christophany would be possible."

4. H. Sahlin, *Der Messias und das Gottesvolk. Studien zur protolukanischen Theologie,* Upsala, 1945, p. 346, is right to emphasize this point.

5. On the theory of the Ascension in John, cf. P. Benoit, *op. cit.,* p. 167f; A. M Ramsey, *op. cit.,* p. 47f.

6. Similarly Mark 16. 19, certainly dating from the second century, refers to the Ascension but without dating it with respect to the Resurrection.

7. On the testimony of the Fathers concerning the Ascension, cf. M. S. Enslin, "The Ascension Story". *Journal of Biblical Literature,* 1928, p. 66-72; H. Sahlin, *op. cit.,* p. 343-346; P. Benoit, *op. cit.,* p. 167-172.

8. Cf. for example M. Goguel, *La foi à la résurrection de Jésus*, p. 354-355; Jackson-Lake, *The Beginnings of Christianity*, Part I: *The Acts of the Apostles, V*, London, 1933, p. 18-21.

9. For example, the unity of the infant Church (2. 43-46; 4. 32; 5. 12), the preaching of the gospel to the Gentiles (10; 11. 1-18; 15. 7-11), the conversion of Paul (9; 22; 26).

10. O. Bauernfeind, *Die Apostelgeschichte* (Theol. Handkommentar V), Leipzig, 1939, p. 175.

11. K. Lake, in *The Beginnings of Christianity*, V, p. 4.

12. Cf., along with others, the studies of J. H. Ropes, in *The Beginnings of Christianity*, III, p. 256-261; K. Lake, *ibid.*, V, p. 2-3; A. C. Clark, *The Acts of the Apostles*, Oxford, 1933, p. 336-337.

13. A. Harnack, *Beiträge zur Einleitung in das Neue Testament*, III: *Die Apostelgeschichte*, Leipzig, 1908, p. 148, n. 1.

14. Cf. W. G. Kümmel, *Theologische Rundschau*, 1948, p. 9, n. 1.--To the list of scholars cited by Kümmel (E. Meyer, M. Goguel, H. W. Beyer, O. Bauernfeind), we should now add M. Dibelius, *Aufsätze zur Apostelgeschichte*, Göttingen, 1951, p. 165 and n. 3.

15. K. Lake, in *The Beginnings of Christianity*, V, p. 1-4; H. Sahlin, *op. cit.*, p. 11-18.

16. H. Sahlin, *op. cit.*, p. 14.

17. K. Lake, *op. cit.*, p. 3-4.

18. Elsewhere in the New Testament ἐπαίρω has as its complement τοὺς ὀφθαλμούς or τὴν φωνήν or τὰς κεφαλάς but never τὰς χεῖρας when speaking of a sign of blessing. In I Tim. 2. 8 (cf. I Clem. 29. 1) it is a case of hands extended in prayer.

19. Apart from Luke 24. 50 Jesus only blesses children (Mk. 10. 16; Matt. 19. 15), but the actions and the words used are different. Acts 3. 26 ("God has sent his Servant to bless you") has a general meaning and refers to the whole mission of Jesus.

20. On the contrary, A. C. Clark, *op. cit.*, p. 407, thinks that the mere fact of the Ascension is the reason for the dis-

ciples' joy, and he sees it as a proof of the authenticity of the words καὶ ἀνεφέρετο εἰς τὸν οὐρανόν at the end of Luke 24:51.

21. Cf. P. Benoit, *op. cit.*, p. 199.

22. Cf. Papias, in Eusebius, *Ecclesiastical History* 3. 39, 15: τα ὑπο τοῦ κυρίου ἤ λεχθέντα ἤ πραχθέντα.

23. Τεκμήριον appears particularly in Josephus, *Ant.* 5, 39 in a very similar expression δια πολλῶν τεκμηρίων (W. Bauer, *Wörterbuch zum Neuen Testament*, 4 Aufl., Berlin, 1952, *sub verbo*). It is quite certain that the Acts preceded the Jewish Antiquities.--συναλίζω can be found in Ps. Clem. Hom. II, 1. This last word is, if you like, a demi-legomenon; it is to be found again in Acts 10. 24 D.--By way of comparison, it should be noted that the passage which, in certain respects, parallels Acts 10. 40-42, has only two hapax legomena: προχειρίζω and συμπίνω.

24. Cf. μετ'ού πολλας ἡμέρας Luke 15. 13; μετ' οὐ πολύ Acts 27. 14.

25. It is true that in 1. 4, D adds φησίν after ἥν ἠκούσατε and also has διὰ τοῦ στόματός μου instead of the simple μου of the so-called Eastern text. The text thus improved by D seems to suggest that the inelegance of the Eastern text was noticed at an early date.

26. Cf. Acts 1.18; 2. 41; 5. 41; 8. 25; 9. 31; 11. 10; 12. 5; 13. 4; 15. 3, 20; 16. 5 (K. Lake and H. Cadbury, in *The Beginnings of Christianity*, IV, p. 7).

27. There is no reason for thinking, with H. Sahlin (*op. cit.*, p. 13, n. 3 and p. 15, n. 3), that this verb belongs to the secondary addition. Συνέρχομαι is quite common in Acts; it is found 16 times there, while it appears twice in Luke and once in each of the synoptics.

28. It should also be noted that Acts 1. 4-5 seems to be a padded version of Luke 24. 49.

29. Cf. W. Bauer, *Wörterbuch. . .*, *sub verbo*.

30. Acts 2. 32-33; 3. 13; 5. 30-31. Cf. A. N. Wilder, *op. cit.*, p. 313-317.

31. There is no reason to be surprised that both traditions, Exaltation and Ascension, are to be found in Acts.

On all points of christology, the work of Luke conveys different traditions, some minor, some of major importance. In fact the move from one form to another was unnoticed, and the Christians of the first century certainly had no idea that the faith of the Church was evolving, even if some expressions were changing.

32. Cf. P. H. Menoud, "L'originalité de la pensée johannique," *Revue de théologie et de philosophie,* 1940, p. 250-251, and *infra.* p. 228-266; O. Cullmann, *Les sacrements dans l'évangile johannique. La vie de Jésus et le culte de l'Eglise primitive,* Paris, 1951, p. 13.

33. In *The Beginnings of Christianity,* II, p. 492 - If we admit that, at the time when Luke's work was divided into two parts, other sections were perhaps added - for example, Luke 1. 5 - 2. 52 - Luke's original work, in its entirety, could scarcely have been any longer than the first book of Josephus' Jewish War.

The Plan of the Acts of the Apostles[1]

The work of Luke is generally divided into two parts which are called "The Acts of Peter" or "From Jerusalem to Antioch" (chapters 1-12) and "The Acts of Paul" or "From Antioch to Rome" (chapters 13-128).[2] But there are serious reasons to doubt whether this division was the plan which the writer himself had in mind. The whole of chapters 6 and 7 and parts of chapters 8, 9, and 11 have nothing to do with Peter. The acts of Paul are also interrupted by an event of major importance, the conference at Jerusalem, in which the Apostle to the Gentiles appears to have played a very minor role. Moreover, this plan seems to reflect the modern concern to find in the Acts of the Apostles the biographies of the two chief Apostles. This is certainly not Luke's preoccupation, since he can abandon Peter at a moment's notice (12. 17). He is only interested in one part of Peter's life and that is all he includes in his plan. In the same way, after reporting in detail Paul's journey from prison in Caesarea to Rome and his arrival in the capital where he preaches "without let or hindrance" (27. 1 28. 31), Luke has nothing to say about Paul's trial. Apparently, therefore, the end of Paul's career has no place in his plan either. In other words, Luke's major interest is in the extra dimension given to the Church by the Holy Spirit through the witness of the Apostles, and not in the Apostles themselves.

During the whole of his career C. C. Torrey defended the thesis that the Acts are divided into two parts, but that the first part, translated from the Aramaic, consists of chapters 1. 1 - 15. 35 and traces the history of the Church from its beginning up to the conference at Jerusalem. To this is added a second part, chapters 15. 36 - 28. 31, which describes how the gospel was carried from Jerusalem to Rome.[3] We may have reservations about an Aramaic substratum being the basis for considering the first fifteen chapters as an entity.[4] But the fact remains that the American scholar was quite right in his suggested division of the Acts, and several writers have already concurred in this opinion.[5] The aim of this present study is to attempt to show that this division seems to correspond better than any other with Luke's ideas and intentions.

Luke begins the book of the Acts by reporting the mission entrusted to His first disciples by the risen Christ, to be His "witnesses in Jerusalem and in all Judea and Samaria and to the remotest parts of the earth" (1. 8). He concludes by describing Paul preaching the Gospel at Rome "without let or hindrance" (28. 31). Evidently, in spite of appearances, there is a connection between this beginning and the conclusion. In Luke's opinion, on the one hand, the order given to the first disciples is carried out, concurrently with them and after them, by a new witness, empowered by the direct call of Christ (9. 15 etc.), although he was not present at the beginning (cf. 1. 21-22; 13. 31). On the other hand, Paul's arrival in Rome is the decisive point between the time when the missionary command was given and the time when it will be fulfilled in the second coming.

Let us return to the text of Acts 1. 8. Luke mentions a point of departure, Jerusalem and three stages along the way: Judea, Samaria, and the whole earth. These stages are geographical and theological at the same time. Jerusalem, which in the Old Covenant was the place where the divine presence was to be found in the temple, is now the place of the divine presence in a new form known to the New Covenant, since it is there that Christ died, that he rose again, that he appeared, that he was taken away in a cloud; it is there that the Spirit descends, that Christ is proclaimed and that the Church first appears. From this place every Christian mission, including Paul's, takes its departure. It is worthy of note, in fact, that the Apostle to the Gentiles should make Jerusalem--and not Damascus or Antioch, for example--the point of departure for his missionary journeys which took him even as far as Illyricum (Rom. 15. 19).

Judea, Samaria, the far corners of the earth are at first geographical stages in the Christian mission. Already in Acts 5. 16 we see the effects of Peter's work being felt in the villages in the neighborhood of Jerusalem. Starting in chapter 8 the mission reaches Samaria, then Caesarea. In chapters 9 to 14 it arrives in Damascus, Phoenicia, Cyprus, and Syria, along with Antioch, Cilicia, and the areas in the south of what we know as Asia Minor.

At the same time as it was making advances on the geographical level, the mission was making headway on the theological level. The gospel preached at first only to the Jews is soon preached also to the Samaritans. The Holy Spirit descends on the latter too, so that the new preaching re-establishes the unity of the people of the Old Covenant. Next, the same gospel is preached to the proselytes and the pagans, so that, by the time of the opening of the conference at Jerusalem, the gospel has already reached all possible manner of men. In other words the missionary command has already been carried out in principle, even if, in practice, the work is not yet finished.

On the geographical level the final stage--the uttermost corners of the earth--could not be achieved in one or two generations. Luke is writing after the destruction of the temple in A.D. 70; there is no feeling of eschatological excitement in his work; the traces of institutional establishment which appear in the apostolic churches show that the era of the Holy Spirit, begun at Pentecost, is intended to last for some time. But before attaining the furthest limits of the earth the Gospel must reach Rome—the capital city. If the Gospel is pronounced and believed in this city, inevitably it will eventually reach all the provinces of the Empire. At the time when the conference at Jerusalem opened, the decisive phase, Rome, was already prepared.

On the theological level the final stage was already achieved when the Holy Spirit revealed that the Gospel should also be preached to the pagans and when the Apostles, in obedience to this instruction, set up rules whereby believers from Judaism and those from paganism could live in harmony within the same Church. The conference of Jerusalem marks this stage, since from that time forward the Church, however far it extends and however long it lasts, will never consist exclusively of Jews or of non-Jews. In this respect the definitive structure of the Church was already set by the beginning of the first century when the conference convened.

Obviously the Jerusalem conference was important in every respect and that is why Luke gives it a central place in his work. It is the turning-point in the history of the propagation of the Gospel as Luke understood it. We shall see this even better if we study the nature of the chapters which follow the account of the conference.

From the time of the Jerusalem conference, according to Acts, Paul's missionary activity takes on new characteristics. At the same time Paul himself is elevated to the new rank of an apostolic Witness (μάρτυς). Paul, from now on, bearing the same title as the Twelve, becomes, in Luke's view, the executor of the missionary commission given by the risen Christ to His first disciples.

Let us examine first of all the character of the Pauline mission. It has been customary, since the 19th century, to divide Paul's missionary travels into four separate journeys, namely chapters 13-14; 15. 36 - 18. 22; 18. 23 - 21. 14 (16); 21. 15 (17) - 28. 31. But there is room for serious doubt as to whether this division follows the writer's intention. If Luke puts to one side, before the conference, the journey with Barnabas, it is because, in his view, this journey is quite different from those which follow the conference. First, it is, in fact, a journey in which the Holy Spirit takes the initiative, a journey which the Spirit orders the church at Antioch to carry out, designating the missionaries he has chosen, namely Barnabas (mentioned first) and Paul (13. 1-2).[6] Secondly, it is a complete journey, from Antioch back to Antioch (13. 3; 14. 26), the only one of Paul's journeys to be so closely restricted. Luke explains the reason for this; it is a prototype, intended to show before everything else that "the Spirit had opened for the Gentiles a door of faith" (14. 27). Certainly many more missionary campaigns will be required before the Gospel is proclaimed everywhere, But the later journeys will only repeat what was established on this first one, when the decisive step was taken: the proclamation of salvation to those who had no previous connection with the Jewish faith. The later journeys will extend the Church geographically; they cannot extend it theologically, because, on the latter level, it has already reached its greatest possible dimension during the first journey, by the admission of the Gentiles. We might also note that this first journey is the counterpart of Peter's mission in Caesarea (10. 1 - 11. 18) to Cornelius, who was also a Gentile, but closer to Judaism since he was "God-fearing" (10. 2). Here too it is the Spirit who directs the Apostle, it is to the church that the Apostle gives an account of his mission, and the conclusion drawn by the church at Jerusalem will be the same as that at Antioch: "So then, to the Gentiles also God has given the repentance which leads to life " (11. 18). Now we can understand why Luke placed the mission of Barnabas and Paul before the Jerusalem conference. Thanks to the missionary work reported in chapters 8 to 14, the Church encompasses Jews, Samaritans, proselytes and Gentiles before the conference assembles. However far the Church spreads it cannot add any different types of believers to its membership. Here and now is the time to pose and to resolve the question of the unity between the Church's Jews and Gentiles.

Paul's journey after the conference has, by the very nature of things, a rather different character. First of all we are speaking of one single journey and not of several separate expeditions. In fact, leaving aside the transfer of Paul as a prisoner from Jerusalem to Caesarea (23. 23-35) and from Caesarea to Rome (27. 1 - 28. 14), all Paul's missionary activity, from the time of the conference up to the moment of his arrest, is, according to Luke, one single journey. There is no support in the text of Acts for the division, traditional among exegetes, into two or even three journeys. More seriously, this division gives a false impression of this part of Paul's career.

According to commonly accepted tradition, the change from the second journey to the third takes place between verses 22 and 23 of chapter 18; that is, right in the middle of one of Luke's sentences. In these two verses which, in their writer's view, have no break, Antioch is obviously neither an end nor a beginning but only a stage along the way. Undoubtedly, in the view of the writer of Acts, Antioch is an important center of Christianity. It is there that for the first time the believers are called "Christians"; it is there that converts coming from Judaism and paganism are united and it is this situation which will give rise to the need to envisage ways of maintaining the unity of the Church. But however important the church at Antioch may be, after the conference Luke does not make it the Apostle's home base.[7] Antioch is only one stage among the other stages that are land-marks along this lengthy journey. Luke emphasizes Antioch's importance by pointing out the length of time Paul spent in particular cities: six months in Corinth (18. 11), two (19. 10) or even three years at Ephesus (20. 31), and once again three months in Corinth (20. 2). In short, according to Luke, the Apostle's wanderings after the conference are really only one long journey from Jerusalem (15. 30) back to Jerusalem (21. 15).[8] The divisions Luke wants to make in this long journey are the "town-stages"[9] which lead the Apostle westward and inflame his desire to go to Rome (19. 21).

We must now emphasize the different nature of the journey undertaken by Paul after the Jerusalem conference. In fact, after Acts 15. 30, Paul appears not only as the head of the mission--no longer as just the companion of Barnabas--but also, and especially, as the spokesman of the Christian mission *überhaupt*. That is why, from this time onwards, Luke gives him the supreme title "Witness for Christ", and that is also why he now records only Paul's story. In Luke's view, from now on, it is Paul who is in charge of the apostolic witness entrusted originally to the first disciples, and who must now carry this witness to the far ends of the earth, which is as far as Rome.

This Lucan plan appears quite clear. As we have said, the point of departure of this great journey, like the point of arrival, is Jerusalem. From Jerusalem it is "the Apostles and the elders" who send "our beloved friends Barnabas and Paul", accompanied by Judas and Silas, to Antioch (15. 25-27), and of the four, only Barnabas and Paul are described as men "who have endangered their lives for the sake of our Lord Jesus Christ" (15. 26). After a stay in Antioch, which was probably not of very great importance since its duration is not specified (15. 30-40), Paul chooses his mission-field and his companions, undoubtedly with the inspiration of the Holy Spirit, but without the intervention of the church at Antioch, as was the case on the earlier journey. Moreover, and this is the important point which makes this later journey different, the preaching of Paul is called from now on a "witness"--the same expression employed for the preaching of Peter.[10] Such was not the case previously. Paul himself is given the title "Witness for Christ" (22. 15; 26. 16). This title, uncommon in Acts, is only given to the first disciples at the beginning (1. 8; 1. 21-22 etc.), to Stephen (22. 20) and to Paul. It is given to the latter two undoubtedly because the writer deems their vision of the glorified Christ equivalent to participation in the earthly ministry of Jesus. If Luke tells the story of the christophany on the Damascus road three times (9; 22; 26), it is not only to emphasize the importance of the event in itself; it is also to show that Paul is thereby equal in rank to the earliest Apostles.

When Paul's position in Acts is studied, it is usually emphasized that Luke omits him from the group called οἱ ἀπόστολοι (15. 2, etc.).[11] On the other hand, Paul on one occasion is given the title of ὑπηρέτης (26. 16), which is only applied to him and to John Mark (13. 5), and never to the Twelve. But this term ὑπηρέτης does not seem to have the same meaning when applied to John Mark and to Paul. John Mark is a helper, an assistant in comparison to the missionaries Barnabas and Paul. Paul is ὑπηρέτης καὶ μάρτυς (21. 16), that is, a "Witness", like the Twelve, but an assistant and not an Apostle like them, evidently because he is a latecomer into the circle of Witnesses.[12] His is a unique case, because Barnabas is never called a Witness. It is this designation of Witness which makes Paul a missionary equal to Peter.

Therefore it is not at all with the intention of belittling Paul that Luke leaves him outside the circle of the Apostles.[13] Moreover, there is no anti-Pauline element in the story of the election of Matthias. In recounting this episode, Luke wants to show, in advance, that Paul is not called to take a place in the circle of the Twelve. Paul is not one of the Twelve because he is in himself, if one can so describe it, another circle. He is "the chosen vessel" (9. 15) bidden, when the time comes, to take upon himself alone the function Christ first entrusted to the early disciples, and to bring the task of the first missionaries to a successful conclusion by bearing witness to Christ as far as Rome. This is what is emphasized in 26. 20: "I preached first to the people in Damascus, and then to those in Jerusalem and in all Judea and to the Gentiles". The parallel with 1. 8 is quite striking.

There can be no doubt that Luke is not unaware that other apostles and missionaries are at work. He describes Peter leaving "for another place" (12. 17)--that is, perhaps, for another mission-field; he indicates that Barnabas and John Mark are at work in Cyprus (15. 39); he knows that there are Christians who have preceded Paul in Rome (28. 15) and that consequently "the chosen vessel" is not the first to preach the Gospel in the city of the Caesars. But it is Paul who, coming from Jerusalem in the fellowship of the Apostles, clothed by Christ Himself in the garb of a Witness, is, in Luke's view, the missionary truly authorized in all respects and the qualified executor of Christ's command to proclaim the Gospel throughout the world. That is why, after the Jerusalem conference, Luke restricts himself to narrating the mission of Paul.

In the light of what we have just said the plan of Acts can be seen quite clearly. Luke's intention is to show how the risen Christ's command to His disciples to be His Witnesses from Jerusalem to the uttermost ends of the earth is carried out. The first part (chapters 1-14) shows how the Gospel takes firm root in Jerusalem and how, from this center, the Gospel is spread, thanks to the efforts of different missionaries, into the eastern provinces of the Empire. It is on the theological level that the Church most quickly attains its perfect stature, by uniting within it both Jews and Gentiles. If it is according to the will of God that salvation is intended for all, the Church, having reached this point in its history, must take any measures necessary to ensure life together, in peace and unity, for believers who have come from the two groups which represent the whole of humanity. That is why the first missionary effort came to a natural end in the Jerusalem conference (15).

If the conference marks an end, it is at the same time a point of departure. The extension of the Church on the geographical level still has to be completed. The Gospel continues to be preached, but no essentially new fact can be produced, except the conquest of the capital of the Empire by the Gospel, a sign that the apostolic witness cannot fail to reach the ends of the earth (15 end - 28). The task of carrying the Gospel to Rome is entrusted to Paul, chosen instrument and Witness for Christ, who, from now on, takes upon himself, from Luke's point of view, the mission first entrusted to the Apostles.

NOTES

1. *New Testament Studies*, I, 1954, p. 44-51, by kind permission of Cambridge University Press, London.

2. Cf. among recent writers: commentaries on Acts by H. W. Beyer, 1935 (*Das N. T. Deutsch*); O. Bauernfeind, 1939 (Theologischer Handkommentar, V); J. Renié, 1949 (Pirot-Clamer, *La Sainte Bible*, XI, I); R. B. Rackham, 14th ed., 1951 (Westminster Commentaries); W. Michaelis, *Einleitung in das Neue Testament*, Bern, 1946, p. 117-118; J. Klausner, *From Jesus to Paul*, 2nd ed., London, 1946, p. 212; W. L. Knox, *The Acts of the Apostles*, Cambridge, 1948, *passim*; M. Dibelius, *Aufsätze zur Apostelgeschichte*, Göttingen, 1951, p. 164 and *passim*.

3. C. C. Torrey, *The Composition and Date of Acts*, Cambridge, Mass., 1916 (Harvard Theol. Studies, I); *Documents of the Primitive Church*, New York, 1941; "The Aramaic Period of the Nascent Christian Church", *ZNW*, XLIV, 1952-3, p. 206-7.

4. Cf. J. de Zwaan, in *The Beginnings of Christianity*, II, p. 44-64; J. Dupont, *Les problèmes du Livre des Actes d'après les travaux récents*, Louvain, 1950, p. 41-2.

5. F. J. Foakes-Jackson, *The Acts of the Apostles*, London, 1931 (M.N.T.C.); L. Cerfaux-J. Dupont, *Les Actes des apôtres*, Paris, 1953 (La Bible de Jérusalem).

6. It is possible that Barnabas is named first because he is already at Antioch as an envoy from the church at Jerusalem (11. 22), and so the mission in 13 - 14 has, like any valid mission, Jerusalem as its point of departure. Cf. also Rom. 15. 19.

7. It is noticeable that the Pauline letters give the same impression. Paul only mentions Antioch once (Gal. 2. 11) and only once mentions the province of Syria (Gal. 1. 21).

8. Jerusalem is also the center of this journey according to the most probable interpretation of 18. 22. Cf. E. Preuschen, *Die Apostelgeschichte* (Handbuch zum N. T. IV, I), Tübingen, 1912, p. 114; R. B. Rackham, *op. cit.*, p. 334; F. F. Bruce, *The Acts of the Apostles*, London, 1951, p. 350; M. Dibelius, *op. cit.*, p. 167.

9. We should point out that the whole Christian mission

in the first century is essentially a city ministry. The word πόλις appears 43 times in Acts, whereas there is rarely any mention of the apostles evangelizing the countryside. Terms to describe non-urban areas are few and far between: κώμη 8. 25; μέρος 2. 19 (Libya), 10. 1 (Asia), 20. 2 (Macedonia); περίχωρον 14. 6; χώρα 8. 1; 13. 49; 26. 20. For the missionaries, and for Paul in particular, the towns were the primary objective, as they felt these were the vital centers it was important to win over before anything else. The Gospel will spread out from them into the countryside. Doubtless this is why Paul could consider his task in the East finished when he had evangelized the large towns "from Jerusalem even as far as Illyricum" (Rom. 15. 19).

10. In 18. 5; 20. 21 and 24; 23. 11 and 28. 23 Paul's activity is described by the verb μαρτυρέω or διαμαρτυρέω which elsewhere in Acts is only applied to the preaching of Peter (and John): 2. 40; 8. 25; 10. 42.

11. Paul, like Barnabas, receives the title of "apostle" in 14. 4 and 14 (οἱ ἀπόστολοι is lacking in 14. 14D). But here the word has the general sense of ambassador (cf. E. Lohse, "Ursprung und Pragung des christlichen Apostolates", *Theologische Zeitschrift*, 1953, p. 273, n. 46).

12. Paul demonstrates the same distinction when he speaks of "those who were apostles before me" (Gal. 1. 17).

13. In this respect we should note that according to Paul himself (I Cor. 9. 5), the missionary travels of the other Apostles and the Lord's brothers seem to have been longer than the Acts would have us believe. Luke may be keeping to essentials, but it is to further Paul's recognition, not to denigrate him.

The Additions to the Twelve Apostles According to the Book of Acts[1]

According to the writer of Acts, the Apostles in the specific sense of that word--that is, those who actually saw Jesus incarnate and risen from the dead, His authorized representatives to the world--were a close group of twelve men. Barnabas and Paul are also called Apostles (Acts 14. 4, 14), but when the term is applied to them it has the broad sense of missionaries, undoubtedly sent out by the Holy Spirit, but commended by a particular church and returning to it to give account of their mission (Acts 13. 1-3; 14. 27). That Barnabas and Paul are not Apostles in the same sense as the Twelve is shown again in Acts 15. 2, where Paul and Barnabas are seen to "go up to consult the Apostles and Elders in Jerusalem," that is to say, to go to see a group of which they themselves are not members. Moreover, Barnabas and Paul are not the only ones of importance in the infant Church whom Luke does not place among the Apostles. James, the brother of the Lord, who appears as the leader of the church remaining in Jerusalem, is also left outside the circle of the Apostles.

However, this closed circle is changed twice. First of all it acquires an addition within, when Matthias is called to take the place vacated by the traitor Judas, who died unrepenting. Secondly the circle is enlarged outside, by the arrival, in Paul of Tarsus, of a new Witness (Acts 22. 15; 26. 16), equal in importance to the first Witnesses and on whom devolves the mission of carrying "to the remotest parts of the earth" the testimony already made by the Twelve "in Jerusalem, and in all Judea, and Samaria" (Acts 1. 8). In fact, after the Jerusalem conference, in the second part of Acts, "the chosen vessel" (Acts 9. 15) alone takes upon himself the task which had been originally assigned to those who had accompanied Jesus from the time of John the Baptist until His ascension (Acts 1. 21). Paul is therefore well and truly added to the "Twelve", even though he does not join their circle proper and does not, in Acts, receive the title of Apostle in its specific sense.

Moreover, the group of the Twelve is not reconstituted after the death of James, the son of Zebedee (Acts 12. 2), who was not replaced as Judas had been.

How can we explain these different and even, at first glance, contradictory facts? Are they the result of different views of Apostleship which the writer of Acts took from his different sources of information, and which he reproduced without attempting to standardize them? Or, on the contrary, in spite of their diversity, do these facts presuppose one and the same concept of Apostleship, the one held by Luke himself? That is the question we would attempt to answer.

First of all let us look at the account in Acts 1. 15-26 of the replacement of Judas by Matthias. In these verses, we see the Apostle Peter explaining to the group of the first believers that Scripture has predicted both the wretched end of Judas and the necessity to entrust his apostolic charge to someone else. After this, the leader of the Twelve states the conditions the new Apostle must fulfill: he must have been a witness with the Eleven of the ministry and resurrection of Jesus. Two names are presented, and the Lord, expressing His will through the drawing of lots, chooses Matthais, who is thus added to the group of eleven Apostles.

The literary unity of these verses is often debated. It is pointed out particularly that the prophecy about the end of Judas (v. 20) is separated from the introductory words

(v. 16) by an account of the traitor's death which could not originally have been part of Peter's words, considering that the Apostle is presumed to be apprising his hearers of an event "known to all the inhabitants of Jerusalem"; and he seems to be translating an Aramaic expression for them, as if Aramaic were not their native tongue. Therefore verses 18 and 19 must be an addition to the original text.[2] In a recent study, C. Masson aligns himself with this view and suggests that the writer of Acts had added even more elements to his original source.[3] On the one hand Peter announces a single text of Scripture (v. 16) and proceeds to quote two (v. 20a and 20b); we must therefore consider both the second quotation and verse 17, which is an attempt to pave the way for the quotation and fits awkwardly into the context, as additions by Luke.[4] On the other hand, in verses 21 - 22. Peter fixes conditions for apostleship which nobody could fulfill, as Jesus had only chosen the Twelve to be with Him all the time; therefore it must be acknowledged that Luke puts into Peter's mouth his own conception, according to which only the Twelve are Apostles in the specific sense of the word.[5] In short, according to Masson, Luke has re-edited an earlier account which can be summarized as follows: in the early days of the Church, when a small group of disciples of Jesus had gathered together round the Eleven, Peter requested that the void created in the ranks of the Twelve by the absence of Judas should be filled, in a way which he indicated. The gathering approved and set forward two candidates. So that the Lord should Himself make the choice, as He had done formerly in the case of the Twelve, they besought Him in prayer to make His will known in the drawing of lots. The lot fell on Matthias and the Collegium of the Twelve was reconstituted (p. 196). In the opinion of the first writer, this reestablishment of the number was the sign that God had not abandoned His people, though they had rejected His Messiah; the reconstituted Collegium of the Twelve was a witness to Israel of the resurrection of Jesus and the faithfulness of God, in spite of the faithlessness of the people (p. 200). But, continues Masson, Luke has retouched the account and given it a new meaning, because the Church of his time was no longer interested in its original sense. In Luke's time Israel was rejecting the Gospel, while the Gentiles were joining the Church in great numbers. The Collegium of the Twelve, with its significance that salvation was destined first of all for Israel, no longer had any special meaning in a Church which had mostly non-Jewish Christians as its members. The interest lost in "the Twelve" was transferred to the Apostles; the old account of the reconstitution of the Collegium of the Twelve became, in Luke's work, the account of the choosing by the Lord of the twelfth Apostle, "for which there no longer seems to be any reason, for why must there be twelve apostles, no more, no less?" (p. 201). And so, concludes Masson, Luke saw in these twelve men not only envoys of Jesus to the Jews, but Witnesses to their Master within the Church and to the whole world (*ibid.*).

This study has the value of drawing attention to the many problems raised by this pericope. But it does not seem to us that the proposed solution will suffice. If, at the time when Luke is writing, the Collegium of the Twelve has no longer any significance, why does the writer of the Acts set these twelve men apart by keeping for them the title of Apostle and by introducing another term, Witness, to relate Paul to the Twelve? On the other hand, it is not only the verse which Masson holds to have been added by Luke which should be charged to the writer of Acts, it is the whole pericope which reflects the preoccupations of a time following the Ascension and preceding Pentecost. Undoubtedly Luke did not invent this situation; he is relying on traditions, doubtless oral, connected with the fate of Judas and his immediate replacement, and drawing especially on insights expressed by believers in his presence. Luke, and perhaps others before him, found the solution of the problem in the words from Psalms quoted in verse 20. These quotations are given in the Greek version. For this reason we would hesitate to attribute them to Peter, even more should we hesitate to suggest different literary sources for the two scriptural attestations. For the two quotations only make sense together. The first proves that Judas died unreconciled to Christ, the second shows the consequence of this--the place left empty must be filled. Therefore we must see Luke's hand throughout the whole pericope. The difficulties in the account, and they are real ones, can be explained by the very nature of the subject: to remind the first believers of the painful subject of Judas, to assert that it is the traitor's apostasy and not simply his death which brings about his fall from the circle of the Apostles, to report the reconstitution of the circle of the Twelve, but, at the same time, stating neither a principle of Apostolic Succession, nor, on the other hand, denying to Paul premature entry into the strictly limited group of "Witnesses" to Jesus. For this last must be reserved. Luke has already said that the Gospel will be preached "to the remotest parts of the earth" (Acts 1. 8), and Luke knows very well that none of the early Witnesses is destined to reach this ultimate objective. Luke must therefore make it clear that Matthias does not prematurely usurp the place which should have been kept for Paul, and that Paul's place is elsewhere than *within* the circle of the Twelve. We must therefore not be surprised if this account is not among Luke's most fluent writings.

The crux of the pericope is the double quotation in verse

20. The two texts are from two different Psalms (Ps. 69. 25 in verse 20a and Ps. 109. 8 in verse 20b), and both are quoted from the Septuagint version.[6] It is probable that the two passages were put together and applied to the troublesome case of Judas in order to resolve it scripturally, and if this was not done "in the first perplexing days" in the life of the first believers,[7] at least it was done by Greek-speaking Christians before Luke.[8] A scriptural justification was necessary to explain these unexpected events: the fall of one of the Twelve and the necessity of replacing him. Now, the same scripture, although in two different passages which traditionally go back to David, has foretold these two events. That is why it is not so strange to see the two passages announced ahead of time as if they were one single passage.[9]

The first quotation shows that the fall of one of the Twelve was predicted and is therefore part of the divine plan. We must re-emphasize one point: it was not simply the death of one of the Twelve which posed a problem for the first Christians. The Apostles chosen by Jesus are for the present time and for all ages to come. This is proved not only by the promise made to them that they should sit on twelve thrones in the kingdom of God and judge the tribes of Israel (Lk. 22. 30; Matt. 19. 28), but also by their very number of Twelve: they are the representatives of the people of God who, at the end of time, will be reconstituted in entirety and unity.[10] It follows therefore that, on the one hand, the circle of the Twelve must always be complete and, on the other hand, that the death itself (apart from apostasy) of one of the Twelve does not constitute a break in the apostolic circle, since the end of an Apostle's life on earth is not the end of his ministry. If James, put to death by Herod Agrippa in 44, is not replaced, it is not because by that time the circle of the Twelve had lost all significance for the Church.[11] Just the opposite. It is because the conviction of the Twelve's unique vocation and their eschatological mission was maintained in the Church that no Apostle was ever replaced, except the traitor Judas.[12] Therefore, if Judas had to be replaced, it is not because he died but because he betrayed Christ and, if we recall the manner of his end here, it is to point out that he died without repenting, an enemy of Christ, a fallen Apostle.

This is established by the quotation from Psalm 69. 25. This Psalm of lament by a servant of God was given a christological interpretation very early; the New Testament, particularly in the passions narratives, cites it or alludes to it frequently.[13] Here, the application of the 25th verse of the Psalm to Judas, declaring that the habitation of the traitor should remain desolate, shows that the renegade has taken his place among God's enemies and that there really is a gap in the cirlce of the Twelve.[14] But this first quotation, by itself, does not say that the gap should be filled.

Viewed in this perspective, the first part of the pericope is clear, with no embellishments, with no deficiencies. Peter approaches the painful and difficult subject of Judas' disappearance by pointing out straightaway that it is written into the divine plan revealed in Scripture (v. 16). Judas has betrayed, even though he was one of the Twelve, and the rather unusual expressions used here to speak of the apostolic vocation (κατηριθμημένος and ἔλαχεν τὸν κλῆρον) show, ahead of time, that Matthias, chosen by lot and added to the Eleven (ὁ κλῆρος ἐπὶ Μαθθίαν and συνκατεψηφίσθη v. 26), replaces Judas and does not occupy a really new place. The account of the death of Judas which follows and which ends with the first quotation from the Psalms (v. 18-20a) makes it clear that Judas thought only of reaping the reward for his betrayal, that he did not repent and that his unnatural death proved his fall from grace.[15]

The second quotation from scripture (v. 20b) has to justify the choice of a new Apostle and, at the same time, point out that the election is an exception, unique, as the fall from grace of the traitor had been. It does not present a principal of Apostolic Succession. Matthias does not succeed an Apostle whose mission would be ended by his death; he takes the place left empty by an apostate and which ought therefore to be occupied.

Luke first emphasizes that there can only be one such replacement, since there has been only one betrayal.[16] Next, the one who replaces Judas should be, like the Eleven, a witness of Christ's ministry since the time of John the Baptist and a witness of the resurrection. These two conditions are not as difficult to fulfill as has been suggested. We should note that the former is expressed in restricted terms, intended to comply with reality. It is not a matter of being a "witness to the whole ministry of Jesus".[17] Only the three closest disciples were that. It is a matter of having lived within the group around the Twelve while Jesus was with them. Luke seems to have chosen his words to allow for the replacement of Judas and at the same time to preclude in advance the pretentions of any other possible aspirants to the apostolate. As for the second condition, it was doubtless easy to satisfy that, for neither Luke 24 nor Acts 1 puts a definite limit on the number of those who witnessed the christophanies and the Ascension. Finally, just as Jesus has chosen the Twelve for preeminence from among a wider circle (Luke 6. 13), "the Lord", that is, Jesus glorified,[18] in the same way here reveals by lot His own choice from among the candidates judged possible by the believers. This procedure, without parallel in the history of the infant Church,[19] also shows that the nomination of a new Apostle among the Twelve, apart from the fact that it can only be done by Jesus, is an event as unique and as exceptional as the defection of Judas. Matthias is a replacement and not a real addition to the circle of the first Apostles, which must remain what it has been from the beginning--a circle of twelve men.[20] In other words, the circle of the Twelve maintains, at the time of Luke, its original historical and eschatalogical significance.

One cannot help being struck by the importance attached by Luke to the reconstitution of the circle of the Twelve. The writer of Acts has had less to say about other events which seem more important to our modern eyes, such as James' accession to the leadership of the Church and the appearance of Elders in Jerusalem. It is not that Luke attaches any particular psychological interest to Matthias himself. The new Apostle plays no part in the book of Acts, as he is never mentioned again. But Luke attaches a very great theological significance to the group of the Twelve as such, reconstituted in its integrity because, in his view, this group is preserving its specific mission. The Twelve are an important permanence within the Church, which will be for ever the Church of Jews and Gentiles.

During His ministry, Jesus chose twelve disciples to be His representatives to the people of God. This mission will not be finished as long as the story of salvation lasts. Hence Luke is of the opinion that the decisive events of the death and resurrection of Jesus must be accompanied by the reconstitution of the circle of the Twelve. In his view, this event is so necessary that only after it has happened can the gift of the Spirit, and the call to Israel in the name of the risen Lord by His twelve Witnesses, take place. On the day of Pentecost, Peter appears before the people "with the eleven" (Acts 2. 14). By their unanimous presence, the Twelve are carrying out the mission for which they were set apart, eleven of them from the time of the ministry of Jesus, the twelfth from the time that Judas became irredeemable by his fall and death.

Certainly, Luke wishes to point out that the Twelve are the witnesses of the resurrection and also the witnesses of everything which Jesus did and taught from the time of John the Baptist, and that, consequently, they are the guarantors of the Christian tradition.[21] But Luke emphasizes also the Apostles' role of being Witnesses from the very beginning, in Peter's speech at Caesarea (Acts 10. 37-41) and in that of Paul at Antioch in Pisidia (Acts 13. 31). In these two passages Luke does not specify that the witnesses were twelve in number. The actual number of witnesses to testify to the reality of the saving acts on which the faith of the believers is based is immaterial. But the representatives of Jesus must be twelve in order to announce to Israel that the salvation accomplished by Christ is for all the people of God and is destined first of all for the Jews.[22] In other words, according to Masson, the eschatological perspective of the early days of the Church, when it was necessary that there should be twelve Apostles sent to Israel,[23] has not been changed essentially by the passage of time. It has been lengthened, but it remains theologically the same, as long as the witness and the call to Israel last. Gentiles may enter the Church in as large a number as God may call, but the fact remains that salvation is always destined first of all for Israel. That is why, of necessity, the Twelve, throughout all the history of the Church, and no matter what may be the numerical proportion of Jews and Gentiles among the believers, keep their same historical and eschatological significance. To lose sight of this fact, would be, for the

Gentile Christians, to come to the hasty conclusion that God had rejected His people.

The theory according to which the Church very soon lost sight of the value of the circle of Twelve[24] does not seem to have much support in the New Testament texts. It is not to be found in Paul. It is true that the Apostle to the Gentiles only uses the expression "the Twelve" once, and probably in a text which he is quoting and which he has not edited himself (I Cor. 15. 5). It is true that, of the Twelve, he only mentions Peter and John. But this lack of interest in the personages of the Apostles does not signify ignorance of the theological value of the circle which they constituted. Moreover, if Paul speaks of the Apostles rather than of the Twelve, it is doubtless for the following reason: he himself is claiming the title and authority of an Apostle and an authority equal to that of those who have been Apostles before him. He has not, and he could not have claimed a place within the circle of the Twelve, because he was mindful of the differences in vocation and missionary task which distinguished him from them. But a Paul who declares that the Gospel is addressed to the Jews first and then to the Greeks (Rom. 1. 16), who makes Jerusalem the starting-point for his own mission (Rom. 15. 19), who considers himself the Apostle to the Gentiles, while Peter is the Apostle to the Jews (Gal. 2. 7), cannot help but see in the circle of the Twelve, or at the very least in its leaders, a sign for Israel.

There is also in Luke a very clear picture of the diversity and the unity of the two apostleships. It is quite clear that the writer of Acts does not grant Paul the Pauline title of Apostle but keeps it for the Twelve. But he shows no trace of anti-Pauline feeling. In the Acts Paul is not subordinate to the Twelve. On the contrary, he alone takes up the task of preaching the Gospel to the remotest parts of the earth, which at first had been entrusted to all of them.[25] Luke makes use of a vocabulary which is properly his. The Apostles for him are the Twelve, and, when Paul speaks of "Apostles of Jesus Christ", Luke speaks of "witnesses".[26] Luke and Paul are in agreement in saying Christ alone chooses his Witnesses or his Apostles. But Luke understood the specific nature of Paul's apostleship as clearly as he comprehended the eschatalogical significance of the Twelve. It is was quite clear to him that the circle of the Twelve should be reconstituted, it was equally clear that Paul could not replace Judas, and that, in spite of certain manifestations, he was not "the one who took over Judas' place".[27] Paul is a circle of himself, separate from but equal to the circle of the Twelve. They have been sent to Israel and its proselytes; he will go far beyond, to the Gentiles.

NOTES

1. "Hommage au Professeur Jean Héring," *Revue d'histoire et de philosophie religieuses*, 37, 1957, p. 71-81, by kind permission of the Faculté de théologie Protestante at Strasbourg.

2. Cf. for example, with slight differences of opinion, M. Goguel, *Introduction au Nouveau Testament*, III, Paris, 1922, p. 174; H. W. Beyer, *Apostelgeschichte* (Das N. T. Deutsch), Göttingen, 1935, p. 11f; O. Bauernfeind, *Die Apostelgeschichte* (Theol. Handkommentar zum N. T.), Leipzig, 1939, p. 26.

3. Ch. Masson, "La reconstitution du collège des Douze d'après Actes 1. 15-26," *Revue de théol. et de philos.*, 1955, p. 193-201.

4. *Ibid.*, p. 194.

5. P. 195-196. Along with verses 21 and 22 Masson attributes two other small additions to Luke, the words τῆς διακονίας ταύτης καὶ ἀποστολῆς (v. 25) and ἀποστόλων (v. 26). Altogether, the original account could only have contained verses 15, 16, 18a, 20a, 23-26.

6. Cf. E. Haenchen, *Die Apostelgeschichte* (Meyer's Kommentar, III, 10 Aufl.), Göttingen, 1956, p. 128-129, and C. H. Dodd, *According to the Scriptures*, London, 1952, p. 58-59.

7. Dodd, p. 59, n. 1.

8. Haenchen, p. 131.

9. Similar cases can be cited in the New Testament. In Romans 10. 11-13, the expression "the Scripture says" introduces the quotation from Isaiah 28. 16 in verse 11 and the quotation from Joel 2. 32 in verse 13. In James 2. 23, the expression "the Scripture was fulfilled, which says" introduces quotations from Genesis 15. 6 and Isaiah 41. 8 (II Chron. 20. 7).

10. Cf. J. Jeremias, *Jésus et les païens* (Cahiers théol. 39), Neuchâtel-Paris, 1956, p. 16-17.

11. Cf. Masson, p. 200-201, and among recent writers E. Lohse, "Ursprung und Prägung des christlichen Apostolates", *Theolog. Zeitschrift,* 1953, p. 265; L. E. Elliott-Binns, *Galilean Christianity* (Studies in Biblical Theology, 16), London, 1956, p. 59.

12. Cf. among others, Rengstorff, *Theol. Wörterbuch,* II, p. 327 and n. 49, and the commentaries by Bauernfeind and Macgregor-Ferris. -- In Paul's view too the death (in faith) of an Apostle does not leave a gap in the circle of Twelve. When the Apostle to the Gentiles claimed to be recognized as an Apostle equal in title and rank with those who had been Apostles before him, James had died. But Paul never claimed the place of James. Among other reasons, it is evidently because after the death of James, the Twelve remained the Twelve, they did not become the Eleven again, as they had after the treachery of Judas.

13. Cf. Matt. 27. 34 and 48; Mk. 15. 36; Jn. 2. 17; 15. 25; 17. 12; 19. 18; Acts 1. 20; Rom. 11. 9-10; 15. 3.

14. Cf. Dodd, p. 59, n. 1. -- If, on the other hand, Luke and the first Christians had shared the opinion of J. L. Leuba (*L'institution et l'événement,* Neuchâtel-Paris, p. 51) that even the betrayal cannot erase the *character indebilis* conferred on Judas by his election to the body of the Twelve, there would never have been any question of replacing Judas.

15. On the different traditions connected with Judas' end see finally P. Benoit, "La mort de Judas", *Synoptische Studien A. Wikenhauser...dargebracht,* München, 1954, p. 1-19. -- We might wonder whether Luke, by maintaining a tradition which holds that the traitor's death was later than the account in Matthew 27 suggests, did not want to provide an answer to the following question: why did the risen Christ Himself not designate the replacement for Judas, before His ascension? Judas has to be replaced not because he died but because he was guilty of betrayal; in any event, it was necessary to wait until he died unrepentant before his fall from grace became irremediable and his place became really vacant.

16. Cf. ἕνα, v. 22; ὃν...ἐκ τούτων δύο ἕνα, v. 24.

17. Masson, p. 195

18. Cf. in connection with this, the decisive arguments of Th. Zahn, *Die Apostelgeschichte des Lucas* (Kommentar zum N. T., V), Leipzig, 1919, p. 63-64. Among recent commentators, Zahn's theory is followed by Renié, Bruce and Macgregor-Ferris. Cf. also L. S. Thornton, "The Choice of Matthias",

Journal of Theol. Stud., 1945, p. 51-59.

19. Masson (p. 196, n. 2) is of the opinion that, in the original version reworked by Luke, Peter was proposing a nomination procedure similar to that followed in the election of the Seven (Acts 6. 3f). But the two cases are really very different. In Acts 6 it is a matter of the Twelve handing over to the Seven an office which, until now, has been theirs. That is why the Twelve themselves decide on the procedure to be followed, and after the Seven have been chosen by the main body of the disciples, the Twelve lay their hands on them, less to ordain them than to hand on to them a share of their own power. Here the ritual keeps its original meaning. In the case of Matthias, it is a matter of finding a man associated with the Eleven, equal with them, and who, like them, can receive his charge only directly from the Lord Himself. That is why there is no question of the laying on of hands on the occasion of the election of the new Apostle. The Eleven did not choose Matthias and they have nothing to hand on to him. It is the Lord who gives him Judas' place, by virtue of which he becomes joined to the Eleven.

20. We should note Luke's insistence on Matthias' occupation of Judas' place (v. 25), and that Matthias' share in the apostolate is made available by Judas' defection (του κλῆρον τῆς διακονίας ταύτης, v. 17; την ἐπισκοπην αὐτοῦ, v. 20; τὸν τόπον τῆς διακονίας ταύτης καὶ ἀποστολῆς v. 25). This collection of expressions is not to be explained by literary considerations or by Lucan additions to the sources, but by theological reasons. Luke wished to avoid the erroneous interpretation which might result from the choice of Matthias and which is reflected in the commentary by F. J. Foakes Jackson: "The selection of Matthias may be intended to show that the infant Church possessed the power alike of organization and continuance" (*The Acts of the Apostles*, The Moffatt N. T. Commentary, London, 1931, p. 9). This exegesis does not seem valid to us. First the Lord alone has the authority and the power to create new Witnesses; secondly, the choice of Matthias is to remedy what has happened in the past; it is not the starting-point for a new organization. It is not a matter, therefore, of "the first ecclesiastical election" (A. Loisy, *Les Actes des Apôtres*, Paris, 1920, p. 175).

21. Cf. E. Haenchen, p. 132. -- We should note that in constituting the Twelve as witnesses of Jesus from the time of John's baptism, Luke is following Johannine tradition (cf. Jn. 1. 35-42). It is one example among many of similarities

between the Johannine and Lucan traditions.

22. Cf. Acts 3. 26; 13. 46, and J. Jeremias, p. 64.

23. Ch.Masson, p. 200.

24, Cf. the articles quoted by Masson and Lohse and, with some reservations, the commentary by Haenchen.

25. Cf. W. Mundle, "Das apostelbild der Apostelgeschichte", *ZNW,* 1928, p. 45f; P. -H. Menoud, "Le plan des Actes des Apôtres", *N. T. Studies,* 1954-55, p. 49f. *supra* p. 121-132.

26. Cf. Acts 1. 8 and 21f, etc. (the Twelve); Acts 22. 15; 26. 16 (Paul).

27. K. Barth, *Kirchliche Dogmatik,* II, 2, Zollikon-Zürich, 1942, p. 530. English translation, *Church Dogmatics* II, 2, Edinburgh, 1957, p. 478. My colleague at Bern, W. Michaelis, and my former student Rev. J.-J von Allmen, have drawn my attention to this.

Jesus and His Witnesses

Observations on the Unity of the Work of Luke[1]

To save the world it is not enough that Jesus should die and rise from the dead; there must be witnesses to these events and these witnesses must be heard. If it is a case of propagating a philosophical religion like the popular stoic wisdom of the Hellenic age, preachers and teachers would be sufficient for the task. But witnesses are necessary in order to proclaim to men that they have been saved not by a doctrine which is timeless but by the intervention of God in history, by events which happened once and for all, at a particular time and in a particular place; that is, men are needed who were present when these events took place and whose preaching is based on the affirmation "We have seen". Christian revelation of necessity has these two aspects: on the one hand the redemptive work of Jesus and, on the other hand, the disciples' testimony to the risen Christ. If Christ died and rose again without witnesses, or if these witnesses, disobeying the order they had been given, had kept silent, redemption would no longer have been possible except at the cost of a new incarnation. In other words the foundation of the Church is at one and the same time the work of Christ and the testimony of the Apostles.

The first Christians saw these two aspects of the Gospel and their unity. The Pauline epistles contain two declarations which are complementary and not contradictory--that the foundation of salvation is Christ (I Cor. 3. 10-11) and also the group of Apostles (Eph. 2. 20). The words with which Jesus addresses Peter, according to Matthew 16. 18, combine the two Pauline affirmations by stating that the Church of Christ will be built on this rock which is Peter.

The writer "to Theophilus", who is an historian open to theological questions, wanted to express in his turn this same idea of the unity of the redemptive work, in a piece of work much more extensive than the Gospel of Mark. By describing in a first book the activity of Jesus and in a second that of His witnesses, he wanted to retrace the whole history of the revelation, to include it, so to speak, in one sweeping overview, from its preparation in the ministry of John the Baptist to the ultimate testimony to Christ in the capital of the world by His last Witness, Paul.

Now we must try to show that Luke's work fulfills His intention. To attempt to establish that we shall put forward two arguments. First of all a negative argument: the book of Acts remains properly an enigma if it is regarded by itself, separate from the Gospel of Luke, as a history of the early Church. Secondly, a positive argument, which will occupy more of our attention: the book of Acts becomes clear if it is considered as a collection of testimonies given to the world regarding the redemptive work of Jesus, testimonies without which the revelation itself would remain incomplete and ineffectual.

Let us look briefly at the negative argument. The book of Acts is not offered as the first history of the Church. Luke is not a forerunner of Eusebius of Caesarea. If it were an account of the beginnings of Christianity, the second book to Theophilus would have some surprising omissions. There would be omissions with regard to the outreach of the Church. In the second part, after the Jerusalem conference (chap. 16-28), the book of Acts is concerned only with the missions of Paul. But there were other missionary enterprises--for instance the one which established the church in Rome. When writing to this church, Paul declares that the report of its faith has spread through the whole Christian world (Rom. 1. 8). Luke himself knows that there are already "brethren" in Italy when Paul lands there (Acts 28. 14-15). In keeping silent about the foundation of the church at Rome Luke acted deliberately and not out of ignorance. In his view, the Gospel really reaches the capital of the world only with the arrival of "the chosen vessel" predestined to give witness before Caesar. In other words Luke is giving a stylized picture of the events. He is writing the story of Jesus' Witnesses rather than that of the growth of the Church.

There would also be omissions in the biographies of the great missionaries outlined in Acts. All the important characters in the story disappear at a particular moment carefully fixed by the writer, before their career is finished and before the historical curiosity of the reader is satisfied. Luke does not say one word about Peter's activities after his deliverance from the hands of Agrippa and his departure for "another place" (Acts 12. 17), and there is no word either on the outcome of Paul's trial, to mention only the most striking examples. But when Peter disappears from the horizon of the Acts, his work is finished in a certain sense, because he has already given testimony to Christ in Jerusalem, in the land of the Jews, in Samaria, and in the house of the Italian Cornelius. What else could Peter do, since he has already proclaimed Christ to Jews, to half-Jews, and to non-Jews, that is to say, to representatives of all manner of men? If his story is left unfinished on the historical level, it is complete in respect to testimony. As for the problem posed by the allegedly abrupt ending of the Acts, we shall return to that a little later.

Let us point out a third category of omissions. Luke

says nothing, or almost nothing, about life within the Christian communities, their worship and their organization. Nothing about the origins of the Seven, nor the appearance of Elders in the church at Jerusalem, nor the accession of James, the brother of Jesus, to the leadership of the Church. He says nothing either about the organization of the Pauline churches, apart from the brief note on the installation of Elders in the communities established by Barnabas and Paul (Acts 14:23). Obviously Luke is hardly concerned to show how the Church lives and develops. The founding of the Church interests him more than its growth. It is enough for him to say that it is born out of the testimony of the Apostles. One other fact confirms this. It is well-known that the book of Acts is made up of a number of speeches. Now, Luke does not report speeches of all the missionaries, but only of the few he singles out by conferring on them the title he regards as highest, that of "Witness". There are only speeches by the Witnesses Peter, Stephen and Paul in Acts. Neither Barnabas, nor Philip, who are not Witnesses, in the specific sense, make speeches which are reported.

We come therefore to our first conclusion: Luke is interested above all in the Witnesses of the risen Christ. It is their testimonies which are the essential part of his book, which mark the stages in it and which dominate all other events.

Luke is the only one of the writers of the New Testament who applies the term "witnesses of Christ" to the Twelve and to Paul. He includes Stephen also, Stephen who would be unknown to us but for the book of Acts. Let us now turn our attention to Luke's view of what a Witness is.

In the writers of the time, the word "witness°(μάρτυς) is a very loose term which can be used in many different ways and whose context determines the exact shade of meaning. In its usual sense, the word means one who testifies to what he has seen and heard, particularly in a court-room. The word μάρτυς therefore is more or less synonymous with the term αὐτόπτης, "eye-witness". However, this term puts the accent on the presence of the witness at the events he is reporting; the term is by definition rigid; either one has seen and one is an eye-witness, or one has seen nothing and does not deserve this title. The word μάρτυς (one who testifies) puts the accent on the testimony given by the one who has seen or heard; this is why the word can have different shades of meaning. In fact, if the witness (μάρτυς), who is giving evidence, can remain objective, he can also take sides, especially if he is testifying on behalf of ideas which he shares or for a person to whom he is bound by ties of common interest or affection. Then the witness is no longer an impartial reporter. He is a guarantor and an authority, a partisan and a disciple, or even an arbiter and a judge.

Let us give two examples taken from the writer closest in time to Luke, manely Flavius Josephus. The Jewish historian claims to be αὐτόπτης, an "eye-witness" of most of the events he reports in the *Jewish War* (C. Ap. 1. 53), but he describes as μάρτυρες, "witnesses" in his favor, pagan writers who describe the antiquity of the Jewish race and who thus corroborate what he himself has written in his *Antiquities* (C. Ap. 1. 4).

Again, in another passage in the *Jewish War* (VI, 134), Josephus makes use of both words meaning "witness", which shows that there is a shift in meaning from one to the other. Reporting an episode in the capture of the Temple, the historian describes Titus leading an attack by night when he is both αὐτόπτης καὶ μάρτυς, "spectator and judge"; Titus, in fact, took part in the fight in order to estimate for himself the zeal of his men and to reward those who would fight all the more valiantly under the eye and the judgement of their commander-in-chief.

These examples show clearly that the witness in the strong sense (μάρτυς) is more than just an eye-witness. The witness does not look on passively and objectively at the events taking place before his eyes; he understands them and he sees their ultimate significance.

Like the Jewish historian Luke recognizes and distinguishes between the two terms. In the preface to his work, he uses the word αὐτόπτης when speaking of those who "were eye-witnesses and became servants of the Gospel" (Luke 1. 3). But he resorts to the word μάρτυς (Luke 24. 48; Acts 1. 8, etc.) to describe the witnesses of the risen Christ, because he wants to make it clear that these are more than simple eye-witnesses like many of the believers in the church in Palestine. Moreover, the disciples were "eye-witnesses" from the moment they first followed their Master. None of them has any need to be solemnly invested with the title of eye-witness; they were that from the simple fact that they were present at the event. When the risen Christ declares to His followers that they shall be His "witnesses" (Luke 24. 48; Acts 1. 8), the term must be understood in its strong sense.

The risen Christ confers the title and the charge of Witness (μάρτυς) on the apostles He chose during the time of His earthly ministry (Luke 6. 13), to whom He appeared, whom He instructed for an extended period, and who will speak in His name when He is no longer with them in person. United to Christ by their first calling and by personal encounter, in the appearances of the Glorified Lord, the mission of the Witnesses is not merely to testify to the historic veracity of the events in the life of Jesus. These events themselves are already known to the Apostles' first audience in Jerusalem and in Palestine. Even when speaking to Cornelius at Caesarea Peter gives a brief reminder of the career of Jesus with these words: "You know what happened throughout all Judaea" (Acts 10. 37). The Apostles must, above all else, testify to the significance of the divine events they have just witnessed and whose meaning and implication their Lord had explained to them at length. They must proclaim, with the authority of those who have seen and comprehended, that Jesus is risen and glorified, that the Scriptures have been accomplished in Him and that the salvation formerly promised to Israel is now offered to all mankind, to Jews and to Gentiles, and to the uttermost ends of the earth.

We should note in passing that, in speaking of the Apostles here, we are simplifying a little the facts as given by Luke. In actual fact, the writer to Theophilus is not much concerned about the precise number of the disciples who were present with the risen Christ in the scenes enacted at the end of Luke 24 and at the beginning of Acts 1. At one time only the Eleven are there (Acts 1. 2-5), at another time other disciples are present as well (Luke 24. 33; Acts 1. 21f). It seems as though Luke wavers between being carried away by the tradition that the Twelve were the only ones to see the risen Christ and another tradition that the Eleven had several companions with them when Jesus appeared to them. But the question is secondary to our main subject. In any case, the number of witnesses is limited, and these few men are the uniquely authorized bearers of the revelation, in that the risen Christ Himself did not enlarge the circle of His Witnesses.

It is maintained, it is true, that these first disciples are only the representatives, in some way, of all believers and that the latter are equally called to be Witnesses for Christ. The first Witnesses only carried out their charge after having received the Holy Spirit. Now, in the Church, all believers participate in the gift of the Spirit. Therefore, it is maintained, it is in the end the congregation of believers, the Church, which finds itself in the succession of the Apostles, taking up their mission of testimony.

But this interpretation does an injustice to Luke's intentions and to the precise letter of his text. Undoubtedly, further on in Acts, the Spirit will be seen to descend not only on the Witnesses of the risen Christ, but also on all believers (Acts 2. 38). However, the gift of the Spirit does not make all the believers Witnesses in the strong, unique sense which Luke gives to the word. The pouring out of the Spirit is necessary so that the Witnesses chosen and commissioned by Jesus on the one hand, and the believers won over by the testimony of the Apostles on the other hand, can both fulfill their own vocation. But this vocation is not the same for them both. Only the Apostles are the Witnesses of Christ. The mission of the believers is to proclaim to the world, by the new life which animates them, the truth and effectiveness of the Apostles' testimony (Acts 2. 42-47). For the Spirit does not create new Witnesses, any more than it created the first ones, seeing that the Spirit does not make Christ appear. Certainly the words: "You shall be my witnesses" recall Isaiah's proclamation to the people of Israel: "'You are my witnesses,' says the Lord". But the parallel is purely formal. The Witnesses of Christ are so by virtue of special selection and preparation, after having seen and heard what was given to them alone to see and hear, and in order to accomplish a specific mission that they alone can fulfill by virtue of what they are. In the eyes of the prophet it is all the members of the race who will testify before the world, through their faithfulness to Yahweh, that Yahweh alone is God. The precise New Testament correspondence to the text in Isaiah is to be found in the pictures of the everyday life of the believers (Acts 2. 42f. etc.), where we see the faithful, by their exemplary Christian life, attesting to the fact that the Apostles' testimony has touched them. The few men whom the risen Christ Himself picked out keep their privilege of being the only immediate Witnesses of the saving acts. New Witnesses can only arise if Christ Himself calls them. We shall see this as we review the circumstances in which three new Witnesses appear: Matthias, Paul and Stephen.

Matthias has to fill the gap left in the circle of the Twelve by the fall of Judas, and his case is not essentially different from that of the Eleven, in spite of appearances to the contrary (Acts 1. 21-26). In fact, Judas' replacement must satisfy two conditions as a preliminary to his selection by Christ to replace Judas. He must have lived close to the Twelve during the time that Jesus was with them and he must have been present at an appearance of the risen Christ. In other words, the one who will become "a witness with us as to His resurrection", as Peter says (Acts 1. 22), must have been first an eye-witness, as were the Eleven themselves when the risen Christ declared to them: "You shall be my witnesses". We must emphasize that in Luke's view this was a prerequisite only for the one who would occupy a place in the circle of the Twelve; it is not required for every Witness. If such were the case Luke could not give the title of Witness to Stephen and to Paul. This requirement being satisfied, Matthias is elevated to the rank of Witness by the Lord Himself, that is to say by Christ glorified, whose will is shown through the drawing of lots, and not by God, in view of the solidarity established by Luke between Matthias and the Eleven. The strangeness of the procedure, which is not used anywhere else in the infant Church, serves to emphasize on the one hand that we have here a unique case, as was the treachery of Judas, and, on the other hand, that Christ alone can elevate a believer to the rank of Witness.

Luke does not hesitate to make Paul a Witness of the same rank as the Twelve, as Paul also was chosen in a particular way: he has seen the glorified Christ and has received His instructions (Acts 22. 14-15; 26. 16-18); he too is sent to give testimony to all men (Acts 22. 15; 26. 17-20) and particularly to the Gentiles (Acts 22:21). Paul, it is true, was not one of Jesus' followers during His earthly life, he is not an eye-witness. But Christ, who showed him the reality of His life in heaven, made him realize at the same time that He was Jesus of Nazareth (Acts 22. 6; cf. 26. 9). It is through personal revelation and not through the testimony of another that Paul knows that: "A certain Jesus, who had died, is now alive" (Acts 25. 19). He is therefore undoubtedly a Witness in the view of the writer of Acts.

That Stephen also should be called at least once a "witness" of Jesus (Acts 22. 20) is surprising at first glance. For Luke makes him a member of the group of Seven which he clearly subordinates to the Twelve. But Luke takes care to separate Stephen from the group by reserving a special place for him. He stresses, as if with a purpose, the multitude of gifts which Stephen possesses and which are the sign of divine election. Stephen is not only full of faith and of the Holy Spirit, as is also another who is not an Apostle, namely Barnabas; Stephen is also clothed in power like the Twelve, in wisdom and grace like Moses and the child Jesus (Acts 6. 5-10). Moreover, Stephen delivers a speech--the longest speech in Acts--and Luke only allows Witnesses of the risen Christ to make speeches. Finally, Stephen sees the glorified Christ, and if this christophany is not exactly the same as those granted to the Twelve and to Paul, in Luke's view it is equally significant in the sense that it is the starting-point of a mission, namely that of the followers of Stephen in Samaria. For these reasons we can see why Luke did not hesitate to put the name of Stephen on the list of Witnesses of the risen Christ along with the Twelve and Paul.

In short, Luke reserves the title of Witness for a few men predestined to see what other believers can only know in this world by adding their own faith to the assertions of the Witnesses. In this sense, the Witnesses are the necessary intermediaries between the living Christ and men destined to share in the salvation brought about by the life, death, and resurrection of Jesus. So even though these Witnesses mark the beginning of the time of the Church by preaching as they are called to do, they still belong to the time of the Revelation by the unique bond which Joins them to Christ. Their ministry is the final act in the Revelation announced by John the Baptist.

Let us now look at the plan and the structure of the Acts. We will see that the enterprises of the three Witnesses or groups of Witnesses, Peter (and the Twelve), Stephen, and Paul form the back-bone of the book, on which everything depends or to which everything relates.

Let us return to the fundamental text of Acts 1. 8 and turn our attention to the program set by the risen Christ for his Witnesses. After Jerusalem, the Holy City, where the Gospel story begins (Luke 1. 5), where Jesus died and rose again, where He first appeared to his Witnesses (Luke 24; Acts 1; cf. 7. 55-56; 22. 18), and where the Holy Spirit was poured out for the first time (Acts 2), there are three stages: the land of the Jews (Judaea and Galilee); Samaria, the land of the schismatics who were regarded as demi-pagan by the Jews; and finally "the remotest parts of the earth".

The last expression is taken from the prophecy of Isaiah 49. 6, where God makes His servant a light to the nations, that His salvation may reach to the ends of the earth. So it is the Gentiles who are referred to in Acts, after the Jews and the Samaritans (cf. Luke 24. 47), the reader should understand that the order given by the risen Christ also previews his supreme testimony and that "the end of the earth" is Rome, where everything comes together and beyond which there is nothing.

These three stages are more theological than geographical. The word of the Witnesses, which is going to resound from the Jewish capital as far as the capital of the civilized world, will reach, in succession, three kinds of men who constitute the human race: Jews, half-Jews and non-Jews. Now the three Witnesses whom Luke presents in succession, Peter, Stephen, and Paul, are not necessary to bring the missionary enterprise to a successful conclusion. Peter, in the name of the Twelve, begins in Jerusalem. The contents of the first five chapters of Acts are essentially his sermons. It could even be said that Peter, to some extent, starts the mission of the other Witnesses, since he also visits the Samaritans (chap. 8), and the home of the Gentile Cornelius (chap. 10). But the intervention of Stephen was necessary for Peter to leave the Holy City and the Jewish environment. The witness of Stephen is of major importance, not only of itself, but also because of its effects. It determines the whole sequence of events up to the arrival of Paul on the scene. The affair of Stephen is the source of the different threads from which the fabric of chapters 8 to 14 is woven. Some of Stephen's scattered followers go to Samaria, with the Apostles Peter and John following them; others go as far as Antioch. At the same time the persecutor, brought to light by the death of Stephen, is conquered by

Christ; the new Witness does not delay in joining the missionaries in the work at Antioch, from where the first great mission to the Gentiles will start (chap. 13-14). Having reached the middle of his story, Luke pauses at the plateau provided by the Jerusalem conference. For, from that time on, the risen Christ's command is plainly obeyed on the theological level; the testimony has already reached the Jews, the Samaritans and proselytes who are half-Jews, and the non-Jews. The Church has already reached its full theological stature since it is the Church of Jews and Gentiles. After Luke has shown that measures necessary to ensure unity of the Church have been taken "by the Apostles and elders at Jerusalem" (15. 22-23; 16. 4), it only remains for him to relate how the task, already finished at the theological level, will be completed on the geographical level through the missions of the final Witness, Paul. Paul, taking upon himself from now on the commission formerly given to all, will go to the remotest parts of the earth, as far as Rome "preaching without let or hindrance".

Such an ending would be surprising if one held to the idea that Luke wanted to write a history of the first missions; he could be reproached for not having reported Paul's appearance before Caesar and the outcome of his trial. On the other hand, this conclusion seems to be the only possible one, if it is conceded that Luke, in his second book, wanted to show how the Witnesses of Jesus obeyed the command of the risen Christ to carry the Gospel from Jerusalem to the ends of the earth, to the Jews, and to the Gentiles.

It is not only the last two verses of Acts which bring the reader's attention back to the mission entrusted to the Witnesses of Jesus (Luke 24. 47; Acts 1. 8) to show that it has been accomplished. The last chapters lead up to this finale by a double series of accounts affirming, on the one hand, that Paul is to give testimony in Rome as he has in Jerusalem (19. 21; 23. 11) and, on the other hand, that he cannot be prevented from going to Caesar by any obstacles placed in his way by the Jews, by any legal contrivances, or by any perils on his journeys (25. 11-12; 26. 32; 27. 24). But in these accounts, the accent is not on the trial awaiting the Apostle, but in the fact that nothing can turn him aside from the setting of his final testimony. In Rome, as everywhere else since Jerusalem, he will be able to proclaim "the Lord's affairs" and he will do it with all inner freedom and without external obstacles, for two full years. This emphasizes in the strongest possible way that the Gospel is authentically proclaimed in the capital of the world and the mission of the unique Witnesses of Jesus is accomplished.

On the other hand, it is quite clear that others who do not bear the name of Witnesses of Jesus have had a part in the missionary work reported in the book of Acts. But however important their role may be, these bearers of the Gospel never act except as associates and deputies of the Witnesses, as disciples and assistants. Philip, "the evangelist, one of the Seven" (21. 8), receives the laying on of hands of the Apostles (6. 6) before preaching the Gospel in Samaria and along the coast of Palestine. Barnabas appears chiefly as an intermediary between Paul and the Twelve (9. 27), between Jerusalem and Antioch (11. 22), and between Antioch and Paul (11. 25). If he goes on a missionary journey with Paul it is always the latter who speaks for both of them (chap. 13-14). When Barnabas leaves Paul, he does not set out for a new mission field but returns to Cyprus (15. 39), where the word of Paul had been revealed in all its power (13. 1-12).

In short, if Luke is not unaware that the Apostles had numerous assistants, known or unknown, and even some forerunners on the road of evangelization (8. 4; 11. 19-20;

26. 14), he does not devote his second book to Theophilus to a general history of the first missions. It is devoted above all to the work of the Witnesses, whom the risen Christ chose for Himself to proclaim His work of forgiveness and salvation to all mankind.

One last question demands our attention. Why has Luke used this term of "witness" in preference to any other--in particular to the term "apostle", in the exclusive sense which Paul gave it when he claimed for himself, as for the Twelve, the title and rank of "apostle of Jesus Christ", in contrast to those apostolic missionaries who were delegates of the churches? Luke, it seems, could have made use of the word Apostle in the Pauline sense since "the apostle of Jesus Christ" according to Paul is the same as "the witness of Jesus" according to Luke. They are the same in the sense that both designations put the Twelve and Paul on equal footing, yet, at the same time, isolate them from the other bearers of the Gospel, with the exception of Stephen in Luke's writings, and of James, the brother of the Lord, and several others in Paul's writings. In any case, it is in no way with the intention of subordinating Paul to the Twelve that Luke denies to the Apostle to the Gentiles the title the latter claimed for himself.

In fact, Luke is aware that the term Apostle has different shades of meaning. He does use it in the general sense of missionary. In this way he presents Barnabas and Paul as "the apostles" (14. 4 and 14) sent by the church or by the prophets and scholars at Antioch. Everywhere else he keeps the title of "apostle" for the Twelve, but with definite specifications; he says "the twelve apostles" (1. 26) or "the apostles in Jerusalem" (8. 14; 15. 2; 16. 4, *passim*), except when the context makes it quite clear that it can only be a matter of the first apostles. Luke knows that there can be apostles and apostles and that the term itself, in spite of the precision with which Paul has endowed it, remains ambiguous. The word "witness" is clearer and more definite. The authority and power of the "apostles in Jerusalem" come from their being Witnesses of the risen Christ.

We should note that, in the final analysis, Paul's view is the same. Not only is he an Apostle of Jesus Christ because he has seen the Lord (I Cor. 9. 1; 15. 8; Gal. 1. 15), but also his well-known declaration--"If Christ has not risen... we are shown to be bearing false witness (ψευδομάρτυρες) about God because we have testified that God raised Christ" (I Cor. 15. 14-15)--leaves one to think that he is aware of the Lucan meaning of the terms "witness" and "witnessing". However he takes for himself the title of Apostle while Luke gives him, along with the Twelve, that of Witness.

This difference in vocabulary has to be explained, finally, by theological norms. Expressions were used differently at the time of the Apostles and after they had disappeared from the scene, because their disappearance itself marked the boundary between the time of Revelation and the time of Faith.

According to Paul and the first generation of believers, the resurrection of Christ and the rule of the Holy Spirit marked the beginning of the present era, and it was not thought that this interim period would go beyond the time of the Apostles. In this perspective, the Witness of Jesus appears above all as the Apostle of Christ who hastens to proclaim His name, while there is still time, in all places where it has not yet been heard.

Luke is writing about twenty-five years after the appearance of the Pauline epistles. Time passes and the world still endures. All the Apostles, except perhaps one, are gone. In this new perspective Luke no longer is looking forward towards the early completion of the missionary task. He is looking backwards to that bygone era when those few extraordinary men lived and worked; the few who had seen and heard the living Christ and on whose testimony the faith of all other believers rests. In order that their faith may be assured, it is not enough from now on to report "the affairs of the Lord Jesus Christ", it is also necessary to report how His Witnesses have proclaimed Him to the world. The fourth evangelist, following after Luke, takes the same point of view, using, in general, the same vocabulary. If the disciples are not called by John "the Witnesses of Jesus", it is on a mission of "witness" that they are sent into the world (John 15. 27; 17. 18), for men can only attain faith through their preaching (17. 20).

John the theologian concludes his gospel with these words of the risen Christ: "Blessed are those who have not seen and yet have believed" (20. 29). These words do not allude to Thomas; he believed after he had seen, like all the Apostles. These words allude to the believers who, without being witnesses to the revelation, will inherit the same salvation as those who were witnesses, by accepting their testimony. The historian Luke, who has so much in common with the Johannine traditions--which of course are earlier than the publication of the fourth gospel--has seen the profound significance of this word. He understood that, in order to strengthen Theophilus' faith, he had to describe the revelation of salvation in its entirety, as Jesus had achieved it and as His elect had handed it on. He had to recall in his two books both the work of Jesus and that of His Witnesses.

NOTES

1. *Eglise et Théologie*, Bulletin trimestriel de la Faculté libre de théologie protestante de Paris, 23rd year, no. 68, 1960, p. 7-20, by kind permission of the Institut Protestant de Théologie, Paris.

"During Forty Days"

(Acts 1. 3)[1]

If it is generally admitted that the book of Acts is the continuation of the third gospel and the work of the same author, there is cause for some perplexity when we read the last page of the gospel and the first page of Acts continuously. The writer begins his second "book" with the customary brief summary of the first one (Acts 1. 1-2); then, instead of furthering his story, he returns to the last conversations of the risen Christ with His disciples and presents a somewhat different version of the ascension (1. 3-12) from that which appears at the end of the gospel (Luke 24. 44-53). In fact, these two parallel passages include, along with identical theological themes--the presence of the risen Christ in the midst of His disciples, instruction to His future Witnesses, the announcement of the gift of the Holy Spirit and the mission to Jews and Gentiles--different information about the duration of the christophanies and the location of the ascension. The latter point is not of primary importance: it matters little whether the risen Christ leads His disciples "as far as Bethany" (Luke 24. 50) or on to "the mount of Olives" (Acts 1. 12), since it was necessary to cross the latter to read the former. The crux of the problem is in verse 1. 3: "It was to the apostles that he had shown himself alive, after his Passion, with many sure proofs, appearing to them at intervals during forty days and speaking of the Kingdom of God". The number of forty days is new when compared with Luke 24, which does not specify how long the christophanies lasted and shows, in this regard, the same indifference as the other versions in the New Testament and the ecclesiastical historians of the first three centuries. What does this mention of forty days mean? Is it a precise statement of time or has it an essentially theological significance? Moreover, what is the origin of this idea: is it invented by Luke, does it represent a tradition which was unknown to Luke until after he had written his gospel, or is it an addition by another hand? We should like to attempt to answer these questions.[2]

I

We shall concern ourselves first with the significance of the forty days. Three facts lead us to give to this chronological statement an essentially theological interpretation.

1. In Acts 1. 3 the risen Christ is addressing His eleven Apostles and not a wider circle of disciples as in Luke 24.

In I Cor. 15. 3-11 the Apostle Paul, quoting and enlarging upon the traditional accounts, makes an explicit distinction between the two groups who were granted christophanies: first those who saw the living Christ and can attest to the reality of His divine life; secondly those who, in the course of their encounter with the risen Christ, were called by Him to be Apostles. For it is quite clear that "all the Apostles" (v. 7), destined to preach the Gospel to the world (cf. v. 10-11), make up a much smaller group than the "five hundred brethren" (v. 6).

Luke makes the same distinction explicitly. He recognizes on the one hand the twelve Apostles chosen by Jesus during His ministry (Luke 6. 12-16; Acts 1. 2) and destined to be His "witnesses" in the highest sense of the word (Acts 1. 8), and beside them he sees other disciples, who were with the Eleven on the occasions when Jesus appeared to them (Luke 24. 9, 33), but who were not called like them to be Apostles. This distinction between simple eye-witnesses (αὐτόπται) and witnesses in the strong sense of the word (μάρτυρες) appears as clearly as we could wish in the episode of Matthias. When he is first presented to the reader (Acts 1. 23), Matthias already belongs to the wide circle of those who have seen the risen Christ (cf. 1. 21 f). But he must be chosen by the Lord in order to take a place in the circle of the Twelve and be made like them "a witness to his resurrection" (1. 22) in the strong sense.

When Luke wants to emphasize the fact that Jesus is risen he assembles both groups of witnesses simultaneously. Such is the case in Luke 24, where we read, three times in a row, that Jesus "rose on the third day" (v. 7, 21, 46). The gospel ends leaving the reader quite convinced that Jesus has entered into the heavenly life, thus fulfilling His own prophecies (v. 7) and those of the Scriptures (v. 46). Moreover this certainty is based on the confirmation of the greatest number of people possible, the Eleven and their companions (v. 9, 33) and the travellers from Emmaus (v. 35).

Another concern is foremost in Luke's mind when he writes the first page of Acts, as the following fact will show. In the summary which he gives of the first book, he deliberately limits the number of those who saw Jesus to the circle of the Apostles (1. 2). They alone are the beneficiaries of the forty days of appearances and instructions (1. 3) and are solemnly instituted "witnesses" (μάρτυρες) of Jesus (1. 8). So that the reader shall not misunderstand, Luke again lists the eleven men (1. 13) he has already named in the gospel. The perspective of Acts 1. 1-13 is rectilinear and is different from that of Luke 24. The accent is no longer on the reality of the resurrection nor consequently on the great number of disciples who saw the risen Jesus. The accent now is on the institution of a small group of Witnesses charged with proclaiming the Gospel to the world and consequently is on the exceptional revelations these Witnesses received from their Master "during forty days". If Luke stresses, from his very first words, the authority conferred on these Witnesses, it is because the book of Acts is devoted, above all, to the work of these twelve men, represented by Peter, their leader, and of the two other "witnesses" whom Christ will call later, Stephen and Paul.[3] It is the missions of the Apostles which form the backbone of the story; it is the speeches made by the Apostles which set the pace for the advancement of the Gospel, for only they have sufficient authority that their missionary sermons are worthy of being reported.

In short, in inserting the statement about the forty days at the beginning of Acts, Luke is theologically motivated in line with his book as a whole: he wants to show that the Witnesses of the beginnings of the Church are the authentic trustees of the teachings of the risen Christ.

2. The specific number of forty has a symbolic significance.

The fact emerges from the text and from the context of Acts 1. 3 that it is the Apostles who need forty days of appearances and instructions, not Jesus Himself,[4] who had "entered his glory" at the very moment of His resurrection (Luke 24. 26). We must also point out that Luke does not mean that the risen Christ spent a continuous period of time with the Apostles,[5] but that there were several appearances at intervals during a period of forty days.[6] This is tantamount to saying that Jesus appeared to His future Witnesses and gave instructions to them forty times.

Forty is a number which occurs often throughout the ancient East and which, in Israel, defines particular periods, of days or years, in the lives of the servants and people of God. There are many well-known examples of its use.[7] The very frequency of its use shows that it is a "round number" of symbolic rather than strictly numerical significance. Forty days is, in particular, the period spent by Moses on Sinai at the time of the covenant (cf. Ex. 24. 18; 34. 28), and this length of time has remained traditionally the normal period of divine revelations. The rabbis, in their commentaries on Exodus, write that Moses, having spent forty days on the mountain, received the words of the Law straight from the mouth of God Himself.[8] We can see an influence of the same idea in the rabbis' practice of repeating their instruction forty times to their pupils so that the latter will know it by heart, and, in their turn, can hand it on in its entirety without alteration.[9] This practice, confirmed by several passages in the Talmud, certainly goes back to early times, since it presupposes an essentially oral transmission of the tradition.

It is very probable that Luke knew of these uses of the symbolic number from his Palestinian sources of information. In any case they provide the closest parallels to his text. For Luke intends to emphasize, by speaking of forty days, that the Apostles received, with respect to their mission, revelations from the risen Christ Himself and that they saw and heard their Master often enough to remember His teaching and to be able to pass it on with complete fidelity.

3. The fortieth day after the resurrection is not a date on the Christian calendar for Luke nor for the Church of the first three centuries.

In the pericope Acts 1. 1-12, the account of the forty

days is not connected directly with the story of the ascension, where we would expect to find it if it had a chronological significance; it could have appeared in verse 12 along with the information about the location. On the other hand Luke is most explicit in dating the resurrection and the giving of the Holy Spirit. In his gospel he mentions three times that Jesus "rose on the third day" (Luke 24. 7, 21, 46), in accordance with the earliest tradition (cf. I Cor. 15. 4). In Acts 2 he places the giving of the Holy Spirit fifty days after Easter and not ten days after the ascension. Luke, and the Palestinian tradition on which he depends,[10] knows that this "fiftieth day" is, as its name indicates, the end of the Weeks which connect it to Easter, of which it is the outcome.[11] Luke does not place the resurrection, the ascension and the giving of the Holy Spirit at three specific dates on the same time-line. He reports two traditional and authentically chronological facts, the resurrection on the third day and the giving of the Holy Spirit on the fiftieth day, both joined to each other by their common dependence on the Jewish paschal cycle. On the other hand the statement about forty days is not directly attached to either Easter or Pentecost; it floats somewhere within the space of fifty days. This is yet another indication that it has a different significance and a different origin from the two accepted chronological dates.

This Lucan chronology, with two fixed points, Easter and Pentecost, but with no definite date between them for the ascension, is the one found in the Church during the first three centuries. The Fathers of this time,[12] with hardly an exception, do not concern themselves with the forty-day time period[13] and place the exaltation of Jesus on the same day as the resurrection or on the day of Pentecost, or even on an undetermined date between these two days. We can deduce from this that, having read Acts 1. 3, they have not interpreted it as a chronological fact but they have understood it theologically as Luke intended.

Confirmation of this conclusion can be found if we turn to the only ecclesiastical writer who, before the fourth century, cites and comments on Acts 1. 3. This is Tertullian. In *Apologeticum* (XXI. 23) he writes as follows: "Jesus spent forty days with some of his disciples...teaching them what they should teach (docens eos quae docerent). Then, having entrusted to them the mission to preach throughout the earth, he was lifted up to heaven in a cloud." Tertullian therefore interprets verse 3 in the sense that the forty days are a time of instruction to make the Apostles qualified spokesmen of Christ, and he mentions the ascension without connecting it to the forty days. Some years later, in *De baptismo* (XIX. 2), he gives the name of Pentecost to the fifty days following Easter which constitute "one single feast day" filled with christophanies, the giving of the Holy Spirit, the ascension and the promise of the parousia, which should happen, like the ascension, at Pentecost. This coinciding of Pentecost and the ascension is another aspect of the problem which we cannot pursue here. We will merely note that Tertullian reports the Ascension and the words of the angels to the Apostles in terms of Acts 1. 11, leaving aside the fact of the forty days even more obviously than in *Apologeticum*. But, by doing this, he confirms the interpretation he gave to the forty days there, namely that they are relative to the instruction given to the Apostles and do not specify the actual date of the ascension of Jesus.[14]

Therefore, Luke's intention to constitute the Twelve the only Witnesses of Jesus who had been duly instructed and invested, by isolating them from the other disciples from the very beginning; the symbolic significance of the number of forty days and the absence of any ritual commemoration of the fortieth day after Easter in the Church of the first three centuries--all of these considerations lead us to conclude that, in the thought of Luke, as Tertullian well understood, the idea of the forty days has a theological and not a chronological significance. It is intended to guarantee the authority of the Apostles' testimony and not to fix the date of the ascension of Jesus.

II

The question of the origin of the idea can be settled fairly easily. In fact, if the number of forty days has the meaning which we suggest giving to it, it is simple to choose between the three possibilities which are, in theory, presented to us: 1) this idea could be an addition to Luke's work; 2) it could be a tradition which was unknown to Luke until after he had finished the gospel; 3) it could be quite simply Luke's own idea.

1. The idea that the forty days could have been a later addition to the Acts, the beginning of which was reworked, can be put forward, as we know, in two different ways. Either the account of the ascension in Acts is thought to be, entirely or in part, an interpolation,[15] or it is thought that Luke originally wrote one connected work that was divided into two books, during the second century, at the time the canon was constituted. In the original work Luke 24. 49 was followed by Acts 1. 6; when the two parts of the work were separated it was necessary to add a conclusion to the gospel (Luke 24. 50-51) and an introduction to Acts (1. 1-5).[16] It is certain that several lexicographical arguments can be put forward in favor of this thesis: the style of Acts 1. 1-5 is particularly involved and includes some linguistic expressions which are rather surprising if they are from the pen of Luke himself. But the suspect text is too short, and Luke's language too

uneven for these comments on style, however accurate they may be, to prevail against the theological coherence of Luke 24 and Acts 1 as a whole. Moreover, the hypothesis of a reworking comes up against two strong objections. It is highly unlikely that the interpolation of the theme of the forty days or the division into two parts of Luke's work, formerly in one whole, could have taken place in the second century without leaving some trace in the manuscripts.[17] The insertion of the account of the forty days into the work of Luke in the second century remains unexplained; in fact we can take our choice: either this account was added because it was important (but then why is it not found elsewhere in the writings of the period?) or it is not mentioned elsewhere because it is not important (but then why is it introduced into the work of Luke?). It is obvious that this hypothesis solves nothing.

2. The idea that the forty days came to Luke's attention after he had finished the gospel[18] is not much more likely. That Luke does not use the number when he is writing his first book does not mean that he did not know about it at that time. It means quite simply that the idea had no value at the end of a gospel.[19] Moreover this hypothesis is supported by the presupposition that the tradition of the forty days has some chronological value. But then we come up against the same difficulty we had with the preceding hypothesis: where could Luke have found this tradition, since it is common knowledge that the early Church was not concerned about the exact length of time of the christophanies?

3. The most likely explanation seems to us to be that the idea of the forty days originates in Luke's own reflections about the exceptional authority which has to be recognized in the first Witnesses of the risen Christ. This theme, in fact, adds dimension and color to his portrait of the "witness" of Jesus in the specific sense of that term.

The gospels report that Jesus' disciples often wondered which of them was the greatest. The Church in the first century was concerned about the same question. Who was foremost? The Twelve whom Jesus chose during His ministry, James, the Lord's brother, because of ties of blood, or those who were inspired by the Spirit? Paul attempted to bring some order to bear by distinguishing at least two kinds of Apostles: the "Apostles of Jesus Christ" who saw the risen Christ and received their mission from Him, and the "Apostles of the churches", Apostles instituted by man.

Using different terminology, Luke makes a similar distinction, as we have pointed out previously. On the one hand he speaks of the "witnesses of Jesus" in the specific sense, those who have seen the risen Christ, who have been called by Him to preach the Gospel and who, as a result, have the necessary authority for Luke to report their missionary sermons in Acts. Luke speaks on the other hand of the simple eye-witness, who did not receive the same calling as the Twelve, and the missionaries, like Barnabas and Philip, who did not see the risen Christ, who do not have the authority of those sent directly by Him, and whose missionary sermons are not reported in Acts.

To make the authority of the "witnesses of Jesus" truly authentic, Luke gives a new expression to the traditional idea that the christophanies were accompanied by the teaching of the risen Christ. It is to His "Apostles" that the living Jesus revealed Himself primarily; it is His "witnesses" who heard Him often enough to be the faithful repositories of His thought and His qualified spokesmen. The simplest and most direct way to say all that was to turn to the expression offered by the Judaism of that time. It was to write "He appeared to them and spoke to them of the Kingdom of God during forty days."

NOTES

1. *Neotestamentica et Patristica. Eine Freundesgabe, Herrn Professor Dr Oscar Cullmann zu seinem 60. Geburtstag überreicht.* Supplements to *Novum Testamentum*, 6, Leiden, 1962, p. 148-156, by kind permission of the publishers E. J. Brill, Leiden.

2. We should say at the beginning that we intend in the present work to make some corrections in the views we expressed on the same subject eight years ago in our *Remarques sur les textes de l'ascension dans Luc-Actes*, Neutestamentliche Studien für Rudolf Bultmann (*BZNT*, 21), 1954, p. 148-156, and *supra*, p. 107-120.

3. Cf. P. H. Menoud, "Jésus et ses témoins," *Eglise et Théologie*, Bulletin de la Faculté de théologie protestante de Paris, 23, 1960, p. 7-20, and *supra* p. 167-176.

4. Some writers are of the latter opinion however. M. Goguel (*La foi à la résurrection de Jésus dans le christianisme primitif*, 1931, p. 354) considers that Jesus, who prepared Himself for His earthly ministry by His forty days in the wilderness, must similarly prepare for His heavenly ministry. But that does not explain why this preparation should be necessary for the risen Christ. We would rather compare Luke 4. 2 and Acts 1. 3 and deduce that the Apostles have to be prepared for their ministry as Witnesses, just as Jesus had to prepare Himself for His messianic ministry. F. Dornseiff (*ZNW*, 35, 1936, p. 136) compares Jesus, who remains for forty days "between two worlds," with Moses, who spends forty days with God on Mount Sinai. But this comparison is weak; Moses was there to receive the Law from God and to return to the people, whereas Jesus, at the end of forty days, will remain with the Father, far from His people. According to J. Manek "The New Exodus in the Books of Luke," *Nov. Test.*, II, 1957, p. 8-23, Jesus, the new Moses, spends forty days between His resurrection and His ascension, just as Israel, led by Moses, spent forty years between the deliverance from Egypt and the entry into the promised land. However, the two events have nothing in common but the number forty, which means nothing, in view of the common recurrence of this number.

5. If it were a question of a continuous stay, we would expect the words ἡμέρας τεσσαράκοντα (cf. Matt. 4. 2). Moreover the expression ἐν πολλοῖς τεκμηρίοις can only refer to a series of christophanies.

6. This was already the opinion of Chrysostom and most of the commentators.

7. Th. Zahn (*Die Apostelgeschichte des Lucas*, 1919, I, p. 42, n. 1), M. S. Enslin ("The Ascension Story", *JBL*, 1928, p. 64-66) and V. Larranaga (*L'Ascension de Notre-Seigneur dans le Nouveau Testament*, 1938, p. 174-207), among others, have drawn up lists of these periods in the Old Testament, Jewish literature and the New Testament.

8. Cf. the texts cited by Strack-Billerbeck, *Kommentar zum Neuen Testament*, III (1926), p. 511 and 530; IV (1928), p. 440.

9. Cf. B. Gerhardson, *Memory and Manuscript. Oral Tradition and Written Transmission in Rabbinic Judaism and Early Christianity*, 1961, p. 105, n. 9, 119 and 135. Gerhardson himself refers to J. Bergmann, "Die runden und hyperbolischen Zahlen in der Agada", *Monatsschr. f. Gesch. u. Wiss. d. Judentums*, 82 (1938), p. 370 f.

10. Cf. G. Kretschmar, "Himmelfahrt und Pfingsten", *ZKG*, 66 (1954-55), p. 211f and 244.

11. Luke's expression in Acts 2. 1 does not mean "the day of Pentecost ends" since it has only just begun (cf. v. 15). It is the weeks after Easter which end with the arrival of the day of Pentecost (cf. the commentaries by Lake-Cadbury and J. Dupont).

12. On the testimony of the Fathers, cf. among others M. S. Enslin, *op. cit.*, p. 66-78; M. Goguel, *op. cit.*,p. 352-355; K. Lake, *The Beginnings of Christianity*, V (1933), p. 18-21; V. Larranaga, *op. cit.*, p. 492-589; P. Benoit, "L'Ascension", *RB*, 1949, p. 169-172.

13. Justin Martyr, *Apol.* 50, 12 and Irenaeus, *Adv. haer.* II, 32, 3 in particular summarize the end of Luke and the beginning of Acts without mentioning the forty days. We should remember too that in a text as late as the Apostles' creed all the stages in the life of the glorified Christ are connected to the resurrection "on the third day", without any more specific dating. The ascension on the fortieth day did not become a tenet of the faith.

14. We should note that the speculations of the Gnostics, who lengthened the time of the christophanies to 545 and 550 days and even to eleven or twelve years (cf. M. Goguel, *op. cit.*, p. 354f; G. Quispel, *Zeitschr. für Religion- und*

Geistesgeschichte, 1954, p. 291), also give this time-period a theological and not a chronological significance.

15. Cf. W. G. Kümmel, *ThR*, 17 (1948-49), p. 9 who cites in this connection E. Meyer, M. Goguel, H. W. Beyer, O. Bauernfeind and E. Hirsch.

16. Cf. H. Sahlin, *Der Messias und das Gottesvolk. Studien zur protolukanischen Theologie*, 1945, p. 11-18; P. H. Menoud, "Remarques sur les textes de l'ascension dans Luc-Actes," *Neutestamentliche Studien fur Rudolf Bultmann*, 1954, p. 148-156 and *supra* p. 107-120; E. Trocmé, *Le "Livre des Actes" et l'histoire*, 1957, p. 30-34.

17. E. Haenchen, *Die Apostelgeschichte* (Meyers Kommentar, III, 12 Aufl.), 1959, p. 115.

18. Cf. among others Wendt, Reicke, Williams in their commentaries on Acts, and P. Benoit, *op. cit.*, p. 193; G. Staehlin, *Interpretation*, 1956, p. 294, n. 11; C. F. D. Moule, *ExpT*, 68 (1956-57), p. 205 and *NTS*, 4 (1957-58), p. 60.

19. Cf. E. Haenchen, *op. cit.*, p. 114.

The Lucan Version of Pentecost and History[1]

Did Jesus' disciples receive the Holy Spirit on the day of Pentecost after the christophanies had ceased, as is reported in the book of Acts, or did Jesus Himself infuse them with the Holy Spirit during His first meeting with them on the evening after the resurrection, as recorded in the fourth gospel? In other words, should we follow Luke, who makes Easter and Pentecost two separate experiences in the lives of the first believers? Or should we concede, on the basis of the Johannine tradition, that Easter and Pentecost coincide in the sense that the disciples were united with their glorified Lord by the Holy Spirit at the very moment they were convinced of the reality of His life in heaven? In the opinion of most exegetes the question is settled, and not in favor of the Lucan theory. It is not that the exegetes admit the historical accuracy of the scene in John 20. 22, but it seems to them that the Johannine symbolism is probably closer to the earliest tradition. In fact, the Apostle Paul mentions the Holy Spirit very often; although he says nothing about a Pentecost as Luke describes it, and he affirms that life in the spirit begins at the same moment as the life of faith, and he sees the work of the risen Christ Himself in the granting of the Holy Spirit (cf. Rom. 8. 4-11, etc.) Our inclination then is to conclude that, in the beginning, the resurrection and exaltation of Jesus, His appearances, the gift of the Holy Spirit and the birth of the Church were all part of one single event. It is only later that the differing elements of this unique experience were presented as the successive events in a historical development whose stages Luke distinguishes when he speaks of the christophanies, the ascension after forty days and the giving of the Holy Spirit on the fiftieth day after Easter.[2]

It is possible, however, that the first two chapters of Acts are closer to the truth than has been suggested. Certainly, we have no intention of defending to the death the historicity of all the details of Luke's account. But it seems to us worth investigating whether Luke is not more faithful to history when he separates by a period of time the two decisive facts which were successively thrust upon the disciples; the first, that their Master was living and exalted at the right hand of God, the second, that their faith must be "proclaimed upon the house-tops" (Matt. 10. 27f; Luke 12. 3).

It is a vast and complex subject. In this study we shall limit ourselves to presenting a few remarks on the points which seem to us the most important.

First of all let us examine Luke's overall plan: Easter, Ascension, Pentecost. We will begin by quoting a work to which we owe a great deal, Haenchen's great commentary on Acts. This exegetical scholar writes: "We must exclude the idea of the existence of an early tradition which placed the giving of the Holy Spirit at a date as late as that suggested by Luke: fifty days after Easter! Luke arrived at this date because he was using the tradition of the forty days (Bauernfeind); consequently, he placed the pouring out of the Holy Spirit on the occasion of the first Jewish feast-day after this delay."[3] This argument is only decisive if it is granted that the forty days (Acts 1. 3) are really connected with the duration of the christophanies and that Luke found this piece of information in the Christian tradition about the christophanies. In our opinion, this does not seem to be the case.[4]

In the first centuries, there is no trace of a tradition of forty days; this number is only known through the work of Luke. It is common knowledge that the early Church did not concern itself about the exact duration of the christophanies. Apart from Luke, no New Testament writer touches the question, and the ecclesiastical writers of the first three centuries place the glorification of Jesus on the same day as the resurrection, or on the day of Pentecost or on an undetermined day between Easter and Pentecost.[5] It is only in the fourth century that the ascension begins to be commemorated on the fortieth day after Easter and that the three festivals are fixed on the calendar. This is so because the Church did not give a distinctively chronological significance to the account of the forty days. It was interpreted symbolically, following the example of Tertullian (*Apologeticum,* XII. 23), who makes the forty days a time of instruction after which the Apostles will be qualified spokesmen for Jesus. Tertullian has understood Luke's intention very well. In fact, in the pericope Acts 1. 1-12, the fact of the forty days is not directly connected to the story of the ascension, where we would expect to find it, but to the statement that the risen Christ gave instruction to His future Witnesses. In other words, this fact was not intended to date the ascension but to show that the Apostles are the authorized Witnesses of their Master. The "round number" of forty days indicates in biblical tradition the normal length of time of divine revelations. The same idea appears, in almost identical form, in the rabbinic tradition; to repeat his teaching forty times is, for a master, to transmit all his knowledge to his disciples so that they, in their turn, can instruct with authority. This traditional number was quite in keeping with Luke's aim in Acts 1 when he described the christophanies already mentioned at the end of the gospel. The gospel must conclude by leaving the reader in no doubt that Jesus has entered into the heavenly life, and that is why Luke emphasizes the great number of disciples who saw the living Christ, the Eleven and those with them (Luke 24. 9-33) and the travellers from Emmaus (Luke 24. 35). On the other hand, the book of Acts, which is dedicated to recounting the undertakings and the sermons of the supreme Witnesses of the risen Christ, must show from its very first page that these "apostles" (Acts 1. 2), these "witnesses" (Acts 1. 8) are really the authorized conservators of Jesus' thought, since it is for them that the risen Christ reserved the plenitude of His revelation. The most simple and the most direct way to do this was to turn to the Jewish traditional expression and to speak of forty days of appearances and teaching. And this expression describes so well the figure of the Apostle-Witness created by Luke that it can legitimately be concluded that it was Luke himself, and not earlier Christian tradition, who used the expression in describing the relationship of the risen Christ to His Apostles.

To be more precise, Luke's historical framework includes only two definite dates and not three: the resurrection "on the third day" (Luke 24. 7, 21, 46) and the gift of the Holy Spirit and the first apostolic testimony "on the fiftieth day". The expression used by Luke in Acts 2. 1 emphasizes that this fiftieth day marks the end of the Weeks between it and Easter; it also marks the fulfillment of the promise of the Spirit made by the risen Christ on the third day (Luke 24. 46-49).[6] In other words, chronologically and theologically, the giving of the Holy Spirit is connected to the resurrection and not to the ascension. On the other hand, the forty days are not placed in direct relationship to either Easter or Pentecost; they float, so to speak, in the fifty-day interval. This is the indication that they were inserted by Luke into an already existing framework. Therefore, from the chronological point of view, Luke invented nothing. He did not mention the forty days of fix the date of the ascension, and he found the dates of Easter and Pentecost in his sources of information. This last statement needs to be justified.

The resurrection "on the third day" is confirmed by tradition prior to Luke (cf. I Cor. 15. 4) and there is no problem here. There are some convincing arguments that the date of Pentecost was probably observed by the church at Jerusalem in the time of Luke. It has often been pointed out[7] that Luke describes the descent of the Holy Spirit on the disciples (Acts 2. 1-4) in the same terms used in Jewish tradition to describe the revelation on Mount Sinai. Now ideas of a new covenant and a new law have no part in Luke's account. It is in the date of Pentecost that the Jewish tradition of Sinai has influenced the Christian tradition of the gift of the Holy Spirit.[8] The chronological information in Acts 2. 1 comes from Luke's sources, he did not invent it. We should note, on the other hand, that Pentecost, along with the Passover, is the only Jewish festival to which the Apostle Paul seems to pay any attention (I Cor. 16. 8; Acts 20. 16), in spite of his reservations with regard to festivals in general (Gal. 4. 10; Col. 2. 16). Finally, we should remember that Pentecost, with the Passover, is the only Jewish festival which became incorporated into Christian tradition. Would this have happened if it had only been known in the early Church because of the work of Luke? This is to be doubted in view of the very vague echo of the Lucan forty days in the Fathers of the first three centuries.

Pentecost would not have become a Christian festival if nothing had happened on that day to change the lives of the first believers. Luke's account is historic in the sense that it was very probably on the day of Pentecost that the Apostles received the spiritual power and the courage (cf. Acts 2. 24) to proclaim the Gospel of Christ for the first time.[9] The objection that the date would be very late[10] is not conclusive. There had to be some interval between the day when the Apostles were personally sure that Jesus was living and the day when they were impelled to proclaim that fact to the world and, in the first instance, to the Jews. To proclaim to the people of Palestine that Jesus of Nazareth was the Messiah could not be simply a case of reporting facts, which in any case were already known to the hearers (cf. Acts 2.22; 10. 37). It was necessary to draw out the salvation aspect of these events, to show how they conformed to the divine plan outlined in the Scriptures--in short, to add to their personal testimony to Jesus' testimonies from the Scriptures. To be a Witness of the risen Christ before the Jews necessitated being a Witness also of what had been foretold in the Scriptures about the Messiah.[11] A proclamation not based on the Scriptures would have been quite unacceptable, and we have no examples of kerygma where scriptural proof is lacking. Undoubtedly, in actual fact, Peter's first sermon was not endowed with all the scholarly interpretation we now read into Acts 1. From all evidence the beginnings of apostolic exegesis were more modest (cf. I Cor. 15. 3-4). Nor have the Apostles taken time from that set aside for reflection, meditation and prayer (cf. Acts 1. 14; 6. 4). What should be surprising is not that apostolic preaching started so late but that it started so soon.

The major objection to Luke's chronology comes from another source. It results from the existence of a rival tradition which connects the gift of the Holy Spirit with the christophanies at Easter and not with the apostolic witness at Pentecost.

We should note first of all that there is no parallel to

the Lucan Pentecost. As Luke understands Pentecost, it is not only the giving of the Holy Spirit, it is the giving of the Holy Spirit *and* the first preaching by the Witnesses of Jesus. The Two events are linked together in the promises of the risen Christ (Luke 24. 46-49; Acts 1. 4-8). They are linked also in the fulfillment of these promises; the pouring out of the Spirit provides an introduction to Peter's sermon; this onrush of power from on high has no effect on the spectators while Peter remains silent (Acts 2. 12-13); it is his testimony which arouses their faith (Acts 2. 37f). Although all the gospels end by stating that the risen Christ appoints His disciples His spokesmen to the world, only the book of Acts tells us when and how the Apostles began their ministry.

The pericope in the fourth gospel (Jn. 20. 19-23) is described as the "Johannine Pentecost",[12] when John writes that the risen Christ breathes the Holy Spirit into His disciples, on the evening of Easter, on the occasion of His first appearance to them. The difference with Luke is obvious. John is supported by Matthew, who places Jesus' declaration to His disciples "I am with you always, until the close of the age" (Matt. 28. 20) at the time of His first appearance to them, albeit several days after Easter, during their journey from Jerusalem to Galilee. It is only through the Spirit that He can remain with them, and it is because this presence of Jesus glorified within them is the presence of the Holy Spirit, that they can henceforth teach all nations and baptize them "in the name of the Father, and of the Son and of the Holy Spirit" (Matt. 28. 19). Although the first evangelist does not express himself as precisely as John, we are justified in saying that he also connects the giving of the Holy Spirit with the Easter appearances.

But that is only one aspect of the question. Johannine tradition would really contradict the account in Acts if, according to John also, the gift of the Spirit impelled the Apostles to give testimony immediately--in short, if John left no interval of time between the first christophany and the first apostolic sermon. That is not so. For the disciples who have just received the Spirit, "who are fully equipped for their mission and have nothing more to wait for",[13] are, eight days later, in the same situation, still in the upper room at Jerusalem (John 20. 26). The epilogue provided by chapter 21 follows the same idea, since it reports that the Apostles go back to their trade as fishermen (21. 1-3) until the time when Jesus comes to call them to the ministry of Witness (21. 15f) to which He destined them by promising them the gift of the Spirit before His passion (John 15. 26-27) and by giving it to them on the evening of Easter. John's description should be taken in its entirety, since we have no indication that the Gospel ever existed without the epilogue.

It is quite clear that John also recognizes, on the one hand, an interval between the resurrection of Jesus and the ministry of the disciples, and, on the other hand, two divine interventions in succession: the first to persuade the Apostles that their Master is living, the second to call them to the effective fulfillment of their vocation. We do find again in John the two stages which Luke distinguishes so carefully. The difference is only in the place reserved for the Holy Spirit within the same historical framework. This place is not the same because when John and Luke speak of the Spirit their interpretation is not the same. John connects the pouring-out of the Spirit with the first christophany, because he understands the gift as the proof that Jesus is glorified (cf. John 7. 39) and as the presence of Jesus among them in a different guise; if the Spirit was delayed and was not breathed into them on the occasion of the first encounter of the risen Christ with His disciples, the latter would be temporarily fatherless, contrary to their Master's promise (John 14. 18). Luke, however, reserves the giving of the Spirit for the time when the apostolic witness will begin, because he sees in the Spirit the divine power which will make this preaching effective.

As for Matthew, who, as we have seen, follows a line parallel to that of John, by showing the Apostles living in the communion of the risen Christ from their first encounter with Him, he closes his gospel without telling us when or in what circumstances the Apostles began their missionary task.

If our analysis is correct, we can conclude that Luke does not stretch things too far by distinguishing between Easter and Pentecost and by showing that the Apostles were called first to believe that their Master was living and then to proclaim that fact to the world. At the end of his gospel, John hints at the same development.

However, Luke yields to his tendency towards stylized history by presenting the Spirit uniquely as the divine power given to Christ's Witness--and to every believer--in view of the task he must accomplish; he neglects the point, which both John and Matthew have included, that the believer encountered by the risen Christ lives immediately henceforth in His Spirit. Thus there is a limitation here similar to that resulting from his silence on the subject of the christophanies in Galilee.

Just as there is no cause to distinguish between the christophanies in Galilee and those in Jerusalem, since the risen Christ met His followers wherever they were, so there is no cause to distinguish between the Johannine Pentecost and the Lucan Pentecost. They express the two revelations which the disciples received or the two experiences they had: they are living in the presence of Christ from the day of His resurrection; after Pentecost they proclaim this to the Jews and to the world with the help of divine power.

NOTES

1. *Revue d'histoire et de philosophie religieuses,* 42, 1962, p. 141-147, with kind permission of *l'Université des Sciences Humaines* at Strasbourg.

2. Cf. for example C. K. Barrett, *The Gospel according to St. John,* 1955, p. 475; J. Knox, *Christ and the Hope of Glory,* 1960, p. 35f.

3. E. Haenchen, *Die Apostelgeschichte* (Meyers Kommentar, III), 13. Aufl., 1961, p. 137.

4. In what follows we are summarizing our study "Pendant quarante jours (Acts 1. 3)", *Neotestamentica et Patristica* (Festschrift O. Cullmann), 1962, p. 148-156; *supra* p. 167-179.

5. This indifference with regard to the duration of the christophanies can only be explained by the persistence of the early idea in the Church that the resurrection of Jesus is, at the same time, His exaltation to the right hand of God, that it is from on high that He reveals Himself to His disciples as the glorified Lord and that the ascension is merely the conclusion of the final christophany (cf. W. Michaelis, *Die Erscheinungen des Auferstandenen,* 1944, p. 83f, and *ThWbNT,* V, p. 355f). It seems to have been admitted that these earthly appearances of the glorified Christ continued right up to Pentecost, that is to say up to the moment when the Apostles started on the work to which they had been called. It is only when His Witnesses begin to proclaim Him to the world that the Lord can withdraw to be with His Father until the time of the Second Coming. This explains the custom in Jerusalem, observed until about the year 400, of celebrating the ascension in the afternoon of Pentecost, after commemorating on the same morning the giving of the Holy Spirit and the first apostolic preaching (cf. Ethérie, *Journal de voyage,* 43, Sources chrétiennes, 21, p. 246f).

6. In this sense cf. Lhose *ThWbNT,* VI, p. 50, and the commentaries on Acts by Zahn, Wendt, Dupont.

7. Cf. the commentaries on Acts and particularly G. Kretschmar, "Himmelfahrt und Pfingsten", *ZKG,* 66 (1954-55), p. 243f.

8. However there is no need to be enslaved to contemporary fashion and to suppose that Luke's source had been in-

fluenced by Qumran. Certainly the Qumran texts (cf. particularly 1 QS I, 7 - II, 19) offer the earliest explicit confirmation that the ancient Festival of Weeks took on a historic characteristic and was connected to the events at Sinai. The people of Qumran celebrated their most important festival at Pentecost, [This name of Hellenistic origin is used for the Jewish harvest festival which is called in the Old Testament the Festival of Weeks.] commemorating at the same time the Mosaic covenant and the new covenant which they were claiming (cf. J. T. Milik, *Dix ans de découverts dans le désert de Juda*, 1957, p. 72-77). In official Judaism we must wait for the time of the Talmud before finding formal evidence that the giving of the Law was celebrated at Pentecost. But there is no doubt that the rabbinic scholars were handing on a very old tradition. The Festival of Weeks could not escape the movement which was changing agrarian festivals into celebrations of the history of salvation, and the place of this celebration in the calendar made it inevitable that it should recall the events at Sinai. The appearance, in the second century before our era, of the new name, Pentecost, recalls the interval between the exodus from Egypt, celebrated at Passover, and the covenant with Moses too clearly not to be a strong indication that from that time on the Festival of Weeks changed its character. If, in official Judaism, Pentecost is rarely mentioned and always remains in the shadow of the Passover, it is because of fidelity to the traditional idea that God's great work for his people is the deliverance from Egypt, of which the covenant on Sinai is but the consequence. The originality of the people of Qumran, in comparison to the other Jews, does not consist in celebrating the events of Sinai, but in celebrating the renewal of those events for the benefit of the only members of the Community of the New Covenant. They therefore tend to see the central event of salvation in the covenant rather than in the deliverance from Egypt. Now, as to the hierarchy of the acts of salvation and the festivals which commemorate them, the infant church follows official Judaism and not Qumran: the resurrection is the event of prime importance, and Easter, the greatest festival. If the influence of Qumran on the church at Jerusalem had been felt as much as has been suggested (cf. G. Kretschmar, *op. cit.*, p. 232 and 246, and particularly J. Van Goudoever, *Biblical Calendars*, 1959, p. 228f), the status of Christian festivals would probably be different.

9. Cf. G. Kretschmar, *op. cit.*, p. 256; H. von Campenhausen, *Der Ablauf der Osterereignisse und das leere Grab*, 2, Aufl. 1958, p. 50.

10. Cf. E. Haenchen, *op. cit.*, p. 137.

11. Cf. B. Gerhardsson, *Memory and Manuscript. Oral Tradition and Written Transmission in Rabbinic Judaism and Early Christianity,* 1961, p. 221f, 226f, 280f.

12. Archimandrite Cassien, *La pentecôte johannique* (Jn. 20. 19-23), 1939. It is true that he identifies Acts 2. 1-4--the pouring out of the Spirit takes place on the evening of Pentecost in the upper room, while Peter's sermon is preached on the next day in the Temple--with John 20. 19-23,(p. 75-91). It seems to us that this exegesis encounters insurmountable difficulties--the following for example: Thomas' disbelief and the disciples' return to Galilee as fishermen after a Pentecost seemingly in the Lucan sense of the word. On the different attempts to harmonize John 20. 22 and Acts 2, cf. particularly Hoskyns and Davey, *The Fourth Gospel,* 2nd ed., 1947, p. 546-547.

13. C. K. Barrett, *op. cit.,* p. 475.

The Meaning of the Verb BIAZETAI in Luke 16. 16[1]

Translators are in agreement, for the most part, in giving to the main part of the verse Luke 16. 16 the following meaning: "The law and the prophets continued until John; from that time the Gospel of the kingdom of God has been spreading..."[2] But opinion is divided on the way to interpret the last phrase of this verse: καὶ πᾶς είσ αὐτῆν Βιάζεται; for the verb Βιάζεται is taken *in bonam partem* and translated "and everyone strives to make his way in," - this is the opinion of the majority[3] - or *in malam partem* in the sense "everyone uses force against it."[4] Finally there are some exegetes who cannot make a choice between these two explanations.[5] In fact the choice does not have to be one or the other of these. In the pages which follow we shall endeavor to justify this third interpretation: "and everyone is expressly invited to come in."

In the parallel text in Matthew 11. 12-13 we read: "From the days of John the Baptist until now the kingdom of heaven has been enduring violent assault (Βιάζεται) and men of violence have been taking it by force (Βιασταὶ ἁρπάζουσιν αὐτήν). All the prophets and the law prophesied it until John." This parallel is not a great deal of help in the interpretation of Luke 16. 16. In fact the two evangelists place this declaration by Jesus in different contexts. Luke puts it at the beginning of several maxims of law (16. 16-18). Matthew places it in a series of observations by Jesus on John the Baptist.

(11. 2-11 and 14-15), which also appear in Luke (7. 18-30). It is a question of a saying of Jesus which has been handed on in isolation by tradition, a saying all the more difficult to interpret as the circumstances in which it was pronounced are unknown, and which each of the evangelists has interpreted in his own way and placed in a context of his own choosing. It is generally admitted that Luke has kept the primitive order of the two parts of the verse; Matthew has inverted them because of the demands of his context. Moreover Luke gives an earlier form of the first part, without a verb: "the law and the prophets until John", and the rather artificial expression in Matthew has been revised. On the other hand the sentence on the kingdom, so difficult, and even obscure, in Matthew, seems to be closer to the original than its equivalent in Luke.[6]

The text in Matthew has not yet been given an explanation which reflects all the opinions. Most exegetes admit that it is a matter of violence committed against the kingdom and that the "violent men" are either demonic forces, or the Jewish adversaries of Jesus, or the Zealots, or Baptizers, or even unidentified aggressors.[7] The opinion of the minority is that, on the contrary, this violence is the force exerted by those who are striving to enter the kingdom.[8]

Our intention is not to enter into a discussion on the meaning as it appears in Matthew, but to emphasize the difference in atmosphere between the text in Matthew and that in Luke. Whether Matthew is speaking of aggressive violence directed against the kingdom, or spiritual force put forth to enter therein, the idea of striving and force dominates the text in Matthew. On the other hand, when Luke speaks of a kingdom which has been evangelized by the preaching of the Gospel, which will open the doors of the kingdom to men, if it is accepted in faith, he gives a quite different interpretation to the mysterious saying. In Matthew the idea of violence is expressed three times by the words βιάζεται, βιασταί and ἁρπάζουσιν, but this idea is only expressed in Luke by the single use of βιάζεται, tempered and weakened to some extent by the verb εὐαγγελίζεται which precedes it. In other words the text in Luke is quite different from that in Matthew and it should be interpreted on its own without any necessity of finding one or other of the Matthean meanings within it.

Let us return to Luke 16. 16b. In this text the accent is on the first section: since the disappearance of John the Baptist Jesus has preached the Gospel of the kingdom. The second section describes the consequences for those who listen.

In this perspective the two current explanations of the words καὶ πᾶς εἰς αὐτὴν βιάζεται, which we mentioned at the beginning, seem equally contrived. For they both presuppose that Jesus' hearers are unanimous either in accepting His message ("everyone strives to make his way in"), or in rejecting it ("everyone rises up violently against the kingdom"). Now the third gospel--like the others, for that matter--does not mention such unanimity for or against Jesus. Certainly Luke observes that the Master's first sermons in the synagogues were favorably received (4. 15); he recalls that, throughout the ministry of Jesus, His miracles aroused enthusiasm in those who witnessed them (4. 36; 5. 26; 7. 16; 9. 43; 18. 43). But this is not enough grounds for the conclusion that "everyone strives", by the decisive welcome given to the preaching of the Gospel, "to make his way into the kingdom". On the other hand, even if it is true that at Nazareth Jesus encounters general hostility (4. 28) and that at Jericho everyone mutters with indignation because Jesus entered the house of Zacchaeus, a sinner (19. 7), these facts are not grounds for concluding that everyone is rising up against the kingdom in rejection of the Gospel.

In fact, according to the prophecy of the elderly Simeon, Jesus is a sign of tension in Israel (2. 34). Throughout His ministry He both attracts followers and suffers rejection. He Himself is listened to or disregarded in the person of His representatives (10. 16); men declare that they are for or against Him (12. 8-9); He came to bring dissension to the earth (12. 56); one of His miracles stirs up adverse feelings (13. 14-17); when He cures ten lepers, only one of them believes in the Gospel (17. 15-18); on the cross, finally, He is flanked by the bad and the good thief (23. 39-43). It is clear, from the beginning to the end of his Gospel, that Luke is showing us how men are divided when confronted with the presence of Jesus, His message, or His miracles. As a result, the words in our verse, which put all the hearers of the Gospel into one single, homogeneous group, cannot have either one or the other of the two traditional exegetical meanings.

Moreover, each of these current interpretations presents its own difficulties. The first one, which reads "everyone strives to make his way into the kingdom", does not fit very well with the words of Jesus which Luke takes from Mark: "Whoever does not receive the kingdom of God like a little child will not enter it" (Luke 18. 17). That the kingdom is a gift of grace to which the believer becomes entitled is recalled by Luke in Jesus' words to His diciples: "Dismiss your fears, little flock: your Father finds pleasure in giving you the kingdom" (12. 32) and "I assign to you a kingdom, as my Father has assigned one to me" (22. 30).

According to the second interpretation: "everyone uses force against the kingdom," Luke would go further than Matthew, for whom only the βιασταί, and not everyone, seek to take the kingdom by force. Now Luke certainly wants to weaken the traditional expression since he speaks from the very beginning of the preaching of the Gospel. He makes use of the same procedure again when he speaks of the dealers driven out of the Temple. In one sentence, he shows us Jesus expelling these intruders (19. 45), then installing Himself in the Temple where He is at home (cf. 2. 46-50) in order to give instruction (19. 47). The Gospel as Luke understood it and hands it on is not a doctrine of violence.

For the rest, according to this exegesis of Luke, these are not Zealots who violently oppose the kingdom of God. According to A. Schlatter,[9] it is only the Pharisees who "frustrated God's purpose", by "refusing John's baptism" (Luke 7. 29-30). But is not πᾶς (everyone) too strong a word to mean just the Pharisees? W. Grundmann,[10] who for his own part suspends judgment, is of the opinion that if we want to go along with Schlatter we must admit that, in reality, everyone is opposing the kingdom--the Pharisees by their pride, the crowd by its indifference and the disciples themselves by their misunderstanding of the Master. But, as we have said, Luke does not have such a schematic view of the different members of Jesus' audience. We must assert that neither of the two interpretations usually advanced is fully satisfactory.

Tertium datur. The way is indicated by H. J. Holtzmann who takes the verb βιάζεται in a passive sense when usually it is given an active meaning and who understands the expression in the sense of the command in Luke 13. 23: "Compel them to come in"--referring to those who will take the places of the discourteous guests at the great feast. The meaning then would be "everyone is compelled to enter the kingdom".[11] To which Lagrange quite rightly objects, "This meaning must be rejected; nobody is brought into the kingdom by force; one is only invited to follow the way to it".[12] βιάζομαι does not contain the idea of compelling force which there is in ἀναγκάζω (14. 23). Lagrange himself notes that, "βιάζομαι should not be taken too seriously". For this verb seems to have acquired a weak meaning over the centuries. In the Septuagint--which Luke had studied diligently--βιάζομαι has the meaning of "to beg earnestly", "to urge", in the sense that Jacob "urges" Esau, after the reconciliation, to accept the gift he intends for him (Gen. 33:11). In a papyrus of the year 22 A.D. (POxy II, 294, 16), Βιάζομαι means "the affectionate constraint of friendship",[14] for a certain Serapian writes, "I am constrained by my friends to enter the service of Apollonios", a man of importance who had access to the palace of the prefect. The composite verb παραβιάζομαι has, in the Septuagint, the same weak meaning as the simple verb; it is thus that Saul yields to the requests of his servants who urge him to take food (I Sam. 28. 23). Now this same verb παραβιάζομαι appears twice in Luke--this is interesting, as the only other places the simple verb βιάζομαι appears are Matthew 11. 12 and Luke 16. 16--and nowhere else in the New Testament. In Luke 24. 29, the disciples at Emmaus constrain the Stranger to enter the inn with them. In Acts 16. 15, at Philippi, Lydia urges Paul and his companions to stay at her house. In both cases it is a pressing invitation and not coercion by force.[15]

It is obvious that these weak meanings of παραβιάζομαι and of the simple verb βιάζεται fit very well into the context of Luke 16. 16, βιάζεται being taken in the passive sense, "Everyone is earnestly invited by the preaching of the gospel to enter the kingdom of God".[16]

The verb βιάζεται in the passive is the same as εὐαγγελίζεται.[17] Nothing is more classic than that this passive should have as its complement the preposition with the accusative.[18] Moreover, the same construction is to be found elsewhere in Luke.[19] The sentence is grammatically correct, even elegant.

This explanation, justified by philology, also offers the

only meaning acceptable in the context. The proclamation of the kingdom has as its consequence an earnest invitation addressed to all men, that is to each individual, for entry into the kingdom of God is a purely personal decision.[20] If everyone does not rush towards the kingdom or forcibly resist it, it is certainly true that the call to believe the Gospel is addressed to everyone, to the Pharisees as well as to the tax-collectors.

There is no doubt that Luke found this verb βιάζομαι in his sources. It appears also in Matthew, and when Luke is showing his independence from earlier traditions he uses the synonym παραβιάζομαι. By keeping the simple verb in 16. 16, he has preserved something of its first meaning. For the preaching of the Gospel to some extent does exert force on the man it reaches, either to accept or refuse the invitation offered to him, and when it is a question of the Gospel, not to answer is tantamount to a refusal. And so it is in a certain continuity with tradition that Luke gives this expression a new and very positive interpretation.

NOTES

1. *Mélanges bibliques en hommage au R. P. Béda Rigaux,* Gembloux, 1970, p. 207-212, with kind permission of Editions J. Duculot, Gembloux, Belgium.

2. We are leaving aside the question of whether the words ἀπὸ τότε have an inclusive or exclusive meaning here, in other words, whether John the Baptist considers himself to be at the beginning of the period of evangelism or at the end of the time of the prophets.

3. Cf. for example: Ambrosius of Milan, *Exposirio Evangelii secundum Lucam,* VIII, 1 (SC, 52, 101); the commentaries of Calvin, Plummer, J. Weiss, Lagrange, Joüon, Klostermann, Creed, W. Manson, Hauck, Rengstorf, Marchal, Goguel (BC), Osty (BJ); and the following works: M. Goguel, *Au seuil de l'Evangile,* Jean-Baptiste, Paris, 1928, p. 66f; M. Goguel, *Jésus,* Paris, ^{2}1950, p. 214, n. 2; Schrenk, in *TWNT,* I, 1932, p. 611; W. G. Kümmel, *Verheissung und Erfüllung,* Zurich, ^{2}1953, p. 114-117; H. Conzelmann, *Die Mitte der Zeit, Studien zur Theologie des Lukas,* Tübingen, ^{3}1960, p. 103; N. Perrin, *Rediscovering the Teaching of Jesus,* New York, 1967, p. 74.

4. Cf. the commentaries of Loisy (*Les évangiles synoptiques* and *L'évangile selon Luc*), Schlatter, Leaney; also Ch. Bruston, *Essai d'explication de passages obscurs des Evangiles,* Paris, 1926, p. 21; D. Daube, *The NT and Rabbinic Judaism,* London, 1956, p. 293; M. Black, *An Aramaic Approach to the Gospels and Acts,* Oxford, ^{3}1967, p. 116.

5. Cf. W. Grundmann, *Das Evangelium nach Lukas* (ThHKommNT, 3), Berlin, ^{3}1966, p. 323.

6. Besides the commentaries on Matthew and the works cited in note 3 *supra* cf. R. Bultmann, *Geschichte der synoptischen Tradition,* Göttingen, ^{3}1957, p. 177f. and *Ergänzungsheft,* p. 25; E. Jungel, *Paulus und Jesus,* Tübingen, 1962, p. 190-193.

7. Cf. R. Bultmann, *op cit., Ergänzungsheft,* p. 25.

8. Cf. E. Percy, *Die Botschaft Jesu. Eine traditionskritische und exegetische Untersuchung,* Lund, 1953, p. 191-197; C. Spicq, *Agapè dans le Nouveau Testament, Analyse des textes* (EB), I, Paris, 1958, p. 165 and C. Spicq, *Théologie*

morale du Nouveau Testament (EB), Paris, 1965, I, p. 214; II, p. 529.

9. A. Schlatter, *Das Evangelium des Lukas aus seinem Quellen erklärt,* Stuttgart, 1931, p. 549.

10. W. Grundmann, *Das Evangelium nach Lukas,* p. 323.

11. H. J. Holtzmann. *Die Synoptiker* (HKommNT, I, I), Tübingen-Leipzig, [3]1901, p. 388. Holtzmann has been followed by E. Käseman, *Das Problem des historischen Jesus* (1954), in *Exegetische Versuche und Besinnungen,* Göttingen, [3]1965, p. 210.

12. M. J. Lagrange, *Evangile selon saint Luc* (EB), Paris, [3]1927, p. 440.

13. M. J. Lagrange, *Evangile selon saint Matthieu* (EB), Paris, [2]1923, p. 222.

14. C. Spicq, *Agapè dans le Nouveau Testament, Analyse des textes,* I, p. 165, n. 2. This text which is readily available - it is, in addition, cited in Moulton-Milligan and since McNeile it has appeared in several commentaries on Matthew - does not seem to have had any influence on the exegesis of Luke.

15. If, with regard to the two uses of παραβιάζομαι, we examine the three occasions on which Luke resorts to ἀναγκάζω, it is easier to see the difference between the two verbs. In Luke 14. 23, the substitute guests are recruited by force, because the master's house must be full. According to Acts 26. 11, Saul forced the Christians to blaspheme, that is to say, to deny that Jesus was the Messiah. Finally, according to Acts 28. 19, Paul was compelled to appeal to Caesar in order to escape a Jewish trial.

16. F. Godet (*Commentaire sur l'Evangile de saint Luc,* II, Neuchâtel, [3]1889, p. 259) already offers this explanation, saying that the context demands it.

17. Deponents, that is passive verbs with an active meaning, can also have a passive meaning (F. M. Abel, *Grammaire du grec biblique* (EB), Paris, 1927, §53g) - Blass-Debrunner, §311 and N. Turner, in J. H. Moulton, *A Grammar of New Testament Greek, III, Syntax,* Edinburgh, 1963, p. 58, recognize present passives in εὐαγγελίζεται in Luke 16. 16 and βιάζεται in Matthew 11. 12, but state without further explanation that the βιάζεται in Luke 16. 16 is a different matter. It is difficult to see why. This is not the opinion

of A. Deissman (*Neue Bibelstudien*, p. 85f. quoted by E. Klostermann, *Das Matthäusevangelium*, Tübingen, ^{2}1927, p. 98).

18. Cf. ἑάλωσαν εἰς Ἀθήνας γράμματα, "letters were seized and sent to Athens", (Xen, HG, I, 1, 23, quoted by F. M. Abel, *op cit.*, §48c).

19. Cf. Acts 2. 38: βαπτισθήτω ἕκαστος ὑμῶν ... εἰς ἄφεσιν τῶν ἁμαρτιῶν ὑμῶν.

20. Th. Zahn, *Das Evangelium des Lukas*, Leipzig-Erlangen, ^{4}1920, p. 580, n. 3.

Justification by Faith
According to the Book of Acts[1]

To deal with the subject of justification by faith according to the book of Acts at the end of a conference devoted to the subject of justification by faith according to Saint Paul, means we must concentrate on one precise topic: what does the work of Luke owe to the thought of the Apostle to the Gentiles?

It may be said that Luke's indebtedness is minimal, even non-existent, if it is held that the writer to Theophilus is a synthesizer and a compromiser who makes the Apostles Peter and Paul speak with identical accents, and fails to appreciate the originality of Paul's preaching. But we do not need to accept this explanation, which has been widely held for the last hundred years, without further examination; we can look at the question again.

We should say at the beginning that it is quite normal to find only a feeble echo of Paul's central message about justification by faith in the Acts. At the outset uncertainty prevails about the identity of Luke. Even if, following tradition, we admit that he is Paul's "physician-in-chief", we should make it quite clear that he is, for the Apostle, a friend rather than a collaborator intimately involved in his work and struggles as were Silas, Titus, and Timothy. Luke never appears as co-writer of any of the epistles; he does not seem to have been present at Corinth, or at Ephesus, where Paul waged his hardest battles and undoubtedly wrote most of his epistles.

Secondly, Luke is not, like Paul, a theologian "by trade". Furthermore he has not read Paul's epistles, "which contain difficult passages," - so difficult that specialists who incessantly scrutinize the text never fully succeed in agreeing on their interpretation. Even in the Apostle's lifetime, his teachings on justification by faith gave rise to misunderstandings. That a Pagan-Christian like Luke has not managed to retain all the subtleties of Paul's preaching on grace and on Jewish Law is not proof that he has betrayed the great Apostle.

Finally, by the time Luke writes his two books to Theophilus, the Apostles Peter and Paul have both disappeared from the scene. Times have changed. The problem of the Law is not as acute as at the beginning, the admission of Pagan-Christians to salvation is no longer under debate. The conciliatory tendency shown in Acts may be explained more by the spirit of the time than by any deliberate intent on Luke's part. Moreover this conciliatory tendency has its origin in Paul's thought, as he shows when he writes to the Corinthians about the unity of the apostolic message: "Whether it is I or they - the other apostles - this is what we all proclaim, and this is what you believed" (I Cor. 15. 11).

All of this means that we should investigate exactly what Luke understood and retained of Pauline thought. Our investigation will be based on the following three points:

I. We shall ask ourselves whether the words put into the mouth of Peter in Acts 15. 10-11 are really Pauline, as has been suggested, or if, on the contrary, they reveal pre-Pauline thinking.

II. We shall see how far the passage on justification by faith in 13. 38-39 is in conformity with Pauline thought.

III. Finally, we shall examine whether the passage in II Corinthians 5. 18-21 could be the inspiration for Luke's idea of a work in two books - the Gospel recounting how Christ accomplished the work of salvation, and the Acts relating how this salvation was proclaimed to the world by Christ's Witnesses.

I

At the time of the Council of Jerusalem (Acts 15) the Apostle Peter recalls that by the conversion of the centurion, Cornelius, (Acts 10. 1 - 11. 18) God showed it to be His will that the Gospel should be proclaimed also to the Gentiles. And Peter concludes with these words (15. 10-11):

v. 10: "Now, therefore, why provoke God, by laying on the necks of these disciples a yoke which neither our fathers nor we have been able to bear?"

v. 11: "On the contrary, we believe that it is by the grace of the Lord Jesus that we, as well as they, shall be saved."

So, through the events at Caesarea - the Holy Spirit descending on uncircumcised Gentiles - God had revealed His plan: the observation of Jewish Law must not be imposed upon Gentiles who are converted; for the Gentiles, like the Jews, are saved by the grace of the Lord Jesus.

We are faced with the following question: is the content of these two verses a Pauline idea put into the mouth of Peter by Luke, as has been suggested?[2] Let us look closely at the two verses, and, first of all, at verse 10. At least the interpreters are agreed on this first point: the idea expressed here, that the Law is an unbearable yoke, is not Jewish. For Israel, the Law is a privilege and a grace, the very sign of its election; it is the Law which sets Israel apart from "those Gentile sinners", and which stamps it visibly as the chosen people. The rabbinic expressions, "the yoke of the kingdom of heaven," "the yoke of the Torah," "the yoke of the commandments," or simply "the yoke," are intended *in bono sensu.* This position is not threatened by any act of breaking commandments, since "the day of Atonement" exists for the forgiveness of any unfaithfulness to the Law.[3]

Paul, the Pharisee, spoke of the Law in similar terms. It was for him a "gain" (Phil. 3. 7); he is conscious of being "irreproachable" in his "zeal" to observe the Law (Gal. 1. 14; Phil. 3. 6).

But what about Paul the Apostle of Jesus Christ? Does he affirm that the Law is an unbearable yoke? Alfred Loisy thinks so, for he says about our verse, "Paul could not have said it better,"[4] and he cites two verses from the epistle to the Galatians: Gal. 5. 1, "Christ has made us completely free; stand fast then and do not again be hampered with the yoke of slavery," and 3. 19, "The Law was imposed with a view to transgressions." In actual fact these two verses say more than Acts 15. 10. The text in Acts presents the Law as a collection of obligations which the Jews themselves could not fulfil; it outlines a contract they are powerless to carry out but it does not explain the reason for their incapability. The texts from Galatians are written into the Pauline theology of Law, of which they are principal parts. In the Apostle's view, the Law is not a religious and moral code which can "confer life" (Gal. 3. 21); its providential, and moreover temporary, role is to magnify transgressions so that the sinner may recognize himself as such before God and may be saved by His grace shown in Jesus Christ. And the yoke of servitude under which the Galatians would fall, if they became obedient to the Law, is equivalent to their life without God when they were unbelievers (Gal. 4. 8-9).

There is another passage in Galatians which Nestlé mentions in a footnote and to which Father Lyonnet[5] and Dom

Dupont[6] draw the reader's attention. It is Galatians 3. 10-12:

> All who depend upon obedience to the Law are under a curse; for it is written, "Cursed is everyone who does not abide by all the precepts of the law and practise them." It is evident, too, that no one can be put right with God by Law, because, "the righteous shall live by faith," and the Law has nothing to do with faith; but "he who does these things shall live by them."

In these verses Paul is declaring: Scripture teaches that the righteous man lives by faith and the Law promises nothing but a curse on whoever hopes to reach salvation through it. The Apostle bases his argument on three declarations from the Scriptures. First he quotes Deuteronomy 27. 26, "Cursed be every one who does not abide by all things written in the book of the Law, and do them." Thus he establishes that those who rely on practising the Law risk condemnation. Why? Because nobody can keep the Law in its entirety? Paul does not say so immediately because the reply is implicit in the last of the three Scripture verses (Gal 3. 12). In the first verse (Gal. 3. 10), the accent is on the curse connected with the legal system, not on the human responsibility to keep the Law, an impossibility which, moreover, does not exist in the thought of Deuteronomy.[7] Paul continues in verse 11 by saying why the rule of works ends in condemnation and not in justification. It is because God has decided thus, by declaring in the words of Habakkuk 2. 4, that "the righteous shall live by his faith." And the Law, the Apostle, quoting Leviticus 18. 5, emphasizes in verse 12, does not rest on faith but on the practice of the commandments. There, basically, is the key to the three verses. It is in principle, by the very virtue of its nature, namely, the rule of works and of action, that the Law can only lead to condemnation. In fact, man either does not keep the Law sufficiently and is condemned by his transgressions, or he keeps the Law with the zeal of a Pharisee, and is condemned by the pride into which he falls through his own righteousness. In short, it is the Law as such, and in so far as it is the rule of works, which can produce nothing but condemnation.

It is obvious that these reflections of Paul, the theologian, on the ineffectiveness of the Law - observed or not - to solve the problem of salvation, go much further than the simple remark in Acts 15. 10 on the impracticability of the Law.

Assuredly Paul the Apostle no longer has the confidence of Paul the Pharisee in the possibility of man being able to satisfy the demands of God by observing the Law. Paul the Apostle also knows that the Law, in fact, never could have been practised. But he is not content with noting the fact. He attempts to understand it. For he knows that God's policy, from the time of Abraham, has been to justify by faith and that the temporary role of the Law in the divine plan of salvation was limited to revealing the fact that salvation can only be based on faith in Jesus Christ. It would be necessary to find in Acts 15. 10 some trace, even if only the beginning, of these ideas, in order to be able to conclude that this verse in Acts is Pauline.

The thought in Acts 15. 10 is basically very general. The writer states that the Law has been seen to be impracticable in the past; to wish to impose it on the believers on whom God has caused the Holy Spirit to descend would be unreasonable, and even blasphemous. The Law is ruled out as a means of salvation and that is an established fact. But this idea is not specifically Pauline; it belongs to the whole of primitive Christianity. Is it possible that it belongs to the thought of Peter himself?

We know too little about the teachings of the Apostle

Peter to be able to make a categorical decision. Peter, the first to believe in the risen Christ, could very well have been the first to understand, perhaps intuitively, rather than by theological reflection like Paul, that the Law was no longer the way to salvation.

Even if we hesitate to see here an echo of the teachings of the prince of the Apostles, it is admitted[8] that Luke is expressing in Acts 15. 10 the theory about the Jewish Law which the Gentile-Christians of the second generation made for themselves, a theory, moreover, which became fixed in Christian tradition: that the Law was a collection of commandments and prohibitions which nobody has ever been able to keep.

Let us go on to the second element in Peter's speech, Acts 15. 11, which is the positive counterpart to verse 10: "On the contrary, we believe that it is by the grace of the Lord Jesus that we, as well as they, shall be saved."

Exegetes are divided about the possible Pauline character of this verse. "Peter speaks like the epistles to the Galatians and the Romans," writes A. Loisy.[9] G. Stählin[10] and H. Conzelmann[11] say only that the verse sounds Pauline. On the other hand, Conzelmann, repeating the opinion of Holtzmann[12] and Preuschen,[13] and comparing 15. 11 and 13. 38-39 writes: "Petrus spricht wie dort Paulus. Lukas kennt nicht verschiedene Typen von Theologie und Terminologie." He adds however: "Die paulinische Antithese zu den Werken fehlt."[14] It is the absence here of the typically Pauline comparison between justification by faith and justification by works which produces a more subtle opinion in Haenchen: "Paulinische Begriffe werden von Lukas übernommen, aber nicht die paulinische Theologie."[15]

In fact, whenever the Apostle Paul speaks of justification or salvation by faith, he never uses the expression διὰ τῆς χάριτος τοῦ κυρίου 'Ιησοῦ. He says that we are justified not by works but by faith in Jesus Christ (Gal. 2. 16; Rom. 3. 22;

Phil. 3. 9), or we are justified by the grace of God (Rom 3. 9), and the grace which saves us is "the grace of God" (Gal. 1. 15; 2. 21; Rom. 5. 15; 5. 2). Except in expressions of benediction Paul only speaks of "the grace of Jesus Christ" in the following cases: he tells the Galatians that God called him "through the grace of Christ" (Gal. 1. 15); he writes to the Corinthians: "You know the grace of our Lord Jesus Christ - how for your sakes he became poor, though he was rich" (2 Cor. 8. 9). He declares that, in reply to the prayer that he should be delivered from the thorn in the flesh and Satan's angel, the Lord - that is Jesus, as the context shows - said to him, "My grace is sufficient for you" (2 Cor. 12. 9). It is quite clear that the text of Acts does not make use of any Pauline expressions. For one thing the Apostle Paul only uses the designation "the Lord Jesus" twelve to fifteen times, though it was already traditional in his time, since it appears in the words of the institution of the Lord's Supper: "I received from the Lord what I also delivered to you, that the Lord Jesus, on the night when he was betrayed ..." (1 Cor 11. 23). In short, the expression, "We believe that it is by the grace of the Lord Jesus Christ that we shall be saved," rather than imitating Pauline expressions, could well pre-date the Apostle. If Christian preaching, in the beginning, unloosed the persecuting zeal of the Pharisee from Tarsus, it was because this preaching was not passive and innocuous but already included, in one form or another, these two elements: 1) The crucified Christ had been seen risen from the dead (cf. 1 Cor. 15. 3-5). 2) It is upon the name of this glorified Lord that the believers call as the author of their salvation (cf. Acts 7. 59; 9. 14 and 21). To deny that before the time of the Apostle Paul Christian preaching had formulated any christological and soteriological theories based on Jesus Christ, is to remove all content and reason for the persecution launched by Paul the Pharisee. In short, far from being taken from Paul, the declaration in Acts 15. 11 must be much older and could well be transmitting an echo of the teaching of Peter.[16]

II

"Understand therefore, brethren, that through this Jesus forgiveness of sins is announced to you; and in Him every believer is absolved from all offences, from which you could not be absolved under the Law of Moses" (Acts 13. 38-39).

These are the concluding verses of Paul's sermon in the synagogue at Antioch in Pisidia, the first of Paul's speeches in Acts. It is evident from his repeated use of the verb δικαιοῦν (and δικαιοῦν combined with ἀπὸ, as in Romans 6. 7), that Luke wished to recall that justification was one of the major themes of Paul's preaching.[17] This is the only place in Acts where he uses this specifically Pauline verb in the sense of man being justified (or absolved) by faith or by works. Apart from this passage, this verb only appears in the New Testament in the writings of Paul, and in the epistle of James (2. 21-25) where he develops the part played by faith and works in justification, with reference to the teachings of Paul. Therefore we have in Acts 13. 38-39 an incontrovertible reference to the theology of Paul. Everyone agrees on that point.[18] But what is its significance? This is where opinions differ. There seem to be three schools of interpretation:

1) Luke did not understand Paul and has seriously altered his ideas.

2) Luke has only a somewhat hazy recollection of Paul's idea of justification.

3) Luke knows that justification by faith is a specifically Pauline expression and, moreover, he is well acquainted

with other aspects of the Apostle's thought.

Let us examine these three interpretations:

1) According to the first interpretation Luke misunderstood Paul and made him say that justification by faith is complementary to justification by the Law; faith intervenes as a means of salvation at the point where the Law of Moses proves inadequate. This idea, put forward for the first time in 1846, reappearing many times during more than a hundred years of exegesis,[19] surfaced again in an article by P. Vielhauer in 1950.[20] This way of interpreting the text, already attacked by Wendt, is totally rejected by recent commentators on Acts.[21]

In fact, grammatically it is not correct to take the sentence in the sense of a partial justification by the Law and a complementary justification by faith. The intended contrast between πάντων and πᾶς suggests rather that the Law does not justify in any way, and that all sinners are absolved of all their sins by faith. Two arguments can be added to that. First, as Wendt says, Paul, in his epistles, never opposes the idea that a partial salvation through works is possible. The Judaizers want the Pagan-Christians, after they have been baptized and endowed with the Holy Spirit, to become additionally observers of the Law, but that is quite another matter. Secondly, as Wilckens and Stählin, in particular, emphasize,[22] there is no trace of synergism in Acts; texts such as 4. 12 ("There is no other name under heaven that has been given to men through which we are to be saved") and 15. 11 ("We believe that it is by the grace of the Lord Jesus that we shall be saved") are decisive in this respect. We can also mention the passage 16. 30-31: "What must I do to be saved? - Believe on the Lord Jesus Christ and both you and your household will be saved," with the antithesis "do" and "believe." This, furthermore, is found in Peter's first sermon: "'Brethren, what are we to do?' - 'Repent,' replied Peter, 'and be baptized, every one of you, in the name of Jesus Christ, for the remission of your sins, and you shall receive the gift of the Holy Spirit'" (Acts 2. 37-38). The four activities in which the believers persevered, "the teaching of the Apostles, fellowship, the breaking of bread, and prayers" (Acts 2. 42), are an expression of the results of salvation, not the conditions for it. In short, it is difficult to see how Luke could assign to Paul a theory of salvation which is neither Pauline nor Lucan.

2) Let us now turn to the second interpretation of verses 13. 38-39: there can only be the merest hint of Paul's theology here. This is the most widely accepted opinion today. It is summed up very well in these words by U. Wilckens: "For Luke, justification by faith is only a Pauline expression which he had heard and which he introduces into the speech in Pisidia to make it into a sermon by Paul; he does not see that, for Paul himself, the justification of the sinner by faith is the result of the death of Christ 'for our sins' as already stated in tradition prior to Paul (cf. 1 Cor. 15. 3), and for the Apostle Christian preaching is a 'word from the cross' (1 Cor. 1. 18)."[23] This same opinion is expressed by Bauernfeind, Haenchen, and Conzelmann in their commentaries; for Luke "justification by faith" is merely an expression, he does not give it any more content than he gives to his usual expression "forgiveness of sins," which he puts into the mouth of Paul as well as into that of Peter (Acts 2. 38; 5. 31; 10. 43), an expression which itself does not appear in the epistles of Paul (except Col. 1. 14 and Eph. 1. 7). This interpretation had already been given by Burton Scott Easton in 1936.[24] The American theologian emphasized particularly that, for Luke, forgiveness of sins is granted by the risen and glorified Christ, while, according to Paul, it is God who

absolves from sin through the cross of Christ. In short, in the view of the writers we have just cited, even although the sermon at Antioch in Pisidia expressly mentions justification by faith, it is not, basically, any more Pauline than the other sermons in Acts.

The explanations we have just summarized are based on actual facts. But the inferences to be drawn from those facts are debatable. Two magnitudes of the same order must be compared to each other. Luke's intention is to give us, in Acts, a report of the missionary sermons whose aim is to awaken faith and which cannot include explanations about the death of Christ. The latter are to be reserved for confessions of faith and for catechetical instruction of the believers. When the Apostle Paul recalls his first preaching in Thessalonica (1 Thess. 1. 5-10), the "word of the cross" is just as much absent as in Acts 13. On the other hand, when Luke describes Paul speaking before the Elders of Ephesus (Acts 20. 28), salvation through the death of Christ is expressed in terms very like those in the epistles (cf. Rom. 8. 32).[25]

Moreover Martin Dibelius has reminded us on several occasions[26] that the writer of Acts wishes to emphasize the unity rather than the diversity of Christian preaching and that his work is illustrated in the words Paul, after citing and developing the original kerygma given to him, uses to conclude: "Whether then it is I or they [those who were Apostles before him] this is the way we preach and the way that you came to believe" (1 Cor. 15. 11). There is only one Gospel and the different proclamations of it only make for variation on the same theme. That is Luke's perspective, and within that perspective, to allow Paul, and Paul only in Acts, to preach of justification by faith, is too much.

3) Finally, let us look at the third interpretation: we have in Acts 13. 38-39 a conscious and intentional indication

of Paul. First let us remind ourselves of two facts: (1) Luke knows that it is the unique mark of Pauline theology to find justification by faith within the works of the Law. This is proved in that he did not insert Pauline expressions into either of Peter's speeches. We must also admire the skill with which he could say, in Acts 15. 10-11, that Peter had preached salvation by faith without using the typically Pauline vocabulary of justification. It is clear that it would be an exaggeration to say that Luke was unaware of differences in theology and terminology when he was reporting the different missionary speeches.

(2) The verses 13. 38-39 are the end of the speech, which explains why the remarks on justification are few. However they deal with two essential points: first, justification by faith concerns all believers, the Jews and the proselytes to whom Paul is speaking now, and the Gentiles to whom he is preparing to go; secondly, the Law is powerless as a means of salvation. Certainly in these verses there is nothing about the role of the Law as an agent revealing man's sin, about Christ the end of the Law, about life in Christ to which salvation leads, or about the new life of the believer justified and inspired by the Holy Spirit. But if Luke's information is limited, it is correct.[27] For the rest, we should remember that, already in his gospel, Luke shows little interest in questions concerning Jewish Law.

We must go one step further. It is possible that the Pauline conclusion was envisaged, in the main body of the sermon, by its point of contact with another element in Pauline thought. We read in verse 33: "God raised up Jesus,[28] as it is also written in the second Psalm: 'Thou art my son; today I have begotten thee.'" This passage, according to which Jesus is proclaimed the Son of God on the very day of his resurrection, is interesting from two points of view.

First, Luke, in Acts, only uses this title of "Son of God" twice, here and in 9. 20, and in both cases it is to show that it is typically Pauline preaching;[29] this way of describing Jesus is common with the Apostle. Secondly, the divine sonship of Jesus is here put into direct relationship of time, and even of causality, with His resurrection; this is also the case in Romans 1. 4,[30] without any explicit reference to Psalm 2. 7 however.[31] It is true that there is general agreement that in Romans 1. 3-4 an early statement of faith, reworked by the Apostle,[32] is to be seen. But the additions made by Paul do not in any way alter the link already established in the early form of the text between the resurrection and the divine sonship of Jesus. This is why the Apostle could include this form of christology,[33] which he generally replaces by affirmation of the pre-existence of Christ. When the Apostle reminds the Thessalonians of the Gospel he preached he writes, "You turned to God from idols, to serve a living and true God, and to await the return from heaven of His Son, whom He raised from the dead, Jesus who delivers us from the wrath to come" (1 Thess. 1. 10). Here also resurrection and divine sonship go hand-in-hand.

What can we conclude from the comparison of these three texts (1 Thess. 1. 10; Rom. 1. 4; Acts 13. 33)? Van Iersel is of the opinion that Acts 13. 33 cannot be taken as unique in Paul and put specifically into Paul's mouth by Luke, because the quotation of Psalm 2. 7 is part of a traditional group of scriptural arguments which Luke uses in Peter's speeches also, in 2. 29-31 and 4. 24-27.[34] "This text must not be isolated; it is part of a chain."[35] Can this statement really be made, seeing that Luke himself remains master of these traditional groupings? He modifies them according to each use he makes of them and in view of the contexts into which he inserts them. The fact remains that Luke well and truly isolates the quotation from Psalm 2. 7, which he only uses once and in one of Paul's sermons; the fact also remains that this relationship between the resurrection and the divine sonship of Jesus, which gives weight to the quotation from Psalm 2. 7, appears again in the Pauline epistles. This agreement between Luke and Paul should at least be noted.

That is not all. We must also mention the following: the speech at Antioch in Pisidia includes traditional accounts which are only found in Paul. This is apparent in the passage (Acts 13. 28-31) where the Apostle recounts the death and resurrection of Jesus. This theme appears in almost all the missionary speeches in Acts. But here the usual motif is enriched by original features some of which only have parallels in Pauline texts (1 Cor. 15. 3-11).

These features are as follows: the Jews condemned Jesus "and asked Pilate to have Him put to death" (Acts 13. 28), while everywhere else in Acts, in Luke 24 and also in Paul (1 Thess. 2. 15) it is the Jews who kill Jesus. "When the Jews had carried out everything which had been written about Him, they took Him down from the cross and laid Him in a tomb" (v. 29). Now, apart from the Gospels, the burial of Jesus is only mentioned twice in the New Testament, here and in 1 Corinthians (15. 3): "He died ... according to the Scriptures and He was buried." We should point out, in passing, the obviously very early feature which is preserved here by Luke: it is the Jews who took Jesus down from the cross and placed Him in the tomb, and not those who were secretly His disciples, as in the Gospels.[36] The speech in Acts continues: "He appeared [ὤφθη] ... to the people who had gone up with Him from Galilee to Jerusalem" (v. 31a). It is the parallel passage to 1 Corinthians 15. 5: "He appeared [ὤφθη] to Cephas and then to the Twelve." The speech adds that those who saw the risen Christ are now His witnesses to the Jews (v. 31b). In 1 Corinthians Paul also declares that the Twelve became preachers of Christ (15. 11).

Certainly, the two passages which we are comparing (Acts 13. 28-31 and 1 Cor. 15. 3-11) are different; one is part of a missionary speech, the other is a confession of faith which Paul states and then develops. But the two texts are constructed from the same plan: "Christ dies, He was buried, He rose from the dead, He is now proclaimed." The equivalent of the Pauline expression that Jesus died and rose from the dead "according to the Scriptures" is provided by Luke in the scriptural proofs given a little further on (v. 33-37). Moreover, these two passages are the only ones in the New Testament, apart from the Gospel texts, which specifically mention the burial of Jesus, and for the same reason: to emphasize the reality of His death. For they both seem to be unaware of the tradition of the empty tomb. In every feature these two traditions go back to very early antiquity. That these two very early traditions have been preserved for us, one by Paul and the other by Luke (and in a speech by Paul rather than in one of Peter's speeches), is another indication that Luke was less ignorant than might have been supposed about specific features, at least, of the Apostle's thought and of the early traditions preserved in Pauline circles.

If Luke composed the speeches of Peter, Stephen and Paul himself, and if he wanted to illustrate the unity of their message, he also knew how to put variety into the missionary sermons, and this is not merely the result of his literary skill. He knew how to draw on good original authorities for characteristic notes on the method of the preachers, notes which were doubtless few, but sufficient, so that, in spite of their considerable basic resemblance, these speeches are not interchangeable. To be more specific, if it is Luke who wove the cloth of the speech at Antioch in Pisidia, more than one of the threads was spun by Paul.

III

Finally, we must say something about the most characteristically Pauline feature in the work of Luke. It is the very existence of the book of Acts. It is without doubt to the Apostle Paul that Luke owes the idea that salvation through faith in the Lord Jesus Christ is as much part of the Gospel to be preached as the life, death, and resurrection of Jesus of Nazareth. In other words, Luke owes to Paul his conception of a Gospel twice as developed as that of Mark and comprising a first book dealing with the redemption accomplished by Jesus Christ, and a second book revealing that salvation proclaimed to the world.

When Luke began to write the work addressed to Theophilus, he probably had as his models only the gospel of Mark and a few other sources which, we have every right to presume, were less detailed. For him - and for Matthew too - the model for gospel writing is Mark. Our proof is in the following: Luke - and Matthew too - had at their disposal other material besides Mark to enable them to envisage a plan different from Mark's. However, neither of them escaped the traditional (i.e. Marcan) framework. It is into Mark's framework that Luke inserted non-Marcan elements; hence the inordinate length of his gospel account of the journey from Galilee to Jerusalem. Likewise Matthew attempted to insert into Mark's plan his own project which envisaged five successive books, and for him, it was the Galilean ministry which he developed at length. The impress of the model was very strong, doubtless because behind the redaction of Mark the preaching of Peter could be felt.

However, if Luke dared not break loose from Mark's format in composing his own account of the ministry and passion of Jesus, he did free himself from Mark's idea of a gospel by exceeding the limit which Mark had set for himself. Luke composed for Theophilus a work in two books, united under the same preface according to custom, the first book devoted to what Jesus Himself did and taught, and the second including the testimonies given to the risen Christ by the Witnesses He Himself had chosen. One moment's reflection is enough to convince us that the idea of a gospel which Luke set for himself is the better one. As Father Spicq puts it so well: "It is not enough to save the world that Christ should die and be raised from the dead. It is also necessary that these facts should be made known and believed."[37]

Now who could inspire Luke with this idea of a complete gospel and give him the courage to write it, going beyond the known model of a gospel? None other than the Apostle Paul. This is not a rash judgment if we read 2 Cor. 5. 18-20, where the Apostle writes: "And all this is from God, who has reconciled us to Himself through Christ, and has appointed us ministers of this reconciliation, to tell how in Christ God was reconciling the world to Himself ... depositing with us the message of this reconciliation." This text speaks for itself; no lengthy commentary is required. Twice Paul declares that the salvation realised by God consists of these two stages which form a whole: a redemptive action accomplished by Christ, and a proclamation of this Gospel to the world by the Apostle.

The Apostle develops the same idea more fully in Romans 10. 4-15. Verses 4 - 7 recall that salvation has already been realised by Christ; He has already been sent by God (cf. Gal. 4. 4) and He has already been raised from the dead. Verses 8 - 15 explain that the preaching of the Gospel is a necessity correlative to the very nature of redemption. It is the one who calls on the name of the Lord who will be saved. Now one can only call on the name of the Lord if one believes in Him, and in order to believe, one must hear the Gospel proclaimed.

That is an inherent requirement of the divine plan, and that is why the Apostle, "to whom God has revealed His son in order that he might preach Him among the Gentiles" (Gal. 1. 15-16), declares elsewhere, "I preach the gospel ... for necessity is laid on me and woe to me if I do not preach the gospel" (1 Cor. 9. 16). In this case, in fact, it would be impossible for men to receive the salvation for which Christ died and rose from the dead. Paul writes again to the Galatians: "If man were justified through the Law, then Christ died in vain" (Gal. 2. 21). It would be the same if men did not learn through the preaching of the Apostles that Christ died and rose again for them.

There is a striking resemblance between the Pauline texts on the unity of the work of redemption, accomplished by Christ and which is preached by the Apostles, and the gospel of Luke in two books. In particular the concise phrases of 2 Corinthians 5. 18-19 could appear as an epigraph for the writing to Theophilus. The gospel of Luke: the work of Christ; the book of Acts: the preaching of His Witnesses.

But it will be said, is not this resemblance between the declaration of Paul and the plan of Luke somewhat exaggerated? And the three following objections will be put forward:

1) The Apostle, according to Paul, is sent by God; the Witnesses in Acts are sent by the risen Christ.

2) Luke, in Acts, refuses to give to Paul the title of Apostle.

3) The Acts are a history of the infant Church and not merely a collection of sermons.

Let us answer these three objections briefly.

1) If Paul receives his vocation from God (Gal. 1. 15f.), and if he is sent by God (2 Cor. 5), in the greetings of his epistles, when he claims the title of Apostle, he presents himself as the Apostle of Jesus Christ. Moreover, according

to Acts, the Apostles are instituted Witnesses either by the risen Christ (1. 2 and 8), or by God (10. 41). Paul, likewise, is presented sometimes as sent by Christ (9. 15; 22. 21; 16. 16), and sometimes as the one predestined by God to be the Witness of the Righteous One before men (22. 14). It is quite clear that Luke and Paul follow the same usage and make the Apostles the instruments of either God or Christ.

2) That he refused to Paul the title of Apostle, equal to the Twelve, which Paul claimed for himself, is a common accusation levelled against Luke. We must make a distinction. The title itself, yes; but it is only a question of vocabulary. Actually Luke created a new title, which Paul does not use, the title of "Witness" (μάρτυς). But the "Witness" according to Luke is the exact equivalent of "the Apostle of Jesus Christ" of whom Paul speaks. The two designations serve the dual purpose of grouping the Twelve and Paul together and of distinguishing these supreme ambassadors of Christ from other missionaries, however enterprising they may be. Luke does not repudiate Paul's claim; he well and truly believes him to be an ambassador of Christ, equal to the Twelve in dignity and in authority; for he makes the Apostle to the Gentiles "the chosen instrument" who, in the end, assumes the mission entrusted at first to the Twelve by the risen Christ to be His Witnesses "to the remotest parts of the earth." Luke uses the term "witness" rather than that of apostle doubtless because, in his time, the term apostle remained ambiguous, in spite of the distinctions made by Paul, and was used to refer to missionaries of no great authority (cf. Didache 11. 3-6). But Luke has remained faithful to the thought of Paul on this point.

3) The Acts are not a history of the Church but a collection of testimonies to the risen Christ. If the Acts were a history of the early Church it would be difficult to explain the omissions. There are omissions, first of all, with regard

to the expansion of the Church; even facts which were known to Luke, like the founding of the church at Rome and in Italy (Acts 28. 14-15), are not reported; omissions are apparent, secondly, in the activities of the Apostles. Peter suddenly disappears from the scene (12. 17), but he reappears at the conference in Jerusalem (15. 7f.), and then we read nothing more of him. Nor do we learn what happened to Paul after his two years in captivity in Rome. There are omissions, finally, about life within the churches; if we did not have the information in the epistles, we would know nothing of the questions which concerned the Pauline communities.

This lack of information can be fairly well explained if we admit that Luke did not want to write a systematic history of the evangelization of the world, nor biographies of the Apostles, nor an account of the daily life of the local churches, but that he had another aim in mind.

It is the testimonies given by the spokesmen of the risen Christ which are the essential body of the book, which mark the stages in it, and which emphasize the advancement of the Gospel. The first five chapters include particularly the sermons of Peter. Then Stephen, through his speech followed by his martyrdom (chap. 6-7), carries the Church out into the world, initiates the evangelization of Samaria, then Antioch, and provides the introduction to the calling of Paul to be an Apostle. In chapter 10, the Gospel is preached for the first time to non-Jews, in a sermon by Peter; in chapter 13, Paul's speech at Antioch in Pisidia launches a new phase in the mission to the Gentiles. So we reach the Jerusalem conference, the high-point of Acts (chap. 15), where the Church already appears in its full theological stature, since it brings together in unity believers coming out of Judaism and their Gentile brethren.

After that Luke has only to show how the work of witness is accomplished on the geographical level by the mission of the final Witness, Paul, who, after proclaiming the Gospel "from Jerusalem as far as Illyricum" (Rom. 15. 19), will finally carry into the capital of the civilized world the message of redemption which is in Jesus Christ. The work as Luke conceived it, probably under Pauline inspiration, ends when "the chosen vessel" preaches "the gospel of the Lord Jesus without let or hindrance."

It is time to draw our conclusions and we will do it in a few words. If the analyses we have presented are more or less correct, it follows that our debt to Luke is enormous. For Luke reminds us that all the Apostles preached the same salvation through faith in the Lord Jesus, and that Paul formulated the idea that the sinner is justified by faith in Christ without the works of the Law. Luke reminds us too, by his Gospel in two books, of the great Pauline truth that redemption consists of two acts: the salvation realized by Christ, and the salvation preached by Christ's Witnesses, so that the hearers and the readers of these sermons might attain the faith which alone can save them.

Undoubtedly it is possible that in the account he gives us of the Apostle's career, Luke may have been at times betrayed by his faulty recollection or by inaccuracy. But from the theological point of view tradition rings true when it declares that Luke in his work gives us a faithful reflection of the Gospel of Paul.

NOTES

1. *Foi et salut selon saint Paul,* Analecta Biblica, 42, Rome 1970, p. 255-276, with kind permission of *Biblica,* Pontifical Biblical Institute, Rome.

2. Cf. among others K. Lake and H. J. Cadbury, *The Beginnings of Christianity.* Part I: *The Acts of the Apostles,* IV, London, 1933, p. 173: "This passage is in some ways the most Pauline in Acts."

3. Cf. H. Strack and P. Billerbeck, *Kommentar zum Neuen Testament aus Talmud und Midrasch,* I, München, 1922, p. 608-610.

4. A. Loisy, *Les Actes des apôtres,* Paris, 1920, p. 579.

5. S. Lyonnet, *Les épîtres de saint Paul aux Galates et aux Romains* (Bible de Jérusalem), Paris, 1953, p. 28.

6. J. Dupont, *Les Actes des apôtres*[3] (Bible de Jérusalem), Paris, 1964, p. 139.

7. Cf. the commentaries on Galatians by Lagrange and, particularly, by Schlier, who is followed by Bonnard.

8. Cf. the commentaries on Acts by Haenchen and Conzelmann.

9. A. Loisy, *op cit.,* p. 580.

10. *Die Apostelgeschichte* (Das Neue Testament Deutsch 5), Göttingen, 1962, p. 262.

11. *Die Mitte der Zeit. Studien zur Theologie des Lukas*[3], Tübingen, 1960, p. 198.

12. *Die Apostelgeschichte*[3] (Hand-Kommentar zum Neuen Testament I, 2), Tübingen, 1901, p. 96.

13. *Die Apostelgeschichte* (Handbuch zum Neuen Testament IV, 1), Tübingen, 1912, p. 94.

14. *Die Apostelgeschichte* (Handbuch zum Neuen Testament 7), Tübingen, 1963, p. 83.

15. *Die Apostelgeschichte*[3] (Kritisch-exegetischer Kommentar über das Neue Testament III), Göttingen, 1965, p. 387, n. 2.

16. We can also give a second proof for the preceding argument. We have in Ephesians 2. 7f. a passage which is not written by Paul's hand - it does not have his style or his stamp - and which, except for one detail, reproduces his thought and "speaks like the epistles to the Galatians and the Romans": "for by grace you have been saved through faith, and this is not your own doing, it is the gift of God - not because of works, lest any man should boast." Here we have "Pauline" themes: salvation by grace and by faith, a salvation which depends on the initiative of God, a salvation which has nothing to do with man's works. Paul's disciple betrays himself by describing his readers as σεσωσμένοι; the Apostle himself speaks of the believers as σωζόμενοι because he does not forget that the believers still await τὴν ἀπολύτρωσιν τοῦ σώματος. Just as we have in Ephesians 2. 7 a direct echo of Pauline ideas, so we have in Acts 15. 11 an old expression from the origins of Christian faith, and an expression which undoubtedly owes more to Peter than to Paul.

17. Cf. H. H. Wendt, *Die Apostelgeschichte*[3] (Kritisch-exegetischer Kommentar über das Neue Testament III), Göttingen, 1913, p. 215, n. 38.

18. Except O. Glombitza, "Akta XIII. 15-41. Analyse einer lukanischen Predigt vor Juden," *New Testament Studies* 5 (1958-1959), p. 306-317. According to this writer, the discussion of the messianic texts in Acts 13. 33-37 allows Luke to introduce one of his own ideas, that of the superiority of the prophetic and priestly office of Jesus the Messiah, raised from the dead by God, over the royal office formerly exercised by David. Luke expresses the same thought at the end of the speech (v. 38-39): the forgiveness of sins which the Law cannot grant, is gained through the redemptive work of the Messiah-priest Jesus at Jerusalem. Luke's theology is very close to that of the epistle to the Hebrews, and those commentators are wrong who find in this finale a more or less direct reference to justification by faith according to St. Paul. This explanation, which lacks convincing arguments, does not seem to have gathered much support.

19. Cf. H. H. Wendt, *op cit.,* p. 215, who cites particularly Schwegler, Zeller, Pfleiderer, Holtzmann, B. Weiss, Hilgenfeld and Harnack.

20. P. Vielhauer, "Zum Paulinismus der Apostelgeschichte," *Evangelische Theologie* 10 (1950-1951), p. 15; in English in the volume: *Studies in Luke-Acts,* Nashville, New York, 1966, p. 41-42. Similarly: E. Schweizer, "Zu den Reden der Apostelgeschichte," *Theologische Zeitschrift* 13 (1957), p. 5, n. 15; G. Klein, "Rechtfertigung," *Die Religion in Geschichte und*

Gegenwart[3], V, p. 827, in connection with Acts 13. 38-39, speaks of an "unverständene Reminizenz."

21. Cf. the commentaries by Bauerfeind, Haenchen, Stählin, and Conzelmann in Germany; Lake-Cadbury, Bruce and Williams in Anglo-Saxon countries; also H. Conzelmann, *Die Mitte der Zeit. Studien zur Theologie des Lukas*[3], Tübingen, 1960, p. 149; C. F. D. Moule, in *Studies in Luke-Acts*, Nashville, New York, 1966, p. 184, n. 46: "This would surely be a perverse exegesis ... an almost anti-Pauline sense." We must also mention A. Loisy, in a passage which is worth quoting in full; it is the only time, to our knowledge, where Loisy comes publicly to the defense of Luke. Loisy writes (*Les Actes des Apôtres*, Paris, 1920, p. 536): "Several scholars (Holtzmann, p. 90; Harnack, IV, p. 48; Preuschen, p. 85, etc.) are of the opinion that the writer admits there is a partial and incomplete justification by the works of the Law, which seriously alters Paul's thought. The truth must be that he does not look at things as closely as that, and that he had not foreseen commentators so quick to be shocked. He had not the slightest intention of reproducing the whole of Paul's system of thought on justification here, nor of referring his readers to the epistles; he reports what he believes he understands of it, what he thinks is good to be retained, and he does not hesitate, once in a while, to use Paul's own words; but he does not deserve to be treated as one whose slightest observations other theologians have the right to criticize so strongly."

22. U. Wilckens, *Die Missionsreden der Apostelgeschichte* (Wissenschaftliche Monographien zum Alten und Neuen Testament 5), Neukirchen, 1961, p. 182; G. Stählin, *op cit.*, p. 185.

23. U. Wilckens, *op cit.*, p. 217.

24. B. S. Easton, "The Purpose of Acts" in *Early Christianity. The Purpose of Acts and other Papers*, London, 1955, p. 87-88. "The Purpose of Acts" appeared alone for the first time in 1936.

25. Cf. W. G. Kümmel, *Theologische Rundschau* 22 (1954), p. 209; J. Dupont, *Etudes sur les Actes des apôtres* (Lectio Divina 45), Paris, p. 145, n. 27.

26. M. Dibelius, *Die Formgeschichte des Evangeliums*[3], Tübingen, 1959, p. 16; *Aufsätze zur Apostelgeschichte*, Göttingen, 1951, p. 142-143.

27. We could apply to Acts 13. 38-39 what C. F. D. Moule said about Acts 13. 33: "It looks, then, as though Luke

may have represented Paul quite correctly, although on one of the shallower of Paul's own levels of thinking" in "The Christology of Acts," *Studies in Luke-Acts*, Nashville, New York, p. 174.

28. 'Αναστήσας must refer to the resurrection because of the context. On this point, cf. E. Lövestam, *Son and Saviour: A Study of Acts 13. 32-37*, Lund-Copenhagen, 1961, p. 37-48; M. Rese, *Alttestamentliche Motive in der Christologie des Lukas*, Diss. Bonn, 1965, p. 117-123.

29. Cf. J. Dupont, *Les sources du Livre des Actes*, Bruges, 1960, p. 75, n. 1.

30. Cf. M. E. Boismard, "Constitué Fils de Dieu (Rom. 1. 4)," *Revue Biblique* 60 (1953), p. 12.

31. Cf. B. M. F. Van Iersel, *"Der Sohn" in den synoptischen Jesusworten*[2] (Supplements to Novum Testamentum 3), Leiden, 1963, p. 67.

32. On this point, cf. Van Iersel, *op cit.*, p. 71-72.

33. On early christologies which connect salvation with the resurrection-exaltation of Jesus, cf. E. Schweitzer, *Erniedrigung und Erhöhung bei Jesus und seinen Nachfolgern*[2] (Abhandlungen zur Tehologie des Alten und Neuen Testaments 28), Zurich, 1962, p. 60; Van Iersel, *op cit.*, p. 49-50.

34. Van Iersel, *op cit.*, p. 67-70.

35. Van Iersel, *op cit.*, p. 68.

36. Cf. M. Goguel, *La foi à la résurrection de Jésus dans le christianisme primitif*, Paris, 1931, p. 129-134.

37. *Les épîtres pastorales* (Etudes bibliques), Paris, 1947, p. 226.

III. JOHANNINE STUDIES

The Originality of John's Thought[1]

Dedicated to the memory of Professor René Guisan

The frescoes on the temple at Ressudens depict a group of Apostles prostrate before Christ. One of the worshippers attracts attention by the strangeness of his position: the ends of his cloak are pulled up over his head so that no one can see his face.

I do not know what was the painter's ultimate intention; but I do not know of a more moving depiction of the anonymous disciple to whom we owe "the Gospel according to Saint John," the unknown witness, who omitted all trace of himself in order to bring us close to the one whose "glory he had seen." I also see in this painting a striking representation of the mystery surrounding the fourth Gospel in all its aspects.

What of the author and the origins of the work? Here is a mystery which tradition does not entirely clarify for us. John's thought also is a mystery: at times it seems to answer to the highest hopes of Israel's Messianism and at others it seems to exceed the highest aspirations of the Greek soul. Whether Jewish or Greek, according to the point of view of the exegete, the work of "John" remains an enigma, especially in its theological content. The history of research on the fourth Gospel shows that critics' opinions depend to a great extent, if not entirely, on their way of interpreting Johannine thought and where they place it in the context of primitive Christian thought.

John - whether he is the son of Zebedee or an unknown disciple makes hardly any difference to the problem - makes his voice heard at the time when the apostolic age has reached its end. He develops his own personal thought which gives his testimony a new accent and a particular strength. We have the feeling that he defines an epoch. But what is it? An arrival point or a point of departure? Is John still to be placed, following the Apostles and Saint Paul, in the field of Jewish thought; and, if he thereby enriches the tradition of the infant Church, does he avoid bringing incongruous elements into it? Or, on the other hand, is John a philosopher, a mystic, a gnostic who adds the hypotheses of Hellenistic syncretism to the Christian message? In short, is John the last witness of the revelation or is he the first theologian of the Greek Church? This is the question we wish to try to answer.

Before coming to the heart of the matter, let us look at the question itself more closely. There are two ways of understanding the possible resemblances between Johannine thought and Hellenestic syncretism, (that is, the vast movement to unify all religions, and in certain respects too, the philosophy which abandons all high aspirations to become scarcely more than a practical way of life). It may be a matter of purely external resemblances, which can be explained by the very nature of things, or it may be a question of fundamental ideas which have been "borrowed." These are two different problems.

We admit that John's vocabulary is Hellenistic in many of its expressions, and that certain Johannine ideas, taken in isolation, are very close to one or another syncretistic idea. John allies himself with the thought of the world at that time on a common foundation of symbols, images, and, in a certain sense, concepts. We only have to think of the expression Logos, of the images of 'the way,' 'the vine,' 'the shepherd and the flock,' of the dualities: life-death, light-darkness, truth-falsehood, of the use of the sacred *I*, for example. But these are obvious resemblances. First because feelings and religious convictions can only be expressed in pictures, in concrete or conceptual images; the simplest images and ideas are best, and inevitably these are limited in number, and they are to be found everywhere in more or less identical form. Secondly, because every man must speak in the language of his time in order to make himself understood; John, witness of the Word incarnate among men, does not escape this general rule.

What is important, therefore, is not simply to recognize, for example, that the Stoics, Philo, the Gnostics, and John all speak of the Logos, but to know why and in what sense they speak of it. A particular point of resemblance can lose all significance if the systems being compared, as a whole, direct analogous thoughts into different channels. Therefore we must turn our attention to the second of the two problems we pointed out a short time ago; that is a comparative study of the specific characteristics of Johannine thought and syncretism. That means we must widen the debate and, first of all, we must see in what ways Christianity differed radically from the world around it.

If the thought of the infant Church took for itself elements from paganism, it did not express itself essentially in pagan terms. It could not do that without repudiating itself. Primitive Christianity and syncretism, despite all they have in common, are defined by different conceptions of religious and metaphysical reality.

To explain this distinction fully it would be necessary to give an account of the intellectual and spiritual heritage of the primitive Church and show its links with Jewish thought; it would be necessary, secondly, to describe the mystical aspirations, the philosophy, the mysteries and the whole gnosis of the Hellenic world. A choice like the one we are going to make is always somewhat arbitrary and forced; however, we hope to bring out, in the following three points, what is really essential:

1) Primitive Christianity knows only one God, creator of heaven and earth. Creation is good; matter itself is good "at its level of existence."[2] Evil is the consequence of disobedience to the divine will; it is not eternal; it will disappear when God establishes His kingdom. Christianity is marked by a temporal dualism: to this present, or earthly, world it sets in contrast the world to come or the world of God. Syncretism, on the other hand, is dominated by an essential dualism; spirit and matter, good and evil, both come from an eternal principle. The tendencies to monotheism in the Greek world do not eliminate this fundamental dualism.

2) For Christianity, salvation is the deliverance from sin, which has broken the bonds joining the created one to his Creator. Salvation is the regeneration of human personality, on which, inevitably, the regeneration of the cosmos depends. Syncretism, on the other hand, presupposes an anthropological dualism. Man is weak, not because he has disobeyed, but because he is flesh. Salvation, for the immortal soul, consists of escaping from the prison of the body.

3) In Christianity, redemption is offered by the historic work of Jesus Christ, who by His incarnation, death, and resurrection has conquered the powers of evil and opened the way to the heavenly world for the believers. Faith makes the

believer a part of this new world now and the resurrection ensures him a place in it "on the last day." Salvation is achieved by the personal participation of the believer in the kingdom of a personal God through a communion of love. Redemption is historical and eschatological. In syncretism, on the other hand, redemption is an idea or a mystery. In order to be saved, the faithful must rid themselves of matter by an intellectual, ecstatic or sacramental technique, which, to all intents and purposes, unites them with the Logos or with the Savior-God of mystery. Salvation is achieved by the absorption of the soul into the great whole of divine unity.

In short, Christianity and syncretism are both religions of redemption which, taking hold of man in his solid, restricted reality, would save him by taking him from an inferior world to a superior world. But, while syncretism presupposes a spatial dualism at the universal level and the human level, and a salvation which is achieved according to mystic and sacramental categories, Christianity postulates a temporal dualism, a moral evil and entrance into the heavenly world by rebirth and resurrection.

It is obvious therefore that we can only speak of the hellenisation of Christian thought in so far as these two dualisms, spatial and temporal (or, if you like, these two *realisms*, mystico-sacramental and historical) come together; in the sense that the facts which belong to the dualism of primitive Christianity begin to be interpreted according to the norms of Hellenistic dualism. In fact, we can speak only of the combining of ideas, for Hellenic mysticism was never substituted for historical realism in Christianity entirely; and if, at certain times in the history of the Church, the apostles of a spirituality called *pure*, because it aimed at being timeless, wanted to cut Christianity off from its historic roots, Christian feeling reacted almost automatically in the certainty that Christianity would cease to be itself if it ceased to be grounded in history.

This apparent parenthetical discussion was necessary in order to enable us to define the Johannine question. We can now state it in precise terms: is the thought of the fourth Gospel dominated by the historical reality of primitive Christianity, or, on the contrary, is it an essay in synthesis between Christian realism and Hellenistic mysticism?

Several exegetes and historians have come down on the side of the second alternative. The strongest interpretation along these lines is without doubt that given by Albert Schweitzer in a chapter entitled: "The Hellenisation of Paul's Mysticism by Ignatius and the Johannine Theology," at the end of his fine volume *The Mysticism of Paul the Apostle.*[3] The eminent theologian's hypothesis is, in brief: Paul's thought owes nothing to Hellenistic mysticism. This was introduced into the Church by Ignatius, and John follows in the footsteps of the Bishop of Antioch. The fourth evangelist wants to show that the historic Jesus does not preach eschatological salvation, as the synoptic Gospels taught, but a mystical doctrine of redemption, working through a "presence" which is Christ-Logos, bearer of the sacraments of everlasting life; the elements of the eucharist, bread and wine, are bearers of the redemptive power of the Logos, which had been physically the person of Jesus Christ, and in a form which the believers can assimilate; the Johannine theory of redemption therefore is the same as the theory of Ignatius, and Johannine thought is a kind of Hellenisation of the purely Christian mysticism that Paul preached.

We propose a diametrically different solution, but, to reach it, we will make use of a course parallel to the one followed by the writer of *The Mysticism of Paul the Apostle.*

By bringing Ignatius into the debate, Albert Schweitzer has appealed to a norm of comparison the value of which cannot be over-estimated. Ignatius has preserved several essential facts of the Christian heritage, but he has had to give up or change others, which could not be assimilated just as they were by a mind already influenced by greco-oriental mysticism.[4] So a comparative study of the ideas of John and Ignatius will serve to show whether John does the same or whether he remains within the perspective of Pauline thought.

The discussion can usefully center on the following three points:

1) the concept of the person and work of Jesus - with his idea of the Logos the evangelist seems at first to place himself firmly on the side of Hellenism;

2) the relationship between mysticism and eschatology in Johannine thought - for the expectation of an eschatalogical salvation John is considered as having substituted a mysticism of salvation realised here and now by the "presence" of Jesus in the believer and of the believer in Jesus;

3) finally the Johannine idea of the eucharist - John, it is said, seems to have given the most sacramental interpretation of the Lord's Supper in the New Testament, by putting into the mouth of Jesus those words whose importance is emphasized by the double *amen*: "Truly, truly, I say to you, unless you eat the flesh of the Son of Man and drink his blood, you have no life in you" (John 6. 54).

We shall look closely at these three aspects of the thought of John, not for themselves, but for their part in the alternative interpretation we have offered as our solution to the Johannine problem.

I

If the writer of the fourth Gospel is considered as being open to the charge of Hellenism it is often because he makes use of the term "Logos" (the Word) in the prologue of his work. At the beginning of this century, any exegete concerned about his reputation subscribed to the peremptory judgment of Jean Réville, for whom the evangelist was, "not just varnished with the theology of Philo, but impregnated to the marrow with judeo-hellenistic religious philosophy." Réville observed however that on "a point of major importance," the idea of the incarnation of the Word, John showed signs, "of a most remarkable independence of thought."[5]

This "independence" has attracted much notice since then. Recent works have not only stressed the difference in meaning between the Logos of Philo and the Logos of John, they have also shown how the two writers differ even in the development of their thought.[6] Philo is dominated by the Jewish idea of the transcendence of God and by the spatial dualism of Hellenism; his interest is in the way in which God sets about freeing the soul from bodily matter and allowing it to return to its primitive purity. So the transcendent God of Philo needs a Logos to serve as intermediary. Intellect itself, this Logos addresses itself to the human intellect in order to separate it from the flesh and lead it, by ways of knowledge and of the practice of virtues, to a vision of God conceived as a complete possession of the divine. The Logos for Philo is, "the result of a logical sequence. It would no longer be good for anything if it became corporeal."[7]

It is quite different with John. His Logos is incarnate, and it is by its work in human form that it becomes mediator. It is not because he speculates about the nature of a pre-existent Logos that John deduces the idea of incarnation; it is because he has seen the glory of a Son coming from the Father shining in the historic person of Jesus that John knows, "the Word became flesh." John is not a reasoner, but a dreamer; his whole thought centers in a vision of the person of Jesus, who is for him not only a fact of history, but a revelation of God in history; and that is not by virtue of an arbitrary assumption but because of necessity within his thinking. John's whole being is permeated with this truth, which he shares with the believers of the Old Covenant and which remained almost unknown outside biblical revelation, namely that, "God does not reveal Himself all at once, nor in a timeless manner through some general idea, but in the course of factual history where He continues His work."[8] The incarnation of the Logos therefore is not just an "original idea" in a theory of salvation, which is otherwise identical with that of Philo, it is the proof that John has a completely different notion of the world and, particularly, of the way in which God intervenes in the world. To be convinced of this, it is only necessary to point out two consequences of the historic idea of the incarnation of the Logos: the very character of the redemptive work of the Word incarnate and the place of this work in the series of God's historic revelations.

The coming of the Son from the Father presupposes the existence of two different worlds: that of God or the world on high, which is the world of life or of life eternal (the two expressions are synonymous for John), and that of the earth or the flesh, the human world, which is doomed to disappear because it does not have *life*.

In order for man to be saved - that is put in possession of life as it is on high - it is necessary for this divine life to come down to man in a form which will be accessible to him and appropriate for the earthly world. The Son, whom God has endowed with life in its fulness, becomes incarnate in Jesus of Nazareth, for this very purpose, to give divine life to men who do not possess it naturally.

John does not explain the origin of the difference between these two worlds, but it is obvious that for him, as for the whole biblical revelation, it is the result of an accident. Creation is good because it is the work of the Logos. Matter of itself is so close to God that the Word becomes matter in order to reveal God. By His incarnation the Logos comes to combat evil, to destroy its historic principle, the Prince of this world, and restore once and for all the unity of the *cosmos*. Although the universal aspect of redemption is less marked than in Paul, it appears like the watermark in a sheet of paper, and it postulates a *telos*, where the Word has just as much part as He has had in the work of creation. The dualities in John are temporal, not spatial, and the eschaton appears as the end of the story of which creation was the beginning.

Moreover, flesh is not of itself identical to sin; in theory, and before the time of biblical revelation, flesh is, so to speak, "neutral" as far as God is concerned; it is not suited for eternal life. Man in his totality is *flesh;* immortality is not a quality which is inherent in man even at his highest; it is the gift of God in Christ, for the only true *life* there is is of God. Sin is conscious opposition to the revelation from above; it is the refusal of the darkness to accept the light; it is an act of disobedience and not a state of nature; it is spiritual and not physical.

With all these cosmological and anthropological presuppositions John sets himself in the line of Paul, and, with him, on ground far different from that of syncretism. Basically, Greek thought hardly knows what to do with the problem of "matter" and ends, like Plotinus, by identifying it with evil.[9] Philo, as we have noted, already seems to be leading towards this identity of terms, and Ignatius sometimes makes use of language which shows very similar concepts. In his eager desire to reach God through martyrdom the Bishop of Antioch begs the Romans not to intervene on his behalf; that would tear him away from God; his desire is to be born to "life," to reach the pure light, by escaping from the world and its "seductions of the flesh," because his earthly passions have already been destroyed and the "fire of the flesh" no longer burns within him.[10] This desire to take hold of God, combined with a contempt for the material body as being essentially an obstacle to communion with the divine, is completely alien to the spirit of primitive Christianity, and, on this point, it is Ignatius and not John who has been influenced by Hellenism.

We reach a similar conclusion if we look at the position of the work of the Word incarnate in the whole series of the divine revelations. When the Jesus of the Gospel of John declares that, "salvation comes from the Jews," he means that the incarnation of the Son does not happen *ex abrupto*, but following a long series of historical interventions by God in Israel. Moses and the Scriptures give testimony to the Son, whose coming and passion are foretold.[11] At the end of the Old Covenant, John the Baptist appears as "a witness to the light and the truth" and it is because the Jews, as a whole, did not remain faithful to his teaching that they reject the testimony of Jesus.[12]

If Jesus appears so harsh towards the *Jews* labelled as unbelievers on almost every page of the Gospel, if he accuses them of being worthy sons of their father, the Devil, a liar and a murderer, it is because, face to face with the most dazzling of God's manifestations, they closed their eyes and would not see. However, they had had witnesses to this revelation, from Moses to John the Baptist; there is no excuse for their unbelief.

The meaning of the anti-Jewish polemic in the fourth Gospel is sometimes misunderstood; John has even been called a Marcionite before his time.[13] This is to forget that John and Marcion opposed Judaism for very different motives; they are not fighting the same enemy under the name of Judaism. Marcion's anti-Judaism is a result of his dualist idea of the world, and his rejection, in practice, of monotheism. John, on the contrary, categorically affirms the unity of God and creation, or, in other words, the unity of God the creator and God the redeemer; the Logos, participating, as we have seen, in the work of creation, comes to "His own" by being incarnate in Israel, where the way had been providentially prepared for Him, so that a "true" Israelite, like Nathaniel, recognises Jesus as "the Son of God," although Jesus gives only a hint of the secret of His personality. So it is not against Judaism as such that John rails, it is against a Judaism which, by its unbelief, has ceased to be authentic Judaism. From now on the legitimate heir of the Old Testament is no longer the Synagogue which, not content with disbelief, drives from its bounds those who confess "Jesus Messiah and Son of God," but the Church, the flock which recognises the good shepherd.

By affirming in this way the unity of the revelation within the two Testaments, John is faithful to the theological meaning of history which governs all his thought; he remains faithfully in the line of primitive Christianity and Saint Paul; he has nothing to do with the preoccupations of thinkers like Philo and Ignatius. Here again the originality of John appears clearly, if his point of view is compared with those of the philosopher of Alexandria and the Bishop of Antioch.

Philo speaks of the continuous action of God in terms often cited in connection with one or another passage in John.[14] But the parallelism does not go very far. Philo sees in Genesis mainly a moral history of the human soul, and in Providence an exigency of human intellect which cannot attribute to chance the degree of perfection apparent in the universe.[15] Strictly speaking, in Philo, there is no history of revelation in which the Logos has the central role, as the relationship of the Logos to God is not expressed in temporal terms.

Ignatius did not break away completely from the Christian idea of historic revelation. He knows that "ancient practices" preceded the "new hope,"[16] "the divine plan in reference to the New Man Jesus Christ;"[17] but these references to a revelation before Christ seem like traditional elements which his own thinking has superceded. The accent is elsewhere. Far from associating the Logos with the work of creation and recalling the historic testimonies which foretold and prepared the way for the incarnation of the Son, Ignatius declares that "Jesus Christ, who was with the Father from eternity, appeared at the end of time;"[18] the Word "issued from the silence."[19] In the historical events between the creation and the eschatological accomplishment, the Bishop of Antioch only pauses at the central element: the incarnation, before and after which nothing happens, for the Gospel is not for him a historical fact, in the Johannine sense of the term, it is the "achievement of perfection."[20]

All of this explains Ignatius' ambiguous attitude with regard to the Old Testament. If he declares that the prophets foretold Jesus Christ, the object of their hope and their expectation,[21] he thinks of them, it seems, less as the antecedent witnesses of Christ than as His "disciples by the spirit,"[22] "inspired by his grace;"[23] Jesus, their Master, has raised them from the dead by His coming,[24] and this should not be understood as a temporal resurrection, but as the access to salvation, for "Abraham, Isaac, Jacob and the prophets" are only saved as they pass through "the door to the Father" which is Jesus Christ.[25] In short, "it is not Christianity which believed in Judaism, but Judaism in Christianity."[26]

That is why the Old Covenant has no historical value of itself. In themselves the precepts of Judaism are outmoded tales which only mislead, "a bad yeast which has grown stale and gone sour."[27] It even seems that Ignatius does not wish to recognize any other "documents" or writings than the Gospel.[28] In any case in his writings there are only about ten citations or allusions to the Old Testament, and, contrary to the practice of the Fathers,[29] he never employs arguments from Scripture in discussions with the Jews.

Basically, Ignatius does not give the positive value to the Old Testament which Paul and John accord to it because his static, rather than historic, concept of revelation does not allow him to appreciate the dynamic connection between the two covenants. If one wishes to discover a Marcionite before his time in Christian literature, attention should be turned to the Bishop of Antioch rather than to any of the New Testament writers. Ignatius, by his inability to understand the Old Testament and, as a result, by his attitude of indifference towards it, is about equi-distant between John and Marcion. "He tends towards an a-historical concept of revelation which is not so very different from that of the gnostics."[30]

II

From the central intervention of God through the incarnation of the Son, we have retraced the course of the earlier historical revelations. Now we must look at John's concept of the final end of the work of salvation. Does he think that salvation is realised in the actual giving of divine life to the believer, or does it depend on a final intervention of the Son? In other words, is salvation for John essentially mystical or does it imply an eschaton?

The question may seem irrelevant. Current opinion tends to contrast the mysticism of John with the apocalyptic eschatology of the synoptic Gospels and Saint Paul; it does not hesitate to get rid of the texts in John which are incontestably eschatological. If, so it is said, John speaks of the resurrection of the dead and of judgment "on the last day" (to mention only the most obvious examples), this does not detract from the main thrust of his thought, which concentrates on preoccupation with salvation here and now. So whether these eschatological texts are the evangelist's own words or whether they are editorial additions they represent simply a concession to traditional ideas, intended to win wider acceptance of his Gospel in the Church; but these are ideas which the main thought of the evangelist has left far behind, because it has converted the Christian hope into reality and interiorized it; it has reached an immediate idea of salvation, very far from the eschatological expectations of primitive Christianity.

We must give Bultmann's interpretation a place of its own at this point. According to him, John's intention is not to spiritualize the eschatology of the infant Church nor to transform it into mysticism but to make it the expression of his own thought. Life, in the Johannine sense, is not a collection of mystic experiences, nor a benefit still to come, it is the *decision* with which the believer is constantly faced. What John calls eschatology is an existential stand with regard to a historic fact which is both already past and yet ever present in the preaching of the word: the advent of the Son; this ever present event is the place and time for a *final decision* between God and the world, between life and death. In other words, Johannine eschatology can be defined as a dialectical relationship between the time in which man lives and the eternity of God, a relationship whose teleological end is only "mythological expression."

Although Bultmann uses the expression and the concept of eschatology, he gives them a quite different meaning from that in the New Testament, where the *telos* envisaged by the faith of the believer always means a temporal and not existential conclusion. Though he takes another route Bultmann reaches the same practical result as the critics who interpret John's thought as mystical: he makes eschatology a reality and deletes passages like John 5. 28f. and 6. 39f. which do not fit into his personal concept of last things.[31]

These very quick outlines of the different interpretations of the eschatology of John show that there is no question about eschatological ideas being present in John's Gospel; so much trouble would not be taken to get rid of them in one way or another if they were not there. What is under discussion is the place and the value given by John to eschatology, and also, as a result, the inner cohesion of Johannine thought. Therefore, our concern here is less to reveal the content of the eschatology of the fourth Gospel than it is to define its significance, and to show the role it plays in John's thought. In short it is a question of the relationship of mysticism to eschatology.

Mysticism is, according to Littré's definition, "the claim to know God without any intermediary, and, to some extent, face to face." In this sense, the different currents in hellenistic syncretism are eminently mystical. While the Stoic, for example, discerns God by his intellect,[32] the neo-Platonist and even Philo perceive Him in mystical ecstasy,[33] and the initiate sees Him in the celebration of a mystic rite.[34] Whatever the form may be, this vision of God is not an experience which necessarily makes demands on man's moral capacity; it is a process of deification by which the higher part of man, his spirit or his soul, becomes one with a consubstantial God, by freeing itself from the material and temporal. It is God's spirituality which makes Him inaccessible to those who are not purified through "gnosis" or the mystical experience.

On the other hand, for John, as for all biblical revelation, God cannot be seen because He is holy,[35] and to "see God" does not mean only to become one with Him substantially, but to be able to stand before Him, to receive His forgiveness and His grace. The salvation which God reveals through His Son can only be won by the believer through the mediation of the Son. The Johannine expressions are only mystical if they are interpreted by themselves, taking them out of the historical context in which the evangelist placed the whole work of salvation. Mysticism is subordinate to history.

"No human eye has seen God; the only Son, who is in the Father's bosom - He has made Him known,"[36] this affirmation by John is the dominant feature of his mysticism. Jesus, who alone knows God, is the only one who can reveal Him to us; He is the only way which leads to the Father; it is by seeing Him that we see the Father.[37] And Jesus can say to His disciples: "Apart from me you can do nothing."[38]

Communion of the Christian with God is only possible through faith in Jesus Christ. To believe is to admit that Jesus is not only "the son of Joseph of Nazareth," - as the unbelievers would agree - but also "the Messiah" and "the Son of God," the one sent by the Father to bring divine life to men.[39] In so far as faith perceives the person of Jesus in this way, it develops a knowledge and a view of its object, and thereby a knowledge and a view of the Father. But it is necessary to make it clear that faith must precede the knowledge and the vision; faith is the first step for a man who wishes to respond to the revelation of God in Jesus Christ;[40] only the believer can *see* Jesus as the Son of God and know Him as such, and thereby receive life from Him, in a word: see the Father through the Son.[41]

Faith is not a unique act, nor a series of acts, without any consequence for the moral life of the believer; it implies constant obedience to the commands of Jesus; it is necessary to live in His word in order to be really His disciple. Faith which reaches its completion in obedience creates between the believer and Jesus a relationship similar to that which unites the Son to the Father; through Jesus, the believer is joined to the very source of life. He is then a man "born of God" or "born from on high"; his earthly birth had made him an earthly man; the new birth makes him a being who takes part in the heavenly world: he is saved.

But this salvation is not completed on the level of history. The eruption of the divine life into man's existence does not break the bonds which join him to the earthly world and to the flesh; the new birth does not change the Christian substantially. He remains, as before, in a form suited to his natural environment: life on earth, and fitted for the only life known on earth.[42] The new birth simply qualifies him to enter the divine world when the earthly world disappears.[43] The believer, who possesses eternal life, must therefore pass through death in order to rise again "on the last day," just as the only Son, who possessed life in its fulness, had to die in order to rise again. Thus eternal life and resurrection, which are so often placed together in the fourth Gospel, are not placed in this relationship because of any arbitrary juxtaposition of the Greek idea of the immortality of the soul and the Jewish belief in bodily resurrection, but as a direct result of the temporal dualism which determines the whole of John's thought. It is also by virtue of this dualism that it is not possible to "spiritualize" "heaven" and "interiorize" the Second Coming by saying that it is replaced by the coming of the Spirit into the heart of the believer, in short to make salvation a wholly present reality.[44] On the contrary, salvation now and the salvation to come are organically linked together, and mysticism which, as we have seen, is subordinate to history, is equally subordinate to eschatology.

If the realisation of salvation is thus divided into two stages, it is so by a necessity of providence, as John indicates in several places. In theory we could envisage that the gift of divine life to the believer would break the bonds which unite him to the flesh; earthly death would therefore be the automatic result of the new birth; the man being born to life from on high would, at the same time, be called to God. But God would be left without witnesses on the earth, which would be abandoned to the Prince of this world. This is why the believer, who is no longer *of* the world, nevertheless remains *in* the world to witness to the Christ who has come, just as Moses and the prophets did until John the Baptist witnessed to the Christ who was to come. In other words, the believer remains in the world to assure the transmission of God's historic revelation.

The disciples who were Jesus' contemporaries believed in Him, because they saw the revelation of God in His person, in His words, and in His works. But a similar intervention will not happen again; the incarnation is a unique event. From now on it is up to the disciples, as history unfolds, to lead new generations to the faith, and, by their testimony, to make the saving value of the incarnation of the Son real. Jesus' declaration to Thomas: "Blessed are those who have not seen and yet have believed,"[45] is significant in this respect. It is not a veiled reproach to Thomas, for he is basically in the same position as the other disciples; they all believed in the resurrection after they had *seen* either the empty tomb or the risen Christ. Jesus' words are addressed to the disciples of the future who will not be granted the vision which was given to Thomas. Nobody has the right to demand a repeat performance, for from now on the faith is based on the testimony of the disciples; and these disciples of the future are pronounced "blessed" because their faith, resulting from testimony to the tradition, secures for them the same gift of life as that of the direct faith of the disciples who were Jesus' contemporaries. Jesus Himself prayed for His disciples of all time, those who would be brought to Him through the preaching of His witnesses.[46]

By making, in this way - and for always - the incarnation of Jesus, and faith in this incarnate Jesus, the permanent objective and subjective conditions for salvation, John leaves no room for the pretentions of mystics and Illuminati to win salvation outside the historic revelation given once and for all; he makes redemption not a series of mystical experiences of infinite variety with a purely spiritual Christ as a common denominator, but a historical and eschatological event.

In this regard John's thought has much in common with that of the infant Church and that of Saint Paul. Doubtless the last of the evangelists can be distinguished from the Apostle to the Gentiles by appreciable shades of difference, but they have similar ideas about the relationship between salvation now and the salvation to come, and between mysticism and eschatology.[47]

The Gospel will begin to be interpreted as offering a

true mystique of salvation, when temporal dualism is exchanged for a different conception of the world and of man, with a different idea of redemption, very close to the theories developed by Hellenistic syncretism. Here again, the first witness to this change would seem to be the Bishop of Antioch.

Ignatius of Antioch, who was indifferent to history, as we have seen, seems even less concerned with the end of history. Although he preserves several elements of the eschatological vocabulary of Paul and John, he obviously does not understand these terms in the same way as they do, because for him, salvation is no longer realised at the eschatological level but at the mystical level.[48] The contrast between the present world and the world to come has disappeared from his horizon; Jesus Christ appeared "at the end of time";[49] the resurrection is not eschatological, it follows immediately after the believer's death, in imitation of that of Christ;[50] for the believer, as for Christ, it is the means of reaching God.[51] The resurrection of Jesus does not mark the beginning of an "eschatological time"[52] as it does in Paul and John, at the end of which is the completion of redemption, but a cycle of ascents towards God: the faithful follower, in imitation of Jesus, reaches "the pure light" and himself becomes *Logos*.[53]

In short, for the historical and eschatological idea of salvation, Ignatius substitutes a "mysticism of the imitation of Christ and of unity." For him, the Gospel is less the proclamation of the Kingdom of God than the realisation of the immortality of man, and the question is no longer how God will establish His Kingdom, but how man can escape from this evil world and reach substantial unity with God. To this question which results from the radical dualism of the Hellenistic and Eastern worlds of that time, Ignatius replies with a mysticism foreign to the thought of the New Testament, and whose motif is related to the more or less gnostic idea of a celestial course which the faithful must follow in the steps of their Savior.[54]

III

Does John, who has taken nothing essential from syncretism to express his ideas about revelation and redemption, owe to syncretism his ideas about the Lord's Supper? This has been asserted. The eucharistic teaching of the fourth Gospel, it is said, is based on the miracle of the multiplying of the loaves,[55] and this miracle is "the prototype of the Eucharist, the mythical event which inaugurated the Christian communion service. Not content with inaugurating it in this way, the Johannine Christ, in a long speech which is connected to the miracle as a kind of commentary, formulates a theory of the sacrament. Nothing is more consistent with the role of the great revealer and the great mystagogy attributed to him; but nothing shows better how essential ritual symbolism and the mystical idea of the sacrament are to the theology, the 'religion' and the 'Christianity' of the fourth Gospel" ... "Here we have utter mystery."[56]

There seems to us to be no basis for this interpretation. If it is obvious that chapter 6 of the Gospel of John is an entity in itself, it is also certain that it does not offer any new information; it is one of the variations on the single theme of the Gospel; the gift of divine life by Jesus. There is no indication to make us suppose that the evangelist here is unfaithful to the general premises of his entire thought; if the "sign" which John describes here is original, it still illustrates the same idea: the manifestation of salvation through the words and work of the Son.[57]

This revelation is developed, as is common in John, in three clearly defined stages: first of all there is the concrete fact; the multiplying of the loaves, and the different events connected with that; the gift of life is presented in the form of the multiplied loaves, and the evangelist informs us that we are witnesses to a sign - that is an act of Jesus which shows His redemptive power (v. 1-25). Secondly we have the explanation of this sign by Jesus in what is known as the sermon on the bread of life (v. 26-65). Thirdly, there is the decision imposed upon the hearers by this appeal from on high; the unbelief of many and the strengthened faith of the disciples (v. 66-71).

The bread of life discourse is divided into two parts. In the first part (v. 26-51), Jesus presents Himself as the bread of heaven given by the Father; whoever eats this bread of life, that is whoever believes in Him, possesses eternal life. In the second part (v. 51-65), Jesus adds that this bread is His flesh which He will give for the life of the world. The realism of the expression becomes even more impressive when Jesus, in reply to the murmurings of the Jews, develops His thought in these terms: "Truly, truly, I say to you, unless you eat the flesh of the Son of man and drink his blood, you have no life in you; he who eats my flesh and drinks my blood has eternal life, and I will raise him up at the last day." The verses which follow, assert again that this flesh and this blood are the essential nourishment for divine life, and the speech ends with this warning: "It is the spirit that gives you life, the flesh is of no avail. The words that I have spoken to you are spirit and life."

The bread of life discourse is so far from formulating any *ex professo* instructions about the eucharist that some excellent exegetes consider it to be an integral part of faith in Christ. This interpretation is to some extent legitimate but - like that of the speech on the Lord's Supper - it does not take into account either the obvious progression from one section of the speech to another or the very fine subtleties of the text.[58] We think that the first part is speaking about faith in Christ and that only the second part alludes to the eucharist. However we would be wrong to give an explanation of the second part without taking into account what precedes it, for the two lessons are linked one with the other. It is a matter of accepting the divine gift brought by Jesus in one way or another; whether by the incarnation, or by the eucharist; what is new is the position of the giver and the recipients. In the first part Jesus is present in person in the middle of His hearers. In the second, Jesus envisages the future and shows how the believers will continue to be nourished by the same bread, after His death and His glorification.[59] We are, on the one hand, in the time of Jesus' earthly life, and, on the other, in the time when the Church realizes the eternal presence of Jesus in the celebration of the eucharist. We see immediately that John makes a very close connection between the incarnation and the eucharist, both of which "signify" the same gift of life from the same Jesus.[60]

The exegesis of this connection will explain the significance of the Johannine eucharist for us. To penetrate the meaning of it we must start with the text itself. One part of Jesus' hearers misunderstood the meaning of His words. What is the nature of this misunderstanding?

His human origin is brought up by the Jews against the Jesus who claims that He is the heavenly bread; against Jesus' affirmation that to have life one must eat His flesh, the Jews argue that that is an impossibility. To be precise these are not two different objections; it is the same criticism viewed from two different aspects. The idea of divine nourishment was familiar to the Jews; the Messiah was to make manna descend from heaven, as Moses had done formerly for the people in the desert, and the Messianic manna would excel over the material manna given by Moses as the eschatological Savior would surpass the first deliverer of the people; but certainly, the gift and the giver must be divine. Now Jesus is "the son of Joseph" and not greater than Moses; His heavenly bread is His own flesh and not manna from heaven, that form of Messianic grace. Let us define these two aspects of the problem and see how Jesus replies to them.

The Jews first of all stumble against the problem of the earthly characteristics of the person of Jesus; the one whose human origins are known cannot come from heaven. In a word, the Jews deny the incarnation. The proof of this is in the urgent appeals by Jesus to the faith of the hearers, which can be heard throughout the whole discourse, from the declaration in verse 29 that *to believe* is, for man, "to do the work of God," to the last words of Jesus, permeated with unspeakable sadness: "But there are some of you who do not believe!" The object of faith is, here again, "Jesus, Messiah and Son of God." Hence this insistence on repeating on almost every line that Jesus is the authorized envoy of God *His* Father, that He comes from heaven, that it is divine life which He brings in an earthly form. This is why in a last desperate attempt to vanquish the unbelief which His testimony has not yet shaken, Jesus ends by saying that it is the spirit that gives life and not the flesh. In short, if the words and the person of Jesus give life, it is because they do not come from the earthly world, but from the divine world which alone possesses life from the Spirit.

There is no contradiction between the declaration that "the flesh is of no avail" and the words which precede it, presenting the flesh of Jesus as the bread of heaven. Of itself flesh can do nothing; or, to speak John's language, faith is not fed by the "son of Joseph" but by the Son of God incarnate in him. This means that, in the eucharist, faith is not nourished by the bread, but by the person of Jesus which the bread *signifies*. In both cases, it is under an earthly aspect and by an earthly mediator that the believers receive the gift of divine life, but this earthly reality is not an obstacle to the transmission of the divine gift. The human reality of Jesus does not prevent him from being the divine Word,[61] and the earthly reality of the eucharist (the bread and the wine) does not prevent it from being the means by which the Son makes His presence real among His followers. While the contemporary disciples saw and heard Jesus in the flesh and, through faith, saw in Him the Son of God "encamped" among them, believers, who were not witnesses of the incarnation, benefit from it by participating in the eucharist, the sign of the continual presence of the Word in the midst of those who believe in Him.

We should note, however, that the eucharist is not another incarnation in a different form. This would be the case if Jesus were present in the elements; but this theory is foreign to Johannine thought. In reality the eucharist is a memorial and a prolonging of the unique incarnation.

Our interpretation seems to be confirmed by the other aspect of the problem which the Jews find in the words of Jesus: the fact that they interpret in a literal sense: "the bread which I will give to you is my flesh." They express their objections in the same terms as those used by Nicodemus, to whom Jesus was explaining the new birth.[62] Instead of clarifying the problem, Jesus repeats the same thought in even more ambiguous terms. The process here again is the same one He followed in the explanation to Nicodemus. The Jews, therefore, are mistaken in interpreting the words about Jesus "the food of divine life" in the same way as Nicodemus interpreted the words about the new birth. In chapter 6, as in chapter 3, the misunderstanding arises from the fact that the *spiritual* meaning is not understood and the hearers interpret in a *physical* sense words which are Spirit and Life. Not a single man can return to his mother's womb to be born again - such an action is by nature impossible, and the new birth is not a miracle which overcomes the powerlessness of nature, but something of a quite different order - nor can the Christian consume a food which is in actual substance the flesh of Christ. What the believer eats in the eucharist is bread, but this bread is the *sign* of the spiritual presence and saving action of Jesus.

To sum up, the Johannine theory of the eucharist can be stated as follows: the Word became flesh; He dwelt among us; in His flesh, that is in His human form, He gave Himself for the life of the world; He returned to the Father; He continues to give the life which He gave through His incarnation to the believers in the eucharist, which is His flesh, that is, it reveals His presence and His action in a way just as real and effective as "the son of Joseph" revealed them to the eyes of the disciples in His own time.

Neither pure symbol, nor sacrament in a magical sense, the eucharist has a double value:

1) As a memorial of the incarnation, it places the believers who communicate in the eucharistic elements on a level of spiritual equality with the first disciples who saw the Word incarnate; in that way it makes real the unity of believers in their assurance of salvation, just as the testimony of faith makes this unity real as far as revelation is concerned.[63]

2) Tangible food of the faith, the eucharist is to faith

what action is to the word in the revelatory work of Jesus.[64] To the two ways (word and work) of divine testimony there are two corresponding ways of accepting salvation: faith, and participation in the eucharist.

Like faith, the eucharist belongs to the realities of "the eschatological time." When the end comes, the signified presence in the eucharist will be replaced by the immediate presence, just as faith will be replaced by sight.

Thus the idea of the eucharist outlined by John is in complete harmony with the dominant characteristics and the main ideas of his thought. He is very far from making the Christian eucharist a mystery and there is no firm indication of any influence of Hellenistic mysticism on this particular point. Moreover the Johannine eucharist is not a materialization or an allegorical spiritualization of the Pauline idea; John linked the idea of the eucharist organically to his own thought by his own personal reflection and meditation; his theory of the eucharist follows a line parallel to the line taken by Saint Paul. Paul himself "is inspired not by the details of the ceremony nor even by traditional explanations, which had been handed on to him, but by its inherent eschatology and mysticism."[65] This is why neither Paul nor John reached the conclusion that Christ was physically present in the elements of the eucharist.[66]

The eucharist can only be understood as a quasi physical food of immortality when redemption itself is conceived according to categories which are more physical than moral, and when salvation is less the creation of a personal communion of the believer with the Savior who regenerates him than a process of making the believer divine in the image of his Savior. Such is the conception of Ignatius of Antioch.

For Ignatius, as we have seen, the Gospel is above all the realization of the immortality of man. Now it is the eucharist which provides the practical realization of this immortality; the eucharist is "a medicine of immortality, and the antidote which wards off death,"[67] for the elements are in reality the flesh and the blood of Christ. If therefore Ignatius reproduces the eucharistic expressions of John,[68] he understands them literally, as Nicodemus understood the teaching about the new birth, because he does not interpret them within the framework of Johannine thought, but according to his own theology. Here we can truly speak of sacramental realism, but here we are very far from Paul and John.[69]

Historical realism or mystico-sacramental realism - these were the alternatives within which we had placed the enigma of Johannine thought. The solution has already been written in the replies we have given along the way. And so we can conclude briefly.

The specific characteristics of Johannine thought are foreign to syncretism, and nothing which is characteristic of syncretism can be found in John.

The thought of Ignatius appears in a quite different light. Seduced and overcome, at least in part, by his environment, the Bishop of Antioch interprets the gifts of the Gospel according to a Hellenistic view of the world and of man, and would exegete them along these lines. He is inclined to make primitive Christianity, which for John is still a history and an eschatology, into sacramental mysticism.

In Ignatius there is no intention, no conscious and avowed design to bring together Christianity and Hellenism, no trace of the attempt to do so which will be made by the apologists in the second century, and which the school at Alexandria will effect later. Born in a pagan land, doubtless even born a pagan, Ignatius quite naturally translates into Hellenistic terms the ideas on which his Christian faith thrives and by which it is expressed. By his attitude "we can measure the extent of the danger which threatened Christianity as soon as it spread outside its Jewish environment: it ran the risk of merely existing according to the need of redemption of the Hellenistic or oriental settings of syncretism in which it found itself, and of being reduced to a kind of mystery religion or gnostic system somewhat more realistic than others."[70]

Was the last witness of the tradition - we can now give this title to John - already aware of the danger? Perhaps. In any case John's work remains a serious, though indirect, warning to those who are tormented with the preoccupation of adapting Christian faith to the aspirations of a particular time; it proclaims that the Gospel is inseparably linked to a historic foundation given once and for all, without which there is no authentic Christianity. It is understandable that Saint Irenaeus saw in John "the intention to establish the rule of truth in the Church."[71]

One last question makes us pause here: who is John? We cannot give the answer - to do so we would need to look at many other aspects of the Johannine problem than the one we have studied here - but we can at least say that our study points the possible answers in a single direction.

The testimony of sublime majesty given to the historic revelation of God in Jesus Christ and to the normative value of this revelation which is provided by the "Gospel according to Saint John" is the work of a mind born and shaped in the land of Judaism. It is only there that the writer could acquire such a profound sense of history, it is there that he found the strength to resist victoriously the pressure exerted on every cultivated mind of that time by Hellenistic syncretism.

NOTES

1. This article reproduces the contents of two studies. One of these was a lecture given at the convocation of the Faculté de théologie de l'Eglise libre of Lausanne on October 20, 1938, under the title: *The Johannine Idea of the Eucharist.* The second was given at a meeting of the Societé des pasteurs et ministres neuchâtelois at Neuchâtel on January 25, 1939, with the title: *The Historic Realism of the Gospel of John.* It appeared in the *Revue de théologie et de philosophie,* n.s. 28, 1940, p. 233-261.

2. This is C. B. Allo's expression, "La philosophie grecque dans le Nouveau Testament," *Annales de l'institut supérieur de philosophie* (Louvain), 1922, p. 293.

3. A. Schweitzer, *Die Mystik des Apostels Paulus* (1930): XIII: Die Hellenisierung der Mystik Pauli durch Ignatius und die johanneische Theologie (p. 324-364); A. Schweitzer, *The Mysticism of Paul the Apostle,* London, 1931.--W. von Löwenich, *Das Johannes-Verständnis im zweiten Jahrhundert* (1932) followed Schweitzer's interpretation: "A. Schweitzer hat wohl aufs Ganze richtig gesehen, wenn er den Trennungsstrich nicht zwischen Paulus - Ignatius einerseits, Johannes andererseits, sondern zwischen Ignatius - Johannes auf der einen Seite, Paulus auf der anderen zieht, und wenn er das Merkmal der ganz anderen Welt bei Ignatius - Johannes in dem starken Zurücktreten des jüdischen Elementes erblickt," (p. 27).--But the members of the opposition have been more numerous; cf. W. Michaelis, "Das Johannesevangelium und die Hellenisierung des Christentums," *Kirchenblatt für die reformierte Schweiz,* 1930, p. 257-264; M. Goguel, *Revue d'hist. et de philos. relig.,* 1931, p. 208, etc.

4. On this point, apart from the works mentioned by W. von Löwenich in his bibliography, cf. Th. Preiss, "La mystique de l'imitation du Christ et de l'unité chez Ignace d'Antioche," *Revue d'hist. et de philos. relig.,* 1938, p. 197-241; H.-W. Bartsch, *Gnostisches Gut und Gemeindetradition im Denken des Ignatius von Antiochen,* Dissert. Heidelberg, 1939.

5. J. Réville, *Le quatrième évangile,* 2ème éd. (1902), p. 105f.

6. M. J. Lagrange, "Vers le Logos de saint Jean," *Revue Biblique,* 1923, p. 321-371; F. Buechsel, *Johannes und*

der hellenistische Synkretismus, 1928, p. 23, 32, 42f; H. Kleinknecht and G. Kittel, in *Theologisches Wörterbuch zum Neuen Testament,* IV, p. 88f. and 134 f.

7. M. J. Lagrange, "Le réalisme historique de l'évangile selon saint Jean," *Revue Biblique,* 1937, p. 340.

8. The expression belongs to Th. Preiss, in the article cited, p. 223f.--On the idea of history as the revelation which is to be found in the Old Testament but is lacking in oriental religions cf. F. Baumgartel, *Die Eigenart der alttestamentlichen Frömmigkeit,* p. 68f. and 75. For his part, F. C. Burkitt, *Church and Gnosis* (1932), has shown that gnosticism has misunderstood this idea of history, and consequently, it substituted religious speculation, nurtured by the science and philosophy of the time, for the "annalistic" faith of the Old and New Testaments, thus destroying the central idea of primitive Christianity that God is revealed through "factual happenings."

9. The eighth treatise of the first *Ennead:* Πόθεν τὰ κακά is nothing but a kind of philosophical sermon on the theme ὕλη = τὸ κακόν; cf. one of the most characteristic texts, *Enn.,* I, VIII, 4: Ὥστε τὸ εἶδος μᾶλλον ἢ τὴν ὕλην τὸ κακὸν εἶναι. [The objection comes from Plato, *Timaeus* 87b] καὶ οὕτως οὐδὲν ἧττον τὴν ὕλην συγχωρεῖν ἀναγκασθήσεται τὸ κακὸν εἶναι. "Evil is then form rather than matter. Even if all these facts are true, it must nevertheless be admitted that *evil is matter.*"

10. Cf. Romans 6 and 7, especially 6. 2: τὸν τοῦ θεοῦ θέλοντα εἶναι κόσμῳ μὴ χαρίσησθε μηδὲ ὕλῃ ἐξαπατήσητε and 7. 2: ὁ ἐμὸς ἔρως ἐσταύρωται καὶ οὐκ ἔστιν ἐν ἐμοὶ πῦρ φιλόυλον. --Ignatius' study of anthropology, the use he makes of the terms σάρξ, ψυχή, and πνεῦμα (in the human sense), also shows that he was greatly influenced by Hellenism; his thought seems trichotomic in *Philad.* 11. 2. New Testament anthropology is not trichotomic; in the only text to be quoted on this subject, I Thessalonians 5.23 (ὁλόκληρον ὑμῶν τὸ πνεῦμα καὶ ἡ ψυχὴ καὶ τὸ σῶμα ἀμέμπτως...) it is more a question of the divine πνεῦμα, within the Christian, and Paul's thought is almost the same as that found in the *Martyrdom of Polycarp,* XIV. 2 (= Eusebius, *Eccl. Hist.,* IV, 15, 33).

11. Cf. John 1. 45; 5. 39 and 46; 7. 38; 11. 18; 17. 12; 19. 24, etc.

12. Cf. John 5. 35.

13. H. Windisch, *Der Sinn der Bergpredigt,* 2. Aufl., p. 103. John would be the third Marcionite in the New Testament, the first two being the writer of chapter 5 of Matthew's Gospel and Saint Paul.

14. Cf. for example, Philo, *Legum Allegoricae* I. 5 and John 5. 17.

15. See, particularly, *Legum Allegoricae* and *De Providentia.*

16. *Magnesians* 9. 1.

17. *Ephesians* 20. 1.

18. *Magnesians* 6. 1.

19. *Magnesians* 8. 2; cf. also *Ephesians* 19. 1.

20. *Philadelphians* 9. 2.

21. *Philadelphians* 9. 2 and 5. 2.

22. *Magnesians* 9. 2.

23. *Magnesians* 8. 2.

24. *Magnesians* 9. 2. Παρών and παρουσία refer in Ignatius to the incarnation.

25. *Philadelphians* 9. 1.

26. *Magnesians* 10. 3.

27. *Magnesians* 8. 1 and 10. 2.

28. Cf. the abstruse text of *Philadelphians* 8. 2.

29. Cf. N. Bonwetsch, "Der Schriftbeweis für die Kirche aus den Heiden als das wahre Israël bis auf Hippolyt," *Theologische Studien Theodor Zahn zum 10. Oktober 1908 dargebracht,* p. 3-22.

30. Th. Preiss in the article cited, p. 225.

31. R. Bultmann, "Die Eschatologie des Johannesevangeliums," *Zwischen den Zeiten,* 1928, p. 4-22 (= *Glauben und Verstehen,* p. 134-152). --On the question as a whole, cf. G. Staehlin, "Zum Problem der johanneischen Eschatologie,"

Zeitschrift für die neutestamentliche Wissenschaft, 1934, p. 225-259.

32. Man perceives God through νοῦς, for νοῦς is in man ἀπόσπασμα θεοῦ, in other words a *particle* of a God who is himself the universal νοῦς-λόγος (Marcus Aurelius, V, 27, 1).

33. Cf. for example Philo's treatise: *Quis rerum divinarum heres sit?*

34. Cf. the account of the initiation into the cult of Isis given by Apuleius (*Metam.* XI, 23): "Accessi confinium mortis et calcato Proserpinae limine per omnia vectus elementa remeavi, nocte media vidi solem candido coruscentem lumine, deos inferos et deos superos accessi coram et adoravi de proxumo." (I approached the boundaries of death and after standing on Proserpine's threshold, I returned across all the elements; in the middle of the night I saw the sun shine dazzling bright; I presented myself face to face with the gods infernal and the gods celestial and I worshipped them."

35. For the contrast between these two types of vision and these two ideas of God, cf. G. Kittel, *Die Religionsgeschichte und das Urchristentum*, p. 95f; R. Bultmann, "Untersuchungen zum Johannes-evangelium, B: θεὸν οὐδεὶς ἑώρακεν πώποτε," *Zeitschrift für die neutestamentliche Wissenschaft*, 1930, p. 169-192.

36. John 1. 18.

37. Cf. John 14. 6f; 16. 5 and 27; 17 *passim*.

38. John 15. 5.

39. Except in two places (John 12. 44 and 14. 2) it is always Jesus and not God who is the object of faith.

40. Verses like John 16. 30 and 17. 8, where knowledge is mentioned before faith, do not contradict this assertion. In these passages it is a question of faith coming out of knowledge; the writer's thought is that knowledge, born of the attachment to Jesus and to His word, that is born of faith, is proper in its turn to affirm faith. --Cf. "La foi dans l'Evangile de Jean," *Cahiers bibliques de Foi et Vie*, I, number 2, p. 27-43.

41. For believers, faith remains the indispensable intermediary in the historic order, and sight belongs to the eschatological order. If God was more immediately

visible in the person of the Word incarnate, whose "glory the first disciples have seen," it is because the benefits of the world to come are already present, in anticipation, at the time of the incarnation. But this vision always comes out of faith; it is significant that only the believers saw the risen Christ. Jesus, "the Saint of God," is the only one to have a direct vision of God; Jesus alone does not "believe" in God but *sees* Him in the properly mystical sense.

42. "Nobody could suppress the laws of existence, which give a carnal mortality to a carnal body, the result of a carnal birth, by a teleology inherent in its whole being." (J. Héring, *Le Royaume de Dieu et sa venue*, p. 211.)

43. This qualification is necessary, since John does not believe that man is endowed with an immortal soul. To make John a Platonist, is the πρῶτον ψεῦδος of spiritualist philosophy, which would like to recognize one of its own in the fourth evangelist. John is a stranger to the synthesis between Judaism and Platonism suggested by the *Wisdom of Solomon* and by Philo. The Johannine idea of life buries its roots in Palestinian Judaism and not in the Hellenistic Judaism of Alexandria (cf. F. Buechsel, *Johannes und der hellenistische Synkretismus*, p. 55; H. Pribnow, *Die johanneische Anschauung vom "Leben"*, p. 41f.).

John is so little an "immortalist" that he speaks of "resurrection to judgment" to illustrate the idea that the unbelievers will understand, at the Second Coming, that they have scorned the divine gift. As the "resurrection" is reserved by definition, in John, for those who, through faith, have accepted this gift of divine life, an incoherency or possible interpolation can be seen in the only text where John speaks of "resurrection to judgment," that is a resurrection which shows a state of condemnation, along with "resurrection to life" which affirms that the believer is definitely given possession of divine life (John 5. 29). It is rather by virtue of what is called so justly his *irony* that John can qualify as a "resurrection" (to judgment) an event which is the opposite of resurrection in the proper sense.

It is worth recalling that John, like Saint Paul, does not envisage a resurrection of the flesh - which would be unthinkable on Johannine or Pauline grounds - but a resurrection of the person (of the body, says Saint Paul) which is not the same thing. "Flesh is of no use at all!"

44. We find it difficult to see in any of the texts in chapters 14 to 16 the idea that Christ comes to find His faithful, one by one, at the moment of their deaths. John

is only concerned with the resurrection "on the last day," and while affirming that whoever has received divine life is not robbed of it by death, he says nothing about the lot of the Christian in the interval between his death and the resurrection at the Parousia. That is a purely speculative problem. Faith envisages these two moments as simultaneous, so to speak, because it cannot imagine the believer ever being deprived of communion with Jesus. The most significant fact for our study is that John does not eliminate the idea of an eschatological and collective salvation in favor of a mystical and individualistic one. The end of redemption is not the believer's attainment of immortality, but the re-establishment of the universal Kingdom of God.

45. John 20. 29.

46. John 17. 21; cf. 20. 31.

47. Cf. M. Goguel, "L'apocalypse paulinienne," *Revue de théol. et de philos.*, 1939, p. 33-47. --The most noticeable difference between Paul and John, from the point of view of our study, is that while John keeps eschatology, he discards apocalyptic.

48. We have already noted that Ignatius means by παρουσία the entrance of Jesus into history. -- Αἰών means: in the plural, eternity, without any idea of contrast with historic time; in the singular, the world as the center of the opposition to God and to Christ, of which Satan is the leader. -- Βασιλεία (once only, in the plural) means "the kingdoms of this world," αἱ βασιλεῖαι τοῦ αἰῶνος τούτου (*Romans* 6. 1); Ignatius never speaks of the Kingdom of God or of Christ. -- Τέλος means the time of the incarnation (*Magnesians* 6. 1) or the end of the believer's life on earth (*Ephesians* 14. 2; *Romans* 10. 3) and never has an eschatological meaning. -- Ἔσχατος, except in the expression ἔσχατοι καιροί, about which we shall have more to say later, has a moral meaning: Ignatius considers himself as "the least" of the faithful (*Ephesians* 21. 2; *Trallians* 13. 1; *Romans* 9. 2; *Smyrnians* 11. 1). -- We could continue further on this point.

49. To be more precise there are two "ends of time" in Ignatius: 1) the incarnation: Jesus appeared ἐν τέλει (*Magnesians* 6. 1); 2) the death of Ignatius (ἔσχατοι καιροί, *Ephesians* 11. 1); it cannot be a question of the eschatological end here because the Church is established and secured (*Ephesians* 12. 1), and Ignatius' exhortations have in view worship and the eucharist, not concern for last things.

This duality results from the mysticism of imitation which makes the fate of Ignatius parallel to that of Jesus.

50. Cf. the passages in the epistles of Ignatius where he speaks of his resurrection and that of the Christians: *Ephesians* 11. 2; *Romans* 4. 3; *Smyrnians* 7. 1. -- In *Polycarp* 7. 1, instead of ἐν τῇ ἀναστάσει "on the day of resurrection" read: ἐν τῇ αἰτήσει "thanks to your prayers" (Lightfoot, Lelong).

51. Cf. *Magnesians* XIV, I; *Romans* 1. 2; 2. 1, etc.

52. Cf. E. Peterson, *Le mystère des Juifs et des Gentils dans l'Eglise*, p. 72: "I call 'eschatological time' the period which began after the first coming of Christ and which ends with His second coming. I call it 'eschatological time' because it is specifically ordered at the end, at the ἔσχατον." This linear idea of time and eschatology which is that of primitive Christianity and of John, is essentially different from the Hellenic idea of cyclical time, in the framework of which Ignatius interprets the Gospel. We might add that the eschatology of the dialectic school and of Bultmann owes much more to this latter concept than to the New Testament idea.

53. *Romans* 2. 1. -- There is a sense of similarity with the Stoic and neo-Platonist idea of the plurality of the *logoi* (cf. H. Kleinknecht, in *Theologisches Wörterbuch zum Neuen Testament*, IV, p. 89.) An affirmation like that of Ignatius would be blasphemous, if not unthinkable, for John, for whom there is only one *logos*.

54. Cf. Th. Preiss in the article cited, p. 218-219 and 209.

55. John 6.

56. A. Loisy, *Les mystères païens et le mystère chrétien*, 2ème éd., p. 287f.

57. We cannot go into here all the questions raised by what John did and did not say about the Lord's Supper. On these problems and on recent research on the subject, cf. E. Lohmeyer, "Vom urchristlichen Abendmahl," in *Theologische Rundschau*, 1937, p. 300-312.

58. In particular the use of the expressions σάρξ and αἷμα (after verse 53), which together correspond to ἄρτος = σάρξ (v. 51). The word σάρξ in itself would be sufficient to designate the eucharist, for it means a complete entity,

like σῶμα in the Pauline expression in I Cor. 11. 24-24 (cf. J. Héring, *op. cit.*, p. 224). If John mentions "the blood" along with "the flesh" it is doubtless because he was influenced by the eucharistic practice in the Church of his time (communion in two kinds). But αἷμα has no specific value and we do not have two different ideas of the eucharist here (the opinion of J. Héring, p. 224, n. 2).

59. The present tense in verses 32-50 puts into sharp relief the future tense of verse 51: δώσω and verse 62 clearly allude to the return of the Son to the Father.

60. This is the reason why John uses the word σάρξ in preference to the word σῶμα which is found in the other eucharistic texts in the New Testament (synoptic Gospels and Paul). The Word was made *flesh;* this flesh which gives life to the world, when Jesus shows Himself there in person, continues to give life through the eucharist.

61. That is why (to digress for a moment) it is not right to accuse the evangelist of docetism. In 6. 42 it is not only the Jews who regard Jesus as "the son of Joseph." For John too the humanity of the Word incarnate is very real. It is not from the point of view of civilian status that Jesus is different for believers and unbelievers.

62. Cf. 3. 4; 6. 52 and also 9. 16; 6. 60; in these four passages, the expression πῶς δύναται (in the final instance τίς δύναται) indicates an absolute impossibility.

63. This is why John gives no words of institution as such, but only an announcement of the eucharist which the Church will celebrate after the death of Jesus. To write his Gospel John puts himself in the position of the believer (and the unbeliever) of his time. He envisages the eucharist as the remembrance not of a particular action on the part of Jesus, but of the gift of His person which Jesus made throughout all His ministry. What Jesus gave on the occasion of the Last Supper (according to the synoptic Gospels) He offered through the entire work of His incarnate life and He offers it still in the eucharist, according to John. Hence the eucharistic teaching, in the fourth Gospel, is intended for a wide audience (actual participation in the eucharistic being reserved for the future and for the believers) just as by the incarnation the Son revealed Himself to the *whole world* (only the believers actually benefiting from the incarnation).

64. The word and the work are not two independent ways

of revelation but two aspects of a single way, by virtue of the principle that God enters history and manifests divine life in signs directly affirming the truth announced in the word. In the same way faith and the eucharist are only one and the same means of grace. The law of the incarnation rules the whole of Johannine thought.

65. J. Héring, *op. cit.*, p. 222. -- In Paul σῶμα means the Church, the body of Christ, while in John σάρξ is the person of Jesus.

66. We mentioned this earlier with regard to John. It is certain also that "any theory about the presence (of Christ) in the elements is outside the horizons of Paulinism" (J. Héring, *op. cit.*, p. 227). "Communion in the actual blood, like in the flesh of Christ is, as far as Paul is concerned, absolutely unthinkable," says M. Goguel in "Le rôle de l'apôtre Paul dans la constitution des sacrements chrétiens (baptême et eucharistie)," *Revue de l'histoire des religions*, CXVII (1938), p. 200. As he sees in Paul a realistic and sacramental idea of the eucharist he adds, "There is something strange in the Pauline system here, which is there by survival and by heritage." But we have no evidence to indicate that the primitive Church understood the eucharist in this sense either before or after Paul. If there is a polemical point in John's explanations, the attack would not be on a sacramental theory which would come to light in the Church, but on the inability of the Jews to understand the meaning and the value of the eucharist (cf. Justin Martyr, *Dial.* CXVII, 3). Ignatius himself has to struggle to make his interpretation of the eucharist prevail (cf. *Smyrnians* VII, 1-2), which seems to suggest that his conception was a new one.

67. *Ephesians* 20. 2; cf. *Ephesians* 13. 1.

68. Cf. *Ephesians* 5. 2; *Romans* 7. 3; *Smyrnians* 7. 1; *Philadelphians* 4, etc. -- It can be noted too that Ignatius is an anti-Docetist as strong as John, but he is so by virtue of his sacramental realism, while John is so by virtue of his historical realism. Nothing shows better that the parallelism of expression in the two authors is a cover for different theologies.

69. Cf. M. Goguel in the article cited, p. 204.

70. Th. Preiss in the article cited, p. 240.

71. "Volens ... regulam veritatis constituere in Ecclesia," Irenaeus, *Adv. haer.*, III, II, I.

Johannine Studies from Bultmann to Barrett[1]

During the last ten years Johannine studies have not been abandoned; far from it.[2] R. Bultmann's commentary on the Gospel and his Theology of the New Testament have revived the debate.[3] In England, Professor C. H. Dodd, of Cambridge, has published his great work, *The Interpretation of the Fourth Gospel*,[4] which he preceded by many valuable studies.[5] More recently, one of the better representatives of the younger generation of British scholars, C. K. Barrett, has devoted an important commentary to the Gospel, of a standard comparable with that of the older works of men like Westcott and Bernard.[6]

The important contribution of these three scholars has been recognised everywhere and has, quite rightly, attracted and held considerable attention.[7] At the same time many other works have appeared, more modest in format but of equally great interest. First of all the commentaries: those by D. Mollat,[8] M. E. Boismard,[9] and L. Bouyer[10] in French; by A. Wikenhauser[11] and H. Strathmann[12] in German; by W. F. Howard A. J. Gossip[13] and R. H. Lightfoot[14] in English. Then there are the introductions to the New Testament by A. Wikenhauser[15] and W. Michaelis;[16] and finally the expositions of Johannine theology by O. Cullman,[17] E. K. Lee,[18] J. Dupont,[19] F. Mussner,[20] F. M. Braun,[21] W. Grossouw,[22] and by J. Bonsirven in his *Théologie du Nouveau Testament*.[23] To this list can be added many important monographs and countless periodical articles.[24]

Enthusiasm for Johannine studies, which has always been ardent, has been further stimulated by the discovery, in the Qumran writings, of a whole world of expressions and ideas which seem as though they can only belong, on a Jewish basis, to the fourth Gospel. Finally the very recent publication of a new papyrus, apparently dating from the beginning of the third century and containing the first fourteen chapters of the Gospel,[25] will not fail to give an added thrust to the study of the Johannine text and of the numerous interesting variants it offers.

It would be wearisome to describe one after the other the characteristics of the new publications or even of the most significant of them. It is better to review the main questions posed by the fourth Gospel and point out the answers given to these questions in recent works.

I. The Literary Question

1) The Composition

Let us start with the solution suggested by R. Bultmann. We recall that, in his opinion, the Evangelist makes use of three main sources, a didactic source - the *Offenbarungsreden*, and two narrative sources - a collection of signs given by Jesus *(Semeia-Quelle)* and an account of the passion independent of the Synoptics. An ecclesiastical editor has touched up the work of the Evangelist and has added to it the texts relating to baptism, the eucharist and apocalyptic eschatology. On the other hand, the editor, and the Evangelist himself before him, left the work in an unfortunate state of disarray which the exegete must put to rights by some necessary transpositions. In short, Bultmann unites to the method of defining the separate sources the art of rearranging the pericopes.

The literary theories of the Marburg Professor have been, and still are, much under discussion. It is interesting to pursue the point further: one of the first expressions of scepticism came from E. Hirsch,[26] who, twenty years ago, in two almost forgotten works on the fourth Gospel, introduced the idea of an editor as well as the Evangelist himself, but along lines quite different from those of Bultmann. In three studies published between 1947 and 1954, and devoted to the composition of chapters 6, 7 and 10 of the Gospel, J. Schneider maintains that Bultmann's analyses destroy the essential unity of these chapters, a unity which is quite obvious if it is recognised that the Evangelist is applying his own rules of composition.[27]

Two important monographs took up the problem of the composition in its entirety and declared in favor of the literary unity of the Gospel. E. Ruckstuhl, in a most meticulous work[28] which had been foreshadowed by two articles in *Divus Thomas* (1945), completes the list of the characteristics of Johannine style that E. Schweizer had already noted, and he showed that they are divided almost equally between the different sources singled out by Bultmann. B. Noack[29] is of the opinion that the existence of *Offenbarungsreden* and a *Semeia-Quelle* is far from proved and that it is much more likely that John draws on the oral tradition which was still alive at the end of the first century, without any recourse to written sources or the Synoptics. On the other hand, at the time when John is writing, the Church already has a history, it is already an intellectual force, and it has already assimilated elements of different cultural origins in order to express its message. In short, John's material comes from this oral, ecclesiastical tradition and not from any written sources, Christian or non-Christian.

In the English-speaking countries the prevailing opinion,

which has never favored any hypothesis distinguishing different sources in the Gospel, seems to be even more cautious than formerly on the question of the rearrangement of pericopes or chapters in John's work. Recent essays by F. R. Hoare[30] and T. Cottam[31] have had few followers. For his part, C. H. Dodd states firmly that the duty of the exegete is to apply himself to understand the Gospel as it is; even if one cannot trace in some places the main thread of the thought it is better to admit one's ignorance of the original plan than to try to reconstitute it arbitrarily.[32] Consequently the Cambridge Professor refuses to make any transposition in the text, even the one which is most generally made, that of inverting the order of chapters 5 and 6.[33] Similarly, C. K. Barrett and R. H. Lightfoot, in their commentaries,[34] consider that none of the proposed changes can be made because the plan of the Gospel is more theological and kerygmatic than geographical and historical.

If many exegetes, of different points of view, today repudiate revising the sources of John and making rearrangements within the Gospel, these same exegetes, nevertheless, are no less aware of certain obvious defects in composition, of a certain unfinished character to the work of John. We must have this in mind when putting forward considerations like the following:[35] the Gospel which we read has a long history behind it; doubtless it was preached for a long time before it was written down; it was probably edited in stages; it is made up of a collection of meditations more or less independent of each other and in a certain sense parallel; some parts certainly did not attain their final form; the writer probably died before being able to put the finishing touch to his work and it was his disciples who ensured its publication.[36]

2) The Prologue

The prologue to the Gospel is a problem in itself. We know that Bultmann sees in the "overture" of John's work a hymn of a Gnostic community in honor of John the Baptist, a hymn which the Evangelist has re-edited to apply to Jesus. This theory - followed by Käsemann[37] and Stauffer[38] among others - is questioned by other scholars who affirm the literary unity of the prologue; they see in it the confession of faith which is developed by the Evangelist in the body of his work and which, consequently, is an integral part of the whole work.[39] It is doubtful, however, whether this explanation can be fully justified, in view of the number of non-Johannine expressions in these verses. Since these expressions, with one exception, belong to the vocabulary of first century Christianity, we are led to conclude that it is a Christian hymn which John had annotated and developed.[40] This answer to the problem is given by two exegetes: H. C. Green[41] and, more recently, R. Schnackenburg.[42] In a most careful study the Bamberg Professor establishes that the Johannine expressions established by Schweizer and Ruckstuhl are not to be found in certain verses of the prologue, namely in those verses which set forth theological ideas which are foreign to the body of the Gospel. These verses (1, 3, 4, part of 9, 10, 11, 14a and d, 16) form the primitive hymn sung by a Christian community in Asia to express its faith in Jesus, using the language of Gnosticism. The Evangelist developed this hymn in three stanzas expressing his vision of the pre-existent and creator Christ (v. 1-5), who is incarnate (v. 6-13) and brings salvation to all believers by His incarnation and glorification (v. 14-18). This hypothesis seems to provide a satisfactory solution to all the difficulties of the problem.[43]

3) *John and the Synoptics*

When speaking of the composition of the fourth Gospel, we must also look at the question of its relationship to the other Gospels. The interpreters remain divided in their opinion on this point; some believe that John is acquainted with the three Synoptics, or at least with one of them, others think that the fourth Evangelist knows only the Gospel tradition and not the Gospels themselves.

The first opinion is represented in all possible variations. John knows Matthew, Mark and Luke;[44] he knows Mark and Luke,[45] he knows only Mark,[46] or only Matthew.[47] In support of the second opinion comes first of all Bultmann, who, in his *Theologie des Neuen Testaments*,[48] keeps the same position on the subject as he took in his commentary on the Gospel. He is of the opinion that it cannot be definitely proved that the Evangelist knew any of the Synoptics; he only knows, and surmises that his readers know, the tradition of the Gospel. C. H. Dodd is of the same opinion; he expressed himself briefly on this point in the appendix of his great work where he develops "some considerations upon the historical aspect of the fourth gospel."[49] He has taken up this subject again in a more recent article where, by a study of four Johannine texts that appear at first glance to be inspired by the synoptic tradition (John 13. 16; 12. 25; 13. 20; 20. 23), he shows that John is handing on, quite independently, a particular form of the common oral tradition.[50] We can but commend the Cambridge Professor when he states that, since the infant Church was not a "bookish community," the nineteenth century exaggerated the extent of literary influence, and that a return to oral tradition is necessary.[51]

The particular resemblances linking John and Luke, or

more precisely linking the Johannine and Lucan traditions, have been emphasized by P. Benoît.[52] In more than one instance, he says, it seems that Luke finds his inspiration in John and not the opposite; John's Gospel is the result of a long preparation, whose beginnings could well have been contemporary with the Synoptics, if not prior to them; if, on the one hand, the final version of John followed Luke's Gospel and could have found inspiration in it, on the other hand, Luke could have known the Johannine traditions which were already in existence, and he could have found inspiration there. In other words, as expressed by E. Osty, there are Lucan expressions in John and Johannine expressions in Luke.[53] The links which exist between the two works, and perhaps between the two writers, remain an open question.

4) Characteristics of the Gospel

a) What is the structure of the Gospel? We have the feeling that the writer is following a plan imposed on him either by his own theological concepts[54] or by the strict rules of composition. Some years ago, E. Lohmeyer found in the Gospel, and also in the Apocalypse, a very definite design, dominated by the number 7, and from this he deduced that the two books formed a literary unit.[55] This division into 7 episodes seems to be much in favor at the moment. It is applied by M. E. Boismard[56] and by R. H. Lightfoot[57] to the body of the Gospel, without taking into account the prologue as such (Boismard) or the prologue and the historical introduction in 1 - 2. 11 (Lightfoot) and chapter 21. The 7 episodes in John according to Boismard are: 1. 19 - 2. 11; 2. 13 - 4. 54; 6 and 5; 7 - 9; 10 - 11; 12 - 19; 20; and according to Lightfoot: 2. 13 - 4. 54; 5; 6; 7 - 10. 39; 10. 40 - 11. 53; 11. 54 - 12. 50; 13. 1 - 20. 31. What strikes us immediately is that each of these plans contains one part which is of inordinate length when compared to the others; the last one in Lightfoot, the next to the last in Boismard. In the latter case the piece is not only too lengthy, but it also spans the only clear division made by the Evangelist himself or his editors, between chapters 12 and 13. We can see that our two writers agree on uniting in one single episode all or almost all of the second part of the Gospel, the farewell speeches and the passion (and the resurrection). In other words this second part cannot be divided like the first and certainly the writer does not follow the same rules of composition throughout. C. H. Dodd realises this. He also adopts the idea of division into 7 parts, but only within chapters 2 to 12, which he calls "the Book of Signs" (2. 1 - 4. 45; 4. 46 - 5. 47; 6; 7 - 8; 9 - 10; 11; 12). In the second part, which he calls "the Book of the Passion," he only makes two divisions: the farewell discourses and the passion-narrative.[58] Dodd's way is undoubtedly best. Certainly the whole Gospel is not strictly organized in an arrangement according to the number 7 which is characteristic of certain parts, for example 1. 19 - 2. 11; other passages cannot be forced into any fixed schema. It could hardly be otherwise if the Gospel was not written all at one time, if it was a posthumous work and if the writer's disciples, with the prospect of publication in one book in view, had been forced to make changes here and there.[59]

b) The Aramaic origin of the Gospel is a perennial subject of discussion. Most of the interpreters have reservations with regard to this hypothesis and maintain that the Gospel was written firsthand in Greek; its Aramaic idioms come from traditions used by the writer or are self-explanatory if the Evangelist is Palestinian.[60] There seems to be less eagerness than formerly to see poor translations of the particle *de* throughout the Gospel.[61] One problem is still puzzling: there are variations within the text of John which could be explained as parallel translations of the same Aramaic original. M. E. Boismard[62] and M. Black[63] are pursuing their researches in this area. But while Boismard asserts that "the fourth gospel was written in Aramaic, then translated into Greek,"[64] Black emphasizes that the Aramaic expressions appear particularly in the isolated words of Jesus (as in the Synoptics also) and that these expressions, handed on orally or in writing in the Aramaic-speaking church, are but the kernel round which the Evangelist composed, in Greek, the great speeches of Jesus.[65] This median opinion could well prevail. On the one hand it explains why only certain passages reveal an Aramaic origin while others are undoubtedly Greek, and on the other hand it agrees with the idea, resulting from other observations, that the Gospel was written slowly and in stages.

5) The Origin of the Gospel

Indications of John's independence from the Synoptics in their present form and evidence of an Aramaic substructure, at least here and there in John's work, lead to the Gospel being placed in a Palestinian setting or within a Christian group originating in Palestine.

Certainly the idea still exists that the geographical indications given by John are fictitious and have only a symbolic significance,[66] that the characters in John have no historical or psychological reality and are merely allegories illustrating the possible attitudes of man face to face with Jesus,[67] and that the "Well-beloved" is the type of the perfect disciple.[68] But a great many scholars, and not only those who customarily defend the traditional positions, admit that the Gospel stands on old and firm traditions;[69] it owes to these traditions an exact knowledge of Palestinian life and geography[70] and precise details about the life of Jesus.[71] It is a testimony equal in value to that of the Synoptics.[72] C. H. Dodd points out that the Johannine traditions have a particular link with southern Palestine[73] and E. Stauffer sees in the Johannine eschatology the expressions of the thought of Jesus Himself, misrepresented in the Synoptics which interpreted it according to Jewish apocalyptic.[74] In short, the Evangelist has put together the recollections of an eyewitness,[75] or he is John's disciple,[76] or he is the apostle John himself.[77] H. Strathmann, who agrees with the last idea, answers the classic objection that one of Jesus' companions would not be able to see in Him the Word incarnate, in the following way: the existence of the Church, on the day after the resurrection, shows that the first believers, and not merely John, saw in their Master a superhuman and divine being. This is the conviction which John expresses in his Gospel, where the facts serve as supports for a sermon about Jesus and in which the apostle uses "a kerygmatic style."[78] In other words, the value of the Gospel is essentially the message it transmits. That makes us turn our attention now to John's theology.[79]

II. *The Theological Question*

John the evangelist is also John the theologian. If his work has been the subject of a great deal of research it is not only because the circumstances in which it was written are unknown and difficult to discern but also because there is an original concept in the work. It is the historian's responsibility to understand the work for itself, to fix it in relationship to the religious currents of the time and to shed light on it with help from the precious texts of Qumran.

1) The Thought of John.

The place of honor among recent works in this field is given to *The Interpretation of the Fourth Gospel* by C. H. Dodd. So far we have scarcely mentioned more than the appendix of this great book which deals briefly with the relationship of the Gospel to the historic tradition of primitive Christianity. The work itself consists of three great parts. The first studies the background of John's Gospel. We will return to this shortly. The second and third parts, which provide the richness of the book and will assure its permanent interest, interpret the thought of John first of all by analysing his "leading ideas." These include symbolism, eternal life, knowledge of God, light - glory - judgment, the Spirit, the Messiah, the Son of Man, the Son of God, the Word. This list of themes which the Evangelist employs and the definitions which go with them prepare the way for the theological commentary in the third part, entitled "Argument and Structure," the design and plan of the Gospel. The salvation expressed by the Johannine themes is realised in the story of Jesus recounted by the Evangelist. After the prologue (the hymn to the Word and the testimonies which follow it in the first chapter) the Gospel consists, as we said above, of the "Book of Signs," chapters 2 to 12, containing seven episodes, and a "Book of Passion" made up of two elements, the farewell discourses and the passion narrative. Each of the seven episodes in the "Book of Signs" constitutes a single unit of action and teaching, however many actual miracles and speeches it contains. Each episode shows Jesus performing works and teaching, for each of them develops the whole theme of the Gospel: Christ revealed, crucified, risen, exalted and communicating eternal life to the believers. The seven episodes therefore are parallel rather than progressive; they repeat the different aspects of one and the same redemptive action. The "Book of the Passion," for its part, develops two elements formed by episodes in the ministry, but in inverse order: the farewell discourses precede the account of the passion. This inversion is not only historical and literary but also theological; it is the already glorified Christ who is speaking to His disciples, by virtue of an anticipatory forecast which the Evangelist can allow himself, for he gives to traditional history and eschatology a new expression, contained in the words, "the time is coming - indeed, has already come." In other words, the time of salvation has already been realised - or, more precisely, is already realised - at the time when Jesus establishes with His disciples the communion of love which is eternal life.[80]

2) The Background of John's Gospel

Let us remind ourselves once more of the interpretation of the main ideas of John in Bultmann's view. The unknown writer of the Gospel belongs to an Eastern Gnostic group, which is dominated by ideas expressed later in the Odes of Solomon and in Mandean and Manichean literature. The Evangelist understands and transmits the Christian message in Gnostic terms, to which he owes his universalist view of the world and particularly his antithetical concepts: light-darkness, truth-falsehood, life-death. He presents Jesus as the Revealer, sent by the Father, through whom the world above, the world of truth, light and life, breaks into the world below to bring salvation to it through revelation.[81]

Dodd looks for the background of John's thought in a different direction. In the first part of his work he discusses the different spiritual worlds which might have made an impression on the Evangelist. The Cambridge Professor quickly dismisses any possible effect of Mandeism, for he accepts it as an established fact that these documents came later; he makes little of the Gnostic influence by pointing out that neither John's dualism, nor the picture he sketches of the Mediator, nor his idea of salvation are Gnostic. He concludes that Rabbinic Judaism, Philo, and particularly Hermetic literature, "the highest religion of Hellenism," are the closest sources, along with Christian tradition. He emphasizes moreover that John's mind is too endowed with originality not to put his own imprint on ideas culled from his contact with other religious forms.

In his important review-article of *The Interpretation of the Fourth Gospel,*[82] Bultmann expresses the opinion that his colleague has underestimated the influence of Gnosticism on John and on the Hermetic writings themselves, and consequently, has overestimated the effect of Platonism and Hermetism. With regard to the parallels established by Dodd between the *Poimandres* and tractate XIII *De Regeneratione* on the one hand, and the Johannine texts on the other, Bultmann has this to say, "This is all instructive but not absolutely convincing."[83] These words recall that at the beginning of his article in 1925 on "The Importance of the Mandaean Sources for the Understanding of the Gospel of John," the Marburg Professor regretted that the Gospel had for so long been linked with Hellenism and with Philo, thus going in the wrong direction.[84]

The Cambridge Professor found a specialist in Johannine studies who is more prepared to go along with him. F. M. Braun has devoted one of his important scholarly

scholarly studies to the question.[85] "The Johannine-Hermetic problem is inevitable," he writes and he explains this connection with more subtlety and reservation as he says, "being very diffuse and doubtless having some Judaic elements, the spirituality in which Hermetism buries its roots overflowed all boundaries, so that John's gospel probably owes something of its sensibility and its literary forms to it."[86] On the other hand, we must take the missionary concern of the Evangelist into account; if John is indebted to Hermetism in any way, it is "in order to be understood by pagans who were of superior intelligence, as well as by others, and without ever deviating from the traditional catechisms."[87] As for C. K. Barrett, he is closer to Dodd than to Bultmann. He expresses himself briefly about the background of John's Gospel.[88] On the one hand he recognises the place held by the themes of the Old Testament, by apocalyptic, and by Rabbinic teaching in John, and on the other hand he allows there is some influence of "popular Platonism," of Philo, of Gnosticism and of Hermetism. He dismisses in a word any possible influence of Mandeism, believing that the works of Burkitt in particular have shown that the Mandean writings depend on Christian sources and not the opposite. He believes that the most likely background for the fourth Gospel is that of Hellenic Judaism and that, somewhat in the manner of Philo and the Wisdom literature, John makes real a synthesis of Jewish and Greek thought in order to show the universal significance of the person of Jesus.[89]

Among the later commentators it is H. Strathmann and M. E. Boismard who give non-Judaic influences the least effect on the thought of John. Strathmann admits that the Evangelist is breathing air through which flow currents of Hellenism and Gnosticism, but that only the Odes of Solomon can be compared to the Gospel, because the Hermetic writings, like the Mandean sources, are of too late a date. John has only taken images and means of expression from his environment. His thought is nourished on the biblical tradition and it is fundamentally original.[90] Similarly, Boismard makes the Old Testament John's essential source; the Word of which the Evangelist speaks is the creating and revealing Word of the Old Covenant,[91] and Johannine typology finds its source in the great themes of the history of Israel.[92] If the work of John is *sui generis* it is because it has to present a unique fact: the coming of the Son of God and its redemptive significance.[93]

3) John and Qumran

The writings discovered in the desert of Judah since 1948 have opened up a new phase in the question of the background of John.[94] The texts of Qumran provide parallels in form and substance to the work of John, which are much more direct than any other Eastern or Hellenic literature.[95] A mind as well-informed and discerning as M. Burrows does not hesitate to write, "The whole manner of thinking and the literary style of the fourth Evangelist are strikingly like what we find in the Qumran texts."[96] We cannot for the moment settle the question of the exact relationship between the Community of the Covenant and Johannine Christianity. What does seem definite, however, is that there existed in the land of Palestine, at the time of the birth of Christianity, a pre-Gnostic form of religion,[97] which found means of expressing itself both in the Old Testament[98] and in a common Eastern source, used by all the religious movements at that time. In other words, Christianity made its appearance in a setting of Palestinian Judaism which had already been influenced by Hellenism and Gnosticism.

The discovery of the Jewish apocalypses at the end of the last century has shed new light on a misunderstood aspect of

Jewish life and thought and has allowed us, in consequence, to reconstitute the eschatological climate in which the first Christians lived. We owe a similar expansion of our knowledge of the Jewish setting to the writings of Qumran. They show us that a community which was essentially Jewish in its scrupulous attachment to the Law and the priesthood, did not hesitate to express its faith in a wealth of ideas taken from the world outside. Consequently, we see that the Christians, very soon, without looking very far, could do the same. The appearance of Johannine thought, or at least the first expression of Johannine thought, in Palestine and at a relatively early date, seems possible and even probable.

The studies of the last ten years have not found the solution to the enigma of the fourth Gospel. The interpreters remain divided in their opinion. Whether the subject is the composition of the Gospel, its connections with the Synoptics, its original language, the circumstances in which it arose, there are always different views. As regards the thought of John and its origin, every possible theory has been put forward in recent studies. Popular Platonism and Philo, Hermetism, Gnosticism, Mandeism - all in their turn have been called upon to explain the thought of John and all of these comparisons have some value. Just as it was necessary to multiply attempts to identify the sources of the Gospel to make its unity emerge, these comparative researches in all directions were necessary to bring out the thought of the Evangelist in its impressiveness and originality. But it can be said of all these comparisons that they are more instructive than convincing. First, all the texts which are placed parallel to John's are later than his. It is not avoiding the question (and it is moreover correct) to say that these texts, whether Mandean or Hermetic, are older than their date of publication; it is very probably the same with the Text of John. Behind the Gospel as we have it is an older Johannine tradition; this seems to be becoming more readily admitted. Secondly, when the same idea is common to John and to Eastern or Hellenistic writings, it is the Gospel which is less wordy, more moderate yet more powerful, more in keeping with the general context of the whole work. If the Gospel of John stands up so well to all comparisons it is because it is not a mosaic of disparate elements, gathered haphazardly from sources known to the Evangelist, or of external influences upon him. The Gospel appears rather as the fundamentally original work of a true genius, one of those beings who create an impression rather than receive one.

The publication of new papyri, in 1935, established that the Gospel dates from about the year 100 and thus disproved the scholarly theories that the Gospel could not have seen the light of day before the middle of the second century. Similarly the discovery of the Qumran writings may well put an end to the searchings in time and space for the true background of Johannine thought. The interest of the Dead Sea Scrolls is that they affirm the introduction into certain currents of Judaism, at the very time when Christianity was about to appear, of a whole collection of images and ideas which also appear in John and which have always been a somewhat surprising element in his work. It was surmised that they were to be traced to movements of thought from beyond Palestine, because Hellenism and Judaism were placed in contrast and there was a tendency to judge all Judaism before 70 in the light of the Pharisaic reaction which followed the fall of the Temple and of the Jewish nation. This was to misunderstand both the power of assimilation always possessed by a living religion, and also its power to spread beyond its immediate field of activity. By revealing the strength of Judaism, the Community of the Covenant also shows that a work like the fourth Gospel could have been conceived and brought to reality by a Palestinian.

If the resurrection of the "Watchers" of Qumran by itself does not bring the solution of the Johannine enigma, it does mark the beginning of a new era in research on the fourth Gospel.

NOTES

1. *L'Evangile de Jean. Etudes et problèmes,* Recherches bibliques, 3, Bruges-Paris, 1958, p. 11-40, published by kind permission of Desclée De Brouwer, Paris.

2. For studies before 1947, cf. P. H. Menoud, *L'Evangile de Jean d'après les recherches récentes* (Cahiers théol. 3), Neuchâtel-Paris, 2ème éd., 1947 and J. H. Scammon, "Studies in the Fourth Gospel," *Angl. Theol. Rev.,* 1941, p. 103-117. For more recent studies, cf. J. Behm, "Der gegenwärtige Stand der Erforschung des Johannes-Evangeliums," *TLZ,* 1948, p. 21-30, W. F. Howard - C. K. Barrett, *The Fourth Gospel in Recent Criticism and Interpretation,* New ed., London, 1955 and the studies of F. M. Braun and E. Haenchen mentioned in the additions to the bibliography *infra.* p. 309. P. Beeckmann, *L'Evangile selon saint Jean d'après les meilleurs auteurs catholiques,* Bruges, 1951, does not concern himself with the most recent works.

3. *Das Evangelium des Johannes* (Kritisch-exegetischer Kommentar über das N.T., II, 10. Aufl.), Göttingen, 1941; 13. Aufl. mit Ergänzungsheft, 1953. *Theologie des Neuen Testaments,* Tübingen, 1953.

4. Cambridge, 1953.

5. Particularly, *The Bible and the Greeks,* London, 1935. For C. H. Dodd's other contributions to the Johannine problem, cf. P. H. Menoud, *passim.*

6. *The Gospel According to St. John. An Introduction with Commentary and Notes on the Greek Text,* London, 1955. Cf. also "The Old Testament in the Fourth Gospel," *JTS,* 1947, p. 155-169; "The Place of Eschatology in the

Fourth Gospel," *Exp. Times,* 59, 1947-48, p. 302-305; "The Holy Spirit in the Fourth Gospel," *JTS,* 1950, p. 9-15; "Zweck des vierten Evangeliums," *Zeits. f. syst. Theol.,* 1953, p. 257-273; "The Lamb of God," *N. T. Stud.,* 1954-55, p. 210-218.

7. Cf. particularly W. Grossouw, "Three Books on the Fourth Gospel," *Novum Testamentum,* 1956, p. 36-46.

8. *L'Evangile de saint Jean,* Paris, 1953 (Bible de Jérusalem).

9. *Le prologue de saint Jean,* Paris, 1953; *Du baptême à Cana (Jean 1. 19 - 2. 11),* Paris, 1956 (Lectio Divina, 11 and 18).

10. *Le quatrième évangile. Introduction à l'évangile de saint Jean,* 2ème éd., Tournai-Paris, 1955.

11. *Regensburger N. T.,* IV, Regensburg, 1948.

12. *Das N. T. Deutsch,* IV, 6. Aufl., Göttingen, 1951. This commentary replaces the one by F. Büchsel in the same series.

13. *The Interpreter's Bible,* VIII, New York-Nashville, 1955, p. 435-811.

14. *St. John's Gospel. A Commentary.* Edited by C. F. Evans, Oxford, 1956.

15. *Einleitung in das N. T.,* Freiburg i. B., 1953.

16. *Einleitung in das N. T.,* 2. Aufl., Bern, 1954. -- Numerous textbooks intended for students and the general public have appeared in English. We should mention at least the new edition, revised by C. S. C. Williams, of the classic work by A. H. McNeile, *An Introduction to the Study of the N. T.,* London, 1952.

17. *Les sacrements dans l'évangile johannique. La vie de Jésus et le culte de l'Eglise primitive,* Paris, 1951 (translation of the second revised edition of *Urchristentum und Gottesdienst,* Basel, 1944). Cf. also the articles which preceded this work: "Der johanneische Gebrauch doppeldeutiger Ausdrücke als Schlüssel zum Verständnis des vierten Evangeliums," *TZ,* 1948, p. 360-372; "La vie de Jésus, objet de la vie et de la foi d'après le quatrième évangile," *Aux sources de la tradition chrétienne. Mélanges M. Goguel,* Neuchâtel-Paris,

1950, p. 52-61; "Sabbat und Sonntag nach dem Johannesevangelium," *In Memoriam Ernst Lohmeyer,* Stuttgart, 1951, p. 127-131. In the same vein as O. Cullmann, cf. J. G. H. Hoffman, "Le quatrième évangile, le Jésus de l'histoire et le Christ, Seigneur de l'Eglise," *Revue réformée,* 1952, p. 1-33 and R. Mehl, "Zur Bedeutung von Kultus und Sakrament im vierten Evangelium," *Evang. Theol.,* 1955.

18. *The Religious Thought of St. John,* London, 1950.

19. *Essais sur la christologie de saint Jean,* Bruges, 1951.

20. *Die Anschauung vom "Leben" im vierten Evangelium,* München, 1952.

21. *La Mère des fidèles. Essai de théologie johannique,* Tournai-Paris, 1953, and the following articles: "Le baptême d'après le quatrième évangile," *Revue thomiste,* 1948, p. 347-393; "L'Eau et l'Esprit," *ibid.,* 1949, p. 5-30; "La Mère de Jésus dans l'oeuvre de saint Jean," *ibid.,* 1950, p. 429-479 and 1951, p. 5-68; "Morale et mystique à l'école de saint Jean," *Morale chrétienne et requêtes contemporaines,* Paris, 1954, p. 71-84; "La vie d'en-haut (John 3. 1-15)," *Rev. sc. phil. théol.,* 1956, p. 3-24.

22. *Revelation and Redemption. A Sketch of the Theology of St. John,* Westminster, Md., 1955. The work of E. C. Colwell and E. L. Titus, *The Gospel of the Spirit. Purpose, Method and Teaching of the Fourth Gospel,* Chicago, 1953, takes up again the ideas Colwell set forth in *John Defends the Gospel,* Chicago, 1936. We cannot mention the numerous commentaries and popular works which are excellent but which bring no new insight to the Johannine problem.

23. Paris, 1951.

24. We should mention at least the following studies: E. L. Allen, "The Jewish Christian Church in the Fourth Gospel," *JBL,* 1955, p. 88-92; H. Van den Bussche, "L'attente de la grande révélation dans le quatrième évangile," *NRT,* 1953, p. 1009-1019; L. Cerfaux, "Le thème littéraire parabolique dans l'évangile de saint Jean," *Coniectanea Neotestamentica,* XI, 1947, p. 15-25 = *RLC,* 1954, II, p. 27-40; "La charité fraternelle et le retour du Christ (Jo. 13. 33-38)," *Eph. Theol. Lov.,* 1948, p. 321-332 = *RLC,* II, p. 27-40; "Les miracles, signes messianiques de Jésus et oeuvres de Dieu selon l'évangile de Saint Jean," *L'attente du Messie (Mélanges J. Coppens),* Bruges, 1954, p. 131-138 = *RLC,* II,

p. 41-50; A. George, "L'heure de Jean 17," *RB,* 1954, p. 393-397; X. Léon-Dufour, "Le signe du Temple selon saint Jean," *Mélanges J. Lebreton I (Rech. sc. relig.,* 1951), p. 155-175; "Actualité du quatrième évangile," *NRT,* 1954, p. 449-468; G. Schulze-Kadelbach, "Zur Pneumatologie des Johannesevangeliums," *ZNW,* 1955, p. 279-280; E. Schweizer, "Orthodox Proclamation. The Reinterpretation of the Gospel by the Fourth Evangelist," *Interpretation,* 1954, p. 387-403; W. Michaelis, "Zur Herkunft des johanneischen Paraklet-Titels," *Coniectanea Neotestamentica,* XI, 1947, p. 147-162; M. F. Berrouard, "Le Paraclet, défenseur du Christ devant la conscience du croyant (Jo. 16. 8-11)," *Rev. sc. phil. théol.,* 1949, p. 361-389; G. Bornkamm, "Der Paraklet im Johannes-Evangelium," *Festschrift für R. Bultmann,* 1949, p. 12-35; J. G. Davies, "The Primary Meaning of Parakletos," *JTS,* 1953, p. 35-38; H. von Campenhausen, "Zum Verständnis von Joh. 19. 11," *TLZ,* 1948, p. 367-392; C. Spicq, "Noli me tangere," *Rev. sc. phil. théol.,* 1951, p. 226-227; A. Vergote, *L'exaltation du Christ en croix selon le quatrième évangile,* Bruges-Paris, 1952 (Analecta Lovaniensia Biblica et Orientalia, II, 29).

25. V. Martin, *Papyrus Bodmer II, Evangile de Jean, chap. 1-14,* Cologny-Genève, 1956. The manuscript, consisting of 108 numbered pages, includes chapters 1 to 14. 26, with a gap of four pages, chapter 6. 11-35. We should note that the papyrus ignores the pericope of the woman taken in adultery and proceeds directly from 7. 52 to 8. 12 in the middle of the second line on page 52. -- We have been informed by the editor that, during the printing of this volume, the Bodmer Library has acquired a new bundle of papyri, which contains quite a number of fragments belonging to the last chapters of the same manuscript by John. Professor Martin is preparing these fragments for publication. -- On the Papyrus Bodmer, cf. the notes of G. Maldfeld which appeared before the text was published: "Ein neues Johannes-Evangelium-Fragment auf Papyrus," *N. T. Stud.,* 1956-57, p. 79-81 and "Papyrus Bodmer II - Joh. Kap. 1-14," *Novum Testamentum,* 1956, p. 153-155, and particularly the studies by K. Aland and M. E. Boismard mentioned in the additions to the bibliography, *infra.* p. 309. In the list of New Testament papyri kept up to date and published periodically in *ZNW* (most recently by K. Aland, 1957, p. 141-191), the Papyrus Bodmer has the number 66.

26. "Stilkritik und Literaranalyse im vierten Evangelium," *ZNW,* 43, 1950-51, p. 128-143 (article written in 1942). Cf. also S. Mendner, "Johanneische Literarkritik," *TZ,* 1952, p. 418-434.

27. "Zur Komposition von Joh. 10," *Coniectanea Nestestamentica,* XI, 1947, p. 220-225; "Zur Frage der Komposition von Joh. 6. 27-58 (59). (Die Himmelsbrotrede)." *In Memoriam Ernst Lohmeyer,* Stuttgart, 1951, p. 132-142; "Zur Komposition von Joh. 7," *ZNW,* 45, 1954, p. 108-119. -- The unity of chapters 6 and 10 is admitted also by J. Jeremias, "Joh. 6. 51c.-58 redaktionell?", *ZNW,* 44, 1952-53, p. 256-257; E. Schweizer, "Das johanneische Zeugnis vom Herrenmahl," *Evang. Theol.,* 12, 1952-53, p. 341-363; L. Cerfaux, "Le thème littéraire parabolique dans l'évangile de saint Jean," *Coniectanea Neotestamentica,* XI, 1947, p. 15-25, (= *Receuil Lucien Cerfaux,* 1954, II, p. 17-26) and P. W. Meyer, "A Note on John 10. 1-18," *JBL,* 1956, p. 232-235.

28. *Die literarische Einheit des Johannesevangeliums. Der gegenwartige Stand der einschlägigen Forschungen,* Freiburg (Schweiz), 1951.

29. *Zur johanneischen Tradition. Beiträge zur Kritik an der literarkritischen Analyse des vierten Evangeliums,* Copenhagen, 1954.

30. *The Original Order and Chapters of St. John's Gospel,* London, 1944 and *The Gospel According to St. John Arranged in Its Conjectural Order and Translated from the Greek into Current English,* London, 1949. -- For other similar studies, up to and including Hoare, cf. the general review by N. Uricchio, "La teoria delle trasposizioni nel Vangelo di S. Giovanni," *Biblica,* 1950, p. 129-163 and 1951, p. 567-568.

31. *The Fourth Gospel Re-arranged,* London, 1952. -- In opposition to the suggestion that certain pages of the original gospel manuscript might have been bound out of order, W. G. Wilson ("The Original Text of the Fourth Gospel. Some Objective Evidence against the Theory of Page Displacements," *JTS,* 1949, p. 59-60) has pointed out that the displaced passages do not fill two entire pages or a multiple of two pages.

32. *The Interpretation...,* p. 290.

33. Along these lines, cf. among recent writers, M. E. Boismard, A. Wikenhauser, H. Strathmann (5. 1-47 after 7. 13). On the other hand W. Michaelis and F. M. Braun (in connection with chapter 3, *Revue thomiste,* 1948, p. 374) remain cautious.

34. C. K. Barrett, p. 14 and 18-20; R. H. Lightfoot, p. 8-10.

35. Along these lines, but with slight variations, cf. H. Strathmann, p. 6; D. Mollat, p. 62; W. Michaelis, p. 117f; C. K. Barrett, p. 20 and 113, R. H. Lightfoot, p. 4f; M. E. Boismard, *Du baptême à Cana,* p. 8-9.

36. The epilogue (chapter 21), particularly, is more and more thought to be an addition to John's work made by one of his disciples. This would explain the strange position of Johannine and non-Johannine characteristics in this chapter. Cf. particularly M. E. Boismard, "Le chapitre 21 de saint Jean. Essai de critique littéraire," *RB*, 1947, p. 473-501, and also G. M. Lee, *JTS*, 1950, p. 62f; C. H. Dodd, *The Interpretation...,* p. 431 and *JTS,* 1953, p. 212f; W. Michaelis, p. 105-106; C. K. Barrett, p. 479-480; R. H. Lightfoot, p. 341-342. -- For the opposite opinion, cf. finally, B. Cassian, "John 21," *N. T. Stud.,* 1956-57, p. 132-136.

37. *Zeits. f. Theol. u. Kirche,* 1951, p. 302.

38. *ZNW,* 1955, p. 14, n. 34 and *TLZ,* 1956, p. 145-147.

39. M. Pohlenz, "Der Prolog des Johannes-Evangeliums," *ZNW,* 1949, p. 98-101. Along the same lines cf. C. Stange, "Der Prolog des Johannesevangeliums," *Zeits. f. syst. Theol.,* 1950, p. 120-141; E. Ruckstuhl, p. 67-97; H. Strathmann, C. K. Barrett, R. H. Lightfoot in their commentaries. On the other hand M. E. Boismard, *Le prologue de saint Jean* (cf. P. H. Menoud, *Rev. théol. phil.,* 1953, p. 253) is of the opinion that verses 6-8 and 15 are not in their right place in the prologue and he revives the idea that verses 6-8 originally preceded verse 19 (cf. also *Du baptême à Cana,* p. 26, n. 1). We should mention the same writer's article, "Dans le sein du Père (Jo. 1. 18)," *RB,* 1952, p. 23-39, where he suggests a new reading for this difficult verse, prompted by the codex of Verceil: "No one has ever seen God, except the only Son; it is He who leads us into the Father's bosom." (Cf. also *Le prologue...,* p. 91-92 and 175.)

40. Like Paul in Phil. 2. 5-11. On this point, cf. finally J. Jeremias, *Studia Paulina,* Haarlem, 1953, p. 152-154.

41. "The Composition of St. John's Prologue," *Exp. Times,* 66, 1954-55, p. 291-294. The primitive hymn comprises the verses 1, 3, 4, 5, 10, 11, 14a and 18.

42. "Logos-Hymnus und johanneischer Prolog," *Bibl.*

Zeits., 1957, p. 69-109. -- We are indebted to the same writer for an excellent piece of work on *Das erste Wunder Jesu (John. 2, 1-11)*, Freiburg i. B., 1951: the focal point of the story is the person of Jesus Himself; in intimate communion with God, whose power He possesses, Jesus submits His actions only to the Father and His "hour" is the time when the Father bids Him begin the work of revelation which will end at the supreme moment of the cross.

43. We should note that R. Schnackenburg keeps the plural version in verse 13, as given in the Greek manuscripts, now based on the Papyrus Bodmer; likewise M. Pohlenz, H. Strathmann, R. H. Lightfoot and J. Schmid, *Bibl. Zeits.*, 1957, p. 118-125. The singular version, interpreted either in the sense of the eternal begetting of the Word, or in the sense of the virgin birth of Jesus, is defended as being the original one by F. M. Braun, "Qui ex Deo natus est (Jean 1. 13)," *Aux sources de la tradition chrétienne. Mélanges M. Goguel*, Neuchâtel-Paris, 1950, p. 11-31 and *La Mère des fidèles*, p. 33-38; M. E. Boismard, "Critique textuelle et citations patristiques," *RB*, 1950, p. 388-408 and *Le prologue...*, p. 54-58 and 64; J. Dupont, p. 51, n. 6; D. Mollat, p. 69. C. K. Barrett (p. 117-118) adopts the plural version but maintains that John could not mention the spiritual birth of the believers without thinking at the same time of the virgin birth of Jesus.

44. R. H. Lightfoot, p. 29f. (John's aim is to give an interpretation of the Synoptics rather than displace them; that is why, for him, Jesus' home is neither Galilee nor Jerusalem, for Jesus is not part of this world, but of the bosom of the Father, cf. p. 34-36.) Cf. also C. Maurer, *Ignatius von Antiochen und das Johannesevangelium*, Zurich, 1949, p. 18; A. M. Farrer, *On Dispensing with Q-Studies in the Gospels, Essays in Memory of R. H. Lightfoot*, Oxford, 1955, p. 55-58; L. E. Elliott-Binns, *Galilean Christianity*, London, 1956, p. 31.

45. H. Strathmann, p. 4; C. K. Barrett, p. 14f., 34 and 37.

46. I. Buse, "John 5, 8 and Johannine-Marcan Relationships," *N. T. Stud.*, 1954-55, p. 134-136: Mark and John would both make use of "some source of Petrine recollections." -- E. K. Lee, "St. Mark and the Fourth Gospel," *N. T. Stud.*, 1956-57, p. 50-58: John knows Mark and another tradition which, occasionally, he prefers to Mark.

47. H. F. D. Sparks, "St. John's Knowledge of Matthew.

The Evidence of Jo. 13, 16 and 15, 20," *JTS*, 1952, p. 58-61: these two texts establish that John knows Matthew 10. 24-25. P. Gardner-Smith points out that the resemblance between these texts is quite natural seeing that the two evangelists were both dealing with the situation of the believer in a hostile world. But their points of view are different and consequently their versions are independent of each other: Matthew's idea is to encourage the Christian missionaries, John's aim is to strengthen the faithful who are struggling against hatred and persecution ("St. John's Knowledge of Matthew," *JTS*, 1953, p. 31-35). -- According to H. C. Snape ("The Fourth Gospel, Ephesus and Alexandria," *HTR*, 1954, p. 1-14), the church at Ephesus is the daughter, by Apollos, of the church at Alexandria; thus the resemblances which exist between John's Gospel, written at Ephesus, and Matthew's, written at Alexandria, can be explained. This also explains the interest they both show in the relationship between Jesus and John the Baptist (John 1 and Matthew 3. 14-15) and in the primacy of Peter (John 21 and Matthew 16).

48. P. 350. Cf. likewise D. Mollat, p. 38f., and W. Michaelis, p. 105.

49. *The Interpretation...*, p. 449f. Already in *According to the Scriptures*, London, 1952, p. 30 and *passim*, Dodd makes the point that the Synoptics and John quote the same texts from the Old Testament independently.

50. "Some Johannine 'Herrenworte' with Parallels in the Synoptic Gospels," *N. T. Stud.*, 1955-56, p. 75-86. -- Other writers reach the same conclusion from a study of different texts: cf. J. Schneider, "Zur Frage der Komposition von Joh. 6, 27-58 (59). (Die Himmelsbrotrede)," *In Memoriam Ernst Lohmeyer*, Stuttgart, 1951, p. 142; R. Gyllenberg, "Die Anfänge der johanneischen Tradition," *N. T. Stud. f. R. Bultmann*, Berlin, 1954, p. 144-147; J. A. T. Robinson, "The Parable of John 10. 1-5," *ZNW*, 1955, p. 240.

51. Article cited, p. 75.

52. "La primauté de saint Pierre selon le N. T.," *Istina*, 1955, p. 325. For example, John 21. 1f. is not dependent on Luke 5. 1-11, but, on the contrary, Luke has combined the story of a miraculous catch of fish from a Johannine source with the scene of the calling of the disciples from Mark 1. 16-20, for Luke 5. 8 is the only case where Luke uses the typically Johannine expression: Simon-Peter. Cf. *RB*, 1939, p. 457-459. -- Cf., along the same lines, M. E. Boismard, *RB*, 1947, p. 499f., and 1956, p. 269.

53. "Les points de contact entre le récit de la passion dans saint Luc et dans saint Jean," *Mélanges Jules Lebreton, I (Rech. de sc. relig.,* 1951), p. 146-154; cf. also A. H. N. Green-Armitage, *A Portrait of Saint Luke,* London, 1955, p. 116. -- D. Mollat (p. 53) and O. Cullmann ("La Samarie et les origines de la mission chrétienne. Qui sont les 'Alloi' de Jean 4. 38?" *Ecole pratique des hautes études religieuses. Annuaire 1953-1954,* Paris, 1953, p. 3-12) recall that Luke and John show the same interest in Samaria.

54. Cf. H. Clavier, "La structure du quatrième évangile," *RHPR,* 1955, p. 174-195, and earlier "Mediation in the Fourth Gospel," *SNTS Bulletin,* I, 1950, p. 11-25 and "Le problème du rite et du mythe dans le quatrième évangile," *RHPR,* 1951, p. 275-292.

55. "Über Aufbau und Gliederung des vierten Evangeliums," *ZNW,* 1928, p. 11-36.

56. *Le prologue...,* p. 136-138.

57. P. 11-21.

58. *The Interpretation...,* p. 289f.

59. For this reason we can only view with scepticism an essay like the one by F. Quiévreux, "La structure symbolique de l'évangile de saint Jean," *RHPR,* 1953, p. 123-165. This writer finds in the Gospel a refined symbolic structure which governs the choice of words and the number of times a word may appear in the text. This would explain the idiosyncracies of John's style and of his composition. It seems to us that this system faces definite objections. First of all the Johannine text has not reached us "in a remarkable state of entirety" (p. 160), any more than any other text from antiquity. The patient and scholarly researches of M. E. Boismard on the Johannine variations show this quite clearly: "A propos de Jean 5. 39. Essai de critique textuelle," *RB,* 1948, p. 5-34; "Critique textuelle et citations patristiques," *RB,* 1950, p. 388-408; "Lectio brevior, potior," *RB,* 1951, p. 161-168; "Dans le sein du Père (Jean 1. 18)," *RB,* 1952, p. 23-39; "Problèmes de critique textuelle concernant le quatrième évangile," *RB,* 1953, p. 347-371. Where the variants are concerned Quiévreux's conjectures are almost always based on the long text, and almost always the short text is the one to be preferred (for example: John 13. 10). Secondly, to reach his conclusions, the writer has to include in the Gospel the episode of the woman taken in adultery and chapter 21. Now, though there is some permissi-

ble doubt with regard to chapter 21, as we have seen above, it is quite certain that the pericope *De adultera* is not Johannine. We will content ourselves with two arguments: it is not in the Papyrus Bodmer and it contains none of the literary characteristics pointed out by Schweizer and Ruckstuhl. -- In connection with this pericope, we should like to draw attention to three articles: S. Läuchli, "Eine alte Spur von Joh. 8. 1-11?" *TW*, 1950, p. 151: Even if Origen knew these verses, he did not read them in John's Gospel. -- J. Jeremias, "Zur Geschichtlichkeit des Verhörs Jesu vor dem Hohen Rat," *ZNW*, 1950-51, p. 148-149: Since the woman is brought to Jesus by "the Scribes and the Pharisees," it is because she is coming out of the court where she has just been condemned according to the Law. But the sentence cannot be carried out, because the Jews no longer have the *jus gladii*. By submitting the case to Jesus, the judges force Him to choose between violating the Law of Moses and violating the command of Rome. The episode is a "temptation" of the same kind as the question of the tax to Caesar. -- T. W. Manson, "The Pericope de Adultera, John 7. 53 - 8. 11," *ZNW*, 1952-53, p. 255-256: The interpretation by Jeremias explains the attitude of Jesus; being invited to usurp the power of the Romans, Jesus accepts; by writing in the sand, he follows Roman juridical practice which lays down that the judge shall write down the sentence and then read it, and Jesus formulates His judgment in such a way that He is not the executor.

60. Cf. J. Bonsirven, "Les araméismes de Saint Jean l'évangéliste?" *Biblica*, 1949, p. 403-432. John wrote in Greek, but his mother tongue was Aramaic and he remained familiar with the Bible in Hebrew, so traces of his linguistic origins can be seen (p. 425).

61. Cf. E. Ullendorf, "A Mistranslation from Aramaic?" *N. T. Stud.*, 1955-56, p. 50-52 (with reference to John 14. 16).

62. "A propos de Jean 5. 39. Essai de critique textuelle," *RB*, 1948, p. 5-34.

63. *An Aramaic Approach to the Gospels and Acts*, Oxford, 1946, p. 54-56 and 207-208.

64. *Du baptême à Cana*, p. 7.

65. P. 208-209. -- Without dealing directly with the original language of John, E. F. F. Bishop, "Jesus Walking or Teaching in the Temple (Mark 11. 27 - John 10. 23)," *Exp. Times*, 63, 1951-52, p. 226-227, is of the opinion that these

two texts (and the parallels of Mark in Matthew and Luke) go back to the same Aramaic tradition and that the same verbal form of *halak* produced two Greek interpretations: Jesus comes and goes (John and Mark) or teaches (Matthew and Luke) in the Temple.

66. N. Krieger, "Fiktive Orte der Johannestaufe," *ZNW*, 1954, p. 121-123: "Bethany beyond the Jordan," is an imaginary place; it is the place where the Jesus whom the Jews do not recognise is to be found (John 1. 19-28). "Aenon, near Salim" (John 3. 23), means that John the Baptist is near to peace, that is to the Christian sacrament.

67. E. Krafft, "Die Personen des Johannesevangeliums," *Evang. Theol.*, 1956, p. 18-32; cf. the different opinion of W. Oehler, "Typen oder allegorische Figuren im Johannesevangelium?" *ibid.*, p. 422-427.

68. Along with Bultmann, Krafft maintains (p. 25-26) that the Well-beloved is the pagan-Christian people, the son given to Judaism in the person of Jesus (to Mary). -- According to E. Käsemann, "Ketzer und Zeuge. Zum johanneischen Verfasserproblem," *Zeits. f. Theol. u. Kirche*, 1951, p. 292-311, the "Elder" (the writer of the Gospel and the three epistles) is one of the appearances in history of the Well-beloved, the perfect disciple (p. 304 and 311). -- On the other hand, the identification of the Well-beloved with Lazarus is not given up: F. V. Filson, "Who was the Beloved Disciple?" *JBL*, 1949, p. 83-88; J. N. Sanders, "Those Whom Jesus Loved (John 5. 11)," *N. T. Stud.*, 1954-55, p. 29-41; and it is even suggested that he might be Matthias (E. L. Titus, "The Identity of the Beloved Disciple," *JBL*, 1950, p. 323-328.

69. R. H. Lightfoot, p. 5-7; J. Schneider, *ZNW*, 1954, p. 117. Cf. also J. Jocz, "Die Juden im Johannesevangelium," *Judaica*, 1953, p. 129-142.

70. S. Temple, "Geography and Climate in the Fourth Gospel," *The Joy of Study. Papers ... Presented ... to F. C. Grant*, New York, 1951, p. 63-72. Cf. also J. Jeremias, *Die Wiederentdeckung von Bethesda, Joh. 5. 2*, Göttingen, 1949. -- P. Parker, "Bethany beyond Jordan," *JBL*, 1955, p. 257-261, suggests an ingenious explanation but one which it is difficult to accept: we must understand "Bethany beyond the Jordan," that is, near Jerusalem, as being the only Bethany of the Gospel.

71. E. Bammel, Φίλος τοῦ Καίσαρος, *TLZ*, 1952, p. 205-

210: In John 19. 12, the Jews give Pilate his official title; it is a question there of a historic word faithfully retained by John. -- J. Blintzer, "Eine Bemerkung zum Geschichtsrahmen des Johannesevangeliums," *Biblica*, 1955, p. 20-35: John 6-7 and Luke 13. 1-5 knew, independently of each other, that Jesus celebrated a fast in Galilee and not at Jerusalem.

72. A. Fridrichsen, "Jesus, St. John and St. Paul," *The Root of the Vine. Essays in Biblical Theology*, London, 1953, p. 57.

73. *The Interpretation ...*, p. 449-452.

74. "Agnostos Christos. Joh. 2. 24 und die Eschatologie des vierten Evangeliums," *The Background of the N. T. and its Eschatology ... in honour of C. H. Dodd*, Cambridge, 1946, p. 281-291.

75. B. Noack, p. 157f; J. Schneider, *In Memoriam Ernst Lohmeyer*, p. 142. -- According to C. Masson, "Le témoignage de Jean," *Rev. théol. et phil.*, 1950, p. 120-127, the Johannine witness is not one of the twelve, but a disciple moved by the Spirit of truth.

76. C. K. Barrett, p. 113; H. E. Edwards, *The Disciple Who Wrote these Things. A New Approach to the Problem of the Authorship of the Fourth Gospel*, London, 1953. -- For E. K. Lee, *The Religious Thought of St. John*, p. 3, this disciple is the Elder, John.

77. The Catholic scholars and H. Strathmann, p. 10 and 23; W. Michaelis, p. 100 and 126; A. C. Headlam, *The Fourth Gospel as History*, Oxford, 1948; H. P. V. Nunn, *The Authorship of the Fourth Gospel*, Oxford, 1952; P. F. Barackman, "The Gospel according to John," *Interpretation*, 1952, p. 63-78; W. M. Smalz, "John, Son of Zebedee," *Angl. Theol. Rew.*, 1953, p. 8-17; R. A. Edwards, *The Gospel According to St. John. Its Criticism and Interpretation*, London, 1954. -- M. Goguel (*Jésus*, 2ème éd., Paris, 1950, p. 108), K. Heussi (*TLZ*, 1952, p. 70), and E. Käsemann (*Zeits. f. Theol. u. Kirche*, 1951, p. 299) remain faithful to the hypothesis of E. Schwartz that John the apostle died in the year 44.

78. P. 23. Cf. along these lines, D. Mollat, p. 48: "Authentic history, but theological and spiritual history. It offers only meagre nourishment to man's curiosity, but it opens up an inexhaustible source for religious reflection."

79. The date of the Gospel is no longer a burning

question. Since the discovery of the Pap. Egerton 2 and of the Pap. Ryl. Gk. 457, it is agreed that the Gospel should be placed about the year 100. It would be even older, if it was admitted that Clement of Rome refers to it (cf. C. C. Tarelli, "Clement of Rome and the Fourth Gospel," *JTS*, 1947, p. 208-209; M. E. Boismard, "Clément de Rome et l'évangile de Jean," *RB*, 1948, p. 376-387).

80. C. H. Dodd himself gave us a quick look at his interpretation of the Gospel of John in the article "Le kerygma apostolique dans le quatrième évangile," *RHPR*, 1951, p. 265-274. Cf. also *The Apostolic Preaching and Its Development*, 6th ed., London, 1950.

81. Along the same lines cf. E. Käsemann, *Verkündigung und Forschung*, 1946-47, p. 182-200 and *Zeits. f. Theol. u. Kirche*, 1951, p. 302; R. M. Grant, "The Origin of the Fourth Gospel," *JBL*, 1950, p. 305-322.

82. *N. T. Stud.*, 1954-55, p. 77-91.

83. P. 80. -- These words could be applied just as well, if not even better, to the Mandean parallels.

84. Cf. *ZNW*, 1925, p. 100.

85. "Hermétisme et Johannisme," *Revue thomiste*, 1955, p. 22-42 and 259-299. Cf. also "Essenisme et Hermétisme," *ibid.*, 1954, p. 523-558.

86. P. 298-299.

87. P. 295. -- R. H. Lightfoot (p. 48-49) says, in a similar vein, that the evangelist is a Jew who wanted to reach the Greeks.

88. P. 22-23.

89. On the contrary, A. W. Argyle, "Philo and the Fourth Gospel," *Exp. Times*, 63, 1951-52, p. 385-386, referring to Julius Grill, is inclined to admit a more marked influence of Philo on John. -- R. M. Wilson, "Philo and the Fourth Gospel," *ibid.*, 65, 1953-54, p. 47-49, replies in terms similar to those of C. K. Barrett, that the work of Philo is important, not as a Johannine source, but as an example of the evangelist's method of putting the terminology of his time to work in the service of the Gospel of the Risen Christ. In a more recent article, "The Fourth Gospel and Hellenistic Thought," *Novum Testamentum*, 1956,

p. 225-227, R. M. Wilson recalls that the Judaism of the first century was encountering the influence of Hellenism and that John did not need Philo in order to know the doctrine of the Logos.

90. P. 10-14. -- H. Preisker, "Jüdische Apokalyptik und hellenistischer Synkretismus im Johannes-Evangelium, dargelegt am Begriff 'Licht'," *TLZ,* 1952, p. 673-678, admits that the Johannine expressions such as light-darkness come from syncretism because John is addressing his Gospel to the Greek world, but the Johannine idea of light has its roots in the Jewish Apocalypse. -- H. Blauert, *Die Bedeutung der Zeit in der johanneischen Theologie. Eine Untersuchung an Hand von Joh. 1 - 17 unter besonderer Berücksichtigung des literarkritischen Problems,* Tübingen, 1953 (typewritten dissertation, summarised by the writer in *TLZ,* 1935, p. 689-690) concludes that John belongs, with his idea of history, to a Jewish setting and not to the world of Gnosticism. -- R. P. Casey, "Gnosis, Gnosticism and the N. T.," *The Background of the N. T. and its Eschatology ... in honour of C. H. Dodd,* Cambridge, 1956, p. 52-80, mentions ideas which are common to Gnosticism and to John and even suggests an influence of John on Gnosticism and not the reverse.

91. *Le Prologue ...,* p. 109f. Cf. also J. Dupont, *Essais sur le christologie de saint Jean,* p. 35-58.

92. *Du baptême à Cana,* p. 39. Cf. H. Sahlin, *Zur Typologie des Johannes-evangeliums,* Upsala, 1950.

93. *Du baptême à Cana,* p. 10.

94. 94. We should remember that the great works of C. H. Dodd and C. K. Barrett were conceived and written before the texts of Qumran could be utilised.

95. On the subject of John and Qumran, cf. particularly F. M. Braun, "L'arrière-dond judaïque du quatrième évangile et la Communauté de l'Alliance," *RB,* 1955, p. 5-44; O. Cullmann, "The Significance of the Qumran Texts for Research into the Beginnings of Christianity," *JBL,* 1955, p. 213-226; A. Metzinger, "Die Handschriftenfunde am Toten Meer und das Neue Testament," *Biblica,* 1955, p. 457-481.

96. *The Dead Sea Scrolls,* New York, 1955, p. 338. Along the same lines cf. W. F. Albright, "Recent Discoveries in Palestine and the Gospel of John," *The Background of the N. T. and its Eschatology ... in honour of C. H. Dodd,* p. 153-171.

97. Cf. B. Reicke, "Traces of Gnosticism in the Dead Sea Scrolls?" *N. T. Stud.*, 1954-55, p. 137-141.

98. A. Metzinger, p. 468-469, emphasizes the importance of the O. T. as a common source for the writings of Qumran and for the N. T. In this connection we should mention that several studies have drawn attention to the close resemblances between Isaiah (which seems to have been well-known in Qumran) and the fourth Gospel; D. R. Griffiths, "Deutero-Isaiah and the Fourth Gospel," *Exp. Times*, 65, 1953-54, p. 356-360; J. A. T. Robinson, "The Parable of John 10. 1-5," *ZNW*, 1955, p. 237-238; F. W. Young, "A Study of the Relation of Isaiah to the Fourth Gospel," *ZNW*, 1955, p. 215-233.

BIBLIOGRAPHY

(The abbreviations are those used in *Revue Biblique*)

W. F. Albright, "Recent Discoveries in Palestine and the Gospel of John," *The Background of the N. T. and its Eschatology ... in honour of C. H. Dodd*, Cambridge, 1956, p. 153-171.

E. L. Allen, "The Jewish Christian Church in the Fourth Gospel," *JBL*, 1955, p. 88-92.

A. W. Argyle, "Philo and the Fourth Gospel," *Exp. Times*, 63, 1951-52, p. 385-386.

E. Bammel, Φίλος τοῦ Καίσαρος, *TLZ*, 1952, p. 205-210.

P. F. Barackman, "The Gospel according to John," *Interpretation*, 1952, p. 63-70.

C. K. Barrett, "The Old Testament in the Fourth Gospel," *JTS*, 1947, p. 155-169.

-- "The Place of Eschatology in the Fourth Gospel," *Exp. Times*, 59, 1947-48, p. 302-305.

-- "The Holy Spirit in the Fourth Gospel," *JTS*, 1950, p. 9-15.

-- "Zweck des vierten Evangeliums," *Z. sys. Theol.*, 1953, p. 257-273.

-- "The Lamb of God," *N. T. Stud.*, 1954-55, p. 210-218.

-- *The Gospel according to St. John. An Introduction with Commentary and Notes on the Greek Text*, London, 1955.

P. Beeckmann, *L'Evangile selon saint Jean*, Bruges, 1951.

J..Behm, "Der gegenwärtige Stand der Erforschung des Johannesevangeliums," *TLZ*, 1948, p. 21-30.

P. Benoit, "La primauté de saint Pierre selon le N. T.," *Istina*, 1955, p. 325.

M. F. Berrouard, "Le Paraclet, défenseur du Christ devant la conscience du croyant," *Rev. sc. phil. théol.*, 1949, p. 361-389.

E. F. F. Bishop, "Jesus Walking or Teaching in the Temple (Mk. 11. 27 - Jn. 10. 23)," *Exp. Times*, 63, 1951-52, p. 226-227.

M. Black, *An Aramaic Approach to the Gospels and Acts*, Oxford, 1946.

H. Blauert, *Die Bedeutung der Zeit in der johanneischen Theologie. Eine Untersuchung an Hand von Joh. 1-17 unter besonderer Berücksichtigung des literarkritischen Problems*, Tübingen, 1953 (diss. en dactylographie).

J. Blintzer, "Eine Bemerkung zum Geschichtsrahmen des Johannesevangeliums," *Biblica*, 1955, p. 20-35.

M. E. Boismard, "Le chapitre 21 de saint Jean. Essai de critique littéraire," *RB*, 1947, p. 473-501.

-- "A propos de Jean 5. 39. Essai de critique textuelle," *RB*, 1948, p. 5-34.

-- "Clément de Rome et l'Evangile de Jean," *RB*, 1948, p. 376-387.

-- "Critique textuelle et citations patristiques," *RB*, 1950, p. 388-408.

-- "Dans le sein du Père (Jo. 1. 18)," *RB*, 1952, p. 23-39.

-- "Problèmes de critique textuelle concernant le quatrième évangile," *RB*, 1953, p. 347-371.

-- *Le prologue de saint Jean*, Paris, 1953 (Lectio divina, 11).

-- *Du baptême à Cana (Jean 1. 1 - 2. 11)*, Paris 1956 (Lectio divina, 18).

J. Bonsirven, "Les araméismes de saint Jean l'évangeliste?" *Biblica*, 1949, p. 405-432.

-- *Théologie du Nouveau Testament*, Paris, 1951.

G. Bornkamm, "Der Paraklet im Johannes-Evangelium," *Festschrift für R. Bultmann*, 1949, p. 12-35.

L. Bouyer, *Le quatrième évangile. Introduction à l'évangile de saint Jean,* Tournai-Paris, 2ème éd., 1955.

F. M. Braun, "Le baptême d'après le quatrième évangile," *Revue thomiste,* 1948, p. 347-393.

-- "L'eau et l'Esprit," *Revue thomiste,* 1949, p. 5-30

-- "Qui ex Deo natus est (Jo. 1. 13)," *Aux sources de la tradition chrétienne. Mélanges M. Goguel,* Neuchâtel-Paris, 1950, p. 11-31.

-- "La Mère de Jésus dans l'oeuvre de saint Jean," *Revue thomiste,* 1950, p. 429-479 and 1951, p. 5-68.

-- *La Mère des fidèles. Essai de théologie johannique,* Tournai-Paris, 1953.

-- "Morale et mystique à l'école de saint Jean," *Morale chrétienne et requêtes contemporaines,* Paris, 1954, p. 71-84.

-- "Essénisme et Hermétisme," *Revue thomiste,* 1954, p. 523-558.

-- "Hermétisme et Johannisme," *Revue thomiste,* 1955, p. 22-42 and 259-299.

-- "L'arrière-fond judaïque du quatrième évangile et la Communauté de l'Alliance," *RB,* 1955, p. 5-44.

-- "La vie d'en-haut (Jo. 3. 1-15)," *Rev. sc. phil. théol.,* 1956, p. 3-24.

R. Bultmann, *Das Evangelium des Johannes* (Meyer's Kommentar), 13. Aufl. mit Ergänzungsheft, Göttingen, 1953.

-- *Theologie des Neuen Testaments,* Tübingen, 1953.

-- "The Interpretation of the Fourth Gospel," *N. T. Stud.,* 1954-55, p. 77-91.

M. Burrows, *The Dead Sea Scrolls,* New York, 1955.

I. Buse, "John 5. 8 and Johannine-Marcan Relationship," *N. T. Stud.,* 1954-55, p. 134-136.

H. van den Bussche, "L'attente de la grande révelation dans le quatrième évangile," *NRT,* 1953, p. 1009-1019.

H. von Campenhausen, "Zum Verständnis von Joh. 19. 11," *TLZ,* 1948, p. 387-392.

R. P. Casey, "Gnosis, Gnosticism and the N. T.," *The Background of the N. T. and its Eschatology ... in honour of C. H. Dodd,* Cambridge, 1956, p. 52-80.

B. Cassian, "John 21," *N. T. Stud.,* 1956-57, p. 132-136.

L. Cerfaux, "Le thème littéraire parabolique dans l'évangile de saint Jean," *Coniectanea Neotestamentica,* XI, 1947, p. 15-25 = *Recueil Lucien Cerfaux,* 1954, II, p. 17-26.

-- "La charité fraternelle et le retour du Christ (Jo. 13. 33-38)," *Eph. Theol. Lov.,* 1948, p. 321-332 = *RLC,* II, p. 27-40.

-- "Les miracles, signes messianiques de Jésus et oeuvres de Dieu selon l'évangile de saint Jean," *L'Attente du Messie* (Mélanges J. Coppens), Bruges, 1954, p. 131-138 = *RLC,* II, p. 41-50.

H. Clavier, "Mediation in the Fourth Gospel," *SNTS Bulletin,* I, 1950, p. 11-25.

-- "Le problème du rite et du mythe dans le quatrième évangile," *RHPR,* 1951, p. 275-292.

-- "La structure du quatrième évangile," *RHPR,* 1955, p. 174-195.

T. Cottam, *The Fourth Gospel Re-arranged,* London, 1952.

O. Cullmann, "Der johanneische Gebrauch doppeldeutiger Ausdrücke als Schlüssel zum Verständnis des vierten Evangeliums," *TZ,* 1948, p. 360-372.

-- "Εἶδεν καὶ ἐπίστευσεν. La vie de Jésus, objet de la vie et de la foi d'après le quatrième évangile," *Aux sources de la tradition chrétienne. Mélanges M. Goguel,* Neuchâtel-Paris, 1950, p. 52-61.

-- "Sabbat und Sonntag nach dem Johannesevangelium. Ἕως ἄρτι (Joh. 5. 17)," *In Memoriam Ernst Lohmeyer,* Stuttgart, 1951, p. 127-131.

-- *Les sacrements dans l'Evangile johannique. La vie de Jésus et le culte de l'Eglise primitive,* Paris, 1951.

O. Cullmann, "La Samarie et les origines de la mission chrétienne. Qui sont les ἄλλοι de Jean 4. 38?" *Ecole pratique des Hautes Etudes. Section des sciences religieuses. Annuaire 1953-54,* Paris, 1953, p. 3-12.

-- "The Significance of the Qumran Texts for Research into the Beginnings of Christianity," *JBL,* 1955, p. 213-226.

J. G. Davies, "The Primary Meaning of Parakletos," *JTS,* 1953, p. 35-38.

C. H. Dodd, "Le kérugma apostolique dans le quatrième évangile," *RHPR,* 1951, p. 265-274.

-- *The Interpretation of the Fourth Gospel,* Cambridge, 1953.

-- "Some Johannine 'Herrenworte' with Parallels in the Synoptic Gospels," *N. T. Stud.,* 1955-56, p. 75-86.

J. Dupont, *Essais sur la christologie de saint Jean,* Bruges, 1951.

H. E. Edwards, *The Disciple Who Wrote these Things. A New Approach to the Problem of the Authorship of the Fourth Gospel,* London, 1953.

R. A. Edwards, *The Gospel According to St. John. Its Criticism and Interpretation,* London, 1952.

F. V. Filson, "Who was the Beloved Disciple?" *JBL,* 1949, p. 87-88.

A. Fridrichsen, "Jesus, St. John and St. Paul," *The Root of the Vine. Essays in Biblical Theology,* London, 1953, p. 57-62.

P. Gardner-Smith, "St. John's Knowledge of Matthew," *JTS,* 1953, p. 31-35.

A. George, "'L'heure' de Jean 17, *RB,* 1954, p. 393-397.

M. Goguel, *Jésus,* 2ème éd., Paris, 1950.

R. M. Grant, "The Origin of the Fourth Gospel," *JBL,* 1950, p. 305-322.

H. C. Green, "The Composition of St. John's Prologue," *Exp. Times,* 66, 1954-1955, p. 291-294.

D. R. Griffiths, "Deutero-Isaiah and the Fourth Gospel," *Exp. Times,* 65, 1953-54, p. 355-360.

W. Grossouw, *Revelation and Redemption. A Sketch of the Theology of St. John,* Westminster, Md., 1955.

-- "Three Books on the Fourth Gospel," *Novum Testamentum,* 1956, p. 35-46.

R. Gyllenberg, "Die Anfänge der johanneischen Tradition," *Nt. Studien für R. Bultmann,* Berlin, 1954, p. 144-147.

A. C. Headlam, *The Fourth Gospel as History,* Oxford, 1948.

E. Hirsch, "Stilkritik und Literaranalyse im vierten Evangelium," *ZNW,* 1950-51, p. 128-143.

F. R. Hoare, *The Gospel According to St. John Arranged in its Conjectured Original Order and Translated from the Greek into Current English,* London, 1949.

J. G. H. Hoffmann, "Le quatrième évangile, le Jésus de l'histoire et le Christ, Seigneur de l'Eglise," *Revue réformée,* 1952, p. 1-33.

W. F. Howard, *The Fourth Gospel in Recent Criticism and Interpretation.* New Edition revised by C. K. Barrett, London, 1955.

W. F. Howard and A. J. Gossip, "The Gospel According to St. John," *The Interpreter's Bible,* VIII, New York-Nashville, 1955, p. 435-811.

J. Jeremias, *Die Wiederentdeckung von Bethesda, Joh. 5. 2,* Göttingen, 1949.

-- "Zur Geschichtlichkeit des Verhörs Jesu vor dem Hohen Rat," *ZNW,* 1950-51, p. 145-150.

-- "Joh. 6. 51c - 58 redaktionell?" *ZNW,* 1952-53, p. 256-257.

J. Jocz, "Die Juden im Johannesevangelium," *Judaica,* 1953, p. 129-142.

E. Käsemann, "Ketzer und Zeuge. Zum johanneischen Verfasserproblem," *Zeits. f. Theol. u. Kirche,* 1951, p. 292-311.

E. Krafft, "Die Personen des Johannesevangeliums," *Evang. Theol.*, 1956, p. 18-32.

N. Krieger, "Fiktive Orte der Johannestaufe," *ZNW*, 1954, p. 121-123.

S. Läuchli, "Eine alte Spur von Joh. 8. 1-11?" *TZ*, 1950, p. 151.

E. K. Lee, *The Religious Thought of St. John*, London, 1951.

-- "St. Mark and the Fourth Gospel," *N. T. Stud.*, 1956-57, p. 50-58.

X. Léon-Dufour, "Le signe du Temple selon saint Jean," *Mélanges J. Lebreton, I (Rech. sc. relig.*, 1951), p. 155-175.

-- "Actualité du quatrième évangile," *NRT*, 1954, p. 449-468.

R. H. Lightfoot, *St. John's Gospel. A Commentary.* Edited by C. F. Evans, Oxford, 1956.

G. Maldfeld, "Ein neues Johannes-Evangelium-Fragment auf Papyrus," *N. T. Stud.*, 1956-57, p. 78-81.

-- "Papyrus Bodmer II - Joh. Kap. 1-14," *Novum Testamentum*, 1956, p. 153-155.

T. W. Manson, "The Pericope de Adultera (Joh. 7. 53 - 8. 11). A Footnote to the Article by Prof. Jeremias," *ZNW*, 1950-51, p. 145-150.

V. Martin, *Papyrus Bodmer II. Evangile de Jean, chap. 1-14*, Cologny-Genève, 1956.

C. Masson, "Le témoignage de Jean," *Rev. Théol. Phil.*, 1950, p. 120-127.

R. Mehl, "Zur Bedeutung von Kultus und Sakrament im vierten Evangelium," *Evang. Theol.*, 1955.

S. Mendner, "Johanneische Literarkritik," *TZ*, 1952, p. 418-434.

P. H. Menoud, *L'évangile de Jean d'après les recherches récentes*, 2ème éd., Neuchâtel-Paris, 1947 (Cahiers théol. 3).

A. Metzinger, "Die Handschriftenfunde am Toten Meer und das N. T.," *Biblica,* 1955, p. 475-581.

P. W. Meyer, "A Note on John 10. 1-18," *JBL*, 1956, p. 232-235.

W. Michaelis, "Zur Herkunft des johanneischen Paraklet-Titels," *Coniectanea Neotestamentica,* XI, 1947, p. 147-162.

-- *Einleitung in das Neue Testament,* 2. Aufl., Bern, 1954.

D. Mollat, *L'évangile de saint Jean,* Paris, 1953 (Bible de Jérusalem).

F. Mussner, *Die Anschauung vom "Leben" im vierten Evangelium, unter Berücksichtigung der Johannesbriefe. Ein Beitrag zur biblischen Theologie,* München, 1952.

B. Noack, *Zur johanneischen Tradition. Beiträge zur Kritik an der literarkritischen Analyse des vierten Evangeliums,* Kobenhavn, 1954.

H. P. V. Nunn, *The Authorship of the Fourth Gospel,* Oxford, 1952.

W. Oehler, "Typen oder allegorische Figuren im Johannes-evangelium?" *Evang. Theol.,* 1956, p. 422-427.

E. Osty, "Les points de contact entre le récit de la passion dans saint Jean," *Mélanges F. Lebreton, I (Rech. de sc. relig.,* 1951), p. 146-154.

P. Parker, "Bethany beyond Jordan," *JBL,* 1955, p. 257-261.

M. Pohlenz, "Der Prolog des Johannes-Evangeliums," *ZNW,* 1949, p. 98-101.

H. Preisker, "Jüdische Apokalyptik und hellenistischer Synkretismus im Johannes-Evangelium, dargelegt am Begriff 'Licht,'" *TLZ,* 1952, p. 673-678.

F. Quiévreux, "La structure symbolique de l'évangile de saint Jean," *RHPR,* 1953, p. 123-165.

B. Reicke, "Traces of Gnosticism in the Dead Sea Scrolls?" *N. T. Stud.,* 1954-55, p. 137-141.

J. A. T. Robinson, "The Parable of John 10. 1-5," *ZNW,* 1955, p. 233-240.

E. Ruckstuhl, *Die literarische Einheit des Johannesevangeliums. Der gegenwärtige Stand der einschlägigen Forschungen*, Freiburg (Schweiz), 1951.

H. Sahlin, *Zur Typologie des Johannesevangeliums*, Upsala, 1950.

J. N. Sanders, "'Those whom Jesus loved' (John 11. 5)," *N. T. Stud.*, 1954-55, p. 29-41.

R. Schnackenburg, *Das erste Wunder Jesu (Joh. 2. 1-11)*, Freiburg i. B., 1951.

-- "Logos-Hymnus und johanneischer Prolog.," *Bibl. Z.*, 1957, p. 69-109.

J. Schneider, "Zur Komposition von Joh. 10," *Coniectanea Neotestamentica*, XI, 1947, p. 220-225.

-- "Zur Frage der Komposition von Joh. 6. 27-58 (59). (Die Himmelsbrotrede)," *In Memoriam Ernst Lohmeyer*, Stuttgart, 1951, p. 132-142.

-- "Zur Komposition von Joh. 7," *ZNW*, 1955, p. 108-119.

G. Schulze-Kadelbach, "Zur Pneumatologie des Johannesevangeliums," *ZNW*, 1955, p. 279-280.

E. Schweizer, "Das johanneische Zeugnis vom Herrenmahl," *Evang. Theol.*, 1952-53, p. 341-363.

-- "Orthodox Proclamation. The Reinterpretation of the Gospel by the Fourth Evangelist," *Interpretation*, 1954, p. 387-403.

W. M. Smalz, "John, Son of Zebedee," *Angl. Theol. Rev.*, 1953, p. 8-17.

H. C. Snape, "The Fourth Gospel, Ephesus and Alexandria," *HTR*, 1954, 1-14.

H. F. D. Sparks, "St. John's Knowledge of Matthew: The Evidence of Jo. 13. 16 and 15. 20," *JTS*, 1952, p. 58-61

C. Spicq, "Noli me tangere," *Rev. sc. phil. théol*, 1951, p. 226-227.

C. Stange, "Der Prolog des Johannesevangeliums," *Z. syst. Theol, 1950, p. 120-141.*

E. Stauffer, "Agnostos Christos: Joh. 2. 24 und die Eschatologie des vierten Evangeliums," *The Background of the N. T., and its Eschatology...in honour of C. H. Dodd,* Cambridge, 1956, p. 281-299.

H. Strathmann, *Das Evangelium nach Johannes,* 6, Aufl. Göttingen, 1951 (Das N. T. Deutsch).

C. C. Tarelli, "Clement of Rome and the Fourth Gospel," *JTS,* 1947, p. 208-209.

S. Temple, "Geography and Climate in the Fourth Gospel," *The Joy of Study. Papers...presented to F. C. Grant,* New York, 1951, p. 63-72.

E. L. Titus, "The Identity of the Beloved Disciple," *JBL,* 1950, p. 323-328.

E. Ullendorff, "A Mistranslation from Aramaic?" *N. T. Stud.,* 1955-56, p. 50-52.

N. Uricchio, "La teoria delle trasposizioni nel Vangelo di S. Giovanni," *Biblica,* 1950, p. 129-163 et 1951, p. 567-568.

A. Vergote, *L'exaltation du Christ en croix selon le quatrième évangile,* Bruges-Paris, 1952 (Analecta Lovaniensia Biblica et Orientalia, II, 29).

A. Wikenhauser, *Das Evangelium nach Johannes,* Regensburg, 1948 (Regensburger N. T., 4).

-- *Einleitung in das Neue Testament,* Freiburg i. B., 1953.

R. M. Wilson, "Philo and the Fourth Gospel," *Exp. Times,* 65, 1953-54, p. 47-49.

-- "The Fourth Gospel and Hellenistic Thought," *Novum Testamentum,* 1956, p. 225-227.

W. G. Wilson, "The Original Text of the Fourth Gospel. Some Objective Evidences Against the Theory of Pages Displacements," *JTS,* 1949, p. 59-60.

F. W. Young, "A Study of the Relation of Isaiah to the Fourth Gospel," *ZNW,* 1955, p. 215-233.

ADDITIONS TO THE BIBLIOGRAPHY (November 1957)

K. Aland, "Der Papyrus Bodmer II. Ein erster Bericht," *TLZ*, 1957, p. 161-184.

-- "Neue Neutestamentliche Papyri," *N. T. Stud.*, 1956-57, p. 280-284.

H. Becher, *Die Reden des Johannesevangeliums und der Stil der gnostischen Offenbarungsrede*, Göttingen, 1956.

J. N. Birdsall, "Photius and the Text of the Fourth Gospel," *N. T. Stud.*, 1957-58, p. 61-63.

J. Blinzler, "Die Strafe für Ehebruch in Bibel und Halacha. Zur Auslegung von Joh. 8. 5," *N. T. Stud.*, 1957-58, p. 32-47.

M. E. Boismard, "Le Papyrus Bodmer II," *RB*, 1957, p. 363-398.

G. Bornkamm, "Die eucharistische Rede im Johannes-Evangelium," *ZNW*, 1956, p. 161-169.

F. M. Braun, "Où en est l'étude du quatrième évangile?" *Eph. Th. Lov.*, 1956, p. 535-546.

-- "L'Evangile de saint Jean et l'ancienne catéchèse romaine," *Revue thomiste*, 1956, p. 643-658.

C. H. Dodd, "A l'arrière-plan d'un dialogue johannique [Jo. 8. 33-58]," *RHPR*, 1957, p. 5-17.

E. Haenchen, "Aus der Literatur zum Johannesevangelium 1929-1956," *Th. Rsch.*, 1955, p. 295-335 [publié en février 1957].

W. Kern, "Der symmetrische Gesamtaufbau von Jo. 8. 12-58," *ZKT*, 1956, p. 451-454.

A. F. J. Klijn, "Papyrus Bodmer II (John 1-14) and the Text of Egypt," *N. T. Stud.*, 1956-57, p. 327-334.

H. Koester, "Geschichte und Kultur im Johannesevangelium und bei Ignatius von Antiochien," *Z. Theol. Kirche*, 1957, p. 56-68.

K. H. Kuhn, "St. John 7. 37-38," *N. T. Stud.*, 1957-58, p. 63-65.

M. F. Lagan, "L'oeuvre du Verbe incarné: le don de la Vie (Jo. 1. 4)," *Rech. sc. relig.*, 1957, p. 61-78.

D. Lamont, *Studies in the Johannine Writings*, London, 1956.

C. Maurer, "Steckt hinter Joh. 5. 17 ein Uebersetzungsfehler?" *Wort und Dienst. Jahrbuch der Theol. Schule Bethel*, 1957, p. 130-140.

P. Parker, "Two Editions of John," *JBL*, 1956, p. 303-314.

T. E. Pollard, "The Exegesis of John 10. 30 in the Early Trinitarian Controversies," *N. T. Stud.*, 1956-57, p. 334-349.

G. Quispel, "Nathanael und der Menschensohn (Joh. 1. 51)," *ZNW*, 1956, p. 281-283.

F. Roustang, "L'entretien avec Nicodème," *NRT*, 1956, p. 337-358.

J. Schmid, "Johannes 1. 13," *Bibl. Z.*, 1957, p. 118-125.

J. Schneider, "Zur Komposition von Joh. 18. 12-27," *ZNW*, 1957, p. 111-119.

S. Schulz, *Studien zur Menschensohn-Christologie im Johannes-Evangelium*, Göttingen, 1957.

E. M. Sidebottom, "The Son of Man as Man in the Fourth Gospel," *Exp. Times*, 68, 1956-57, p. 231-235 et 280-283.

-- "The Ascent and Descent of the Son of Man in the Gospel of St. John," *Angl. Theol. Rev.*, 1957, p. 115-122.

E. L. Titus, *The Message of the Fourth Gospel*, New York, 1957.

W. A. Wordsworth, "The Bodmer Papyrus and the Prologue of John's Gospel," *Novum Testamentum*, 1957, p. 1-7

IV. ASPECTS OF NEW TESTAMENT THEOLOGY

ΜΙΑ ΕΚΚΛΗΣΙΑ[1]

The New Testament never states in exact words that the Church is and should be one. The expression μία ἐκκλησία is nowhere to be found in the New Testament. However it does not follow that the early Christians attached no importance, or very little importance, to the unity and the oneness of the Church. On the contrary, according to the New Testament, unity is of the very essence of the Church. Because it is the Church of Jesus Christ, the Church is one in principle and should be one in reality also. The unity of the Church, in the New Testament, appears to be a gift and an obligation at the same time. The biblical writers speak of the unity of the Church both in the indicative and in the imperative. The theological affirmation of unity is accompanied by the exhortation to unity.

In order to attack the sectarian spirit of the Corinthians, Saint Paul does not call on an ideal of human concord and brotherhood, in the manner of the Stoics reflecting upon the cosmopolitan unity of the human race. The Apostle peremptorily declares that the Church cannot be divided because Christ, who constitutes the Church, is not divided. There is, and there can only be, one Church, because there is only one Lord. In fact, by asking the question, "Is Christ divided?"

(I Cor. 1. 13) - a question to which an affirmative answer would be absurd - Paul reminds us that the unity of the Church is a function of the unity of Christ, and he emphasizes the duty of those who are "in Christ" to maintain the unity of His "body." It is the same in the fourth gospel. The necessity and the obligation for unity are combined in the prayer of the Johannine Christ (Jn. 17. 11, 22.)

Moreover, the unity of the Church is expressed in the New Testament in a series of images which leave no doubt about the feeling of the first Christians that the Church cannot be divided or allowed to take manifold forms. The New Testament speaks of the Church as a building, a vine, a flock, a wife, a body, and always in connection with Christ. Christ is the corner-stone of only one building, he is the single vine to which the branches must be attached in order to live, he is the true shepherd who has only one flock, he is the husband who has only one wife, he is the head of one single body.[2]

If the New Testament then feels so strongly about the unity of the Church, why is that unity never mentioned in so many words, without being wrapped in imagery? Why does the New Testament not make use of the expression μία ἐκκλησία?

It is not really surprising that we do not find this expression in the fourth gospel. In fact, although John affirms that Jesus came to reunite in one body the scattered children of God (Jn. 11. 52), and although he adds that this unity should be as close as that between the Father and the Son (Jn. 17. 11, 22), he never uses the word ἐκκλησία.

But Paul's case is quite different. Paul uses the word ἐκκλησία extensively, and if he did not introduce it into the language of Christianity, he gave it its integral resonance which would last for ever. The Apostle had the perfect opportunity to introduce the expression μία ἐκκλησία. He could include it in the series of seven acclamations in Ephesians

4 which can be describing nothing but the unity of the Church. "I entreat you," writes Saint Paul, "to maintain the unity of the Spirit in the bond of peace. There is *one body* and *one spirit,* just as you were called to the *one hope* that belongs to your call. There is *one Lord, one faith, one baptism, one God* and Father of us all, who rules over all, acts through all, and dwells in all." (Eph. 4. 1, 3-6.)

It could be said that Paul had no need to insert "there is one Church" in this list since he writes "there is one body." But the problem is to find out, if possible, why the Apostle, when he talks of the unity of the Church here and elsewhere, uses the expression ἓν σῶμα. He also says εἷς ἄρτος, but never μία ἐκκλησία. It can always be supposed that the fact that an author does not use a certain expression is entirely fortuitous. However, in this particular case, there are perhaps some positive reasons to explain the omission.

First, the certainty that unity belongs to the very essence of the Church, that the Church by definition is *one,* was so strong that the expression μία ἐκκλησία would have been redundant. It will be pointed out that Paul believed in the unity of the Church just as much as in the unity of God, the Lord, the Spirit, baptism, faith, hope and the single body made up of all those called by God in Christ and renewed through His Spirit, since, as believers, they have all received the same baptism and participate in the same hope. The text of Ephesians proves, in fact, that the need was felt to recall the objective facts on which the unity of the spirit, which the believers were urged to maintain, was based. The question to which we are seeking an answer should therefore be framed as follows: why was it necessary to affirm the unity of the divine persons and the acts of salvation and not judged necessary to affirm the unity of the Church?

If we look more closely, we can see that the seven expressions of unity in Ephesians 4 have a controversial element in each of them. This is indicated in the introductory exhortation of the first three verses of the chapter, and particularly these words in verse 3: σπουδάζοντες τηρεῖν τὴν ἑνότητα τοῦ πνεύματος. What must be "maintained" against the denials of the heathens or the Jews, and safeguarded in purity from misinterpretation by perverted Christians - sinners and heretics - are those "unities" which are the expression of the true Christian doctrine and discipline. These "unities" are named specifically, for the reason that they are being, or can be, challenged. It is "for us" - the believers - "that there is but one God, the Father and one Lord, Jesus Christ." And Paul, when he reminds the Corinthians of this fundamental Christian confession of faith, contrasts it with the beliefs of the pagans in many gods and in many lords in heaven and on earth (I Cor. 8. 4-6.) This is the point at which the Christian faith meets pagan ideas head on, and this is why the Apostle must say that there is *one* God and *one* Lord.

The unity of faith and of hope follows naturally from the unity of the Lord. There is no worthwhile faith and hope, among all those offered to man for his allegiance, except faith and hope in Jesus Christ alone (cf. Col. 1. 27 etc.). Therefore it was necessary to state that there is but one faith and one hope. The Christian faith leads to only one baptism - baptism in Christ (Rom. 6. 3; Gal. 3. 27), a baptism which makes all those who are baptized partakers of "one spirit" so that they form "one body" (I Cor. 12. 13.) It was necessary to recall specifically that Christian baptism is the only true baptism and that it is administered only once, not only because Judaism and the eastern religions also recognized a kind of "baptism," but also because, in the first century, it was thought that one could be a Christian without being baptized in the name of Jesus and thus receiving the Holy Spirit. In this respect there are some brief and somewhat puzzling notes in the book of Acts (18. 25; 19. 2-6) in connection with Apollos, teaching τὰ περὶ τοῦ 'Ιησοῦ though he knew only the baptism of John, and with those "disciples" at Ephesus, who "had not even heard that there is a Holy Spirit."

There is "one Spirit," the Holy Spirit, which comes from God, and which is opposed by the spirit of Satan appearing in different forms: the spirit of the world (I Cor. 2. 12), the spirit of slavery (Rom. 8. 15), the prince of the powers of the air, the spirit at work in the sons of disobedience (Eph. 2. 2), or the spirit of evil which causes heresy (cf. I Tim. 4. 1). To say, as the Apostle does in Ephesians 4, that there is but one Spirit, is to put into precise terms the warning developed in the first Epistle of John - "Beloved, do not believe every spirit; test the spirits to see whether they are from God...for the spirit of the Antichrist...is already in the world" (4. 1-3).

There is "one body," the "body of Christ" of which Christians are the members (I Cor. 6. 15), and their membership in the body of Christ forbids them to become members of any other "body" (I Cor. 6. 16).

In short, the numerical adjective which precedes each of the seven acclamations in Ephesians 4 is not there just to recall the unity and the oneness of the persons and the facts of the Christian faith; it is also there to point out that these persons and facts only have their reality within Christianity, although the words which describe them may be used by others apart from the believers.

On the other hand, when speaking of the Church, it was not necessary to say that there was only one, because the word ἐκκλησία, with the genitives τοῦ θεοῦ or τοῦ Χριστοῦ expressed or understood - and they are always understood if they are not specifically mentioned - depicts a reality absolutely *sui generis*, an *ordo salutis* linked by definition with the person of Jesus Christ, and which, consequently, has no equivalent, no parallel, no rival anywhere.

The pagans have no Church. Certainly the word ἐκκλησία exists outside the biblical domain, but in a secular sense. Even if there are any "so-called lords" in the world, they do not incorporate a "Church" in their person. Even if Caesar is given the title Kurios, Caesar's subjects are not a Church. The Jews no longer have a Church. Although Israel was the ἐκκλησία τοῦ θεοῦ at the time of the promise (cf. Acts 7. 38), the unbelief of the people in the face of that fulfilled promise has guaranteed their downfall. Henceforth the dignity of the people of God has passed to those who believe in Jesus Christ. It is they who are "the Israel of God" (Gal. 6. 16) while "those who say that they are Jews are not, but are Satan's synagogue" (Rev. 2. 9; cf. 3. 9). There never has been and there never will be more than one Church of God. When Israel is finally converted, it will not be in order to regain its unique privilege of being the chosen people; it will be in order to be a member of the one Church of the Jews and the Gentiles. The heretics also have no Church. Undoubtedly the Christianity of the first century was already feeling the effects of centrifugal force. There was a tendency towards "heresy," that is to say freely chosen opinion, in contrast to revelation "given to the saints once and for all;" there was yielding to "error" by turning away from "the way" of the Gospel; there were attempts to introduce into the Church "divisions" which would break the unity of the body of Christ, if the apostolic vigilance failed. But this does not seem to have been the case. The "heretics" of the first century were not schismatic. Neither the Judeo-Christians in Galatia, nor the angel-worshippers at Colossae, even if they sought to win over the Church to their particular views, did not undertake to set up another Church in the face of the apostolic Church. It is remarkable also that, while the New Testament numbers among the eschatological griefs the appearance of false Christs and heresies, it never goes so far as to say that, as a result of the work of these false Messiahs, another ἐκκλησία might rise up later, against the only Church worthy of that name.

In short, since there does not exist and cannot exist any other Church but the Church of Jesus Christ, it is not necessary to speak of "*one* Church." It is enough to say "*the* Church."

Therefore it is not because of indifference to the unity of the Church that the writers of the New Testament never use the expression μία ἐκκλησία. On the contrary, if they did not think of creating the expression, it is because they did not need it. They were quite convinced that the Church is one by definition and that it is a reality which is uniquely and specifically Christian.

NOTES

1. *Hommage et reconnaissance à Karl Barth*, Delachaux et Niestlé, Neuchâtel-Paris, 1946, p. 87-91.

2. Cf. P. H. Menoud, *L'unité de l'Eglise selon le Nouveau Testament*. Etudes théologiques et religieuses, 1946. *infra* p. 318f.

The Unity of the Church
According to the New Testament[1]

Hardly had Saint Ignatius of Antioch given the Church the title "catholic" when Marcion openly destroyed the unity of the body of Christ and set up his schismatic Church in opposition to the apostolic Church. From that time on the Church went from division to division almost to the point of crumbling away. In order to maintain the biblical idea that the Church is and should be one, there was recourse to expedients; it has been said that the Church is both invisible and visible, and the division of the visible Church does not affect the catholicity of the invisible Church.

These distinctions which resulted from the separation between doctrinal affirmation and historical reality are not only unknown in the New Testament; they are completely contrary to the concept and the reality of the Church as these appear in primitive Christianity. For the New Testament the Church is visible, and this visible Church is *one*. This is why through all succeeding generations of Christians there have been those who looked back nostalgically to the original undivided Church and sought the secret of unity there.

The Church of the first century was not in an exceptional situation. It was formed, like the Church of all ages, of men very different in temperament and expression, and on its way it encountered obstacles capable of destroying its unity. In the beginning there was the problem of the admittance of Gentiles to salvation; at Corinth, the divisive spirit arose; everywhere, there was burgeoning heresy. But none of these problems caused a schism. The New Testament does not recognize two churches bringing together the Jews and the Gentiles separately, but one single Church of Jews and Gentiles. At Corinth, Paul was able to show to his own followers, or to those who followed Cephas or Apollos, a vision of the indivisibility of the body of Christ. Everywhere the vigilance of the Apostle anticpated the heretics and postponed their devastation.

There are more profound reasons for the unity of the Church than favorable historical circumstances. The supreme reason for unity appears in the policy followed by Saint Paul at Corinth. To attack the sectarian spirit, the Apostle makes no appeal to an ideal of agreement and concord, as the Stoics regard the cosmopolitan unity of the human race. On the contrary Paul makes his appeal to the unity of Christ. He states categorically that the Church cannot be divided because Christ is not divided. That says it all. The unity of the Church is a function of the unity of the Christ who constitutes it. The unity of the Lord is extended in the unity of His Church. Unity comes from above. But the Church must submit to this necessity for unity. It must make real in its actual life the unity which is given to it. It must become what it already is, or it risks being no longer the Church of God in Jesus Christ.

To speak of the unity of the Church according to the New Testament means dealing with the following two questions in turn:

I. What is the nature of the theological requirement which is the basis of the unity and the union of all who believe in Christ?

II. How did the Church of the first century succeed in

maintaining the unity which its Lord desired and in living in a way worthy of its calling.

I. *The theological basis of unity*

Paul's declaration in I Corinthians 1. 13 ("Is Christ divided?") means that the Church can be neither divided nor manifold, because Christ cannot be so. The unity of the Church is therefore based on the unity of Christ, by virtue of the solidarity existing between the Lord and the Church. This idea is expressed in the New Testament in three ways, which correspond to three ideas of the Church. The Church, in fact, bears out these three definitions which overlap each other:

1) it is the people of God of the New Covenant in Jesus Christ;

2) it is all believers whom Jesus Christ has saved by His death and Resurrection;

3) it is the body of the Saints governed by the Spirit of Christ.

The idea of the Church's unity is to be found in these three definitions.

1) *The people of God*

God carries out His work in history according to the unchanging principles of election and promise. The line of divine election, which starts with Abraham and the patriarchs, passes through Moses and Israel, continues in the prophets and the "remnant" of the people, and ends in Christ and His Church. By confessing that Jesus of Nazareth is the Messiah of Israel, the Church becomes the Messianic people, the legitimate heir of the covenant of the promise, the Israel of

God."

The Church is Abraham's only heir. "Through your posterity all the nations of the earth shall be blessed," says Peter (Acts 3. 25), quoting Genesis 22. 18, and he adds that the believers are these chosen heirs. Paul emphasizes, with regard to the same text: "It does not say: 'and to offsprings,' referring to many; but it says, referring to one: 'and to your offspring,' which is Christ" (Gal. 3. 16). Christ here is the epitome of all Christians. Abraham has but one heir: Christ, and Christ in His entirety, that is to say Christ Himself and those who belong to Him (cf. Gal. 3. 26-29; Rom. 8. 17).

That the Church henceforth takes the place of Israel as the people of God is the unanimous testimony of the New Testament, from Peter's speeches in the book of Acts up to the last pages of Revelation. The texts are so well known that we do not need to cite them, particularly the great texts in the epistles to the Romans and the Galatians. The Church, the people of God, is, on the one hand, a people in continuity with Israel: it is the people who are living out the fulfilment of the promise. But, on the other hand, the Church is a new people: its limits are set only by the principle of election on which it is constituted, to the exclusion of all national or racial distinctions. This is already evident in the scene at Pentecost where the Spirit is seen to descend on those who have flocked to Jerusalem from the four corners of the earth (Acts 2). It is the idea emphasized by Paul when he says that Christ has broken down the dividing wall between Jews and Gentiles and made a new people, the one and only people of God, uniting all believers (Eph. 2. 14f). The theology of the people of God presupposes the existence of a single Church of the Jews and the Gentiles.

In short, the theology of the people of God, which presupposes the unity of the Church, bases this unity on the unity of Christ and on the common destiny of Christ and His followers.

God never chooses a man merely for the purpose of his own individual salvation. From the vessels of election which He fashions for the purpose of His glory, God makes His ambassadors, so that they can make His name known and create for Him a people over whom He can reign. This was God's policy towards Abraham, who was chosen not just for himself, but particularly for the sake of his posterity. This was God's policy toward Moses, who fulfills his vocation by the summons he hands on to Israel. Still following the same line, the Son of Man in the Jewish apocalypse brings together "the holy ones on the last day." When the new covenant has been ratified Christ appears at the head of the new people of God - the Church. The policy of God still follows the rule of unity: one patriarch and one lineal descent, one prophet and one "church in the desert" (Acts 7. 38), one Son of Man and one holy people, one Christ and one Church.

Three further remarks on the subject of the Church as the people of God:

i. The New Testament often describes the Church in pictorial forms. The Church is likened to a building (ναός, οἰκοδομή, οἶκος τοῦ θεου, cf. "the heavenly city," "the new Jerusalem"), to arable land or a vineyard, to a flock, to a betrothed girl or a wife. All these images have the factor "one" attached to them. Christ is the corner-stone of only *one* building, he is the *one* vine of which His faithful are the branches, he is the true shepherd who has only *one* flock, he is the betrothed or the husband of only *one* woman. In short, each of these images in its own way illustrates the central idea of the theology of the people of God: God calls together *one* people in Christ.

ii. The theology of the people of God explains why the Christians, from the beginning, described themselves with the word ἐκκλησία, and not with the word SYNAGOGUE like the purists and those who made a profession of their righteousness. The latter, since the time of the Maccabees, separated themselves from the rest of the people in "synagogues of righteous men," or "synagogues of doctors of the law" (I Macc. 2. 42; 7. 12). The word SYNAGOGUE could not possibly be used to describe the Church of God. For it is God Himself who "calls" (Acts 2. 39) men to come into His ἐκκλησία, and the Church will consist of as many people as God is pleased to call. Nobody has the right to set arbitrary limits to the divine call, following human criteria. Moreover a "synagogue," which is a break made in the people of God, has to have a particular characteristic and these particular characteristics bring about, or at least make possible, a plurality. The Church is *one*.

iii. But, it will be said, the expression "the churches" also appears in the New Testament. This is true, but the expression ἐκκλησίαι does not mean a plurality of Churches, but merely a plurality of places where the Church comes together. What constitutes the Church is the call of God in Jesus Christ. The number of those who answer this call and their geographical dispersion could not change the idea of the Church in any way. The Church, in its full theological meaning exists in each local church. It is not because of a lack of vocabulary that the first Christians ignored the distinction we make when we speak of Church and congregation (Kirche und Gemeinde). On the contrary, it is to emphasize that the Church, wherever there are followers of Christ, is one and the same reality, whose unity exists despite scattered local churches. The plural "churches" makes no change in the unity and indivisibility of the Church; it merely indicates a geographical dispersion due to conditions of life here on earth and therefore temporary. This is why the end of the Diaspora and the reunion of the Church at the Parousia are the subject of Christian hope, as the well-known prayer in the Didache says, "Let your Church be brought together from the ends of the earth into your kingdom" (IX. 4).

2) *The unity of Christ*

By His redemptive work Jesus Christ has established *one* single Church. Jesus Christ *alone* is the basis of the salvation of all men, and He alone establishes the unity of all whom He saves. This idea, which can already be seen behind the theology of the people of God, is expressed in the New Testament in several ways which are different in form but fundamentally the same.

In Peter's speech reported in Acts 4. 11-12, he declares that the only salvation is in the one who has become the corner-stone, that is the firm foundation of the building under construction which is the Church. These few words are an outline of the description of the Church as a spiritual house which appears in the first epistle of Peter (2. 4-10).

Paul develops the idea of the solidarity between Christ and the Church along three parallel lines, each of which ends with the affirmation of the unity of the Church. These three lines of thought are as follows:

a) the comparison of Adam and Christ. Just as one single man is the origin of the fall of every man, one man alone brings about salvation for all (Rom. 5. 15-19; cf. I Cor. 15. 22; II Cor. 5. 14; I Tim. 2. 5-6). Along with this comparison of Adam and Christ we should mention the comparison in II Corinthians 11. 2, where the Apostle describes Christ as the only Betrothed of the Church, who should not be led astray, like Eve, by the cunning wiles of the serpent. The image of marriage shows that unity belongs to the Church just as it does to Christ.

b) The affirmation that the believers are one in Jesus Christ (Gal. 3. 28), that they are one body in Christ and that Christ is the head of that body (Rom. 12; I Cor. 12; Col. 3. 15, etc.). In these texts the image of the "body" - no doubt inspired by the use of the word "body" in the liturgy of the eucharist, seeing that the celebration of Holy Communion presupposes the perfect unity of the members of the body - is hardly more than an image. It has a double significance: first it shows that the Church only exists and subsists through Christ, the head of the body; secondly it shows that the members themselves form one single, organic whole. In short, the image expresses both the unity *of* the Church and the unity *within* the Church. But often - for example in Galatians 4. 19 and in Colossians and Ephesians - the equation: the Church = the body of Christ is more than just an image. The Church really *is* a body. It is the organ of the glorified Christ, the means by which He can be present on earth. It is not forcing Paul's thought to make the following equivalent: Christ is now incarnate in the Church, as He was incarnate in Jesus during His earthly life. This is why Saul of Tarsus is persecuting Jesus Himself when he attacks the Church which is His body. The expression: the body of Christ, which - it is hardly necessary to recall - is only applied to the Church and never to the believer, is one of the highest expressions of the unity of the Church, and an expression which reveals as clearly as possible the christological basis of this unity.

c) The strong affirmation that the unity of Christ is continued in the unity of the Church. In the triad "one Lord, one faith, one baptism" (Eph. 4. 5), the unity of the faith and the unity of the baptism signify the unity of the Church, since the believers share the same faith in Christ and have all been baptized in the name of Jesus. And the reason for the unity is the dominant affirmation of the series: one single Lord. The gospel of John is no less affirmative. The aim of the work of Christ is to bring back into one unity the far-scattered children of God (11. 52) so that there may be one flock under the true shepherd (10. 16). The unity of the faithful proceeds, as in Paul, from the communion they have with Christ, and their unity should be as close as that between the Father and the Son (17. 11, 22). Throughout the New Testament, the result of the redemptive work of Jesus Christ is to call into existence the one and only Church of the single Savior.

3) *The unity of the Spirit*

In the New Testament, the Spirit and the Church have a very close relationship with each other. They are the two organs of the Lordship of Christ glorified, and take His place, so to speak, on earth, during the interval between the resurrection and the second coming. The Church without the Spirit would be a corpse. The Spirit without the Church would be a force without a means of expressing itself on earth. It is through the Spirit that the life of Christ is given to the Church. It is in the Church that the Spirit carries out its work.

This is why the Spirit and the Church always appear together in the New Testament. The Spirit and the Church are: 1) announced and promised by Jesus (Jn. 7. 39; Matt. 16. 18); 2) manifested together in history (Acts 2); 3) associated in the work of salvation (I Cor. 12. 12f; Eph. 4. 4, etc.) and 4) united in the same expectation of the Parousia ("The Spirit and the Church say: Come" - Rev. 22. 17).

The "unity of the Spirit" (Eph. 4. 4) of necessity therefore implies the unity of the Church. The Spirit, which is the Spirit of Christ, and the Church, which is the body of Christ, are both of them one, as Christ is one.

There is more. Because it is the Spirit of Christ and because it works in the Church of Christ, the Spirit governs the whole life of the Church and that of the believers and places the sign of unity over that life. The Spirit creates and maintains, in the Church, one single faith, one single baptism, one single hope and the same communion throughout all the faithful. Faith unites the whole Church in confessing the Lord who has been preached, and this is why the book of Acts declares, in praise of the Church, that it is continuing in the Apostles' doctrine. Baptism in the name of Jesus remains in the Church as the visible sign of the union of the believers with Christ. Baptism, uniting all Christians to the unique Christ and to His unique death, manifests unity as well as constituting it. "All of you who have been baptized into Christ have clothed yourselves with Christ...you are one in Christ Jesus" (Gal. 3. 28). The New Testament does not specifically mention the unity of the eucharist, either because the Lord's Supper is the supreme sacrament of unity, or because the unity of communion is already expressed by the very word "communion," which Paul uses in explicit connection with Jesus Christ (I Cor. 1. 9; 10. 16). This communion with Jesus Christ inevitably leads to the communion of the faithful with each other. They are of one heart and mind (Acts 2. 42f), unified in one feeling (Phil. 1. 27; 2. 2f), keeping "the unity of the Spirit" (Eph. 4. 3). The unity *of* the Church creates unity *within* the Church.

Let us summarize what we have said so far. Whether we see in the Church a people called together by God in Jesus

Christ, or the faithful who are one with the Christ who has redeemed them, or Christians governed by the Spirit of Christ, the Church is always *one,* because the one who calls it together, who saves it and who maintains it by the Spirit until the Parousia, is *one.* There is and there can be only one Church, because there is only one Lord.

II. *The historical realization of unity*

We must now deal with the second question we set for ourselves - was the Church of the New Testament, in practice, one?

Let us be more precise. We must distinguish between unity and uniformity. Without any doubt there were differences of doctrine within the Church of the first century - the christologies of Paul and John, for instance, do not correspond exactly, and they are the prevailing expression of the primitive Christian faith. It is likely that the organization of the Pauline churches is not identical in every way with the organization of the churches in Palestine. We might also mention a few disturbing facts which, as far as I know, have never been explained satisfactorily - for instance, the apparent lack of concern of the Apostles at the time of Stephen's trial. There is also the seeming lack of interest among the Christians in Jerusalem (except for James) and among those in Rome, at the time of Paul's arrest and imprisonment. These few small facts prove at least that the infant Church was not immune to contrasts in personalities and differences of opinion. But this fact is no cause for surprise. The first Christians would not have been human if things had been otherwise. As we read the exhortations in the epistles we see that the "saints" were "called" to sainthood but did not necessarily achieve it.

When the question is asked, "Was the New Testament Church one and united?" we would counter in this way: "Was the theological necessity for unity of itself so strong that it prevented a break in the unity of the Church?" And if the answer is "yes," how and why did unity triumph over the forces of division?

Our inquiry will bear on the following three points: 1) the exhortations to unity in the New Testament; 2) the consequences of the entry into the Church of a new Apostle, Saint Paul, and of a large number of Gentile-Christians; 3) the attitude of the Church to rising heresy.

1) *The exhortations to unity*

The Church must establish its unity as a concrete fact. It must remain one and united. Otherwise the affirmation that it is one will be nothing but pure theory; and as unity belongs to the very essence of the Church, the Church itself would run the risk of crumbling away. If the Church is the organ of Christ glorified on earth, it is obvious that this organ must be able to fulfill its mission, which is to make Christ visible to men. This would not happen if the body, which is the Church, were prey to ravages from within or, worse still, if it were divided into separate parts. This is so true that, during the course of centuries, when the ecclesiastical body of christ has been broken, theologians have to dream up either the theory of an invisible Church, or the concept of the soul of the Church, in order to safeguard the theory of the unity of the Church, in spite of its actual divisions.

In the New Testament, the unity of the Church is both a gift and an obligation. The New Testament speaks of unity in the indicative and in the imperative. It is where the theological affirmation of unity resounds more forcefully that the exhortation to unity can be most clearly heard. The well-known series of seven affirmations of the unity of the Spirit, of the Lord and of God in chapter 4 of the epistle to the Ephesians is introduced by an appeal for union and unity, "I urge you then...to maintain the unity of the Spirit in the bond of peace." The necessity for unity and the obligation to maintain it are brought together in the same way in Christ's prayer in the Gospel of John (John 17).

The unity of the Church, as we have said, has its basis in the unity of Christ. The unity of Christ is also the central motif of the exhortations to unity. This motif appears nowhere more clearly than in Paul's well-known reprimand to the Corinthians: "Is Christ divided?" The appeal to unity is not based on any general considerations, such as the value of harmony or the advantages of union, but on the theological truth that Christ, one in His person, must also be one in His body, which is the Church.

The unity which Christians must make real and preserve from all division is always based "in the Lord" or "in Christ." To mention but one example, look at the wonderful exhortation addressed to the Philippians - "If there is any encouragement in Christ, any incentive of love, any participation in the Spirit, any affection and sympathy, make my joy complete by being of the same mind, having the same love, being in full accord and of one mind." In short, says Paul, "Have this mind among yourselves which you have in Christ Jesus" (Phil. 2. 1-5). Since you are one in Christ be one in your Church.

The last reason for unity given in the exhortation is that Christ's glory will shine all the more brightly in the world if the Church in which He is incarnate is perfect in unity. The unity of the Church is an important element in the witness which the Church is to give to the world (John 17. 21).

2) *The Church of Jews and Gentiles*

It has been suggested that the greatest threat to the unity of the infant Church was the arrival on the scene of a new Apostle, Saint Paul and the entrance into the Church of a large number of Gentile-Christians. Certainly the unity of the Church was not broken, since two Churches were not formed. But how did unity prevail, and at what cost?

A. *Paul, the new Apostle*

According to the book of Acts there are two conditions necessary to make a believer into an Apostle: 1) he must be a witness of the resurrection (Acts 1. 22; 2. 32f. etc.) and 2) he must have been with Jesus during His earthly ministry, from the time of John the Baptist (Acts 1. 21; 10. 37 etc.).

Paul only fulfills the first condition. He saw the Lord (I Cor. 9. 1; 15. 8), but that was after the time of the incarnation. Would the difference in his calling have caused a rift between him and the Twelve? In Paul's view, it is the Lord Himself who has called him to be an Apostle to the Gentiles (Gal. 1). He holds his ministry from the Lord Himself and not by an investiture by men, even if they are leading citizens of Jerusalem. But at the same time Paul knows that he has not been called to preach a new religion, but that he is entering an already established tradition. This is why he is convinced that he would be running in vain if the ministry to the Gentiles, which had been entrusted to him, was not recognized by those who were Apostles before him (Gal. 1. 17; 2. 2). Paul would not have made the journey to Jerusalem and the approaches to the Apostles there, as recounted in Galatians 2, if he had not felt that mutual understanding and recognition of apostleship and field of mission were indispensable to the unity of the Church. And Paul had foreseen this rightly, since the "pillars" extended the right hand of fellowship to him.

However, there is still a difference between Paul and the Twelve. Paul was not one of Jesus' Witnesses from the beginning, he did not take part in the first events of the infant Church, and he had also persecuted it. This is why the Apostle Paul, always with the maintenance of the unity of the Church in view, attaches so much importance to the traditions coming from Jerusalem. Starting in chapter 11 of the first epistle to the Corinthians, he mentions several times the traditions by which faith and the discipline of the Church should be guided. At the beginning he declares, in quite general terms, "I commend you because you maintain the traditions even as I have delivered them to you" (11. 2). First, dealing with the tradition of the Lord's Supper, he writes, "I received from the Lord that which I also delivered to you" (11. 23), which means: "What I have taught you about the eucharist I received from a tradition which goes back, through the first Apostles, to Jesus Christ." Next he turns to the tradition of the christophanies (15. 1f) and after mentioning Christ's appearances, Paul adds: "Whether it was they (the Apostles in Jerusalem), or I, this is what we preach and this is what you believed" (15. 11).

Paul shows the same concern to walk in step with those at Jerusalem on the questions of the life of the Church. The authority, for example, on the subject of a woman veiling her head in Christian gatherings, or a woman keeping silent in church, is the custom of the "Churches of God" (I Cor. 11. 16) or the "Churches of the Saints" (14. 34), and Paul means by these the Churches where the Gospel originated (I Cor. 14. 36), the "Churches of Christ in Judea" (Gal. 1. 22). If the traditions and customs of the Palestinian church are the authority for the whole Church, it is because, says Paul, the Gospel originated there. Paul always recognized the primacy of Jerusalem, at least historically. When, in the epistle to the Romans, he retraces the circuit of his missionary journeys in the East, before turning his eyes toward the West and Spain, he writes: "From Jerusalem and as far round as Illyricum, I have fully preached the Gospel of Christ" (Rom. 15. 19). If Jerusalem can be considered the departure point of the Pauline mission it is because Jerusalem, the custodian of spiritual blessings, has shared these with the churches of the Gentiles (Rom. 15. 27). It follows therefore that the Gentile-Christians, in their turn, should send a share of their material benefits to the Christians in Jerusalem (II Cor. 9. 12-13; Rom. 15. 25-27). In setting up the collection Paul has not only instituted a work of fraternal charity; he has made the new Christians realize the important role of Jerusalem in the history of salvation.

So the Apostle Paul, the late arrival to the apostolic circle, has not been a brother of independent spirit; he has been a man of ecclesiastical tradition. Far from being a divisive force in the Church, Paul, the supreme theologian of the unity of the Church - since he forged the doctrine of the Church as the body of Christ - has also been the creator of the actual unity of the Church. "We owe to Paul the preservation of the good relationships, perhaps even of the unity, between the church at Jerusalem and the churches of the Gentiles."[2] This is shown also by the way in which Paul solved the problem of the admittance of the Gentiles into the covenant of grace.

B *The new Christians*

The entry of former Gentiles into the Church must have presented a very serious problem. As we have seen, the Church of Christ is God's Israel. So that the new Christians could be on equal terms with their brothers who had come out of Judaism it was necessary that they too be connected, in some way or other, with the people of God and thereby made heirs to the promises of the old covenant.

There were two ways of looking at this problem in the primitive Christian Church: i) At Jerusalem we see the realization of the promises and the fulfillment of Judaism, that is to say its providential culmination, in the gift of the Holy Spirit at Pentecost and in the appearance of the Church. But the Law and Jewish customs are not totally abolished; the people continue to go up to the temple and to take part in Jewish religious life. The only point of difference between the Christians and the Jews is their faith in Jesus the Messiah. If we take this point of view it is clear that the Gentiles must go by way of the synagogue to enter the Church. ii) Paul's point of view is quite different. It also seems to be that of the Hellenists who founded the church at Antioch, but our knowledge is based only on Paul's attitude and arguments. Paul too is of the opinion that the Church is the people of God. But he makes distinctions in the heritage of the old covenant which were not known in Jerusalem. For he thought more deeply about the significance of Christ's death and resurrection. He understood that if Christ, by dying on the cross, according to the Scriptures, has made the promises a reality, He has, on the other hand, put an end to the reign of the Law by fulfilling it, so that from now on the Law can make no further demands. Christ is the end of the Law. He has closed the parenthesis opened by the Law which came 430 years after the promise. But, although the Law is abolished, the promise which preceded it remains. By putting an end to government by the Law, Christ has renewed the link with government by faith, which had been in force at the time of Abraham. It follows then that Christians are set free from the Law and, at the same time, become heirs to the promise.

There are two consequences of this distinction made by Paul between the Law and the promise: 1) The Law as a means of salvation does not belong in the Gospel, and the Gentiles do not need to pass through it to reach Christ. 2) Through Christ, who has made the promises a reality, the Gentile-Christians are sons of Abraham and share in the bounties of the old covenant in the same way as the Judeo-Christians. Thus the unity of the Church is preserved.

This was undoubtedly the essence of Paul's argument which won the approval of the "pillars" at the time of the Jerusalem conference, since Peter, James and John did not require Titus to be circumcised. The whole essence of the theology of the people of God is maintained by Paul. In comparison, the observance of the Law by the Judeo-Christians and its non-observance by the Gentile-Christians is only a minor distinction. If the Apostles at Jerusalem did not require the Gentile-Christians to be circumcised, Paul, for his part, never taught that the Jews who became Christians should necessarily give up their observance of the Law. For, "neither circumcision counts for anything, nor uncircumcision, but only a new creation" (Gal. 6. 15). "In Christ Jesus neither circumcision nor uncircumcision is of any avail; but only faith working through love" (Gal. 5. 6).

In other words, from now on practical problems raised by the proximity of Judeo-Christians and Gentile-Christians in the same Church are in the order of charity, mutual support and consideration for each other. There is no problem of theological truth. This question was resolved by the principle that all Christians are equal, being all the heirs of Abraham. The problem of the relationship between Judeo-Christians and Gentile-Christians is one of charity. This is the meaning of the order given by James to Paul, according to Acts 21. 25, and Paul's frequent exhortations to the "strong" to sustain the "weak." It is in this sense too that we should interpret the incident at Antioch. If we take care not to over-dramatize we see that Paul reproaches Peter "much more for an inconsistency in conduct than for an error in principle, and their disagreement, though strong, on a matter of the right behaviour in particular circumstances, did not bring about any quarrel or open hostility."[3] Moreover, Paul never gives any indication that would lead us to believe that the "fellowship" established between the two of them at Jerusalem was broken at Antioch.

There remain the Judaizers with whom Paul contended in Galatia and at Corinth. We should not see in them followers of James or Peter - since Paul treats them as "false brethren" (Gal. 2. 4; II Cor. 11. 26) and "false apostles" (II Cor. 11. 13; cf. 11. 5; 12. 11) - but rather turbulent, rebellious groups, whose leaders were doubtless the Pharisees who had become Christians, as mentioned in Acts 15. 5. These Judaizers appear in a quite different light. They require that the Law should be the condition of salvation for all Christians. They go far beyond what charity requires. They preach a "different gospel" from the apostolic Gospel or redemption through Christ. This is why Saint Paul does not hesitate to lay a curse on them (Gal. 1. 6f; cf. II Cor. 11. 2-5). But with these Judaizers we have reached the boundary between authentic Christianity and heresy.

3) *The Church and heresies*

There is no possibility of dealing here with all the problems raised by the appearance of heresy within the Church. It is enough to say that if the Apostles fought against any doctrine which deviated from "the faith delivered once for all to the saints," it was because the new ideas threatened the essential attribute of the Church: its unity.

To preach a different Christ from the one proclaimed by the testimony and the tradition of the Apostles, and to replace that tradition by other ideas about the person and work of Jesus is also to destroy the unity of the Church, since the basis of that unity is the unity of Christ. Heresy is always an attack leveled at the unity of Christ and the unity of the Church.

In the New Testament three words are used to designate heresy: *hairesis, schima* and *planè*: "heresy" as such, "schism," and "deviation;" all three show an opposition to the Christ of the Church as well as to the unity of the Church.

Etymologically the word "heresy" means the philosophical or religious doctrine to which one subscribes after free investigation, by personal preference. Heresy therefore is the opposite of the Gospel; for although the Gospel is also a doctrine, it is a doctrine which neither the believer nor even the Apostle chooses for himself, but which is the expression of the free choice made by God of the means to save mankind. For man to make a choice here would be for him to move out of the divine plan of salvation which foresees one single Christ and one single Church. This is why heresy is one of the "works of the flesh" (Gal. 5. 19); it will be, at the end of time, one of the signs announcing the coming of Antichrist (I Cor. 11. 19; II Peter 3. 3).

Heresy is blameworthy because it brings about "splits" and "schisms" which destroy the unity of the body of Christ and which, so to speak, cut off the members from the body (I Cor. 1. 10; 11. 18; 12. 25). Heresy and schism come from the same spirit of "deviation" from the truth (II Cor. 6. 8; Eph. 4. 14; I Tim. 4. 1; Jas. 5. 20; I John 4. 6; Jude 11 etc.). To "err" is to turn aside from the "good way" of the Gospel (Acts 9. 2 etc.); it is to yield to the enticements of the Enemy and to abandon Christ and His Church. The boundary between confessing Christ and denying Him is at the same time the boundary between the "sacred doctrine" and heresy, between loyalty to the Church and the "carnal" zeal of a partisan and sectarian spirit. This is why the New Testament contains so many exhortations not to deviate from the instructions which have been received (Rom. 16. 17; Jude 3 etc.), exhortations which are linked with urgings to unity. For the doctrine and the discipline of the Church depend on its unity.

If the infant Church has always exposed any form of heresy and denounced it as such, it is precisely because the Church has a sense of being one, and because it feels an obligation to make its unity real. It knows that the centrifugal forces which may appear within it come from none other than Antichrist and are only the premonitory signs of his ultimate assault against the people of God. On the other hand, to defend the unity of the Church is also ti give testimony to Christ.

It is time to draw our conclusions.

Our rapid investigation of the doctrine of the Church in the New Testament has shown us that this doctrine, however we may look at it, postulates the unity of the Church. The Church is one, because the Lord who calls it into being, who saves it and who preserves it until the second coming, is one.

The unity of the Church is one with the unity of Christ.

On the other hand the Church of the first century encountered as many obstacles in its path as the Church of the following centuries, and obstacles which were powerful enough to break its unity. History testifies, however, that schism did not happen. Common faith in the same Savior triumphed over the powers of division. It is because Christ, the basis of the unity of the Church, occupied the central place in the faith of the believers, that they were obedient to the demands of unity.

In short, the unity of the Church is both a gift and an obligation. There is no paradox in this conclusion, nothing which places the Church outside the law that governs all degrees of revelation. Just as the believer does not have to seek his salvation in order to find it, nor have to merit his salvation in order to obtain it, but receives it by grace, grace that obliges the believer to live in a manner worthy of his calling, so too it is with the Church. The Church is called to unity at the same time as it is called into existence; it is for the faithful to order their ecclesiastical behavior according to the demands of unity which the Lord formulates for His Church. In the final analysis, the Church of the New Testament remained one because it surrendered to the fundamental principle of the Gospel - become what you already are.

The unity of the Church was broken when the close connection which exists and should exist between grace and commandment, between the gift of God and the duty of men, was no longer felt as forcibly as in the first century. If it is not possible for us - and perhaps not asked of us - to repair in one day the secular splits in the body of Christ, it is required that we should pray without ceasing that God should give unity to His Church and maintain in us "the unity of the Spirit in the bond of peace."

NOTES

1. *Etudes théologiques et religieuses*, Montpellier, 21, 1946, p. 265-282.

2. L. Cerfaux, *La théologie de l'Eglise suivant saint Paul*, Paris, 1942, p. 59. - We owe a great deal to this very fine work.

3. M. Goguel, *Revue d'histoire et de philosophie religieuse*, 1934, p. 476.

Infant Baptism in the Early Church[1]

Nowhere does the New Testament specifically state that infants should be baptized. Nowhere does it forbid the practice. It does not formulate a specific opinion about baptism; it ignores the sacrament or at least seems to ignore it.

It would be premature to conclude from the foregoing that infant baptism did not exist in the Church of the first century. Several reasons could be given for the silence on this subject even if the Apostles, or at least their successors, unhesitatingly admitted infants to baptism. For example, perhaps it was thought that the age of the one baptized made no difference to the baptism itself, even if the subject were *infans*. It is also possible that the silence in the New Testament may be due to chance. If the first epistle to the Corinthians had not been preserved for us we would only know about baptism for the dead from the very brief accounts of it in the Fathers - accounts as brief as that of Paul himself - and, undoubtedly, we would not have hesitated to deny that such a practice could go back as far as the first century and could have been tolerated by Saint Paul. Therefore we must have reservations about making use of the *argumentum e silentio*.

One further remark before coming to the heart of the matter. The question of infant baptism in the early Church - and in the contemporary Church - does not lead to the dilemma: adult baptism *or* infant baptism, as the adversaries of pedobaptism would have us believe. The Church never has given up and never will give up the baptism of adults. First, because the Church is by definition missionary and it receives believers of every age through baptism. Secondly, if the Church allowed only infant baptism, it would have to fix an age beyond which faith and salvation could no longer be reached, and it would forget that the New Testament itself opens the door to converts at the eleventh hour. In the view of pedobaptists adult baptism and infant baptism are not mutually exclusive. A pedobaptist is one who baptizes infants *also*, not exclusively.

The New Testament never mentions infant baptism. We do not know what the practice was in the first church. But four centuries later, the council of Milevis, in 416, called down a curse on whoever refused to baptize infants, and Saint Augustine, who died in 430, gives the weight of his authority and the guarantee of his orthodoxy to infant baptism. If the Church was not pedobaptist from the beginning we should find evidence that infant baptism appeared at a given moment, as an innovation - that the new practice appeared in the Church, became accepted, gained ground gradually and finally prevailed; in the writings of the Fathers there would be traces of struggles and controversies aroused by this practice which was unknown to the first Christians; it should be possible to fix the time when the Church's change took place. If the alternative was the case, then no trace of disputes about it will be found in the ecclesiastical writings; it will not be possible to determine exactly when the practice started; theologians will refer to it as to an early, even apostolic practice. In this case the conclusion must be that it is more than likely that infant baptism existed in the early Church from the beginning. We must therefore make an historical investigation.

First we must state one general fact: discussions about

baptism were not lacking in the early Church. If baptism for the dead, to which Paul alludes, left no traces in ecclesiastical doctrine, it did win over certain heretics, who practised it from the second century. But this baptism was vigorously attacked by the Fathers as being based on a false interpretation of the Pauline text. Tertullian, for example, pointed out to the Marcionites that the "dead" must be understood as bodies summoned to rise again; Epiphanius and Irenaeus, in opposition to the Valentinians, maintained that the "dead" means catechumens who are on the point of death.[2] Moreover the Fathers rose up against other perversions of Christian baptism, like the multiple baptisms of the Gnostics.[3]

Much more important was the controversy on the validity of the baptism performed by the heretics, the supreme "baptismal controversy."[4] In the third century it set in opposition to each other not only theologians and bishops, but churches themselves. In the West, the church of Rome was set against the churches of Africa; the Romans recognized the validity of the heretics' baptism, while the Africans, who were of the opposite opinion, rebaptized repentant heretics who returned to the Church. The point of view of the church at Rome prevailed at the council of Arles in 314. The council determined, in its canon 8, that heretics who had been baptized according to the trinitarian formula should be admitted into the Church by a simple laying-on of hands. If they had not been baptized according to this formula a second baptism should be administered. In the East, the same problem occurred, but it took longer to be resolved.

If the question of the baptism of heretics developed in this way and brought about the meeting of a council, it is because different and opposing answers could be given to the question, seeing that no solution was offered in the Scriptures or in tradition. In fact, with the exception of Marcionism, heresies took shelter within the Church during the first two centuries; it was within the Church that the first heretics had received baptism. We have here, in certain respects, a parallel case to that of infant baptism, which also cannot be resolved by recourse to explicit scriptural texts and undisputed interpretation.

However, it seems that, in the early Church, the subject of infant baptism was no cause for controversy - certainly not for controversy which resulted in conciliar discussions concluding with official pronouncements. Pedobaptism does not appear as the specific doctrine of one particular group or sect; it does not lurk within some regional church, determined to triumph at the expense of the unity of the faith and of ecumenical communion. This unanimity of opinion with regard to baptism is all the more significant in view of the great number of divergent opinions on doctrine, discipline and liturgy which fueled ecclesiastical debates during the first four centuries; it can almost be said that there is no point of dogma or ethics which did not arouse controversy. The question of infant baptism is among the small group of problems which least concerned the synods and the councils.

But we cannot dismiss the problem of the existence of infant baptism in the early Church with these few observations. We must see what the ecclesiastical writers themselves have to say.

Hippolytus of Rome is the first to mention explicitly the baptism of children, in the *Apostolic Tradition,* written about the year 215.[5] This brief work informs us about the liturgy and the discipline in Rome at the beginning of the third century. Chapters 20 and 21 respectively deal with the subject of those who are *to be baptized,* and "The conferring of holy baptism." We must quote these chapters in full in order to make a correct interpretation of the brief passage on the subject of infant baptism.

20. *Concerning those who are to be baptized*

When those to be baptized have been set apart, let their way of life be considered: *have they lived worthily while they were catechumens, have they honored widows and visited the sick, have they been full of good works*? If those who present them for baptism testify that they have lived in this way, let them hear the gospel.

Starting with the day on which they have been set apart let them be exorcised each day by the laying on of hands. As the day when they are to be baptized draws near let the bishop himself exorcise each of them to ensure that they are purified. If there is any one who is not truly pure he should be separated from the rest; he has not listened to the word in faith because the Stranger is still within him.

Let those who are to be baptized be instructed that they should bathe and wash themselves on the fifth day of the week. If a woman is menstruating she should be set apart and baptized on another occasion.

Let those who are to be baptized fast on Friday and Saturday. On Saturday let them come together in one place with the bishop who will bid them kneel and *pray*. Let him lay his hands on them and bid every evil spirit be gone from them and henceforth never return to them. When he has finished the exorcism, let him breathe on their faces, make a sign on their foreheads, their ears and their noses and then bid them stand up. They will keep a vigil all night while hearing readings and instructions. Let those who are to be baptized bring with them just the vessel which each should bring for the eucharist; it is right that whoever is worthy should offer an oblation at that time.

21. *Concerning the conferring of Holy Baptism*

When the cock crows let them come near to the water which should be pure and flowing. Let them remove their clothes and let the children be baptized first. If they can give the answers for themselves they should do so. Otherwise the parents or some other member of the family should speak for them.

Next let the adult men be baptized and finally the women, after they have let down their hair and removed their gold and silver ornaments and jewels. No one shall go down into the water wearing any foreign object.

At the time fixed for the baptism let the bishop ask a blessing on the oil, place it in a vessel and call it the Oil of Thanksgiving. Let him take more oil, exorcise it and call it the Oil of Exorcism. A deacon shall take the Oil of Exorcism and stand at the left of the presbyter and another deacon shall take the Oil of Thanksgiving and stand at the right. Let the presbyter take each of those who are to be baptized, turn with him to the west, and bid him make a renunciation, saying: "I renounce you, Satan, and all your works." After this declaration let him be anointed with the Oil of Exorcism, with the words: "Let every evil spirit depart from you." Then let the deacon lead him to the bishop or the presbyter who is standing near the water. Likewise a deacon shall accompany him down into the water. The one who is to be baptized shall go down into the water and the one who is to baptize him shall lay his hand on his head and ask: "Do you believe in God, the Father Almighty?" And the one to be baptized shall reply: "I believe." Then let him baptize him once, keeping his hand laid on his head.

Then he shall ask: "Do you believe in Jesus Christ, the Son of God, born of the Virgin Mary by the Holy Spirit, who was crucified and was buried and who, on the third day, rose from the dead, ascended into heaven and is seated on the right hand of the Father, and who will come to judge the quick and the dead?"

> And when he has said: "I believe," let him baptize him a second time.
>
> Then he shall ask again: "Do you believe in the Holy Spirit, the Holy Church and the resurrection of the body?" Let him who is being baptized say: "I believe" and then he shall be baptized a third time.
>
> Then, after he has come out of the water, let him be anointed by the presbyter with the Oil of Thanksgiving, with the words: "I anoint you with this holy oil in the name of the Father, the Son and the Holy Spirit."
>
> Let each of them dry themselves, put on their clothes and go into the church.

The statements at the beginning of chapter 21 are quite explicit: children who are old enough to confess their faith, and even those who are too young to be able to do so - the *infantes* will be baptized. There is nothing in chapter 20 however, to suggest that, at the beginning of the third century, the church of Rome would baptize children indiscriminately. The passages we have italicized in the reproduction of the text remind us that the candidates for baptism must, as catechumens, have led an unblemished life, carried out good works, and listened to the word in faith. Moreover, the catechumens prepare themselves for baptism with fasting, prayers and a watch-night spent in attending to readings and instructions.

If these conditions can be strictly followed by children who are old enough "to answer for themselves," this is not the case with the *infantes*. Nevertheless, according to Hippolytus baptism is administered to them as it is to adults. The sentence in chapter 21: "Let their parents answer or someone from their family," does not make it clear whether these parents have already received baptism or if, along with their children, they are among the candidates. In any case, the young ones are the children of either baptized Christians or catechumens.

We must emphasize that Hippolytus mentions this baptism of children and even of very young infants not in any way as a novel practice whose introduction has to be justified. The baptism of children seems to him to be a matter of course, a normal happening which is beyond dispute. The only point he makes is that children should be baptized before the adults, both men and women. The conclusion to be drawn is that in Rome, at the dawn of the third century, infant baptism is accepted as a traditional institution which does not warrant any discussion of principle.

Let us now go further back and look at the testimony of two Fathers of the second century: Justin Martyr and Irenaeus of Lyons.

Describing the way in which Christians follow the teaching of Christ with regard to purity, Justin writes in his *Apology*, "Many men and women, now in their sixties and seventies, who have been disciples of Christ from their childhood [οἱ ἐκ παίδων ἐμαθητεύθησαν τῷ Χριστῷ], have preserved their purity."[6] In the early Church, as in the New Testament Church, one is not a disciple of Christ without having been baptized. Therefore it is not straining the meaning to say that the proven Christians of whom Justin speaks had been baptized "from their childhood." The only question to which the text does not provide an answer is whether, at the time of their baptism, they were old enough to speak for themselves or not. The expression "Disciples of Christ" which Justin uses is more inclined to imply the first alternative, but the second is not out of the question. These disciples of Christ who were baptized "since their childhood," remained pure until their old age. If they reached the advanced age which Justin mentions at the time when he is writing the *Apology*, that is in the middle of the second century, their baptism must have taken place, at the latest, at the beginning of the same century.[7]

The testimony of Irenaeus is just as important. These are the words of the Bishop of Lyons:[8] "For he came to save all by Himself: all, I mean, who through Him are newborn unto God: infants, and little ones, and boys, and youths, and older men. Therefore He passed through every age, being first made an infant unto infants, to sanctify infants; among little ones, a little one, to sanctify such as are of that same age, being made to them an example both of piety, and of righteousness, and of obedience: among youths, a youth, becoming a pattern to youths, and sanctifying them in the Lord. Thus also He was an Elder among elders, in order to be a perfect Master in all things, not in setting forth the truth only, but in age too, sanctifying the elder persons as well, becoming an example to them also. Lastly He came even unto death, that He might be the first-born from the dead, having Himself the preeminence in all things, the Prince of life, first of all, and going before all."

"In this passage," writes Rodolphe Clément,[9] "the allusion to baptism is not definitely expressed or obvious; it is none the less real however if we look closely. The thought of Irenaeus is that Jesus went through every age of man in order to sanctify all ages in His person, and to make salvation available for all through union with Him. It is therefore possible, according to Irenaeus, for children in the cradle to be reborn through Christ, that is to find union with Him. For later ages, for older children, for youths and for those of mature years, Christ's *example* is there with the fact of salvation by the new birth; but for very small children (*infantes*) the example and instruction are useless. If therefore they are to be 'born again in God through Jesus Christ,' to be joined and united with Christ for eternal life, that can only be accomplished, according to Irenaeus, by baptism." The Bishop of Lyons also emphasizes elsewhere the close connection existing between baptism and rebirth. He explains the two expressions in terms of each other and he qualifies baptism with "rebirth in God" (*regeneratio in Deum*), an expression which he uses explicitly in this passage to indicate that the work of Christ is concerned with people of every age.[10]

It seems clear that, in the time of Irenaeus, at the end of the second century, there was no hesitation about baptizing children, not only children old enough to confess their faith, but also *infantes*. It is interesting to note that the five ages in the life of man, as described by the Bishop of Lyons, are summarized in the three ages of Hippolytus. The Bishop of Lyons is not arguing in favor of the establishment of a new practice, any more than the theologians of Rome did. He speaks of infant baptism as an undisputed practice which is apparently already a tradition in his time.

Let us go on to Africa and see what Tertullian has to say. He wrote a treatise on *Baptism* during the first years of the third century, before he became a Montanist. Chapter 18 of this treatise is devoted almost entirely to infant baptism:

> It follows that deferment of baptism is more profitable, in accordance with each person's character and attitude, and even age: and especially so as regards children. For what need is there, if there really is no need, for even their sponsors to be brought into peril, seeing they may possibly themselves fail of their promises by death, or be deceived by the subsequent development of an evil dispostion? It is true our Lord says, *Forbid them not to come to me*. So let them come, when they are growing up, when they are learning, when they are being taught what they are coming to: let them be made Christians

> when they have become competent to know Christ. Why should innocent infancy come with haste to the remission of sins? Shall we take less cautious action in this than we take in worldly matters? Shall one who is not trusted with earthly property be entrusted with heavenly? Let them fist learn how to ask for salvation, so that you may be seen to have given to one that asketh. With no less reason ought the unmarried also to be delayed until they either marry or are firmly established in continence: until then, temptation lies in wait for them, for virgins because they are ripe for it, and for widows because of their wandering about. All who understand what a burden baptism is will have more fear of obtaining it than of its postponement.[11]

It is surprising that this passage has been mentioned as a testimony against the existence of infant baptism at the time. On the contrary, Tertullian proves that such baptism was practised, since he suggests giving it up. He does not question the legitimacy nor the value of infant baptism; he merely declares that a later baptism is better (*utilior*). It is his opinion that it is better to postpone baptism not only until children are able to know Christ and to confess their faith, but even until the time when candidates for baptism will be out of reach of the greatest temptations.

Tertullian's arguments must be examined closely. They are two in number. First, children are by nature innocent, and consequently have no need of regeneration (*Quid festinat innocens aetas ad remissionem peccatorum?*). The innocence of children is Tertullian's own idea. It has no roots in the thought of Jesus or in the teaching of the Apostles. It is not to be found in the Fathers who are more or less contemporary with Tertullian. On the contrary, it is because he admits that infants in the cradle are already in need of regeneration that Irenaeus develops his theory that the Son of

God came to save man at all stages of life. That is the general opinion. It can be found particularly in Origen or Saint Augustine. This idea, with its obvious biblical connections, was doubtless one of the principle factors in the victory of pedobaptism in the Church.[12]

The baptism of young people is another ill-advised practice which Tertullian cannot encourage. It is better to wait - this is his second argument - until the catechumens have passed the age when they are prone to commit the grievous sins for which, after baptism, there can be no expiation. The unique grace connected with baptism must not be used up prematurely. This is why baptism carries such "weight." (*Si qui pondus intelligant baptismi, magis timebunt consecutionem quam dilationem*).

We can see here the beginning of the ideas of penitence which Tertullian will develop first of all in *De paenitentia* - which seems to belong, like *De baptismo*, to his first period of literary activity, before he left the Church - and secondly in *De pudicitia*, which is "a clearly Montanist treatise."[13] The Tertullian of *De paenitentia* still believes that a public confession and its accompanying humiliation ensure for the Christian God's pardon for all his sins. But when he writes *De pudicitia* Tertullian takes away from the sinner all hope of forgiveness in this world and consigns him to the justice of God. This rigorous attitude brought Tertullian up against Callistus who had just, by a "peremptory edict,"[14] allowed fornicators and adulterers to return into the Church through penitence.

The germ of the rigorous ideas of Tertullian the Montanist can be seen in his thoughts on baptism and the advisability of delaying it. These ideas seem to have enjoyed a certain amount of favor in the third and fourth centuries. They even led to Christians delaying their baptism until they were on their death-beds. There is a passage in the Confes-

sions of Saint Augustine which is most instructive on this point:[15]

> I was signed with the sign of his cross, and was seasoned with his salt even from the womb of my mother, who greatly trusted in thee. Thou didst see, O Lord, how, once, while I was still a child, I was suddenly seized with stomach pains and was at the point of death--thou didst see, O my God, for even then thou wast my keeper, with what agitation and with what faith I solicited from the piety of my mother and from thy Church (which is the mother of us all) the baptism of thy Christ, my Lord and my God. The mother of my flesh was much perplexed, for, with a heart pure in thy faith, she was always in deep travail for my eternal salvation. If I had not quickly recovered, she would have provided forthwith for my initiation and washing by thy life-giving sacraments, confessing thee, O Lord Jesus, for the forgiveness of sins. So my cleansing was deferred, as if it were inevitable that, if I should live, I would be further polluted; and, further, because the guilt contracted by sin after baptism would be still greater and more perilous...
>
> I ask thee, O my God, for I would gladly know if it be thy will, to what good end my baptism was deferred at that time? Was it indeed for my good that the reins were slackened, as it were to encourage me in sin? Or, were they not slackened? If not, then why is it still dinned into our ears on all sides, "Let him alone, let him do as he pleases, for he is not yet baptized"? In the matter of bodily health, no one says, "Let him alone; let him be worse wounded; for he is not yet cured"! How much better, then, would it have been for me to have been cured at once--and if thereafter, through the diligent care of friends and myself, my soul's restored health had been kept safe in thy keeping, who gave it in the first place! This would have been far better, in truth.

This passage from the *Confessions* is interesting from two aspects. It repeats the reasons put forward for delaying baptism and it shows how far from the original concept of baptism one can come when baptism is considered the supreme means of wiping out the sins of a lifetime at the final hour. While regretting that his own baptism had been delayed, Saint Augustine refutes Tertullian's arguments and places himself in the succession of Saint Paul. The Apostle brings to bear all the weight of the exhortation to live a new life when he reminds the Galatians of their baptism: "All of you who have been baptized in Christ, put on Christ."[16]

The two arguments advanced by Tertullian in *De baptismo* are most questionable: the innocence of children and the advantages of a delayed baptism.[17] It is surprising to find such weak arguments coming from the pen of such an experienced polemist who, in his fight against Callistus, for example, points out so vehemently the divergence of the new penitential practice instituted in Rome from the teachings of Scripture about unpardonable sins. Tertullian does not support his opposition to infant baptism by Scripture or by tradition. He would surely not have failed to do so if, in his time, infant baptism had appeared as something novel and had given rise to questions of principle. Obviously this was not the case.

It is in the writings of Origen, who died about the year 253, that we find the first confirmation of the apostolic origin of infant baptism.[18] We will cite three important passages:

In Leviticum homilia, VIII, 3:[19]

> I heard David cry: 'I was brought forth in iniquity, and in sin did my mother conceive me.'[20] So David shows that all who are born in flesh are contaminated by the stains of sin and iniquity, and he confirms what we have already said several

> times, namely that 'no one is clean and without blemish, even if his life has lasted but one day.'[21] To this we might add: since the Church's baptism was administered for the remission of sins, what reason is there to baptize children, as was customary in the Church (*secundum ecclesiae observantiam etiam parvulis baptismum dari*)? The grace of baptism would be unnecessary if there was not something in small children which necessitated remission of sins.

In Lucam homilia, XIV:

> Small children are baptized for the remission of their sins. But how and when did they sin? What reason is there to purify children unless it is because, as we have said, 'no one is clean and without blemish, even if his life has lasted but one day.'[22] Small children also are baptized (*propterea baptizantur et parvuli*) because baptism washes away the stains of birth; for 'unless one is born of water and the Spirit, he cannot enter the Kingdom of heaven.'[23]

Ad Romanos, V, 9:

> We must believe David when he says, as we have mentioned before: 'My mother conceived me in sin.'[24] This is why the Church received from the Apostles the tradition of also baptizing small children. These men, to whom the secrets of divine mysteries had been confided, knew that everyone was tainted by sin and must be washed clean by water and the Spirit.

In these three passages Origen's thought is quite clear: man is by nature a sinner, he needs to be reborn, and rebirth is connected to baptism by water and the Spirit. The point that the scholar is anxious to make is the undisputed fact of original sin which makes regeneration through baptism necessary. He brings two proofs to bear: 1) the authority of Scripture which affirms that man is conceived and born in sin and that he is a sinner, even if his life lasts only one day; 2) the practice of the Church, inherited from the Apostles, of baptizing even children. Origen invokes the letter of Scripture and the pedobaptist tradition as authorities which have no need of proof. For far from thinking that the Church received the tradition of baptizing children also from the Apostles, he makes this tradition an argument to establish that children themselves are contaminated by sin. To rationalize in this way Origen must have been sure that his assertions of the infant baptism tradition could not be contradicted.

If we recall that the great scholar was very well-read and had travelled much among the metropolitan churches of the East, that he had a critical mind and was writing less than two centuries after the death of the Apostles, we cannot but be impressed by his testimony. Even if we hesitate to accept literally the words. "The Church received the tradition of infant baptism from the Apostles," and if we prefer the freer expression, "they baptize children according to the custom of the church," we can hardly avoid coming to the following conclusion: Origen provides one of the firmest foundation for the theory that infant baptism did not have to be introduced at a given moment into the Church because, in practice, it had been there from the beginning.

Shortly after the death of Origen, the third council of Carthage, in 256, declared that baptism should be administered to infants even before their eighth day, if necessary. The council had come together not to deal with the lawfulness of infant baptism, which was not in debate, but to provide an answer to the question posed by the priest Fidus - whether or not it was permissible to baptize before the eighth day. The opinion of the council and the reasons for that opinion are set out by Cyprian in his *Epistula LXIV ad Fidum*. The Bishop of Carthage stresses particularly the argument of Irenaeus that every man can share in the grace of God in Jesus Christ since God "takes no account at all of difference in age;" then, putting baptism and circumcision side by side, Cyprian writes:

> For because the eighth day, that is, the first after the sabbath, was to be that, whereon our Lord would rise again and quicken us and give us the spiritual circumcision, this eighth day, that is, the first after the sabbath, and the Lord's day, was promised in a figure. Which figure ceased, when the reality afterwards came, and when the spiritual circumcision was given to us. On which account we think that no one should by that law which was before ordained be hindered from obtaining grace; nor should the spiritual circumcision be hindered by the circumcision in the flesh, but every one is by all means to be admitted to the grace of Christ.[25]

Several decades later, Gregory of Nazianzus, on the other hand, asks that baptism should be delayed until the age of three. He writes:

> Are we to baptize them too? Certainly, if any danger presses. For it is better that they should be unconsciously sanctified than that they should depart unsealed and uninitiated...But in respect of others I give my advice to wait till the end of the third year, or a little more or less, when they may be able to listen and to answer something about the Sacrament.[26]

Whether children are baptized soon after birth or whether they are baptized at the age of three, there is general agreement, in the third century, that they should not be denied baptism. Infant baptism, already firmly established by the time of Origen, had only to be sanctioned by the authority of Saint Augustine to be considered as a rule of the Church universal and a command of the Lord and the Apostles.[27]

We can pause here and draw our conclusions. The first centuries have not preserved any memory of controversies concerning pedobaptism. We do not see infant baptism being introduced into the Church at a particular moment and striving to become lawful, as we would expect of a new practice. On the contrary, the Fathers and the theologians agree in witnessing to the antiquity of infant baptism, and even Tertullian, who advises against it, does not regard it as a recent novelty in conflict with an earlier tradition. By administering baptism to children, the early Church did not feel it was deviating from its origins; it was assured that it was maintaining an undisputed custom going back to apostolic times.

The only conclusion to be drawn is that the thought of the early Fathers on the subject of infant baptism does not show a break with the thought of the primitive Church and that infant baptism was probably practised from the very beginning. The silence in the New Testament on the subject, a silence more apparent than real,[28] merely suggests that infant baptism appeared entirely lawful and normal and gave rise to no opposition.

NOTES

1. *Verbum Caro*, no. 5, 1948, p. 15-26, by kind permission of the Presses de Taizé.

2. Cf. J. Thomas, *Le mouvement baptiste en Palestine et Syrie (150 av. J.-C.-300 ap. J. -C)* Gembloux, J. Duculot, 1935, p. 393-396.

3. Cf. J. Thomas, *op. cit.*, p. 398-404.

4. Cf. J. Tixeront, *Histoire des dogmes dans l'antiquité chrétienne*, I (8ème éd.) Paris, J. Gabalda, 1915, p. 378-389.

5. Hippolytus, *Traditio apostolica.* The emphases are by Philippe Menoud.

6. *Apol.* XV. From Early Christian Fathers, Volume I, The Library of Christian Classics, newly translated by Cyril C. Richardson, Published in the United States by The Westminster Press, 1953, p. 250. Used by permission of the publisher.

7. In another passage in the *Apol.* LXI, *op. cit.*, p. 282, Justin writes:

> How we dedicated ourselves to God when we were made new through Christ I will explain, since it might seem to be unfair if I left this out from my exposition. Those who are persuaded and believe that the things we teach and say are true, and promise that they can live accordingly, are instructed to pray and beseech God with fasting for the remission of their past sins, while we pray and fast with them. Then they are brought by us where there is water, and are reborn by the same manner of rebirth by which we ourselves were reborn; for they are then washed in the water in the name of God the Father and Master of all, and of our Saviour Jesus Christ, and of the Holy Spirit.

In this passage, Justin speaks of the preparation of

catechumens for baptism in more succinct terms than Hippolytus, but yet he indicates the essential elements which will be developed by the Roman theologian (practice of the Christian life, fasting and prayer.) Nothing in what the apologist says here about baptism would prevent it being administered to children, at least to children old enough to answer for themselves.

8. *Adv. haer.* II, 22, 4. In the English translation we have made use of *Five Books of S. Irenaeus, Bishop of Lyons against Heresies*, translated by John Keble, Oxford and London, James Parker and Co. 1872.

9. R. Clément, *Etude biblique sur le baptême ou le pédobaptisme et l'Eglise,* Lausanne, G. Bridel, 1857, p. 252-253.

10. Cf. *Adv. haer*, I. 21, 1 (Keble, p. 64) "Now that this kind is forged by Satan to the denying of Baptism, our new Birth unto God, and to the rejection of the whole Faith, we will declare in the course of our refutation of them, in the proper place." Cf. also *ibid.* III. 17. 1 (Keble, p. 272) "And again giving His disciples power to regenerate into God, He said unto them, 'Go and teach all nations, baptizing them in the Name of the Father, and of the Son, and of the Holy Ghost.'" - The same equating of baptism and regeneration appears in chapter LXI, 1-3 of the *Apology* of Justin cited above.

11. *De baptismo*, XVIII. 6-13. In the English translation we have used Tertullian's *Homily on Baptism*; the text edited with an introduction, translation and commentary by Ernest Evans. London, S.P.C.K., 1963, p. 41. Reprinted by permission of the publisher.

12. The declaration of the innocence of children comes from the same doctrine of man as the other declaration by Tertullian about the *anima naturaliter christiana,* and this anthropology is not biblical. Here we agree absolutely with Th. Preiss, *Verbum Caro*, 1947, p. 118. - To suppose that this "age of innocence" has no need of the remission of sins, it would be necessary to ask the following question: at what age does a human being cease to be innocent and have need of regeneration? On the theological level, this would be setting a false problem, similar to the philosopher's well-known question: when a grain of wheat falls it makes no noise; but we hear the noise made by an overturned bushel of wheat; how many grains of wheat must there be before they make a noise as they fall?

13. P. de Labriolle, *Tertullien, De Paenitentia, De pudicitia,* Paris, A. Picard, 1906, p. xvi.

14. *De pudicitia,* I. 6.

15. *Confessions*, I, 11. From *Augustine: Confessions and Enchiridion,* Vol. VII, The Library of Christian Classics. Newly translated and edited by Albert C. Outler. Published simultaneously in Great Britain and the United States of America by SCM Press Ltd., London, and The Westminster Press, Philadelphia. First published in 1955, p. 40-41. Used by permission.

16. Galatians 3. 27.

17. We should note that Tertullian's idea is poles apart from that of modern Baptists who make of baptism the sanction of a regeneration which has already taken place.

18. We cannot at this time dwell on the enigmatic words of Clement of Alexandria: "If anyone be a fisherman, let him make an image of the Apostles and of the children drawn out of the water." ἀποστόλου μεμνήσεται καὶ τῶν ἐξ ὕδατος ἀνασπωμένων παιδίων) *Pedagogia* III, 10. The English translation is Clement of Alexandria, *Christ the Educator*, translated by Simon P. Wood, New York, Fathers of the Church, 1954, p. 246. This is probably an allusion to the fact that Peter was called by Jesus to be a fisher of men and also an allusion to infant baptism. For it is in the allegorical image of a fisherman that the Christian elder administering baptism was viewed (cf. *Dictionnaire de théologie catholique*, II, 1, col. 236.) By these two allusions, which overlap, is Clement saying that Peter, fisher of men, also draws children from the water - in other words, that infant baptism finds its origin in the practice of Peter? We cannot state this categorically in view of the brevity of the passage in Clement.

19. English version by the translator.

20. Psalm 51. 5.

21. Job 14. 4-5.

22. Job 14. 4-5.

23. John 3. 5.

24. Psalm 51. 5.

25. *The Epistles of S. Cyprian, Bishop of Carthage and Martyr,* Oxford, John Henry Parker, 1844, p. 197.

26. *Orationes*, XL, 28. The translation into English is from *A Select Library of Nicene and Post-Nicene Fathers of the Christian Church*, Second series, vol. VII, New York, The Christian Literature Company, 1894. *op. cit.*, p. 370.

27. Cf. R. Clément, *op. cit.*, p. 238-239.

28. The testimony of the Fathers clearly supports the exegetes who interpret in the pedobaptist sense texts such as Mark 10. 14; I Cor. 7. 14; Col. 2. 11-13, to mention only the strongest references to infant baptism in the New Testament. On this subject, cf. the article by Th. Preiss, *Verbum Caro*, 1947, p. 113-122.

Church and Ministry According to the New Testament[1]

Foreword

For several years now the question of the pastoral ministry and the organization of the Church has claimed the attention of the French-speaking Reformed Churches. Recently the subject was discussed by our learned colleagues of Geneva, Montpellier and Neuchâtel.[2] They discussed whether elders should be elevated to the ministry of "leaders of the Church," thus producing a "true revolution in Reformed discipline," or whether, on the contrary, protestant tradition is not right when it makes the presbyterial counsellors the "administrators of the Church," and makes the pastoral ministry *the* Christian ministry.

We have no intention, in this study, of entering this debate. We do not want to defend a tradition or propose changes. Our aim is quite different. We shall try to understand and set forth the essence and the nature of the Church and of its ministry in the light of the New Testament and, as far as possible, leaving aside any special interest, confessional or otherwise, which was foreign to the first Christians. We are fully aware that the Scriptures do not contain sufficiently clear and complete information on the subject which concerns us, and that they do not present a blue-print which succeeding generations have merely to follow. But we believe that the study of the problem of ministry and church government, which Protestantism can no longer delay reviewing, must begin with the study of the Scriptures. Also we would suggest that a historian of the origins of Christianity hardly sees beyond the horizon of the first century.

The subject matter of this study is the content of three addresses, followed by discussion, at the annual theological conference of the Belgian Christian Missionary Church which was held at Lustin (province of Namur) from the 26th to the 28th of April, 1948. We ask our listeners, among whom were so many former students and old friends, to accept the offering of these pages, as a reminder of those peaceful days we spend together in that sunny retreat in the Ardennes.

Introduction

There are few questions as perplexing as that of ministry and church order in the first century. The documents at our disposal only bring to light a few facts which are difficult to reconcile and to interpret. We must be content with casual references when we would prefer detailed explanations. There is nothing systematic about our information; it is almost by chance that we are enlightened on one point and remain in ignorance about another. For example, Saint Paul casually mentions that "the Lord's brothers" also undertook missionary journeys.[3] This detail, certainly a historical fact, is most valuable. If Paul had not mentioned it we would think that "James, the Lord's brother" had never left Jerusalem, for, according to the book of Acts he lived continually in the holy city. But how many other details in the life of the infant Church will remain for ever unknown because our sources are fragmentary?

Moreover, many of the theories put forward about the organization of the early Church and the nature of its ministry are to a greater or lesser extent influenced by interests other than historical ones. We are all inclined, even unconsciously, to adapt the Scriptures to fit ideas we hold by virtue of our own confessional allegiance.

On the other hand, minds are more inclined to meet when it is a question of defining the Church of the New Testament. We can speak quite rightly of a *consensus* which seems to be established on this point.[4] There is general agreement that the expression "the Church" means the people of God of the new covenant gathered together in the name of Jesus; that Jesus, from the time when He saw Himself as the Messiah, gathered round Him the eschatalogical community; that the Church, foretold and foreseen in the group of the disciples, appears immediately after the Passion as the place where the Spirit is at work so that the apostolic witness may resound with force and power.

If it is wise to go from the known to the unknown, we must start from the idea of the Church, to find out how it organized and governed its life.

The problem as a whole is not without some analogy to the single problem of infant baptism in the early Church. "It is in fact necessary to ask whether infant Baptism is attested by our primitive Church sources. Now the New Testament texts allow us to answer *this* question with certainty in neither one way nor the other, and we must simply accept this fact. Even the passages which speak of the Baptism of 'whole houses' allow no unambiguous conclusion to be drawn, at least in this respect. For we do not in fact know whether there were infants in these houses. These passages may be used only to explain the *doctrine* of Baptism. They are not effective proof of the practice of infant Baptism in apostolic times." "All discussions about Baptism should begin with this question, viz. with the theological definition of the essence and meaning of Baptism."[5] It is established by this study that "both adult and infant baptism are to be regarded as equally biblical."[6]

The facts given in the New Testament on the subject of ministry are so diverse and so vague that, by starting with them, we could conclude that the infant Church was simply a gathering of free spirits, living in a state of anarchy, without any concern to organize their life as a community or to submit to any guidance other than that of the "Spirit." This conclusion would be wrong however, as is proved first of all by the fact that the Church in the first century survived the threat of division, even of complete dispersal, which hangs over all unorganized communities, and secondly because the Church of the second century appears everywhere as a properly constituted body, and in Asia in particular as a hierarchical society under episcopal leadership. This organization could not have become established spontaneously; it had to have roots in the preceding century.[7] In other words, the principle of ecclesiastical organization is connected to the very idea of the Church.

Herein lies the reason why the study of ministry should begin with what the New Testament has to say about the nature of the Church.[8] For the ministers at work in the Church mirror the characteristics of that Church. It is the ministers who are ordained to the Church and not the reverse.

If the Church is the place chosen by the Spirit to proclaim the redemption accomplished by Jesus Christ, we will not see the ministers of the Church wasting their time fulfilling the unnecessary office of mediation that is already accomplished. On the other hand, we will see the Church itself, elevated by its Lord to the rank of the people of God, exercising the spiritual priesthood of thanksgiving. We will see the Apostles giving testimony to the Risen Christ. As the Apostles disappear, we will see other ministers building on the foundations which were provided once and for all, and organizing the life of the Church.

I *The Church*

The people of God in the old covenant already bore the name which describes the people of God called together in the name of Jesus Christ in a new covenant. But "the Church in the desert," (Acts 7. 38) could only foreshadow and foretell the Church of Christ. In order for the latter to appear in history, it was necessary that, in the fulness of time after redemption was achieved, the Spirit should be poured out upon the believers gathered together in the name of the Risen Christ.

In the history of salvation, the Spirit and the Church belong to the same era, that between the resurrection and the parousia, which can be called indiscriminately the time of the Spirit or the time of the Church. Whichever expression is used, the realities which both contain are emphasized.

The Church without the Spirit would be a body without life force. Its members could come together in order to recollect the events of the past. But these facts would only be valuable as historical information. They would have no power of salvation. The Church without the Spirit would be nothing but a sociological fact.

The Spirit without the Church would be a power with no permanent means of expressing itself. It could work well with isolated believers or even isolated generations of believers. But its work would lack any organic link with that salvation made real once and for all in history; it would reveal Christ glorified, without showing His unity with the Jesus of tradition. The Spirit without the Church would create nothing but communities of mystics.

This is why, in the New Testament, the Spirit and the Church are always ordained to each other and inseparable from each other.

1. The Spirit and the Church are both foretold and promised by Jesus (John 7. 39; Matt. 16. 18). The passage in John declares that the glorification of Jesus, His death and resurrection, are required so that the Spirit can be given to the believers, the Church. The verse in Matthew shows the edification of the Church in the future; it will only take place after the passion, which is foretold for the first time immediately after the words on the Church.[9]

2. After the glorification of Christ, the Spirit and the Church appear in the history of salvation together, in order to define the final period (Acts 2).

3. From now on the Spirit and the Church are closely associated. The Spirit guides the Church. It has often been pointed out that the main character in the book of the Acts is not Peter or Paul but the Spirit which strengthens the Church and causes it to grow (Acts 9. 31), which inspires resolutions to maintain the unity of that Church (15. 28), which strengthens and guides the Apostles and the evangelists in their missionary undertakings (4. 8; 6. 10; 7. 54; 8. 18; 10. 19; 11. 12; 13. 2-4; 20. 22), which establishes the ministry necessary for the Church (6. 6; 20. 28), and which dispenses prophetic warnings (11. 28; 21. 4-11). The epistles of Paul confirm the testimony of the book of Acts on this point. Every time the message of redemption in Christ, which is the foundation of the Church, is proclaimed, the power of the Spirit can be seen (cf. Gal. 3. 3-5; I Thess. 1. 5, etc.). The same events are repeated everywhere, for there is only one Spirit and one body, one Church (Eph. 4. 4).[10] The Church is

the temple of the Spirit (I Cor. 3. 16; cf. Eph. 2. 22). It is the body of Christ - the earthly form of Christ the Spirit. It is this Spirit which endows the Church with its gifts (I Cor. 12).[11]

4. Finally the Spirit and the Church are one in their expectation of the second coming (Rev. 22. 17).

From the time of the resurrection to that of the second coming, the common mission of the Spirit and the Church is to proclaim the redemptive work of Christ. In order to save the world it is not enough that Christ should die and rise again from the dead. It is also necessary that these events, which happened once and for all, should be revealed to the world so that the faith which saves may be established. The Church is the place where the Spirit is at work.[12] The Spirit of the glorified Christ is not a force which acts by chance and haphazardly. It is a power which works within the environment it has made for itself so that it can guarantee the necessary continuity and permanence of its actions. Neither the Church nor the Spirit are single events, even less are they a series of unconnected and transitory events. They are acts of God joined and linked together in a historical chain which has a beginning and an end.

The Spirit brings to the Church the grace of divine freedom. The Church assures for the Spirit the benefits of tradition. Freedom of inspiration and fidelity to tradition have belonged together since the very beginning of the Church.

The Church, the new people of God, gathered together in the name of Jesus Christ, is in continuity with Israel. The Church sees the ancient promises made to the people of the old covenant being fulfilled within itself.[13] Also the Church is in continuity with the earthly work of Jesus, mentioned so often in the speeches of Peter.[14] Those who are qualified to be Apostles are those who not only were witnesses to the resurrection but also had been with Jesus since the time of John the Baptist.[15] The first characteristic of life in the Church, according to Acts 2. 42, is perseverance in the teaching of the Apostles: zeal in unfaltering adherence to the faith preached by Peter that "God has made this Jesus Lord," this Jesus whom the Jews crucified, but whom the Apostles had already followed along the roads of Palestine.[16] The Spirit is at work now in order to link this present time to the earlier events of the history of salvation. Tradition is created by the Spirit.[17]

In this respect, the case of the Apostle Paul is most striking. As soon as the Spirit of Christ called him into faith and to apostleship, Paul entered the Church through baptism.[18] The missionary journeys laid on him by the Spirit have their point of origin in the Church.[19] But the Apostle to the Gentiles, who receives his ministry from the Lord Himself, and not by human commission, even that of the dignitaries in Jerusalem,[20] knows that he is not called to preach a new religion but that he is taking his place in an already existing tradition. He is convinced that he would run in vain if his ministry to the Gentiles were not recognized by those who had been Apostles before him.[21]

In his teaching Paul is concerned to maintain unity with and fidelity to the original traditions. Starting with chapter 11 of the first epistle to the Corinthians, he mentions on several occasions the traditions which should regulate the faith and the discipline of the Church. First of all he declares in a general way: "I commend you for maintaining the traditions even as I have delivered them to you" (11. 2). Next, in connection with the tradition of the institution of the Lord's Supper, Paul writes: "I received from the Lord what I also delivered to you" (11. 23f.), which means: what I have taught you about the eucharist I have myself received from a tradition which goes back, through the first Apostles, to Jesus Himself.[22] Then he deals with the tradition on the resurrection appearances (15. 1f.), and after mentioning Christ's appearances Paul adds: "Whether it was I or they (the Apostles at Jerusalem), so we preach and so you believed."

Paul shows the same concern to follow the line of the authorities at Jerusalem on questions concerning the life of the Church. For example, the regulations about a woman wearing a veil in assemblies of Christians, or about a woman keeping silent in the Church, are customs of the "churches of God,"[23] and the "churches of the saints;"[24] by this Paul means the churches where the word of God originated,[25] the "churches of Christ in Judea."[26]

If the traditions and the customs of the Palestinian church become the authority for the whole Church it is because, according to Paul, the Gospel originated there. Paul has always recognized the pre-eminence of Jerusalem, at least historically.[27] In the epistle to the Romans, when he retraces the course of his missionary journeys in the East, before turning his attention towards the West and Spain, he writes: "from Jerusalem and as far round as Illyricum I have fully preached the gospel of Christ."[28] If Jerusalem can be considered as the point of origin of Paul's mission it is because Jerusalem the guardian of spiritual blessings, has handed on these blessings to the churches of the Gentiles.[29] It follows that the Gentile-Christians, for their part, should share their material blessings with the Christians at Jerusalem.[30] By instituting the collection, Paul not only created a work of brotherly charity, he also made the new Christians realize the important part played by Jerusalem in the history of salvation.[31] In short, the Apostle Paul, the late arrival in the circle of the Apostles, was not a free-spirited brother. He was rather a man of ecclesiastical tradition.

The question has often been asked whether the Church, according to the New Testament, is a society or an institution.[32] This dilemma cannot be resolved. Ideas about a society and an institution can be complementary. Although the sociological category may be inadequate to describe the Church, yet the Church finds its reality in a society. On the other hand, having been founded once and for all, and with a specific mission in view, thus having a beginning and an end, the Church has the characteristics of an institution; it is more than a mystic reality. It is not enough to define the Church as "the living body of Christ."[33] Of course it is that, but it is more than that, "because it makes a divine plan into a reality, and Christ is the one who carries it out."[34] It is not wrong then to consider the Church as a historic institution ordained to eschatological ends and governed by the Spirit. Far from being a hindrance to the Spirit, the institution of the Church is the place intended, by the will of the One who established it, for the Spirit to exercise its power. It can happen that the spiritual character of the Church may predominate to the detriment of its institutional character, and vice versa. Nevertheless the Church, in essence, possesses both of these characteristics.[35]

II. *The Priesthood*

The priestly office and the ministry of the word are both parts of the whole history of salvation. They are linked to each other by virtue of an inner bond which can be found in both covenants but which is not the same in both.

In the old covenant, the prophetic ministry is found within the framework of the priestly office, without breaking out of it. The prophets continually proclaim that a purely ritual religion is an offence to God. But they do not cry out for an abolition of the ritual. They exhort the people to go up to the Temple with pure hearts and clean hands. The words of Jesus: "If you are offering your gift at the altar, and there remember that your brother has something against you, leave your gift there before the altar and go; first be reconciled to your brother, and then come and offer your gift,"[36] follow along the line of the prophets. Nobody within Israel and Judaism, not even the Essenes,[37] ever protested against the principle of sacrifice. The writer of the epistle to the Hebrews does not question the characteristic of divine institution of the priesthood of the old covenant. He only affirms that it was a temporary institution, preceded by the priesthood of Melchizedek and destined to be replaced in its turn by the definitive priesthood of Christ, foreshadowed by Melchizedek. The writer judges the Levitical sacerdotal worship in the same way in which the Apostle Paul judges the Law of Moses. He considers it a parenthesis, willed by God, between the justification by faith granted to Abraham and the justification of those who believe in the crucified and risen Christ. Sacerdotal worship continued to exist throughout the whole of the old covenant. It reminded the people of God that the true redemption had been promised but not yet realized. It foretold this redemption; it was the symbol of the perfect sacrifice which would be offered at the appointed time.

In the new covenant the balance of power between the priestly office and the ministry of the word is reversed. The time of the Church is inaugurated by the pouring out of the Spirit, because Christ has died and has risen from the dead. Constituted after the sacrifice on Calvary, the new people of God live by the priestly work accomplished once and for all by Christ, who elevates the believers to the rank of "priests of God the Father." If the priesthood of believers continues to exist in the new covenant it is as a reference to the unique priesthood of Christ and as a testimony given to this priesthood. Just as Christ dies by the law to free us from the law and make us walk in the new life of obedience, so the priesthood of Christ puts an end to expiatory sacrifices because redemption for all has been obtained for ever. In the new covenant there is only a "spiritual priesthood," a "sacrificial offering of faith," (Phil. 2. 17), by which the priesthood of Christ becomes effective until the end of time.

Let us look at our subject more closely and examine what has been written about it. Evangelical tradition has preserved a declaration by Jesus about the destruction and the rebuilding of the Temple, and the fourth gospel seems to have kept the primitive form of the story.[38] To embark on a complete exegesis of this passage would involve us in a lengthy exposition. Essentially Jesus seems to be announcing the end of the sacrificial system of the old covenant and the foundation, by His death and resurrection, of a new covenant. It has been suggested that in the spiritual temple of which Jesus speaks, according to John 2. 19, one can see an expression similar to the Pauline idea of the Church being the body of Christ.[39] However that may be, the passage on the Temple at Jerusalem expresses the central thought of the New Testament, that the work of Christ inaugurates a new way of serving God, a radically different form of worship based no longer on animal sacrifice but on the sacrifice of Christ. This idea, which is implicit in all types of New Testament theology,[40] was given its explicit and classic expression in the epistle to the Hebrews.

The writer of the epistle to the Hebrews presents Christ

as the high priest of the new covenant, and His work as the perfect and unique priestly office. He is at one and the same time the Son of God (1. 2) and truly man, since he suffered (2. 14-18). He is the High Priest confirmed by an oath from God (7. 20-22); He is holy and without sin (4. 15; 7. 26), but Christ sacrifices His own blood (9. 11-14) once and for all (7. 27; 9. 12) in order to sanctify once and for all those who believe in Him (10. 10-11).

While the Levitic priesthood, which had none of the characteristics of the priesthood of Christ, procured for the people of Israel only a "carnal" ritual purity and did not sanctify the very being of man (9. 13), that is, did not lead to perfection (10. 1), the priesthood of Christ brings about a perfect and definitive expiation which sanctifies the believers (2. 11; 10. 10, 14, 29; 13. 12). The distance which separates God from sinners is removed for those who are "sanctified" in this way; they can serve God in forms of worship which will be acceptable to Him (9. 14; 18. 28).

Nothing remains to be done in the work of redemption, and this work does not need to be repeated. Christ is priest for ever, exercising a priesthood which has no successor.

Thus the new covenant has only one priest, Christ Himself, and one priestly office, that of Christ, the only redeemer and mediator between God and man.[41] The Church is asked only to believe in the salvation offered by Christ and to glorify God for it. This is the real meaning of priesthood.[42]

We read in I Peter 2. 5-10: "Like living stones be yourselves built into a spiritual house,[43] to be a holy priesthood (ἱεράτευμα ἅγιον), to offer spiritual sacrifices acceptable to God through Jesus Christ...you are a chosen race, a royal priesthood (Βασίλειον ἱεράτευμα), a holy nation, God's own people, that you may declare the wonderful deeds of him who called you out of darkness into his marvelous light." In verse 9 the writer cites the words from Exodus 19. 6, where Jahweh announces to the people of Israel that if they keep his covenant and obey him they will be "a kingdom of priests and a holy nation." This promise is not realized for the people of Israel, because of their unbelief (cf. I Pet. 2. 6-7), but for the Church, which lives in communion with God, because it is sanctified by the redemptive work of Christ. The passage is not concerned with priests as intermediaries between the people in the Church and God. All the people are a body of priests, not in order to share and continue the mediation of Christ, but to announce to a race of men who still have not accepted salvation that this mediation has been accomplished.[44]

The Church can be called a priesthood and the believers can bear the title of priests[45] because they are intimately connected with the priestly office of Christ, not, we repeat, to renew it, as if Christ were an inadequate mediator and His redemptive work unfinished, but, on the contrary, to attest to the world that the work of salvation has already been accomplished and that it is sufficient. Without this priesthood of the Church, the priesthood of Christ would be without witness to the world. The priesthood of the Church is the means by which Christ Himself proclaims His redemptive action and reveals its power. This is the idea expressed by Paul when he makes the Church the body of Christ, the organ by which the Spirit-Christ is present in the world after His glorification; as it was present, during the incarnation, in the earthly body of Jesus. Just as it is the Church and not the believer which is the body of Christ, so it is the whole Church and not the single believer which is a priest. In other words, it is by the Church, by the unanimity of believers gathered together in the name of Christ, that testimony can be given to

Christ in its fulness.

The title of "priests" borne by the believers and the Church gives to this testimony its highest expression. The believers are no longer sinners who are in need of a priest to intervene with atoning sacrifices so that they can come into communion with God. They are already saved and sanctified by the only High Priest who has made any further act of redemption unnecessary, for "all is accomplished." The proof is that the Church itself is the priest. Until Christ, the priesthood was a propitiatory office. After Christ and because of His perfect mediation, the priesthood is the office through which the believers testify, by their acts of thanksgiving, to the salvation already realized.

To this new definition of ministry there is a corresponding new definition of worship. Sanctified by Christ, clothed in the Spirit, the Church "serves the living God" (Heb. 9. 14) by the "spiritual sacrifices" (I Pet. 2. 5) of thanksgiving and the gift of service.[46]

The coming of Christ put an end to the secular distinction between priests and laity. This distinction had its place in the old order when, as redemption had not yet taken place and sanctification was inaccessible to man, the people of the old covenant could only present themselves before God hiding behind the protective screen of the Levitic priesthood. In the Church of Jesus Christ, this distinction no longer has the slightest significance. By accomplishing His priestly office, Christ has created a holy people, a Church of priests, who present themselves before the living God in order to serve Him.

Saint Paul declares that the Church marks the end of distinctions based on race and religion, "there is neither Jew nor Greek...you are all one in Christ Jesus."[47] There are no more Jews, because the believers who are of Jewish origin have gone beyond the narrow bounds of their legal religion. There are no more Greeks, because the Gentile Christians have been grafted on to the ancient stock of Israel. There is but one single Church of Jews and Gentiles. There is a similar thought expressed in the first chapter of Peter and in the Revelation to John, that in the Church there are no longer priests and laity, but that all the believers are "a royal priesthood, a holy nation, God's own people."[48]

To maintain the obsolete distinction between priests and laity in the new covenant would be to declare the priesthood of Christ inadequate or invalid and would be to take a backward step in the history of salvation. It would be making the same mistake as continuing to practice, in the new covenant which already possesses the grace of baptism, the circumcision of the old covenant, which was only the foreshadowing of baptism, just as the Levitic priesthood was only the foreshadowing of the priesthood of Christ. "It is against God's plan, denies the history of salvation, discards the fact that Christ died and rose from the dead."[49]

From now on the only distinction which is valid is the one which places on one side the believers, those for whom the redemption of Christ is a reality, *the* reality, who are consequently a royal priesthood and a holy nation; and on the other side the unbelievers, those for whom the redemption which is in Jesus Christ does not yet exist, and to whom it must be proclaimed by the Church.

The new Christian idea of priesthood appears again in several passages in the epistles of Paul,[50] which shows that this idea was more widespread in early Christianity than might have been thought at first.[51] Saint Paul writes to the Romans that grace has been given to him "to be a minister of Christ Jesus (λειτουργὸν 'Ιησοῦ Χριστοῦ) to the Gentiles in the priestly service of the gospel of God (ἱερουργοῦντα τὸ εὐαγγέλιον τοῦ θεοῦ), so that the offering of the Gentiles may be acceptable, sanctified by the Holy Spirit."[52] Paul means that his apostleship takes on a priestly character because he proclaims to the Gentiles the redemption realized in Christ on their behalf. The Gentiles who become believers must offer their bodies "as a living sacrifice, holy and acceptable to God."[53] This is the "acceptable worship" of the new era inaugurated by the priesthood of Christ. In this passage the priesthood of the Church is carried out both by the preaching of the Apostle and by the consecration to God of the Gentiles, incorporated by the Spirit into "the holy nation."

The same thought is to be found again in the difficult text of Philippians 2. 17. The Apostle has cause to think that preaching the Gospel will cost him his life and that he will be the victim of his own apostleship. However, he rejoices and he invites his readers to rejoice with him, for, if he is put to death, he says it will be "to crown that sacrifice which is the offering up of your faith." In other words, Paul offers himself to God in sacrifice and preaches the Gospel until his death; for their part the Philippians offer themselves to God, in the sense of Romans 12, which we have just cited. The Apostle pours out his blood as an accompaniment to the sacrifice which the Philippians offer to God in their life as Christians. The Apostle *and* the Gentiles, won over to the faith by his preaching and now members of the holy nation of the believers, together fulfill the priestly office of the Church.[54]

Finally there are other more simple texts which also bear witness to the "spiritual" character given to the worship service in the new covenant.[55] The offering taken among the churches of the Gentiles on behalf of the church at Jerusalem is, in Paul's view, "a service which is holy indeed, because of the religious thanksgiving and the increase in feelings of kindliness which it produces."[56]

So the idea of the priesthood of the believers in the new covenant is always ordered by the idea of the unique priesthood of Christ to which it has its reference. The "priesthood of the Church" gives glory to God for the work of redemption through which it has become "a holy nation." This sanctified nation attests, by its very existence, that the era of witness and service has taken the place of the era of sacrificial propitiation.

III. *Apostleship*

Through its priestly office the Church turns to God to give thanks for the redemption realized in Jesus Christ. But this office is not the whole mission of the Church. As the earthly form of the glorified Christ, the Church testifies to men of the redemption accomplished for all mankind. The Church was born to serve, just as its Master came to serve. It must preach the Gospel to all nations to the uttermost parts of the earth; it must establish itself on the foundation laid for it; it must continue in the teaching of the Apostles and remain faithful to the truth revealed once and for all time; it must remember the poor and provide for the needs of the "saints;" it must maintain the unity of the spirit in the bond of peace; it must ensure that everything is done in an orderly fashion.

The "service" of the Church, the ministry of the new covenant, was carried out first of all by the Apostles, and then, when the Church spread beyond the circle of the first believers, by a multitude of ministries. The priesthood of the Church is one and collective - the ministries of the Church Church are multiple and individual. If there is *one* priesthood, there is *one* apostleship and *many* ministries.

The first leaders of the Church of the New Testament, in the name of Christ its head, were the Apostles. Undoubtedly it was the preaching of the Apostles which founded the Church and established it. As the Church grew it was from the apostleship that other ministries came and they were always subordinate to the apostleship. Finally, when the Apostles themselves disappeared from the historical scene, others did not come forward to take their title and their precise function. When the orginial Apostles are gone, the Church will have bishops and not Apostles. Apostleship holds a unique place in the Church and in the history of salvation.

Who is an Apostle and what conditions must he fulfill to bear this title? What is the function of the Apostles? What happened at the death of the Apostles? Questions like these need to be answered.[57]

In the earliest writings of the New Testament, the epistles of Paul, we find the word "Apostle" used with two different meanings. Paul speaks of "apostles of the churches" giving to the term the general meaning of "one who is charged with a mission."[58] More often he speaks of "apostles of Christ," Apostles in the specific sense of those who occupy the first rank in the scale of ministries.[59] Among these Paul undoubtedly places the Twelve and probably James, the Lord's brother, "who were Apostles before him,"[60] unknown missionaries like Andronicus and Junius,[61] and himself. We know how strongly he himself claims the title of Apostle, and Apostle "not by human appointment or human commission, but by commission from Jesus Christ."[62] If Paul claimed, and received, the title of Apostle it was because he saw the Lord, who called him to be an Apostle to the Gentiles.[63]

The link between the apostleship and the post-resurrection appearance of Christ is made by Paul with undoubted clarity in the important passage in I Corinthians 15. 1-11, where he lists the appearances of the Risen Lord. One might accept, after the several proofs demonstrated, and particularly those by M. Goguel and W. G. Kümmel,[64] that Paul is citing an established tradition of the early Church in verses 3 to 5 and developing it in verses 6 to 11. In fact the beginning of the passage is "what one may call the confession of faith of the early Church,"[65] while the rest, and particularly what Paul says about his own vision, can hardly have been part of this confession.[66]

The tradition reported by Paul speaks only of appearances of Christ to Cephas (Peter) and to the Twelve. By what he adds, Paul enlarges the circle. He emphasizes that others have seen the Risen Lord and received a missionary call from Him,[67] then he asserts that he himself was added last to the group of witnesses of the living Jesus. As W. G. Kümmel notes quite correctly, the way in which Paul takes his place not immediately after the Twelve, but following "all the Apostles" - who are already a larger group - proves that the early Church, at the time of Paul's conversion, already comprised more Apostles than the Twelve. Consequently Paul did not invent his broader view of apostleship; he inherited it from the infant Church.[68]

Another observation leads to the same conclusion. If, at the time of Paul's conversion, it had been admitted that the circle of Apostles was limited to the Twelve, the idea would never have come to Paul to call himself an Apostle. He could have proclaimed himself a prophet and maintained that the prophet was higher than the Apostle; he could never have laid claims to apostleship.[69]

The conclusion to be drawn from I Corinthians 15 therefore is that the Apostles are a group, wider than the Twelve yet a limited group, of witnesses of the Risen Lord called by

Him to preach the Gospel.

It is true that a somewhat different idea of apostleship appears in the book of Acts. According to this conception, to be an Apostle, it is not enough to have seen the Risen Lord, it is also necessary to have been with Him during His ministry since the time of John the Baptist (Acts 1. 21-22).

But the two ideas of apostleship are not as contradictory as it may seem at first glance. In fact, the quality of being an Apostle was not denied to Paul during his lifetime by the Twelve, and was never questioned in even the earliest tradition.[70] This quality of Paul being an Apostle "should logically have been challenged,"[71] if the idea of the apostleship as an institution had been fixed at a given time.[72] Since this is not the case, it must be allowed that there is an element common to the apostleship of the Twelve and that of Paul which is more essential than their differences.

On the one hand, although the Twelve were called by Jesus during His own ministry, it is not this first calling which makes them Apostles: it is their vision of the Risen Christ and the giving of the Spirit, as we see in the first chapters of Acts; they show us that those who were chosen by Jesus[73] only began their missionary activity after Pentecost.[74] On the other hand, although Paul asserts that he holds his ministry from the Lord Himself and not from men, that he is an Apostle of Christ and not simply an Apostle of the churches, yet he does not forget that the Jesus who appeared to him and whom he preaches is the historical Jesus. He acknowledges the fact that Jesus gathered to Him disciples who became Apostles before Paul, at the time when he, the zealous Pharisee, was attempting to destroy the Church of God. He knows that Christ's call brings him into a tradition. He attaches so much value to being added to this tradition that he is convinced his missionary activity would be in vain if his apostleship was not recognized by the first Apostles.[75] For Paul this recognition is, in some way, the equivalent of the second condition for Apostleship according to Acts 1. 21-22.[76]

Apostleship always has a double aspect: traditional and spiritual, or spiritual and traditional. The disciples who followed Jesus from the time of John the Baptist were not Apostles until after they received the Spirit. Paul, who was called to apostleship by Christ, the Spirit, seeks and finds "communion" with the Apostles at Jerusalem so that he does not "run in vain." In short, the two concepts of apostleship come together at this one essential point: an Apostle is one who has seen the Risen Lord and has received the command to testify to Him.[77] The two concepts of apostleship also agree on a second point, which is the consequence of the first: the apostolic circle is a closed circle. Paul recalls that there have been Apostles before him, but he never says that there will be any after him. On the contrary, he is convinced that he is the last of the Apostles. The companions he takes with him on his journeys are performing a missionary task, as he is, but they are never called Apostles. Even Timothy and Titus do not bear this title.[78] The book of Acts reports that Matthias was chosen to replace Judas,[79] but it does not say that a successor was named for James, the brother of John, who was put to death by order of Herod Agrippa I.[80] If the christophanies ceased and if the condition to be an Apostle was to have seen the Risen Lord, the apostolic circle could not extend beyond very narrow limits or ever be renewed when death removed the witnesses of the Risen Christ. In other words the Apostle occupies a unique place in the history of salvation and fulfills a unique function in the Church.

"Everyone who calls upon the name of the Lord will be saved! But how are men to call upon him in whom they have not believed? And how are they to believe in him of whom they have never heard? And how are they to hear without a preacher? And how can men preach, unless they are sent?"[81] In these terse phrases, Saint Paul states why the Christian mission, that of the Apostles and of the preachers who followed them, is indispensable for the realisation of salvation in history. There must be a "hinge" between Christ who died and rose again and humanity for whom the redemption was accomplished, that is, between men who belong to the time of Christ and to the time of the Church. The Apostles supply this need: witnesses of the Risen Christ and first preachers of the Gospel. If Jesus Christ rose again without witnesses, or if the witnesses kept silent, for all practical purposes there would be no Gospel and no salvation. "To save the world it is not enough that Christ should die and rise again. These facts must be revealed to man and man must believe."[82] If it was a matter of spreading a philosophical religion, like the Stoic wisdom common in Hellenistic times, preachers and teachers would suffice for the task. To announce to the world that it has been saved not be a timeless doctrine but by the intervention of God in history, through events which happened once and for all time at a given moment and in a given place, witnesses are necessary, that is to say, men who were present when these events took place and whose preaching can be summed up in the words: "We have seen." In the infant Church the word Apostle is often replaced by the phrase: "those who are witnesses of the resurrection," just as "those who have believed" designates the members of the Church.[83] The foundation of the Church is the death and resurrection of Christ and also the testimony to these events given by the Apostles.

There is no contradiction between Paul's words: "Jesus Christ is the foundation"[84] and the texts which assign this role to the Apostles.[85] In I Corinthians 3. 10-11, Paul writes that "he has only had to take the foundation laid by God Himself in the person of Jesus Christ, living, dead and risen from the dead, and place it in the hearts of men by preaching, as the foundation of salvation and of the Christian faith. The participle κείμενον, *which is laid,* refers to the work of God, and the verb θεῖναι, to the work of the preacher who lays the foundation of the Church in testifying to God's work."[86] When the foundation is laid, it only remains (for the missionaries who are not witnesses of the resurrection, like Apollos for example?) to build on it, without laying any further foundation. The image in Ephesians 2. 20 is the same: the believers are stages in the construction which rests on the foundation of the Apostles and the prophets; the connection of this text with chapter 3, verses 4-5 of the same epistle indicates that the Apostles are the foundation of the Church, by virtue of the bond which links them to Christ.[87]

Associated with Christ in the foundation of the Church, the Apostles carry out their mission with all the power of Christ. Their word is the word of God;[88] therefore it is effective and is accompanied by acts of divine power, which are "the signs of a true Apostle."[89] There is no function in the Church that the Apostle does not undertake. In the infant Church the Apostles at first exercise every kind of ministry and it is as the Church grows that they delegate certain functions to others. For his part, the *Apostle* Paul is acting as a *prophet* when he proclaims the mystery of the conversion of Israel[90] or the mysteries of the resurrection and the second coming,[91] and as a *teacher* when he explains to the Romans that Christ is the end of the Law and to the Colossians that Christ is above all cosmic powers. In principle all types of ministry belong to the Apostles, who hold them from the glorified Christ, and they can hand them on to those whom they bring into their ministry, except for the ministry of witness which, by definition, cannot be transferred.

Finally, the Apostles exercise their commission over the whole Church,[92] although in practice they have to divide the labor between them.[93] By this ecumenical function the Apostles in the first century are the authority which is superior to the ministry of local churches, and they maintain a community of faith and discipline among these churches.[94] They make the unity of the Church real and prevent it from dissipating into a scattering of local gatherings without any corporate links.

The authority of the Apostles comes from their unique place in the history of salvation and from their specific function as witnesses of the Risen Lord, of the Christ who has chosen them and commissioned them, and not from any sacred characteristic which is theirs alone. In the Church there is religious equality between all the believers, as we have indicated in the previous section.

The Church can have no other Apostles than the original ones because an Apostle is one who has seen the Risen Christ and the appearances have ended. This conclusion was undoubtedly already drawn in the first century. In fact, Paul is convinced that he saw the last of the christophanies. Moreover, to make the Apostles the foundation of the Church is tantamount to saying that the appearances will not happen again; for a foundation is laid once and for all. Apostleship is unique in the history of the Church just as the resurrection of Christ, to which it testifies, is unique, and just as the incarnation, of which the resurrection is the culmination, is unique. Until the second coming the Church lives through the redemption realized by Christ and attested by the Apostles.

This is why we do not see new Apostles arise when Christ's Apostles disappear into history. The case of Matthias is unique.[95] This addition to the apostolic circle was intended to close a gap made in God's work, the circle of Twelve, by the enemies of Christ.[96] It does not raise the principle of apostolic succession. On the contrary, the conditions for apostleship which are specifically mentioned: to be a witness both of the ministry of Jesus and of His resurrection emphasize as clearly as possible that apostleship is, by definition, an institution connected with the origins of the Church.[97] We might even wonder whether the emphasis put on the first of the two conditions (to have "accompanied the Lord Jesus from the time of the baptism of John") is not intended to discourage would-be Apostles, as the words in John 20. 29 emphasize that there will be no more christophanies and it is pointless to use their cessation as an excuse not to believe. In short, given what an Apostle is, he could have no successor who would be an Apostle like him.[98]

But, while being a witness of the Risen Christ, the Apostle exercises a general ministry which goes beyond the boundaries of the local churches. The New Testament shows us that the apostolic function can be seen in the mission of Timothy and Titus. That particular function is transferable. It is not bound by the theological condition that the Apostle-Witness can have no successor. It is a permanent necessity in a Church of succeeding generations of men.

IV. *Ministry*

The Apostle occupies a unique place in the history of salvation because he has seen the Risen Christ and thus he participates in the founding of the Church. But the Apostle also begins to build the Church through his ministry. This work of building must be continued as long as the present era lasts. It requires other capacities besides those of the Apostles. Even if the Church has no other Apostles than the original Apostles, it has other ministries besides Apostleship.

1. *Service and Ministry*

The New Testament in its entirety has only one general term to describe the activities exercised in the Church. It is the word for *service* (διακονία) which is applied equally to the ministry of the Apostle, to the differing functions of certain specific believers, and to the duty of all believers in general.[99] The Church is not a society which has active and passive members. It is the living body of Christ and all the members have their own function. To serve is a vocation and an obligation for all believers.[100] For they are all disciples of the One who "came not be be served but to serve others" and who made service the highest norm in his kingdom: "whoever desires to be great among you must be your servant."[101]

This requirement is contrary to the natural inclinations of the human heart.[102] Only those who are claimed by Christ and transformed by His Spirit can respond to it. To serve is only possible by the grace of God. This is why expressions for service and charisma are complementary, and even equivalent, in Paul.[103] The first epistle of Peter gives the classic expression of this relationship between duty and grace in the words: "Whatever be the gifts which each has received, you must use them for one another's benefit, as good stewards of God's manifold kindness."[104]

Gifts are not in opposition to service, any more than

inspired testimony is in contrast to administrative duties.[105] All ministry proceeds from the Spirit, for nobody can serve the Church without responding to a call. The Spirit has been given to the Church, where it has revealed its presence and its power through the gifts distributed among the believers.[106] The ministries are spiritual and the gifts are ecclesiastical. The two expressions of service and gift designate the same reality; "service" describes the nature and "gift" describes the origin of the ministries given to the Church.

The real distinction lies elsewhere. The New Testament used the one word *diaconia* with two quite different meanings. Although all the believers are in the service of the Church, the Church recognizes the particular ministries of certain men dedicated to an essential task and fulfilling an indispensable duty.

We saw in the preceding section the reasons why apostleship was necessary for the Church. The redemptive work accomplished by Christ would be in vain, if it were not proclaimed to the world so that the world might believe and be saved. This is what Paul develops in Romans 10. 14-15 which we have cited. Without the apostolic ministry there would be no Church. This is why the Apostles, as well as the Christ whom they preach, constitute the foundation of the Church. The Church exists in history from the moment when the Apostles proclaim that "Jesus Christ is Lord"[107] and there are people who accept their testimony. But the apostolic preaching is not merely the announcement of a fact. It is also the explanation of that fact and the exposition of its consequences. To the Jews the Apostles show, through the Scriptures, that the Lord Jesus is the Christ, the Messiah of Israel, and that the revelation of God in the old covenant is fulfilled in the new revelation which calls the Church together. To the Gentiles, the Apostles assert that Jesus Christ is the Lord of all the inhabited earth and of the whole universe, and to Him all power has been given in heaven and on earth. As for those who already believe, the Apostles exhort them unceasingly to continue in the faith which has become the rule of their lives. The Apostle, who founds the Church by his testimony, sets it firmly on its foundation by his teaching and his exhortation.

Although the Apostles' personal affirmation that Christ is risen and that He has been seen in glory cannot be repeated (and has no need to be, as it is given by witnesses who can be believed) - in other words, although the Apostle-Witnesses have no successors - the teaching and the exhortation must be repeated as long as the history of the Church unfolds and the Church continues to grow. The Church could not have been founded without the apostolic ministry, its growth would have stopped if other ministers were not at work to further and continue the work of the Apostles. By his ministry as teacher and leader of the Church, the Apostle inaugurates a series of other ministries, as indispensable as his own to the building-up of the Church.

This is why ministry is considered by Paul to be a divine institution, along with apostleship. He writes to the Corinthians: "God has appointed in the Church first apostles, secondly prophets, thirdly teachers."[108] In the epistle to the Ephesians we read: "Christ has appointed some to be apostles, some to be prophets, some to be evangelists, some to be pastors and teachers."[109] If these various ministries are given to the Church it is - continues the epistle to the Ephesians - "in order to equip God's people for work in his service, for the building up of the body of Christ."[110] The Church must be an edifice and not a pile of building materials, a shapeless mass of believers. Its normal development along the lines of what it should be requires that certain functions are carried out regularly and are truly stable and permanent ministries.[111] This is particularly the case with ministers of the word, without whom the Church would not be the Church.

Just as Christ acts through the Spirit in the Church, as we have seen in the first section, so, in the spiritual institution which is the Church, ministries established by God or by Christ are indispensable. The two most frequent images used for the Church in the New Testament are that of a building and that of a body, both of them showing that God wants an organized Church and that He watches over it Himself by instituting apostleship and ministries. Ministries do not appear as a late development, like institutions which would gradually be substituted for the widespread distribution of charismatic gifts. Paul's epistles give evidence of the existence of already organized ministries, since, according to Galatians 6. 6, the teacher has the right, like the Apostle, to earn his living by the Gospel.[112]

The two images of the building and the body also remind us that even if ministries are indispensable they have no monopoly on "work in his service for the building up of the body of Christ." The building which the Church is consists of "living stones."[113] In the body of Christ, all the members have their proper function and all the members of the body are treated with honor.[114] If the word *diaconia* can be applied both to specially constituted ministries and to the service given by the believers, it is because there is no essential difference between the two functions. It is a matter of difference of vocation in those who exercise the functions. Although the Church of the New Testament makes no distinction between priests and laity, as we have seen in the second section, yet it does distinguish between those exercising a specific ministry and the believers.[115] Certainly not in the sense that only the first are in the service of the Church and the others benefit passively from their ministry; but in the sense that all serve according to the different vocations to which they are called. These different vocations in the Church had already been expressed in the particular calls which Jesus addressed to his hearers. He asked all of them to order their thoughts and their lives in view of the kingdom to come; He made the seventy-six disciples preachers of the Gospel; He set apart the Twelve to be His Witnesses.

We must now examine in detail the information to be found in the New Testament concerning ministry. We shall first investigate the Pauline epistles, then the Acts of the Apostles and the Catholic epistles and finally the pastoral epistles.

2. *The Pauline epistles*

In chapter 12 of the first letter to the Corinthians, the apostle Paul draws up three lists of functions exercised in the Church (v. 8-10; 28 and 29-30).

After recalling that the Spirit manifests its presence in the Church by gifts and service of different kinds (v. 4-5), Paul enumerates a first series of activities: "the word of wisdom, the word of knowledge, special faith, gifts of healing, the exercise of miraculous powers, prophecy, the power to distinguish true spirits from false, the gift of tongues, the interpretation of tongues" (v. 8-10). The Apostle undoubtedly does not intend this to be an exhaustive list of gifts and services at work in the Church. His intention is rather to show how richly and how bountifully the Spirit is at work. These manifestations of the Spirit must have been listed as they came to mind since faith is mentioned in the middle of the series. In fact faith is not one gift among others: it is the very condition which makes the spiritual life possible. When the Apostle reaches the end of the theory he is developing he puts everything in order and makes the necessary distinctions. He writes in verse 28: "And by God's appointment there are in the Church, first apostles, secondly prophets, thirdly teachers. Then came miraculous powers, and then an ability to cure diseases or render assistance, or powers of organization, or varieties of the gift of tongues." There is no change in construction in this sentence, as has been suggested.[116] There is only the intention not to put two series of ecclesiastical functions on the same level. First of all Paul enumerates what may well be called the three ministries of apostle, prophet and teacher. He asserts specifically that these three ministries have been instituted by God and he enumerates them - and only them - to emphasize their importance and to set them apart. We will find them under the same or different names in almost all the epistles of Paul.

If an Apostle is placed at the head of the list it is not only because he is a founder of the Church by his witness; it is also because the Apostle is the doctrinal, administrative and disciplinary authority in the Church.[117] Undoubtedly the prophets are inspired preachers, who express themselves in a language which can be understood by all and not in the "varieties of tongues" of glossolalia.[118] The teachers seem to have a double mission: not only to interpret the Christian message in the light of the Old Testament,[119] but also to reveal and explain the whole message accepted by the believer in faith. It is the function closest to that of the Apostle, as the Apostle also is an instructor when he establishes a church.[120]

In the second part of his enumeration Paul makes a list

of gifts; he describes them in abstract terms, for doubtless they are spontaneous and sporadic manifestations of the Spirit which do not have the permanence of a specific ministry; he does not number them because they are too abstract to form a regulated series. These spiritual gifts are quite different from the three ministries in the first list. Without these gifts the Church would be the poorer; without the word of the Apostle who founds it and of the teacher who edifies it, the Church would not survive.

We have proof of this when we examine the summary in verses 29 and 30. The three ministries stand first, and in the same order. On the other hand the list of gifts is no longer exactly the same. "The ability to render assistance, or powers of organization" is replaced by the gift of interpretation of tongues. Fundamentally, by their very nature, charismatic gifts cannot be strictly classified. What matters for Paul is to remind us that these gifts are manifested in the Church, and to mention some of them specifically by name.

If the three lists in chapter 12 are compared with each other, it will be noticed that apostleship never appears among the gifts - we mentioned this previously and we saw why it was so - and that prophecy and teaching are gifts as well as ministries. We must not conclude from this that to speak of ministries in the time of Paul is an anachronism, and that the churches which he founded only knew the freedom of spiritual gifts. Other texts prove that this is not the case. It must only be stated that those who are seen to be prophets and teachers, established by God, do not have a monopoly in preaching and catechesis. These functions can also be carried out by believers who received a particular gift for this purpose.

The first letter to the Corinthians also gives us some indirect information about ministry. When Paul writes: "Christ did not send me to baptize, but to preach the gospel" (1. 17), he reminds us that his essential task is to carry the Gospel of salvation where it has not yet been proclaimed - in other words, to found the Church - and that the administration of the sacraments, although the missionaries can take care of it,[121] is reserved rather for other ministers, for those who work at the edification of the Church. But neither Paul, nor the New Testament, ever state precisely which minister's function it is to baptize or to celebrate the eucharist.[122] If we remember that early Christian thought does not, like modern thought, separate the word and the sacrament,[123] we would be inclined to think that, in the absence of the Apostles, the prophets and teachers would take care of the celebration of baptism and the eucharist.[124] This would be one more reason which would explain the higher ranking attributed to the prophets and teachers.

In Romans 12. 6-8, Paul enumerates the following "gifts," speaking of them as functions or of the men who fulfill those functions: "prophecy, administration,[125] the one who instructs, the one who exhorts, the one who gives, the one who leads,[126] the one who gives help in distress." This list is less complete than the one in I Corinthians 12. It is couched in very general terms, perhaps because Paul is not so well-informed about the inner life of the church at Rome. For the rest, in this passage, the Apostle is concerned with urging the believers to come together in a harmonious whole, one body in Christ. He does not intend to deal with the organization of the Church.

"The leader" appears again in I Thessalonians 5. 12, where Paul commends his readers "to respect those who are working so hard among you, and in the Lord's fellowship are your leaders and counsellors."[127] Elsewhere Paul speaks of the apostolic missionary work as "labour."[128] Here it is a matter of "labour" carried out by the Thessalonians in their own church; it is concerned mainly with spiritual leadership and brotherly counsel.[129] It does not appear to be a matter of specific ministries as such, but of the free activity of the Spirit.

On the other hand, we find in Ephesians 4. 11 a list of true ministries, along the lines of the list already encountered in I Corinthians 12. 28a: "Christ has appointed some to be apostles, some to be prophets, some to be evangelists, some to be pastors and teachers." The ministries listed here seem more numerous than those in I Corinthians. But it should be made clear at the outset that the expression "pastors and teachers" refers to one category of people. It is the teachers, who, by their instruction, shepherd the flock of God which is the Church. The word "pastor" is only an image evoked by the image of the flock, common in Scripture, to designate the people of God.[130]

We should next note that the expressions "apostles" and "evangelists," although they do not mean the same person, describe the same function: to carry the Gospel to places where it has not yet been proclaimed. The evangelist differs from the Apostle in that he is a missionary of the second rank, so to speak, since he was not a witness of the Risen Christ. This is why Philip, one of the Seven, is called an evangelist.[131] But as the only other evangelist mentioned in the New Testament is Timothy,[132] who seems to be more a leader of the Church than a propagator of the faith, we can see in this term "evangelist" a mere image or general term which does not refer to a specific ministry.[133] So we find in the passage in Ephesians only the three ministries mentioned in I Corinthians, those of the Apostle, prophet and teacher.

In the church at Philippi there are "bishops" and "deacons."[134] These two ministries are not mentioned anywhere else in Paul, unless it is in the pastoral epistles. We also know that the church at Cenchreae had a deaconess in the person of Phoebe[135] but this does not throw much light on the verse in Philippians. There are countless interpretations of the text.[136] One fact seems clear: it is a matter of two different ministries and not a single one described in two equivalent terms; the opening of the epistle is too concise to contain needless repetition. Of the two ministries the one of deacon is doubtless subordinate since it is mentioned second.

Leaving aside the original meaning of bishop, which refers to the one who watches over to protect or to supervise,[137] and remembering that Paul is urging the Philippians like all the readers of his letters, not to turn aside from the Gospel they have received[138] - for it is necessary, in Paul's view, as in the thought of all early Christianity, to continue in the apostolic faith in order to remain within the authentic Christian life - we might conclude that the bishops at Philippi ought to see particularly that the Philippians continue in the Gospel which has been preached to them. In other words, the ministry of the bishop is not essentially different from that of the teachers at Corinth and Ephesus.[139] Whatever the specific ministry may be Philippians 1. 1 "which there is no valid reason to suspect, establishes the existence of a stable ministry already in the time of Paul."[140]

We have further support for this conclusion: in Galatians 6. 6, the Apostle declares that "whoever receives instruction in the gospel should share with his instructor all his temporal blessings." This passage shows that a real ministry of teaching existed in Paul's lifetime, and that this ministry enjoyed the same right as apostleship: to make a living from the Gospel.[141] This verse also reveals the primary importance given, from the very beginning, to the teaching ministry, since it is the only one, apart from that of the Apostles, to be remunerated.[142] This presupposes that the catechetic ministry was recognized as such by the Church. Another text just as conclusive is to be found in the epistle to the Colossians (4. 17). Paul writes: "Tell Archippus: 'Attend to the duty entrusted to you in the Lord's service (ἐν κυρίῳ) and discharge it to the full.'" We should note that the Apostle does not say "by the Lord," as if it were a matter of a simple gift, but "in the Lord" which means the charge given to Archippus is a true ministry recognized by the Church,[143] as the ministry of Timothy will be at Ephesus.[144]

3. *The Acts of the Apostles*

Let us move on to the information we find in the book of Acts and in the other epistles in the New Testament. Prophets and teachers are to be found in the church at Antioch,[145] and prophets at Ephesus[146] and at Caesarea.[147] The writer of Acts here places himself in the line of the Pauline tradition of ministry. But there are two original elements in the book of Acts: it mentions the Seven along with the Twelve, and also elders.

In the opinion of the writer of Acts the rapid growth in the number of believers gave birth to a new kind of ministry in the church at Jerusalem. The Seven are charged with "waiting at table" so that the Twelve can devote themselves exclusively "to prayer and to the ministry of the Word."[148] However, as the account continues, the Seven do not merely fulfill the precise function for which they were added to the Apostles, but they perform also the work of evangelists, they are ministers of the word like the Twelve.[149] The simplest explanation of this rather singular fact is undoubtedly as follows: the writer of Acts sees in the early Hellenistic missionaries, who were not as important as the Apostles, the forerunners to some extent of the deacons who, in the Church of his time, are charged with a ministry of assistance, under the direction, one would suppose, of bishops or elders. It should be noted that the writer of Acts never gives the Seven the name of deacon and that deacons are never mentioned in the book of Acts.[150]

Elders were to be found in the church at Jerusalem,[151] but the book of Acts sheds no light on their origin.[152] They appear suddenly as the heads of the Church (11. 30) in a passage where the Apostles are not mentioned, probably because they are detained far away by their missionary journeys.[153] It is into the hands of the elders that Barnabas and Saul place the collection taken at Antioch on behalf of the brethren in Judea. Elsewhere the elders assist the Apostles (15) or James (21. 18) in the leadership of the Church; they are subordinate to the Apostles but distinct from the rest of the believers.[154]

According to the book of Acts there are also elders in the Pauline churches. We read in Acts 14. 23 that Paul and Barnabas "appointed elders for them in each congregation" on their return from their first missionary journey. Acts 20. 17 informs us that it was the elders who were in charge of the church at Ephesus. This precise information poses a problem seeing that Paul, in his epistles, except the pastoral epistles, never mentions elders. It must be admitted that either the writer of Acts transposes into the past the situation as it is in his own time, when the local churches are under the direction of elders,[155] or it must be supposed that the book of Acts calls elders those servants of the Church to whom Paul gives a different name. To support this idea we can cite the following: the elders at Ephesus (20. 17) are also called bishops (20. 28) and their mission is to be shepherds of the Church (20. 28). We have seen that the church at Philippi has bishops[156] and that, in the epistle to the Ephesians, the teachers are also described as shepherds.[157] So we see a certain equivalent use of the terms elder, bishop and teacher and a certain identity of function in these three types of ministry. For "to shepherd the flock of God" (20. 28) is to defend it against the dangers of the heresy which is being proclaimed (20. 29-31). It is the primary ministry of the word and of teaching which shows itself everywhere under different names.

If we restrict ourselves to the information found in the book of Acts we might conclude that the church in Palestine did not have the variety of gifts and ministries which enriched the Pauline churches. Perhaps this is only an impression because we have, in the book of Acts, only a brief account and few descriptions of the life of the infant Church. The evangelical tradition, nurtured on the soil of Palestine, brings a valuable addition to this. Thus the parable of the judgment reminds us in its own way that everyone should give to the service of others whatever gift he himself has received, by feeding the hungry, giving shelter to the stranger, visiting the sick and those in prison.[158]

The epistle to the Hebrews and the catholic epistles add nothing new to the information provided by the epistles of Paul and the book of Acts. Teachers are mentioned in the epistles to the Hebrews and the epistle of James.[159] The first epistle of Peter and the epistle of James confirm the existence of elders; their mission, according to I Peter, is "to tend the flock whose shepherds you are,"[160] and according to the epistle of James, they have the special task of praying for the sick and laying hands on them.[161]

4. *The pastoral epistles*

The ministries of which we read in the Pauline epistles and the Acts of the Apostles exist in terms of the apostleship which dominates them. The supreme authority within the Church is the Apostle. In order for the organizations of the Church to take shape the Apostles had to have disappeared or be about to disappear. This is the new situation presupposed by the pastoral epistles and this is the reason why they should be examined last.[162] The chief ministries mentioned in the pastoral epistles are those of deacon, elder and bishop, dominated by the ministry of apostolic delegates such as Timothy in Asia and Titus in Crete.

The characteristics of the deacon are strictly outlined in I Timothy 3. 8-13. Deacons must be men of high principle and highly regarded by their fellows, not given to double talk, not addicted to too much wine nor greedy of base gain. They must be carefully examined before being entrusted with their charge. Similar qualities are demanded of the women, although it is not clear whether the concern is with the wives of the deacons, or with women who are themselves deacons, or deaconesses.[163] This passage puts more emphasis on the qualities required of a deacon than on the functions he exercises in the Church. As the requirements are more practical than intellectual we might conclude that the functions of the elder are in service and administration rather than in instruction.[164]

Elders are mentioned in I Timothy 5. 17-22 and in Titus 1. 5-6. We read in I Timothy 5. 17: "Elders who do well as leaders should be reckoned worthy of a double honor,[165] in particular those who labor at preaching and teaching." It seems from this verse that the elders have varying qualifications for their tasks, and that these are varied too, since the double salary (or honor) is for those who preach and teach. Here again we see the preeminence given to the ministry of the word, which is quite legitimate seeing that the Church is founded on the Gospel message and that through that message it is edified and forewarned of the dangers of heresy. Timothy himself is to come to the defense of elders against whom accusations are brought lightly, but any of them "who persist in sin" must be rebuked in the presence of all.[166] The elders came together as a body and laid their hands on Timothy,[167] probably under the leadership of the Apostle himself.[168] This is all the information we have about this group of elders which, as such, plays no further role in the leadership of the Church.

Titus, for his part, is to appoint elders in each town and must choose men of blameless life, who have had only one wife,[169] and whose children are "believers and free from every reproach of profligacy or of disorderliness."[170] But the epistle to Titus has nothing to say about the function of elders.

Episcopacy is mentioned in I Timothy 3. 1-7 and in Titus 1. 7-9. The first point to be noticed is that these passages speak of the bishop in the singular while the pastoral epistles always speak of elders and deacons in the plural. The passage in I Timothy declares that to aspire to the office of bishop is an excellent ambition; then the qualities required for a bishop are enumerated. First they are the same as those for elders according to Titus 1. 5-6. But others are added: the bishop must be hospitable - that is he must welcome believers coming from other churches - a good teacher; not a recent convert; he should have a good reputation with people outside the Church. We might conclude from this that the special functions of the bishop are to teach and to be a representative of the Church to other Churches and to non-Christians.

The epistle to Titus gives more or less the same information. It emphasizes two points in particular: the bishop is God's steward, which means he is the head and the authorized representative of the Church; the bishop must not only be able to teach but also refute objectors. What connection is there between the bishop and the elders? We must differentiate between the two titles although the passage in Titus 1. 5-9 first points out the qualities required of an elder and continues in these words: "for the bishop must be..." But other indications must be taken into account. First the use of the singular by the writer of the pastoral epistles when he speaks of the bishop.[171] Next, the differences we have noted between the functions of the bishop and the elders. In fact the bishop is not limited to teaching, like the elders, but he must also refute heresy, which presupposes he has a wider knowledge or is more skilled in argument. Then, it is the bishop and not the elders who acts as the representative of the Church. Therefore it seems most likely that the bishop is not an elder but that he exercises a particular ministry which is his alone: he is probably the head of the local church.[172]

Other facts bring weight to this supposition. According to the testimony of the book of Acts (21. 18), James very soon, even during Paul's lifetime, became the sole head of the church at Jerusalem, above the elders. At the beginning of the second century Ignatius of Antioch affirms the existence of a single bishop; "Ignatius does not plead in favour of a monarchical episcopate, but merely claims the right of the bishop to absolute obedience."[173] This shows that in the time of the bishop of Antioch they were already accustomed to the idea that the local church had one leader and not several. Therefore there is no need to be reluctant to take the pastoral letters literally when they speak of the bishop in the singular.

These letters mention still another ministry, that of apostolic delegate, which is exercised by Timothy at Ephesus and by Titus in Crete. We know very little about these two men, yet we know enough to see that their ministry is like no other. Although Timothy and Titus have to teach and to fight heresy like the elders and the bishop their special ministry goes even further. Timothy must be the leader for the elders as Paul had been for the 'bishop/elders' at Ephesus.[174] For his part, as we have already indicated, Titus must appoint elders in every church,[175] that is he is to perform the function which, in the opinion of the writer of Acts, was reserved for the Apostles.[176] Finally, Timothy must "hand on what he has learned from the Apostle to men who will, in their turn, be competent to teach others,"[177] which shows that the charge given to him by the Apostle must be continued throughout the Church.

In short Timothy and Titus continue the work undertaken by Paul when, not content with founding the Church by his witness, he started to build it up by his teaching and his exhortations and by his concern with organizing it. Although Timothy and Titus are not Apostles like Paul they are his successors in the building up of the Church and there will be others coming after them, as is shown in II Timothy 2. 2 cited above.

The Gospel, the message of salvation, becomes a written book after the time of Paul, since the Apostle distributes his letters in which his testimony is written for all time. To pass from hand to hand and from generation to generation this message, now written down, has need of no other intermediaries than the believers. It is the original testimony, fixed once and for all. This is why the apostolic witness which was indispensable to the birth of the Church has no other form during the life of the Church than the Scripture. We made this point at the end of the third section.

But it is a ministry which ensures that the Gospel which

is handed on is also preached, explained, understood, and defended against possible distortions by men whose inspiration is sure and whose capabilities are recognized. This ministry remains necessary throughout the life of the Church, so that the Church may continue to grow on the foundation laid once and for all. Because salvation is part of history, tradition is a vital element in Christianity. Therefore, apostleship, in so far as it is also the ministry of the building-up of the Church, continues. This is proved in men like Timothy and Titus and in Timothy's assigned duty to ensure that there would be others to succeed him.

Two facts which are confirmed by the pastoral epistles will pave the way for episcopacy as it was known in the Church in Asia from the beginning of the second century: the appearance of a single bishop, which would give shape to Christian episcopacy, and the idea of tradition, which would give it its content.

It is time to conclude our examination of the different kinds of service and ministry described in the New Testament. What strikes us immediately is the richness of the life of the Church in its beginnings. The ministries exercised in the Church are numerous, varied, not very clearly defined and not clearly differentiated one from another. This is true of every new-born organization. It must be added that the circumstances in which the early Church came to life were not the same everywhere. Although the patriarchal organization of the synagogue may have served as a model for the churches in Palestine, Paul gave to the Gentile churches the sense of divine order which must rule in the body of Christ as in all creation. Not that the Apostle ever wanted "to extinguish the Spirit;" he merely reminded the Corinthians, "blown about by many winds of doctrine," that the Spirit breathes into the Church to edify it.

The infant Church has no one technical term to describe those who serve it. It borrows from current usage and that explains, at least in part, why the names to describe ministry are so diverse. But the plurality of ministries is an expression of the essence of the Church and of the mission proper to is.

The Church is led by the Apostles and then by their successors as we have pointed out. The New Testament does not recognize the immediate government of the Church by the Spirit, any more than it recognizes the immediate action of the Spirit in the world without the Church. The Church cannot exist without ministers of the word which must be preached and taught. The new life, born of the Gospel, is expressed through ministries of charity and administration as multiple and diverse as the tasks of the Church may demand.

V. *Christocracy*

One last question remains: what organization joins all types of ministry together, what is the authority which invests them with their office and, consequently, what is the form of government in the Church, according to the New Testament?

The Apostles were chosen by Christ Himself to be His witnesses to the world and His ministers in the Church.[178] At the time when Christ chooses an Apostle He endows him with His grace and power so that he will be able to endure all the tribulations of a missionary and also accomplish all the miracles which accompany the preaching of the Gospel. These hardships and these miracles are "the marks of a true apostle."[179] It is through these that the Apostle gains the recognition of those who had doubts about the source of his mission. The Church can only recognize the Apostle as an envoy of Christ;

the Church does not have to give him his name.[180]

There is no exception to this rule, and the writer of Acts does not fail to emphasize that the one who replaced Judas in the circle of the Twelve was also chosen by the Lord. They drew lots after they had prayed, so that it was the Lord Himself who chose Matthias.[181] The role of the Twelve or of the hundred and twenty disciples is limited to finding two men who satisfy the conditions laid down by Peter: they must have been with Jesus since the time of John the Baptist and also have been witnesses of the resurrection. These conditions themselves are not lightly imposed and cannot be so. It was Jesus Himself who called those who were to follow Him; the christophanies did not take place "before all the people" but only before a small group of witnesses "chosen by God."[182] To recall these two conditions for apostleship is to emphasize that the Church does not have the power to create Apostles, and that in this particular case it can only put forward those who have already been the subjects of one divine election. Nor does the term "election" in the sense of choosing by the Church altogether fit the case of the Seven.[183] Certainly they are chosen by the "brethren." However the latter do not designate just any of the believers but men "full of the Holy Spirit and of wisdom," that is to say men already set apart in some way. In putting forward their names, the Church is only acknowledging a decision already made by the Holy Spirit.[184]

It is also the Holy Spirit who decided that Barnabas and Saul should undertake missionary journeys[185] and who appointed the 'bishop/elders' in the church at Ephesus.[186] Although, in the first case, the choice of the Holy Spirit was given to the Church by a prophetic revelation during the celebration of worship, there is no explanation of how the elders at Ephesus received their charge. The writer of Acts doubtless is of the opinion that the Holy Spirit acted through the ministry of Paul, seeing that he shows us Paul and Barnabas, as they return from their first missionary journey, appointing elders in each town and installing them with prayer and fasting.[187] This verse is important. It shows that the power held by the Apostle, by virtue of his calling, gives him the ability to discern, through prayer, the will of the Lord, and to be, in effect, the intermediary through whom Christ gives to the Church the ministry it needs.

It is, without any doubt, by virtue of the same ability that Paul chooses Timothy and Titus as his successors, in the sense that we have described, and hands on to them, along with the mission to lead the Church, the precise duty to see that the ministry is continued. When the Apostle stipulates that Timothy should hand on the teaching he has received to men who are competent to instruct others,[188] he undoubtedly means that his disciple must find these men for himself. This is also understood in the passages in which Timothy and Titus are charged with the appointment of elders, by the laying on of hands,[189] as the Apostle had done, according to the book of Acts. Thus at the moment when the office of Apostle will disappear from the historic scene, his power of government does not pass into the hands of the Church as a whole, but to men endowed with a special ministry.[190]

The pastoral epistles only provide information about two ecclesiastical appointments. How were other appointments made? We have no idea; but it is doubtful whether the congregation of believers ever possessed a true right of election.[191] But on the other hand, if this right had existed in the first century, it is difficult to understand why the Church of the centuries which followed should allow itself to be deprived of that right.[193] But the Church is not entirely passive; it is intimately associated with the decisions taken and undoubtedly was invited to give its approval to decisions reached by those who led it.[194]

However brief and fragmentary it may be the information in the New Testament reveals the situation to be as follows: ministers are called before they are charged; it is the Apostles or their delegates who "by prophecy" or otherwise recognize those chosen by the Holy Spirit, and who appoint the ministers; it is those who are endowed with ministry who hand it on to others; by its approval the Church accepts the ministers given to it.[195]

This amounts to saying that authority in the Church comes from on high. It belongs to Christ the Spirit, who is the head of the body, the Church. It is passed to those whom Christ Hîmself has chosen, the Apostles, and then to those who are called to assist them or to succeed then. The Church is a christocracy and, more precisely, an apostolic christocracy.

There is no contradiction between the principle of christocracy and the assertions in the New Testament that every believer possesses the Holy Spirit. If it is true that there is only one Spirit, with which all have been endowed, it is also true that there are varieties of gifts and ministry. In other words, if all the believers have an equal share in the power of regeneration which is at work in the Church, it is so that they can exercise the different functions necessary for the building-up of the Church in order and harmony. All the members of the body receive the Spirit equally, so that all the members may live, and not so that differences in position and function between the different members may be suppressed.[196]

In short, because the Church is the body of *Christ*, the authority which governs it is imposed from on high. Because the Church of Christ is a *body*, the body will not survive unless the different members all carry out their specific functions. Hierarchical christocracy, which is expressed here and there in different texts in the New Testament, is the very expression of the theology of the Church.[197]

At the time of the infant Church, it does not seem that the rite of the laying on of hands was always practised at the conferring of an ecclesiastical charge.[198] As a rite for the transmission of power, the laying on of hands is only mentioned in a few passages in the Acts and the pastoral epistles. According to Acts 6. 6 the Twelve laid their hands on the Seven and thereby conferred on them their mission to take care of the poor.[199] According to Acts 13. 3, Barnabas and Saul receive the laying on of hands - whether by the congregation at Antioch or only by the prophets and teachers, the text does not make it clear - at the time of their departure on their missionary journey. Here is is a matter of a particular mission of which the writer of Acts indicates the completion.[200] It is not apostleship itself which is conferred on Barnabas and Saul.[201]

As we have already pointed out above we learn from the pastoral epistles that Timothy was inaugurated to his charge by the laying on of hands,[202] and that he is to repeat the ceremony on the elders whom he appoints.[203] This laying on of hands is the rite of the transmission of power from one minister to another,[204] which later became the ritual sacrament,[205] but which, in the first century, was not yet in general use.

Conclusion

At the beginning of this piece of work, we stated the principle that the study of ministry and ecclesiastical organization should start with what the New Testament has to tell us about the Church. We can conclude by showing that, in fact, the types of ministry which developed in the Church and the form taken by the Church are expressions of the very essence of that Church.

The Church is a charismatic institution. It has a fixed place in history but it is animated by the Spirit which pours down unendingly from on high to give it life. Just as Christ appointed Apostles to be the foundation of His Church, so the Spirit guides the Church through the men it inspires. But those who are chosen for this are not called to be a brotherhood of free spirits. Paul, converted by Christ on the road to Damascus, is ordained to the ecclesiastical tradition which he received from those who were Apostles before him. The Spirit designates those who will follow in the succession of the Apostles, and it is by the Apostles themselves that they are instructed and exhorted to keep the faith revealed to the saints once and for all and to ensure that this established tradition will not be broken. The organization of the infant Church thus shows a perfect balance between inspiration and tradition.

The book of Acts (10. 44-48) reports that the Spirit descended on Cornelius and his household after they had heard the Gospel preached by Peter. The Apostle drew the conclusion that there could be no opposition to these Gentiles receiving baptism and being accepted into the Church which took its origins from the Easter faith and the events of Pentecost. When applied to our subject this account has the value of a parable. It shows, better than any elaborate explanation, that the Spirit and tradition come together to give to the Church the leadership and the organization which are proper for it.

If Peter had been a pure charismatic he would have concluded that as Cornelius had received the Spirit he would be exempt from baptism. Baptism therefore would have disappeared from the Church of the Gentiles and that Church would have been quite different from the original Church. Similarly, to organize the Church as a group of free spirits is to detach it from the historical foundations on which it rests according to the New Testament. This changes not only the form but also the essence of the Church.

If, on the other hand, Peter had been a pure traditionalist, he would not have been willing to recognize the working of the Holy Spirit if baptism had not been previously administered and he would have been opposed to the divine initiative, to which sovereignty in the Church belongs. To organize the Church as a purely human institution is to forget that the Church lives by the inspiration of the Spirit.

The New Testament does not give a specific model according to which the Church should be organized and administered in every facet of its life. The very development of church life and its necessary adaptation to new circumstances would make detailed instructions of this kind deceptive and useless. It was sufficient to show how the first generations of Christians had understood that the Church should remain open to the Spirit yet administered and organized in such a way as to remain the Church founded by the Apostles, edified by the ministers and enriched by the gifts of all the believers.

NOTES

1. *Cahiers théologiques*, 22, Delachaux & Niestlé, Neuchâtel-Paris, 1949.

2. H. D'Espine, *Les Anciens, conducteurs de l'Eglise*, Neuchâtel-Paris, 1944 (Cahiers théologiques de l'actualité protestante, 7); J. Barnaud, J. Cadier, H. Leenhardt, L. Rimbault, "Pasteurs et Anciens," *Etudes théologiques et religieuses*, Montpellier, 1946, no. 2; J. D. Burger, *Le ministère chrétien*, Neuchâtel, 1948.

3. I Cor. 9. 5.

4. F. M. Braun, *Aspects nouveaux du problème de l'Eglise*, Fribourg, 1942. This work, which is very well researched and reveals a calm, objective judgment, contains a bibliography which completes the one given by O. Linton, *Das Problem der Urkirche in der neueren Forschung. Eine kritische Darstellung*, Uppsala, 1932. Works after 1942 are listed in E. Schweizer, *Das Leben des Herrn in der Gemeinde und ihren Diensten. Eine Untersuchung der neutestamentlichen Gemeindeordnung*, Zürich, 1946 (Abhandlungen zur Theologie des Alten und Neuen Testaments, 8). There are several works which are more recent or which are not included in the bibliographies we have mentioned: L. Cerfaux: *La théologie de l'Eglise suivant saint Paul*, Paris, 1942 (Unam Sanctam, 10); B. S. Easton, *The Pastoral Epistles. Introduction, translation, commentary and word studies*, New York, 1947; R. N. Flew, *Jesus and His Church. A study of the idea of the Ecclesia in the New Testament*, 2nd ed., London, 1943; M. Goguel, *Jésus et les origines du christianisme. La naissance du christianisme*. Paris, 1946 (cf. our review, *Revue de théologie et de philosophie*, 1947, p. 173-182); *Jésus et les origines du christianisme, L'Eglise primitive*, Paris, 1947 (cf. our review, *Revue de théol. et de philos.*, 1949); G. Johnston, *The doctrine of the Church in the New Testament*, New York, 1943; E. F. Scott, *The nature of the early Church*, New York, 1941.

5. O. Cullmann, *Le Baptême des enfants et la doctrine biblique du baptême*, Neuchâtel-Paris, 1948 (Cahiers théologiques de l'actualité protestante, 19-20, p. 20). From the English translation: *Baptism in the New Testament*, (Studies in Biblical Theology 1, p. 24). London, SCM Press, 1950. Reprinted by permission of the publisher.

6. *Op. cit.*, p. 61. English translation p. 70.

7. Let us mention once again the analogy with the problem of baptism. The most decisive argument in favor of the New Testament origin of infant baptism is the fact that in the early writings of the Church there are no signs of any disputes about the baptism of children, but, on the contrary, the theologians are seen to refer to this practice as an old established custom, indeed an apostolic custom, Cf. our article: "Le baptême des enfants dans l'Eglise ancienne," *Verbum Caro*, 1948, p. 15-26, and *supra* p. 341-362.

8. Cf. R. N. Flew, *op. cit.*,p. 130: "Since the various communions are divided from one another by varying convictions as to the ministry, it is assumed that discussion must be concentrated on questions of the origin and nature of the ministry of the Church. But the New Testament shows us a better way. It is surely more important, both for the attainment of historical truth and for the discovery of the way of reconciliation, that attention should first be concentrated on the essential nature of the Church which the ministry serves, and only after that, on the relation of the ministry to the Church."

9. This is undoubtedly the reason why Matthew placed the *logion* on the Church here, out of all traditional context. Cf. O. Cullmann, *Königsherrschaft Christi und Kirche im Neuen Testament*, Zollikon, 1941, p. 22 - On the question of the authenticity of the passage, cf. O. Linton, *op. cit.*, p. 157-183; F. M Braun, *op. cit.*, p. 81-98; R. Bultmann, "Die Frage nach der Echtheit von Matth. 16. 17-19," *Theologische Blätter*, 1941, p. 265-279, and M. Goguel, *L'Eglise primitive*, p. 184-203.

10. Cf. our article "Mia ekklesia," *Hommage et reconnaissance à Karl Barth*, Neuchâtel-Paris, 1946 (Cahiers théologiques de l'actualité protestante, hors série 2), p. 87-91, and *supra* p. 311-317.

11. Cf. also I Pet. 1. 12; Hebr. 6. 4.

12. "...the Church is the place of the Holy Spirit, even if that Spirit can blow 'wherever it chooses.'" (O. Cullmann, *Le baptême des enfants et la doctrine biblique du baptême*, p. 20.) However in our opinion it does not seem likely that John 3. 8 means "the Spirit blows wherever it chooses." It is better to give to *pneuma* the proper meaning of "wind," along with Chrysostom and several modern exegetes from F. Godet to R. Bultmann. This is the only meaning which will fit the con-

text; is it possible to say that "you hear the sound of the Spirit, but you do not know where it comes from or where it is going?" Nicodemus knew, as did every learned man in Israel and even every pious Jew, that the Spirit comes from God and descends on those whom God wishes, the prophets for example. On the contrary it is obvious that *pneuma* means the Spirit at the end of verse 8. But this shift from the proper meaning to the figurative meaning - emphasized by the use of οὕτως - is characteristic of John (cf. 3. 3-5; 4. 10-15, etc.).

If we accept this interpretation of John 3. 8, we reject the idea maintained by E. Stauffer (*Die Theologie des Neuen Testaments*, Stuttgart, 1941, p. 146) that, in John, the Spirit is not uniquely "*kirchengeschichtlich*" as in the rest of the New Testament. Stauffer applies this same idea to John 4. 23 and 10. 16 also. But these two verses do not seem to be concerned with the free action of the Spirit outside the Church. The first means that only those who accept the revelation brought by Jesus can really know the Father and worship Him as He should be worshipped; in the second verse Jesus declares that His mission is to seek out those who do not already belong to Him and bring them into the one flock, which is the Church. The idea is the same as that in 11. 52.

13. Acts 2. 17f., 25f., 34f.

14. Acts 2. 22-24; 3. 13-15; 4. 27-28; 10. 36-40.

15. Acts 1. 21-22.

16. Acts 2. 36.

17. Cf. O. Linton, *op. cit.*, p. 127.

18. Acts 9. 17-18.

19. Acts 13. 2-3; Rom. 15. 23-24.

20. Cf. Gal. 1.

21. Gal. 2. 2.

22. Cf. G. Kittel, *Die Probleme des palästinischen Spätjudentums und das Urchristentum*, Stuttgart, 1926 (Beiträge zur Wissenschaft vom Alten und Neuen Testament 3. 1), p. 64-65.

23. I Cor. 11. 11.

24. I Cor. 14. 34.

25. I Cor. 14. 36.

26. Gal. 1. 22.

27. On this whole question cf. L. Cerfaux, *op. cit.*, p. 209-211.

28. Rom. 15. 19.

29. Rom. 15. 27.

30. II Cor. 9. 12-13.

31. On this point, cf. K. Holl, "Der Kirchenbegriff des Paulus in seinem Verhältnis zudem der Urgemeinde," *Sitzungsberichte der preussischen Akademie der Wissenschaften*, 1921, p. 936-938 and 942.

32. Cf. E. Schweizer, *op. cit.*, p. 53-55.

33. E. Schweizer, *op. cit.*, p. 54.

34. M. Goguel, *L'Eglise primitive*, p. 14.

35. Cf. M. Goguel, *op. cit.*, p. 10.

36. Matt. 5. 23-24.

37. Cf. Josephus, *Jewish Antiquities*, 18. 1, 5(§ 19).

38. Mark 14. 58; 15. 29, and par.; John 2. 19; cf. Acts 6. 14. - On this question, cf. the commentaries and also: E. Lohmeyer, "Die Reinigung des Tempels," *Theologische Blätter*, 1941, p. 257-264, and *Kultus und Evangelium*, Göttingen, 1942 (this work has not been available to us); O. Cullmann, *Urchristentum und Gottesdienst*, Basel, 1944 (Abhandlungen zur Theologie des Alten und Neuen Testaments 3), p. 47f.

39. O. Cullmann, *ibid.*, p. 47-48.

40. In Acts 3. 1 the Apostles go up to the Temple to take part in the service of prayer and not in the sacrificial worship. A fragment of the gospel of the Ebionites has preserved these words of Jesus: "I came to abolish sacrifices. If you do not cease your sacrifices, anger will not cease to fall down upon you." But the account by Hegesippus presents James spending his life in the Temple not offering sacrifices for the people but making intercessions on their behalf. These facts show that among the Jewish Christians themselves there was a feeling that sacrifice and Christianity were incompatible (M. Goguel, *L'Eglise primitive*, p. 273).

41. In the New Testament the words ἱερεύς and ἀρχιερεύς are only applied to Jewish priests and high priests, and to Jesus in the epistle to the Hebrews. Only a few passages, to which we shall return later, make all the believers - and not just a few of them - priests (I Pet. 2. 5, 9; Rev. 1. 6; 5. 10; 20. 6) Similarly the classical terms used in the Septuagint and in Hellenism to designate the priestly office - λειτουργέω, λειτουργία - are only applied to the worship of the old covenant and to the priesthood of Christ, apart from a few instances to which we shall also refer later. These facts have often been noted (cf. E. Schweizer, *op. cit.*, p. 19f. and the writers he mentions). What may be added is that in the particular cases which concern us, we never encounter the expressions, ἱερεῖς and λειτουργέω, λειτουργία together in the same context, which shows that the new covenant does not recognize a priestly class appointed to an office denied to ordinary believers, the so-called laymen. We shall return later to the distinction between priests and laity in the Church.

42. Cf. the expression λειτουργία τῆς πίστεως in Phil. 2. 17, which we will examine later, and the article by K. L. Schmidt, θρησκεία in *Theologisches Wörterbuch zum Neuen Testament*, 3, p. 155-159.

43. It is better to make οἰκοδομεῖσθε in verse 5 an indicative (Bengel, Usteri, J. Monnier in their commentaries, R. N. Flew, *op. cit.*, p. 159) than an imperative (Gunkel, Hauck, Schweizer in their commentaries). In the latter case the aorist would be required rather than the present. Even if we allow the imperative, the meaning hardly changes at all. The writer urges his readers to become (verse 5) what they already are (verse 9) according to the general principle of New Testament exhortations.

44. Cf. G. Schrenk, *Theologisches Wörterbuch zum Neuen Testament*, 3, p. 250-251.

45. Rev. 1. 6; 5. 10; 20. 6 - These three verses express the same idea as the passage in I Peter.

46. Cf. Rom. 6. 13; 12. 1; Hebr. 13. 15-16, 21, and G. Schrenk, *Theologisches Wörterbuch zum Neuen Testament*, 3, p. 283; R. N. Flew, *op. cit.*, p. 160.

47. Gal. 3. 28.

48. I Pet. 2. 9. On the distinction between priests and laity in the early Church, cf. G. Schrenk, *Theologisches*

Wörterbuch zum Neuen Testament, 3, p. 284. For current opinion on the question one should read the fine article by P. Jaccard, "Fidèles, mais point laïques," *Cahiers protestants,* 1944, p. 257-273.

49. [Translator's note] This is a translation into English of the French version, O. Cullmann, *Le baptême des enfants et la doctrine biblique du baptême,* p. 59. The original German is somewhat briefer and could be rendered simply as "it is against God's plan of salvation."

50. These are passages where traditional expressions of the language of worship appear: ἱερουργέω Rom. 15. 16), λειτουργία, λειτουργέω, λειτουργός (Rom. 15. 16, 27; II Cor. 9. 12; Phil. 2. 17, 25, 30).

51. We should also point out that in Hebrews 2. 17 the writer presents Jesus to his readers as the High Priest without any preamble, which allows us to suppose that we have here a general theme in Christian teachings, rather than an idea original to the writer to the Hebrews.

52. Rom. 15. 16.

53. Rom. 12. 1f.

54. The idea of the sacrifice offered by Paul is expressed by εἰ καὶ σπένδομαι and that of the sacrifice of the Philippians by ἐπί τῇ θυσίᾳ καὶ λειτουργίᾳ τῆς πίστεως ὑμῶν. Ἐπί has here the temporal meaning which describes the circumstances surrounding an event (F. M. Abel, *Grammaire du grec biblique,* Paris, 1927, p. 236). J. B. Lightfoot, (*Saint Paul's Epistle to the Philippians,* 10th ed., London, 1890, *ad loc.*) has already noted the resemblance of our text and I Peter 2. 5, but in the sense that only the Philippians represent the royal priesthood here.

55. II Cor. 9. 12: ἡ διακονία τῆς λειτουργίας ταύτης; Rom. 15. 27; cf. Phil. 2. 25, 30. The religious meaning of λειτουργία and allied terms, in these passages, seems preferable to the secular meaning, to which some commentators and H. Strathmann, *Theologisches Wörterbuch zum Neuen Testament,* 4, p. 234, adhere.

56. E. B. Allo, *Saint Paul, Seconde épître aux Corinthiens,* Paris, 1937, p. 236.

57. On the subject of apostleship, apart from the works mentioned in the Introduction, cf. K. H. Rengstorf, *Theologisches Wörterbuch zum Neuen Testament,* 1, p. 397-448.

58. II Cor. 8. 23; Phil. 2. 25. Cf. also II Cor. 11. 5, 13; 12. 11 and *Didache* 11. 3-6.

59. I Cor. 12. 28; Eph. 4. 11.

60. Gal. 1. 17 and 19.

61. Rom. 16. 7. But perhaps these two should be placed with the "apostles of the Church" in the sense of II Cor. 8. 23, (R. N. Flew, *op. cit.*, p. 137).

62. Gal. 1. 1, etc.

63. Gal. 1. 15 to 2. 10; I Cor. 9. 1f; 15. 1-11. Cf. Acts 9. 27.

64. M Goguel, *La foi à la résurrection de Jésus dans le christianisme primitif*, Paris, 1933 (Bibliothèque de l'Ecole des Hautes Etudes, Sciences religieuses, 47), p. 241-248; W. G. Kuemmel *Kirchenbegriff und Geschichtsbewusstsein in der Urgemeinde und bei Jesus*, Zürich-Uppsala, 1943 (Symbolae Biblicae Upsalienses, 1) p. 2-7.

65. M. Goguel, *op. cit.*, p. 246.

66. Cf. M. Goguel, *op. cit.*, p. 246; W. G. Kuemmel, *op. cit.*, p. 5.

67. W. G. Kuemmel (*op. cit.*, p. 7) points out the importance of the missionary command along with the vision of Christ to constitute an Apostle. The five hundred who saw the Risen Lord "all at one time" certainly were not all Apostles. Cf. also E. Schweizer, *op. cit.*, p. 72, n. 14. -- At the same time it is possible that Andronicus and Junias, who are Apostles according to Romans 16. 4, could have belonged to this group, and perhaps also Barnabas, named an Apostle in Acts 14. 14, although the latter seems more doubtful.

68. *Op. cit.*, p. 7.

69. Cf. M. Goguel, *L'Eglise primitive*, p. 91.

70. Cf. Clement of Rome 5. 3-7; 42. 1-2; 47. 1; II Clement 14. 2; Ignatius, Ephes. 12. 2; Rom. 4. 3; Polycarp, Phil. 3. 2; 9. 1; 11. 2-3; II Pet. 3. 15-16.

71. M. Goguel, *L'Eglise primitive*, p. 96.

72. Cf. M. Goguel, *L'Eglise primitive*, p. 91-96.

73. Acts 1. 13.

74. Acts 2.

75. Gal. 2. 1-2.

76. Cf. our article: "L'unité de l'Eglise selon le Nouveau Testament," *Etudes théologiques et religieuses*, 1946, p. 275-276, *supra* p. 331-332. E. Schweizer (*op. cit.*, p. 72, n. 14) asserts that the life of Jesus plays no part in the epistles of Paul and that, in his view, only the death and resurrection of Jesus are essential. It seems to us, on the contrary, "that the Apostle is much more familiar with the life of Jesus than a superficial reading of the epistles might lead us to suppose," (M. Goguel, *Jésus de Nazareth, mythe ou histoire?* Paris, 1925, p. 124,) and that in Paul's thought the incarnation (and not only the death) plays an essential part.

77. Cf. particularly I Cor. 9. 1 and Acts 2. 32; 3. 15; 4. 20; 5. 32; 10. 41.

78. Neither is Apollos an Apostle (cf. O. Linton, *op. cit.*, p. 75) and I Corinthians 4. 9, alleged by M. Goguel to establish this fact (L'Eglise primitive, p. 90, n. 1) does not prove anything. We also find it difficult to agree with the affirmation "Paul does not acknowledge the idea of a limited circle of Apostles nor that of an apostleship which could not last more than one generation" (*ibid.*). For the opposite point of view, cf. also E. Schweizer, *op. cit.*, p. 74, n. 24.

79. Acts 1. 21-26.

80. Acts 12. 2.

81. Rom. 10. 13-15.

82. C. Spicq, *Saint Paul. Les épîtres pastorales*, Paris, 1947, p. 226.

83. Cf. the first chapters of Acts.

84. I Cor. 3. 10-11.

85. Eph. 2. 20; Matt. 16. 18. Here Peter alone is the foundation of the Church.

86. F. Godet, *Commentaire sur la première épître aux Corinthiens*, Neuchâtel, 1886, 1, p. 165.

87. Ephesians 2. 20 remains difficult whether it is understood as Christian prophets - as the parallels 3. 5 and 4. 11 suggest - or as prophets of the old covenant. We find no other trace in the New Testament of the idea that the prophets (whether of the old covenant or the new is of little importance, the difficulty remains the same) are so very closely associated with the Apostles. Hebrews 1. 1 recalls that the prophets of the old covenant and the Son belong to two different periods in the history of salvation (cf. Polycarp, Phil. 6. 3 where the writer distinguishes between the apostles who preached the Gospel and the prophets who foretold it). Paul gives a different rank to the Apostles and the Christian prophets (I Cor. 12. 28). Most recent writers do not hesitate to see the Christian prophets in Ephesians 2. 20. Cf. for example: H. Rendtorff, in *Das Neue Testament Deutsch*, 1935, 2, p. 497; E. F. Scott, in *The Moffatt New Testament Commentary*, 1930, p. 177; L. Cerfaux, *op. cit.*, p. 113; R. N. Flew, *op. cit.*, p. 183; E. Schweizer, *op. cit.*, p. 36, n. 24; F. J. Leenhardt, *Etudes sur l'Eglise dans le Nouveau Testament*, Genève, 1940, p. 71; O. Cullmann, *Königsherrschaft Christi und Kirche im Neuen Testament*, p. 21, n. 27; M. Goguel, *L'Eglise primitive*, p. 55, 104 and 199. The opposite opinion is held by K. L. Schmidt, "Le ministère et les ministères dans l'Eglise du Nouveau Testament," *Revue d'histoire et de philosophie religieuses*; 1937, p. 318, n. 5.

88. I Thess. 2. 13; Gal. 1. 9-10; Acts 4. 29.

89. II Cor. 12. 12; Gal.3. 5; I Thess. 1. 5; Acts 4. 29; 5. 12, etc.

90. Rom. 11.

91. I Thess. 4 and 5; I Cor. 15.

92. Cf. Acts 1. 8; Rom. 1. 14; I Cor. 9. 19-22.

93, Cf. Gal. 2. 7-8.

94. Cf. I Cor. 11. 2, 16; 14. 34, 36; 15. 11.

95. Paul's case is different; he was not called to replace an Apostle who had died.

96. Cf. the importance given to the death of Judas and to the fact that his betrayal was part of the divine plan (Acts 1. 16-20). Judas served as the "guide to those who arrested Jesus;" he was the one who carried out the work of those who "gathered together against the Anointed, the holy servant Jesus." (Acts 4. 27).

97. There is proof of this in the fact that nobody was called to succeed the Apostle James, the son of Zebedee and the brother of John, who was put to death at the order of Herod Agrippa I, probably in the year 44 (Acts 12. 2). The death of the Apostles poses a problem. It is strange that neither the New Testament nor the earliest ecclesiastical writers have anything to say about it; Clement of Rome (chapter 5) betrays his ignorance (for another interpretation, cf. O. Cullmann, "Les causes de la mort de Pierre et de Paul d'après le témoignage de Clément Romain," *Revue d'histoire et de philosophie religieuses,* 1930, p. 294-300). The only one whose fate we know is James, the son of Zebedee. Herod Agrippa, who was responsible for his death, died soon afterwards, struck down by divine punishment (Acts 12. 20-23). Could not the real reason for this punishment be that Agrippa, by laying hands on an Apostle, struck down one who was destined to live until the second coming of Christ? John 21. 21-23 supports this theory. This passage seems to be intended to assuage the doubts and fears resulting from the disappearance of one Apostle, whom Jesus had promised should live until He came again. Primitive Christianity at first thought the second coming was imminent. Paul shared this belief but later abandoned it, at least as far as he himself was concerned (cf. O. Cullmann, *Christ et le temps*, Neuchâtel and Paris, 1947, p. 122). It is possible that the first Christians believed that the Apostles would not die. If so, it would be expected that they would escape the rigors of the tribunal, if they were brought to trial. With this assurance that they were guaranteed divine assistance, there would be a certain lack of interest in the fate of the Apostles who were arrested. When the Apostles were executed and belief in their "immortality" vanished, it was too late to collect precise information about their final days. Undoubtedly they spent them deprived of the company of their Christian brethren. This would explain our total ignorance about the way in which the earthly lives of Peter and Paul came to an end.

98. O. Cullmann (*ibid.*, p. 122) notes quite rightly that the early Church remained faithful to the New Testament idea of the apostleship, when, in the creation of the canon, it set down the apostolic testimony in writing. We might add that the Scripture is to the Apostles what the sacraments are to the person of Jesus.

99. Διακονία, διακονεῖν and διακονος can designate ministry in a general sense I Cor. 12. 5; Eph. 4. 12, etc) and consequently all specific ministries: apostleship (Acts 1. 17 and 25; 20. 24; 21. 19; Rom. 11. 13; II Cor. 4. 1; 5. 18; 6. 3; 11. 8; I Tim. 1. 12. The ἀπόστολος is also διάκονος: I

Cor. 3. 5; II Cor. 11. 23; Col. 1. 23 and 25; Eph. 3. 7) which is primarily but not exlusively the "ministry of the word" (Acts 6. 4); and also an individual ministry which has no particular name, like that of Archippus at Colossi (Col. 4. 17) or of Timothy at Ephesus (I Tim. 4. 6; however, according to II Tim. 4. 5, Timothy is an evangelist, this word also being a "picture-word"); or again "attending to the tables" (Acts 6. 1-2) and all the services resulting from brotherly kindness (Acts 11. 29; 12. 25; II Cor. 8. 4 and 20; Rom. 15. 25; cf. also I Cor. 16. 15; Hebr. 6. 10).

The expression χάρισμα which we shall discuss shortly, only appears in Paul and in I Peter. In these same epistles, we also find the adjective οἰκονόμος (I Cor. 4. 1; Titus 1. 7; I Pet. 4. 10); but οἰκονόμος is only an image derived from that of οἶκος to designate the Church, just as, we shall see, the word ποιμήν is only an image inspired by the comparison of the Church to a flock.

100. Attention has often been drawn to this point. Cf. O. Linton, *op. cit.*, p. 195f; K. L. Schmidt, *op. cit.*, p. 322f, and E. Schweizer, *op. cit.*, p. 23f.

101. Mark 10. 43-45. This thought appears again in Paul: God has made the Apostles the least among men (I Cor. 4. 9) and has given them the first place in the Church (I Cor. 12. 28).

102. The natural feeling is expressed in the words of the Sophist: "How can a man be happy, if he must be the servant of another?" (Plato, *Gorgias* 491c, cited by W. Beyer, *Theologisches Wörterbuch zum Neuen Testament*, 2, p. 81.)

103. I Cor. 12. 4-5. Cf. Rom. 12. 6; I Cor. 7. 7; 12. 31. - We must point out that apostleship is never called a χάρισμα. The explanation given for this is that apostleship is an ecumenical ministry while charisma is exercised in the setting of the local church (M. Goguel, *L'Eglise primitive*, p. 124, n. 3). But Timothy's ecumenical ministry is called a charisma "a gift of God" (I Tim. 4. 14; II Tim. 1. 6). If apostleship is not described as a particular gift of God, it is because it is, so to speak, the sum total of all charismas, being properly ἡ χάρις (Romans 15, etc.) a calling directly by the Risen Lord.

104. I Peter 4. 10.

105. Cf. O. Linton, *op. cit.*, p. 206f; O. Michel, *Das Zeugnis des Neuen Testaments von der Gemeinde*, Göttingen, 1941 (Forschungen zur Religion und Literatur des Alten und

Neuen Testaments, N. F., 39) p. 64-66, and "Gnadengabe und Amt." *Deutsche Theologie*, 1942, p. 133-139, especially p. 135: "Auftrag, Vollmacht, Charisma und Amt sind im Urchristentum keine Gegensätze".

106. R. N. Flew (*op. cit.*, p. 183) writes, in connection with Ephesians 4: "The One Body is the home of the One Spirit and the gifts are possessed by the Church as a whole." E. Schweizer (*op. cit.*, p. 86) says the same in connection with I Cor. 1. 7: "Die Gemeinde als Ganzes ist Trägerin der Dienste." If it is true that the Spirit is given to the Church, which is the body of Christ, it seems that the gifts of the Spirit in fact rest on all the members of the body of Christ, on all the believers. "The Spirit is manifested in each one (ἑκάστῳ) for the good of all" (I Cor. 12. 7; cf. 12. 11; 14. 26; Eph. 4. 7.) The gifts with which the Spirit enriches the Church are shared among the believers, just as the senses and the functions of the human body are shared among all the members (I Cor. 12. 18; Eph. 4. 16.) Paul's analogy leaves no doubt about this.

107. Cf. Acts 2. 36; Phil. 2. 11, etc.

108. I Cor. 12. 28.

109. Eph. 4. 11.

110. Eph. 4. 12.

111. This same necessity for "harmony" and "order" leads Paul to subordinate the gift of tongues to the gift of prophecy (I Cor. 14. 40), for "he who speaks in a tongue edifies himself, but he who prophesies edified the Church." (I Cor. 14. 4).

112. Cf. M. Goguel, *L'Eglise primitive*, p. 160: "Without organization, regulation and leadership the work of the missionary Apostles would have created nothing that would have endured. The Apostle Paul was not content with creating churches; he also organized them."

113. I Pet. 2. 5.

114. Cf. I Cor. 12. 12-25.

115. Cf. Phil. 1. 1; Acts 15. 22 etc.

116. Several commentators (Godet, MacFadyen, etc.) see an anacoluthon in the sentence but they are in error. The first part of the classic formula πρῶτον μεν...ἔπειτα (cf.

James 3. 17) is developed in οὓς μὲν πρῶτον, δεύτερον, τρίτον after which comes the adversative ἔπειτα which is repeated in order to make clearer the distance between the two listings.

117. Cf. I Cor. 5. 4-5; 7. 1; etc.

118. The prophets disappeared quite early. From the time of the second century the word always means the prophets of the Old Testament (cf. O. Linton, *op. cit.*, p. 103.)

119. Cf. R. N. Flew, *op. cit.*, p. 144.

120. I Cor. 4. 17; II Thess. 2. 15; cf. Col. 2. 7; Eph. 4. 21, and K. H. Rengstorf, *Theologisches Wörterbuch zum Neuen Testament,* 2, p. 149 and 160.

121. Paul himself (I Cor. 1. 14f), Peter and the Twelve undoubtedly (Acts 2. 38f), the evangelist Philip (Acts 8. 12f; 8. 38), Ananias (Acts 9. 18) all performed baptisms. Paul perhaps celebrated the eucharist at Troas (Acts 20. 7 and 11.)

122. It is not until the second century that we find precise information on this subject, at least as far as the eucharist is concerned. According to Ignatius of Antioch, the eucharist is presided over by the bishop or his delegate (Smyrn. 8. 1). According to Justin Martyr the eucharist is celebrated by "the one who presides over the gathering of the brethren" and "the ministers whom we call deacons distribute the consecrated bread, wine and water to all the participants, and carry it to those who are away" (Apol. 65. 3 and 5). The Bishop of Antioch does not seem to be referring to this role of the deacons in *Trallians* 2. 3 (as G. Bornkamm thinks, *Theologisches Wörterbuch zum Neuen Testament*, 4, p. 831,) for this passage is more along the lines of I Cor. 4. 1 and I Tim. 3. 9.

123. Cf. M. Goguel, *L'Eglise primitive*, p. 392f.

124. This idea is supported by the *Didache* 10. 7 and 7. 1.

125. Either in the general meaning of "service" or in the particular sense of giving assistance.

126. Προϊστᾶσθαι can be taken in the sense of presiding over the gathering of the believers (cf. for example M. Goguel *op. cit.*, p. 114 and 125; E. Schweizer, *op. cit.*, p. 48, n. 15) or of spiritual guidance (M. Dibelius, *Handbuch zum Neuen Testament*, 11, 3 Aufl. p. 30). The second meaning is perhaps preferable in view of the context. It would apply also in I Thess. 5. 12.

127. We can see here one single category of believers who carry out three activities (those who work so hard among you, lead you and counsel you) or two categories (those who work so hard among you - that is those who lead you - and those who counsel you) or even three separate categories: those who in a general way are at your service (cf. διακονία Rom. 12. 7), those who lead you (cf. Rom. 12. 8), and those who counsel you (cf. ὁ παρακαλῶν Rom. 12. 8).

128. Cf. I Thess. 3. 5; I Cor. 15. 10; Gal. 4. 11; Phil. 2. 16; Col. 1. 29; I Tim. 4. 10; II Tim. 2. 6.

129. Elsewhere this counsel is either the mutual duty of all the believers (I Thess. 5. 14; II Thess. 3. 15; Rom. 15. 14; Col. 3. 16) or one of the functions of the Apostle Paul (I Cor. 4. 14; Col. 1. 28; cf. Acts 20. 31).

130. Cf. M. Goguel, *op. cit.*, p. 115-116. Christ Himself is the shepherd of His flock (John 10. 2f) or the great shepherd of the sheep (Hebr. 13. 20; I Pet. 5. 4). According to Acts 20. 28 and I Peter 5. 2 it is the elders who are charged to watch over the flock of the Lord, that is to say give it its spiritual nurture. The Church exists by "continuing in the teaching of the Apostles" (Acts 2. 42; cf. the many passages in the epistles where Paul constrains his readers not to forget the teaching he has given them). The task of the teachers, according to Paul, seems to be to nourish the Church with the apostolic teaching. The image of the shepherd thus brings the ministry of the teacher, known in the Pauline churches, closer to the ministry of the elder, attested by the Acts and the catholic epistles.

131. Acts 21. 8.

132. II Tim. 4. 5.

133. Cf. M. Goguel, *op. cit.*, p. 115; R. N. Flew, *op. cit.*, p. 144.

134. Phil. 1. 1.

135. Rom. 16. 1.

136. Cf. the commentaries.

137. M. Goguel, *op. cit.*, p. 120.

138. Cf. particularly Phil. 3. 2f.

139. According to popular opinion, the bishops and deacons would be concerned with financial and administrative questions. But it is doubtful whether these concerns would be so complicated - even ignoring the gift sent to the Apostle by the Philippians - that the creation of a double ministry was necessary. The concern to establish first a ministry of the word would have been more urgent, and the deacons would have been sufficient to take care of financial matters.

140. M. Goguel, *op. cit.*, p. 125.

141. Cf. I Cor. 9. 11; II Cor. 11. 7f; Phil. 4. 10f; I Thess. 2. 6, 9; Rom. 15. 27. It is Paul's constant teaching that in the Church temporal benefits are owed to the one who brings the spiritual benefits. It is on this principle that not only the right of the Apostles to receive a remuneration is founded, but also the idea of the collection on behalf of the believers at Jerusalem.

142. Cf. also I Tim. 5. 17.

143. M. Goguel, *L'Eglise primitive*, p. 126.

144. Cf. I Tim. 4. 14; II Tim. 1. 6.

145. Acts 13. 1; cf. 11. 27-28; 15. 32.

146. Acts 19. 6.

147. Acts 21. 10.

148. Acts 6. 1-4.

149. Cf. Acts 7; 8; 21. 8.

150. On The Seven and their origin, cf. particularly O. Bauernfeind, *Die Apostelgeschichte* (Theologischer Handkommentar zum Neuen Testament, 5), Leipzig, 1939, p. 99-105 and M. Goguel, *La naissance du christianisme*, p. 190f.

151. Acts 11. 30; 15 *passim*; 21. 18.

152. They correspond to the elders in the Jewish synagogues, and like them are probably chosen from among the oldest members, so that the word πρεσβύτεροι still keeps its proper meaning. Cf. the contrast with νεώτεροι, Acts 5. 6.

153. Cf. I Cor. 9. 5.

154. Acts 15. 22.

155. M. Goguel, *L'Eglise primitive*, p. 135; B. S. Easton, *The pastoral epistles*, New York, 1947, p. 226.

156. Phil. 1. 1.

157. Eph. 4. 11.

158. Cf. Matt. 25. 31-46 and R. N. Flew, *op. cit.*, p. 147.

159. Hebr. 5. 12 and James 3. 1. "It is still far from certain whether this refers to a specific function" (M. Goguel, *L'Eglise primitive*, p. 117). The expression "leaders" of the Church (Hebr. 13. 7, 17) is only an image, like the word "Shepherd".

160. I Pet. 5. 1-4. These elders could be just the older members of the church, for the exhortation to the older ones is followed by an appeal to the younger men, and the writer, who calls himself an Apostle at the beginning of the letter, refers to himself as a "fellow-elder" in 5. 1. Far from being exclusive the two meanings of the word "elder" can come together; the oldest members of the church will have assumed leadership (M. Goguel, *op. cit.*, p. 117 and 136). The word πρεσβύτερος has also the two meanings of "old man" and "head of the church," in the openings of the second and third epistles of John, and in Revelation 4. 4; 5. 5; 7. 11, where the aged in heaven are the representatives of the elders of the Church (cf. M. Goguel, *op. cit.*, p. 136).

161. James 5. 14.

162. Our intention is not to deny absolutely the possible Pauline authorship of the pastoral epistles. The question is too complex for a simple answer. There is undoubtedly, a Pauline element in these epistles and the dilemma - are they authentic or not - is very difficult to resolve. The solution should be sought along the lines suggested by J. Jeremias (*Das Neue Testament Deutsch*, Göttingen, 1935, 3, p. 3f): Paul, prevented from writing himself by very strict imprisonment, would have entrusted his thoughts to a scribe - and a different scribe from that one or those who had been at his disposal hitherto - who would have edited the epistles from the oral message of the Apostle. We might go a little further than Jeremias and wonder how much the scribe, before writing the letters, took into account the new situation in which the churches found themselves after the removal of the one who had been their common authority and their mutual and living link. Also we might wonder how much the scribe altered the oral message entrusted to him, in view of the new

questions which had to be asked and resolved. However that may be, the pastoral epistles remain the last word of the New Testament on ecclesiastical organization.

163. In support of "deaconesses" it could be pointed out that I Timothy 5. 3-13 mentions also an order for widows (cf. M. Goguel. *L'Eglise primitive*, p. 128-129 and 132-133).

164. It is sometimes deduced from I Timothy 3. 13 ("those who have filled the deacon's office well will gain for themselves a high standing...") that the best deacons can be promoted to the office of elder or bishop (cf. M. Goguel, *op. cit.*, 129 and n. 4). Against this interpretation it might be pointed out that the verb περιποιοῦνται is in the present and not in the future (C. Spicq, *op. cit.*, p. 102) and that the pastoral epistles require of elders and bishops other qualities than those of a deacon, particularly the ability to preach and teach. It is only later that the diaconate becomes the preliminary step to the priesthood (cf. B. S. Easton, *op. cit.*, p. 134).

165. Τιμή can have the meaning of honor or honorarium. The exegetes are divided in their opinion (cf. M. Goguel, *op. cit.*, p. 263, n. 1; C. Spicq, *op. cit.*, p. 175-176). The meaning we give to it in our translation seems to us to be imposed because of verse 18 (cf. B. S. Easton, *op. cit.*, p. 159).

166. I Tim. 5. 20.

167. I Tim. 4. 14.

168. II Tim. 1. 6 - It must be pointed out that the laying on of hands took place διὰ προφητείας [under the guidance of prophecy] (I Tim. 4. 14). According to I Timothy 1. 18 Timothy had been the object of prophecies, which marked him out for his ministry, just as, according to Acts 13. 2, the Spirit, speaking through the prophets at Antioch, had asked that Barnabas and Saul should be set apart for missionary work. Apart from these two verses, the prophetic ministry is not mentioned in the pastoral epistles. These passages must be understood either in the sense that the prophets had marked out Timothy previously (C. Spicq, *op. cit.*, p. 48), or, as seems preferable, in the sense that the prophets are Paul and Timothy themselves, in other words, it is the Apostle and his disciples who received divine revelations with regard to the choice of Timothy (B. S. Easton, *op. cit.*, p. 118).

169. The expression μιᾶς γυναικὸς ἀνήρ means that the aspirant to the office of elder must not have been married for

a seond time, either as a widower (M. Goguel, *L'Eglise primitive*, p. 556 and 557), or as a result of divorce from a non-Christian wife (B. S. Easton, *op. cit.*, p. 84 and 212-215).

170. Titus 1. 5-6.

171. It is doubtful whether the writer is using the singular in a collective sense (K. L. Schmidt, *art. cit.*, p. 238; E. Schweizer, *op. cit.*, p. 109, n. 9 etc.) since he never uses a collective when speaking of elders and deacons.

172. It has often been suggested that the bishop is the president of the body of elders. This hypothesis cannot be confirmed or denied.

173. M. Goguel, *op. cit.*, p. 147.

174. I Tim. 5. 17, 19-20; cf. Acts 20. 19-31.

175. Titus 1. 5. - Timothy must presumably do the same since he is warned "not to lay hands upon any one too hastily" (I Tim. 5. 22).

176. Cf. Acts 14. 23.

177. II Tim. 2. 2. - This verse is difficult and even obscure. E. Schweizer (*op. cit.*, p. 76f.) understands it as the transmission of the Pauline gospel and says: "this is what happens when, in the Church, one generation hands on the New Testament to another" (p. 77). But this interpretation ignores the details of the text. If it were a question of the transmission of the Gospel message, which becomes the Scripture of the new covenant, the words διὰ πολλῶν μαρτύρων would not be necessary, seeing that Paul has preached in public and set forth his gospel in epistles intended to be spread abroad. Moreover, the Pauline gospel, like the whole New Testament later, was intended for all men and not only for ἱκανοὶ... καὶ ἑτέρους διδάξαι.

It must mean something more than the transmission of the Gospel message, in an oral and then later written form. There are two possible explanations. Either the writer means that Timothy and after him other "Christian ministers are responsible for the strict preservation" of the Christian truth (C. Spicq, *op. cit.*, p. 341); or the writer has in mind specific instructions, probably about those who, like Timothy, will be charged with instructing and leading the Church. For them Timothy will be the master as Paul has been for him.

However, it is not enough to say merely that the concern of the writer is that "the work of evangelism should continue" (J. Jeremias, *op. cit.*, p. 36; A Schlatter, cited by E.

Schweizer, *op. cit.*, p. 76, n. 14) since the writer has just asserted that the work cannot continue unless men are found who are capable of carrying it further, and that Timothy must see to it that such men are found.

178. Cf. Acts 10. 41-42; Gal. 1, etc.

179. II Cor. 12. 12; cf. Acts 2. 43; 5. 12-16, etc.

180. On the "apostles of the churches," cf. *supra*, p. 300.

181. Acts 1. 21-26. - It is not clear whether κύριος applies here to Jesus or to God. In support of the second interpretation we would cite the parallel in 18. 8, where God is called καρδιόγνωστης. In support of the first, we would recall that Jesus has just been called κύριος in verse 21, that we have here the verb ἐκλέγω, used in 1. 2 for the choosing of the Twelve by Jesus, and that the infant Church calls upon the κύριος 'Ιησοῦς (Acts 9. 14; 22. 16; cf. 7. 59, 60; 14. 23; I Cor. 1. 2; Rom. 10. 13). It is difficult to make a definite decision and perhaps it was the intention of the writer of Acts not to do so.

182. Acts 10. 41.

183. Acts 6. 1-6.

184. Cf. E. Schweizer, *op. cit.*, p. 98. He expresses himself somewhat differently, p. 90.

185. Acts 13. 2.

186. Acts 20. 28.

187. Acts 14. 23. It is not correct to say that this verse could also be given the following interpretation: the believers could have chosen their elders themselves, under the guidance of the Apostles. The presence of αὐτοῖς after χειροτονήσαντες does not permit of any other meaning for the phrase than "having chosen elders for them." Cf. the commentaries of Wendt, Jacquier, Foakes-Jackson, Lake and Cadbury, Bauernfeind, and W. L. Knox, *St. Paul and the Church of Jerusalem,* Cambridge, 1925, p. 216, n. 38; E. Schweizer, *op. cit.*, p. 96, n. 1 and p. 98, n. 11; M. Goguel, *op. cit.*, p. 406.

Certain writers attempt to belittle the importance of the verse by saying that this method of choosing can be explained "in view of St. Paul's essentially autocratic temperament" (Knox) or by the fact that these are newly founded churches which are not yet firmly established (Schweizer). These observations would prevail if we could see the establishment of a system of election by the believers themselves, when the churches were set free from the so-called apostolic despotism or when they were sufficiently strong. In fact, however, in the New Testament, we can find no trace of democratic elections, in the modern sense of the term, when it is a matter of promoting men in the ministry of the Church.

188. II Tim. 2. 2.

189. Titus 1. 5; cf. I Tim. 5. 22.

190. E. Schweizer's assertion (*op. cit.*, p. 90: "...dass in der Regel die Gemeinde als ganze die Berufung des Herrn zu besonderen Diensten ausführt, diese Berufenen wählt, einsetzt und entsendet, aber auch immer wieder prüft") seems too dogmatic. Schweizer cites in support of his thesis Acts 6. 1-6; 1. 23f; 15 *passim*; II Cor. 8. 18f; 8. 23; I Cor. 16. 3. We have stated above how we understand the first two verses of Acts. In Acts 15, Paul and Barnabas lead the delegation from Antioch to Jerusalem "to see the apostles and elders" (v. 2); it is "the apostles and elders" who come together to discuss the matter (v. 6), and what is known as 'the Jerusalem decree' is promulgated by "the apostles and elders" (v. 23). Certainly the members of the church are present (v. 22), but the apostles (and the elders) appear as the leaders of the church. The account in Galatians 2 - which Schweizer does not mention here - gives the same impression. We should note in passing that this concern of the apostles to settle questions resulting from the growth of the Church, proves that their task is not merely to found the Church but also to begin its edification.

In II Cor. 8. 18-23 and I Cor. 16. 3, the believers do in fact choose their own representatives. But these are delegates who are to accompany Paul to Jerusalem, to carry the collected gifts, who are therefore charged with a contingent mission and not with any permanent ministry.

191. As Harnack thought, cf. O. Linton, *op. cit.*, p. 189f; cf. also p. 109.

192. Not even Acts 6. 1-6. We must also mention this point: it is the Twelve who leave "to the whole body of disciples" the task of "choosing" (ἐπισκέπτομαι v. 3, is not synonymous with ἐκλέγω in Acts 1. 2 and 24) those on whom the apostles themselves will lay their hands. If there is a right, in the opinion of the writer of Acts, this right belongs to the apostles, who, in the circumstances, hand it over in part to the church.

193. Cf. O. Linton, *op. cit.*, p. 110.

194. Such is the case, according to Acts 15. 22, when it is a question of communicating to the Gentile Christians the decisions of the Jerusalem conference and to name delegates for that. The text says: τότε ἔδοξε τοῖς ἀποστόλοις καὶ τοῖς πρεσβυτέροις σὺν ὅλῃ τῇ ἐκκλησίᾳ and not καὶ τῇ ἐκκλησίᾳ. Cf. Clement of Rome, 44. 3: συνευδοκησάσης τῆς ἐκκλησίας πάσης.

195. This is perhaps what is expressed in its own way in Revelation, "here is the secret meaning of the seven stars... which are the angels of the seven churches" (1. 20). The bishops would be called angels, because they are the messengers sent by God to the churches.

196. The situation is similar to that of women who are saved and in the Church, in Paul's view. "There is no longer male and female...you are all one in Christ Jesus" (Gal. 3. 28). However this equality "in Christ" does not abolish the hierarchy instituted by God and according to which man is the head of woman, Christ is the head of man, and the head of Christ is God (I Cor. 11. 3). Salvation in Christ is the same for a woman and for a man, for members of the congregation and for ministers, but this theological equality does not bring with it sociological equality which would destroy the order desired by God in humanity and in the new humanity of the Church, and by virtue of which everyone occupies the rank assigned to him or her.

197. The theory according to which the infant Church would have been a democracy is difficult to support from the texts. It must be said that a truly democratic organization of the Church in the first century would have been impossible. The idea of democracy is based on the following two precepts: 1) sovereignty is in the people, 2) all men are equal. But the first Christians were convinced that sovereignty is in Christ the Spirit, and that believers differ from each other in vocations and gifts, although they are all the children of their Father in Heaven and adopted by Him in Jesus Christ. Democratic ideology and New Testament theology are too different to be united. The proof of this can be seen in that the penetration of democratic ideology into Christian thought has completely denatured (we might almost say disgraced) the New Testament theology of the Church.

198. On this question, cf. M. Goguel, *L'Eglise primitive*, p. 401-410.

199. Cf. M. Goguel, *op. cit.*, p. 405. - According to M. Goguel, if there was no laying on of hands when Matthias was added to the apostolic body, it was "because the writer of Acts was of the opinion that at the time the event took place the Apostles were not yet endowed with the Spirit, which they were not to receive until Pentecost" (*ibid.*, p. 405, n. 2). It seems to us, however, that, for the writer of Acts, it was not so much a matter of the Eleven transmitting power but rather a choice made by the Lord Himself, similar to the choosing of the Twelve by Jesus during His earthly ministry.

200. Acts 14. 26. - Cf. R. N. Flew, *op. cit.*, p. 147.

201. The laying on of hands by Ananias to Paul (Acts 9. 17-18) is an act of healing, not of transmission of power.

202. I Tim. 1. 6; II Tim. 4. 14.

203. I Tim. 5. 22.

204. E. Schweizer is of the opinion that the whole congregation takes part in the laying on of hands. He writes (*op. cit.*, p. 76) in connection with I Timothy 4. 14: "Schon bei seiner Einsetzung ist also die *Gemeinde* mitbeteiligt" (the italics is the writer's). The text only mentions elders. He also writes (p. 116, n. 38): "die Gemeinde ist letzlich Ordinator" and he refers to Acts 13. 3 and 6. 6. Perhaps, strictly speaking, this could be true in the first case but certainly not in the second.

205. Cf. M. Goguel, *op. cit.*, p. 408.

The Early Church and Judaism[1]

Introduction

"It is outrageous to profess the name of Jesus Christ and to live like a Jew. For it is not Christianity which believed in Judaism but Judaism which believed in Christianity, in which all peoples of every tongue who believe in God are united."[2]

This passage from St. Ignatius of Antioch is the earliest document where Christianity and Judaism appear, side by side, as two distinct and separate religions. The words of the Bishop of Antioch make it clear that from the moment when the two religions become distinct from one another they are not merely separated by indifference one to the other. Saint Ignatius makes it quite clear, at the very moment when for the first time he gives to the new religion the name that will be ratified throughout the centuries ahead, that there is utter incompatibility between Christianity and the Judaism from whence it arose and with which it was at first confused. "It is outrageous to profess Jesus Christ and live like a Jew." He had already said, earlier in the same epistle: "If we still live today according to the rule of Judaism we admit that we have not received grace."[3]

If it is impossible to unite the two religions, it is because Christianity is the providential outcome of Judaism, which it has, so to speak, emptied of its substance as it is itself called into being. Since the appearance of Christ it is not really possible to believe in God without belonging to

Christianity. This principle is valid not only for the Gentiles but primarily for the Jews themselves. From the bosom of the chosen people a minority at least believed in the Gospel, thus showing that normal development leads from Judaism to Christianity. For the rest, according to the Bishop of Antioch, it is the way already pointed out by the prophets of Israel, who "lived in accordance with Christ" and were "inspired by His grace."[4] In short, they "were the disciples in spirit" of Jesus Christ and "awaited His coming to teach them."[5]

So, at the dawn of the second century, Ignatius of Antioch is the witness to a separation which has already taken place and which will continue permanently between the Church and the Synagogue. Christianity and Judaism from now on are two rival and concurrent religions, each of them plumbing the depths of the same Scripture for arguments to affirm their own position and destroy that of the other. This conflict has just been masterfully described and explained,[6] and we do not propose to go over it again. A different question holds our interest. We can formulate it as follows: when and how was this rivalry established between the believers in Christ and the Jews - a rivalry which would lead to separation and open struggle?

The break, it seems, does not date from the very beginning. The Apostles in Jerusalem and the first disciples, says the book of Acts, "kept up their daily attendance at the Temple...praising God and being regarded with favor by all the people." (Acts 2. 46; cf. 3. 1 f). Those who confess Jesus Christ do not immediately live apart from the Jews. It is inside the synagogues at Damascus that Paul intends to carry out his persecuting activities (Acts 9. 2). After he becomes an Apostle he is not forbidden to enter the synagogues. It is only toward the end of the first century, under the patriarchate of Gamaliel II (about 80 - 110) that the Christians are excluded from the Jewish community.[7] Saint Paul himself, according to the writer of Acts, did not hesitate to carry out certain purification rites at the Temple in Jerusalem (Acts 21. 16-17), which may be following the rule of conduct that the Apostle to the Gentiles made for himself: "to be like a Jew with the Jews in order to win Jews; to men under the Law as if I were under the Law...in order to win those who are under the Law" (I Cor. 9. 20).

Yet these verses, which might suggest, at first glance, that a Judeo-Christian formula was possible, only reveal one side of the real situation. Peter, who attends the Temple, declares before the High Priest that he will be obedient to God, while preaching that Christ is risen from the dead, rather than to the Sanhedrin by whom he had been forbidden to speak and teach in the name of Jesus (Acts 4. 17; 5. 28-32). The Apostle Paul writes that the Jews everywhere objected to the preaching of the Gospel and thus became enemies of their fellow men and drew the anger of God on themselves (I Thess. 2. 14-16). So signs of conflict appeared at the time of the first generation of Christians. The rivalry between the infant Church and Judaism which was later to lead to a complete break was established during that time.

Why did this happen? Was the break due to unfavorable historical circumstances, to the intransigence of the people involved, in the sense that it would not have happened if external events had been different or if the Apostles had been more conciliatory? Or were there fundamental theological reasons for the separation which only came to the surface gradually, as the infant Church became more aware of the specific characteristics of the Gospel it believed and proclaimed, and as it inevitably and irresistably moved away from Judaism?

We should like to devote the following pages to this problem. A whole volume would be required to do it justice but we will confine ourselves to a brief outline. To remain true to the title we have chosen we shall start from the time when the Church exists as a historical reality, that is to say when there exists in Jerusalem, and soon also outside the Holy City, a group of Apostles and believers who have faith in Christ and who proclaim that faith. Thus we shall leave aside the question of the attitude of Jesus Himself to the Jews and Judaism. This very delicate question needs to be treated separately.

I. *Love of Israel and anti-Judaism*

What were the feelings of the first generations of Christians towards the Jews and Judaism? This is the first question we must ask ourselves, and which we must attempt to answer, without over-simplifying the issue.

In fact, the believers' attitude could not be very simple. They could not help feeling that they were at the same time in continuity with and in opposition to the people and the religion which had been and remained in a certain sense their own.

In continuity, first of all, because the Christ they confess as their Lord is the Messiah of Israel, who has come to fulfill the promises of the prophets. The new covenant, sealed by Jesus with His blood, had been announced, before His coming, at a time which will soon be known as the old covenant. Therefore the Gospel is not strictly speaking a new religion. It is the normal culmination of revelations given by God since the day when, in Abraham, He chose a people for Himself and made them heirs to His promises, now realized in Jesus Christ and the Church. This is so true that even the Gentile

Christians were considered as having Abraham for their father (Rom. 4. 1). In short, it is one and the same plan of salvation that governs all God's relationships with His people, from the beginning until the appearance of the Church, "the Israel of God" (Gal. 6. 16), in which it is God's plan to bring together all peoples. In these circumstances, the believers cannot but feel they are linked to Israel by bonds of solidarity and love founded in God and therefore irrevocable.

In opposition, secondly, because the Christ in whom they believe has been rejected by His own people, who persist in their unbelief despite the testimony to the Risen Christ given by the Apostles and despite the testimony given by God Himself by assuring the Church of its existence, its permanence and its growth. To confess Christ means to be opposed to Judaism which rejects Him; it is necessary to enter into conflict with Judaism whenever it attempts to prevent the preaching of the Gospel or at least to hinder it where there is no opportunity to put a complete stop to it. In these circumstances it is not surprising to see the believers' love of Israel tempered by a strong feeling of disapproval towards the unbelief of the Jews, in a single word, by anti-Judaism.

But it must be strongly emphasized at the outset that these two Christian attitudes, love of Israel and anti-Judaism - which we have briefly described and to which we shall return - have an essentially and uniquely religious foundation. God, who spoke in earlier times through the prophets, has now revealed Himself through His Son, "on the human level born of David's stock" (Rom. 1. 3); it is again to Israel that He has addressed His supreme word. At the same time it is in Israel that opposition to the Gospel of Christ is born and that tenacious unbelief persists, which will make Christian propaganda among the Gentiles more difficult.

By this christological foundation the Christian attitude towards Israel and especially the anti-Judaism of the infant Church differs radically from any other anti-Jewish sentiment known in history. These feelings of the first Christians cannot just be described as "anti-Semitism" and equated with the reactions of the secular enemies of Israel.[8]

The ethnic aspect is totally absent from the careful and subtle analysis which M. Simon has given of anti-Semitism in the ancient world and particularly in the Greek and Roman world,[9] and in his opinion it has no economic foundation either. The complaint of the Roman world against the Jews was not that they were Semites and devoted themselves to business; it was that they were "a people who worshipped without images, the people of the Law"[10] and that they lived, by their strict observance of the Law, on the fringe of society. "This anti-Semitism betrays a spontaneous, elementary and intuitive reaction of social defence rather than a reflective preoccupation with defence on religious grounds...it is feeling and not doctrine."[11] The attitude of the first Christians was quite different. Their love of Israel and their anti-Judaism are governed by their doctrine of Christ, while on the social level we find a certain Christian and Jewish solidarity in the face of the Gentile world: the same aversion to idolatry, the same resistance to any temptation to religious or social syncretism; Paul, arrested by the Roman authorities, reveals that he is a Jew from Tarsus (Acts 21. 39) before he takes advantage of his status as a Roman citizen (Acts 22. 25).

From the time of the second century the anti-Jewish Christian controversy will not hesitate to add to it certain charges already advanced by the Gentiles; but it is and will remain basically theological - the Jews are the murderers of the Lord.[12]

This ultimate indictment already appears in the New Testament. But it does not have the force that it will have later. Peter, according to the book of Acts, certainly does not speak without recollecting that the Jews put to death the Lord Jesus whom God raised from the dead (Acts 2. 23; 3. 15; 4. 10, 27; 5. 30; 10. 39). The same motif appears in Stephen's speech (Acts 7. 52), in the Apostle Paul (I Thess. 2. 15) and in the gospels of Matthew (27. 25) and John (9. 12, 15). But this could hardly be used as the basis for placing the New Testament within the body of anti-Semitic literature. For it is not a matter simply of an accusation. It is a matter primarily of recalling a historic fact: Jesus of Nazareth was condemned to die and the Jews have a part, whatever that may be, in His condemnation. But, above all else, this death is part of the divine plan of salvation. This is why the reminder of His saving death is accompanied by an appeal to believe. The death of Christ does not further condemn the Jews; it invites them to repentance.

This motif is emphasized particularly in the speeches of Peter (Acts 2. 38; 3. 19; 4. 12; 5. 31). Stephen's speech is interrupted, but we are free to suppose that Stephen would not have spoken, if he had not intended to convert his hearers to the Son of man. The same Paul, who writes to the Thessalonians that the Jews have put to death the Lord Jesus and are hindering the preaching of the Gospel, "to Jews became like a Jew...so that I may save some." (I Cor. 9. 20, 22). He declares to the Romans that he would forego his own salvation if he could by that means save his kin, the Israelites (Rom. 9. 3). Although the gospel of Matthew has the people of Jerusalem cry out: "His blood be upon us, and upon our children" (27. 25), yet it emphasizes at the same time that Jesus was sent "to the lost sheep of the house of Israel" (15. 24; cf. 10. 6). As for the fourth evangelist, he recalls that the attitude of the Jews is the result of their refusal to believe (12. 37-43); he is writing his gospel so that his readers, including the Jews, "may believe that Jesus is the Christ, the son of God" (20. 31).

In short, according to the New Testament, the crime of the Jews is not the crucifixion of Christ; it is their unbelief in the face of the Revelation and the preaching which proclaims it. This is why the New Testament does not linger over the accusation of murder but subordinates it to the missionary emphasis. In other words, in Christian literature of the first century, anti-Judaism is tempered, even overlaid, by love for Israel.

That these two sentiments come together in the attitude of the first Christians we shall see even better as we review the testimony in Peter's speeches in Acts, then that of the epistles of Paul and finally that of the gospel of John.

In Peter's speeches, anti-Jewish feeling is expressed by the constantly repeated accusation that the Jews put to death the One whom God sent to save them. We have just stated this, and shown also that Peter continually mentioned the death of Christ not in order to condemn the Jews, but to call them to repentance and to belief. It is love of Israel which stirs him to speak as he does. The Jews to whom he speaks are his "brethren" (Acts 2. 29; 3. 17). He declares to them: "And now, brethren, I know that it was in *ignorance* that you did it, as was the case with your rulers also. But in this way God has fulfilled the declarations He made through all the prophets, that His Christ would suffer. Repent therefore,..." (Acts 3. 17-18).[13] This assertion that the Jews acted in ignorance seems, at first, to contradict what the same Apostle said in his first speech after Pentecost: "Jesus of Nazareth, a man accredited to you from God by mighty works and marvels and signs which God did among you through Him, *as you yourselves know,* this man, delivered up through God's settled purpose and foreknowledge - you...have put to death. But God has raised Him to life" (Acts 2. 22-24). The call to repentance comes later, in verse 38. Here, Peter is not speaking of the ignorance of the Jews; he asserts, on the contrary, that the Jews have witnessed the miracles accomplished by Jesus which should make them recognize Him as the envoy of God.

The contradiction between the two speeches is more apparent than real. Whether the Jews acted in ignorance or whether, having seen the miracles of Jesus, they did not understand their ultimate significance, they can be excused, in the Apostle's view, and their true fault is neither ignorance nor misunderstanding. Moreover they have their counterpart, so to speak, in the theme common to the four gospels, that the disciples themselves remained partially blind in the presence of Jesus of Nazareth and only really understood Him in the light of the resurrection. It is the same with the Jews. Their unbelief, moreover, is part of the divine plan as announced in the Scriptures. What puts an end to "those times of ignorance" (Acts 17. 30) is not the earthly ministry of Jesus, it is the preaching of the Apostles which explains that God, through the death and resurrection of Jesus, is calling men to repentance and to salvation. The fault of the Jews is not their ignorance or their misunderstanding of the Revelation hidden in a humble human form, but their unbelief in the face of the Gospel which is now openly proclaimed. This is why the Apostles too "cannot help speaking" (Acts 4. 20). They have been sent not to condemn the Jews, but to testify before them that "in no other is salvation to be found" than "in Jesus of Nazareth whom you crucified, but whom God has raised from the dead" (Acts 4. 10, 12). Once again, the accusation of having had a part in the execution of Jesus is overlaid by a call to salvation in Christ.[14]

The anti-Jewish theme and the theme of love for Israel are both very clearly defined in Saint Paul.

First let us follow the theme of anti-Judaism. In the earliest of his epistles, I Thessalonians, the Apostle writes (2. 14-16): "You, brethren, followed the example of the Churches of God in Christ Jesus which are in Judea; seeing that you endured the same ill-treatment from your own countrymen as they did from the Jews, who killed both the Lord Jesus and the prophets and drove us out; these men are displeasing to God, and enemies of all mankind; for they try to prevent our preaching to the Gentiles that they may be saved. They thus continually fill up the measure of their sins, and God's anger will eventually strike them down [has overtaken them for good and all]."

There is no reason to think that this passage has been interpolated or that the epistle itself is not authentic, as has been suggested on occasions since the time of F. C. Baur. The epistle has the Pauline touch, and this passage on the courageous faith of the Thessalonians and the unbelief of the Jews is the natural consequence of verse 13, where Paul writes that his readers received his preaching for what it really is - the very word of God.

Although this passage, in its ideas and vocabulary, to some extent evokes the charges formulated in the Greek and Roman world against the Jews,[15] it is oriented in a quite different direction from that Gentile controversy. Paul says that the Jews have killed the Lord Jesus and the prophets, which is an essentially Christian accusation,[16] and then he charges them with doing all in their power to hinder the preaching of the Gospel. If they are "the enemies of all mankind," it is because, by their opposition they prevent the

Gentiles from participating in that salvation which they have not desired for themselves.[17] So Paul's anti-Judaism has a theological basis.

The same idea appears in the epistle to the Galatians (4. 29). The Apostle sees in Isaac the prefiguration of the Church, and in Ishmael the prefiguration of Judaism. Paul is interpreting the verse in Genesis (21. 9) which records how the young Ishmael played with Isaac, according to the Jewish tradition that spoke of the persecution of Isaac by Ishmael.[18] According to the Apostle, this persecution foretells the persecution which the Jews are now waging against the Church and more particularly, as is suggested in Galatians 5. 11 against the Apostle to the Gentiles.

That Saint Paul would come up against Jewish hostility almost everywhere is confirmed by the book of Acts, which records that the Apostle was a victim of "ambushes by the Jews" at Antioch in Pisidia (13. 50), Iconium (14. 2), Lystra (14. 19), Thessalonica (17. 5), Beroea (17. 13), Corinth (18. 12; 20. 3), Ephesus (19. 9; 20. 19) and Jerusalem (21. 27; 23. 12). There is no reason not to take these events as historically accurate, seeing that it was not the Jews who took the initiative in the opposition to Paul in other cities such as Athens and Philippi.

But the trials undergone by the Apostle at the hands of the Jews do not make him forget that Israel is the people of the promise and that God does not reject His people, for "never does God repent of His free gifts or of His call" (Rom. 11. 29). The Apostle to the Gentiles emphasizes as if by design that the Gospel which he preaches is a power to salvation "for the Jews first, and then for the Greeks" (Rom. 1. 16, etc.). Here again the book of Acts is well informed when it shows us Paul, on his arrival in a new city, speaking first to the Jews in the synagogues and the proselytes. But the Jews, in their great majority, do not believe this Gospel to which they have the primary right. It is certain that the Apostle's almost perpetual inability to convince them caused him great grief. Perhaps his anti-Judaism is, in actual fact, the negative expression of his desperate sadness. This feeling is certainly evident in chapters 9 to 11 of the epistle to the Romans.

At the beginning of this authoritative treatise Paul gives free rein to the love and the solidarity which bind him to Israel. He solemnly declares that he himself would rather be "accursed from Christ," deprived of the communion of Christ, that is excluded from salvation, if by this renunciation he could bring about the conversion of his natural kinsfolk - the Israelites. All God's revelations and institutions of salvation in history have been for them, and among them Christ was born (Romans 9. 1-5). This introduction brings the Apostle to the problem which, beyond any shadow of a doubt, tormented him throughout his missionary life: the rejection of Christ by the people whom God has showered with His gifts. The Apostle can find no explanation for this problem. He welcomes the solution which God Himself gives him when He reveals to him the "mystery" of the temporary resistance and of the ultimate conversion of Israel. God makes it the Apostle's responsibility to make known this mystery in order to minimize the problems which the unbelief of the chosen people would not fail to cause among those who did believe, and in order to magnify the glory of God whose ways are unfathomable (Rom. 11. 23-36). Undoubtedly Israel was never more loved "in Jesus Christ" than by the Apostle who wrote these three chapters. The Apostle who, in the first epistle to the Thessalonians, as we have just seen, only expressed himself so vehemently about the unbelief of the Jews, because their unbelief was delaying the moment when the One who was life itself to him, would be life to them and life to all mankind.

It seems that as the Apostle's career advanced, and before the "mystery" of the ways of God with regard to Israel had been revealed to him, it became impossible for him not to see, in the unbelief of those for whom the way to belief was paved, the work of Satanic powers determined to cause the failure of the plan of salvation realized by God in Christ. In the first epistle to the Corinthians (2. 8), it is no longer the Jews who "crucified the Lord of glory," as in the first epistle to the Thessalonians, but cosmic forces of the present age whose power will not last. This opposition to the Gospel is itself part of the "mystery" of the wisdom of God which has been revealed to him (I Cor. 2. 7).

Similarly, according to the second epistle to the Corinthians, it is "an angel of Satan" which inspires the Jews' opposition to the Gospel both by the obstacles they put in the missionaries' way and by their own unbelief (II Cor. 12. 7). It is in this context that the difficult passage about "the thorn in the flesh" and "Satan's angel" which torment the Apostle, can be explained.

In the first six verses of this chapter Paul speaks of the wonderful revelations granted to him, which might tempt him to boast. But so that this should not happen "there was given me," he says, "a thorn in the flesh, an angel of Satan to torture me...Concerning this, three times have I besought the Lord that it might leave me. But He has said to me: 'My grace is sufficient for you, for my power is perfected in weakness'" (v. 7-9).

Since earliest Christian times there has been speculation as to what this thorn and this angel of Satan might be. Almost all our contemporary exegetes and historians contend that it is a matter of an illness which the Apostle suffered during his whole life, from which he could not be delivered, despite his ardent prayers, and which was the great handicap of his missionary career.[19] This explanation has become so prevalent that its weak foundations are forgotten. The New Testament states specifically on only one occasion that Paul was ill; in Galatians 4. 13-15, the Apostle says that it was "in a state of bodily infirmity" that he first preached the Gospel in Galatia. The manner in which he mentions his illness does not make it sound like a chronic affliction. It is true that allusions to the Apostle's weak health could be seen in the passage in II Corinthians 4. 7-12, where he writes: "but we have this treasure in fragile vessels," "we are always carrying about in our bodies the sufferings of the death of Jesus," "death is at work in us." But here he means the troubles, the weariness, the perils, even the peril of death, which are the lot of missionaries, and of Paul in particular, and which gradually take their toll on the body. This is the most natural meaning, supported also by the context. It must also be pointed out that wherever, in the epistles and in the Acts, there are any changes in the Apostle's plans for his journeys, and this is frequently the case, these changes are never attributed to illness. The career of the Apostle Paul is not the story of an invalid. Finally the thorn and the Satanic angel appear in a context concerned on the one hand with the extraordinary revelations granted to Paul (v. 1-6) and the distinctive signs of apostleship which he possesses as much as, if not more than the "Archapostles" at Corinth (v. 11-12), and on the other hand with the "infirmities, insults, distresses, persecutions and grievous difficulties endured for Christ's sake" (v. 10), that is with the trials connected with the exercising of apostleship. From all evidence the thorn and the Satanic angel are numbered among these trials and are even the most grievous of all that the Apostle has to bear.

According to early exegesis, based on the Greek Fathers, and particularly Chrysostom and Theophylact, Paul is referring to the sufferings inflicted on him by his adversaries, who are seen as being in the service of Satan. Some contemporary interpreters are returning to this explanation. They think, for example, that Paul has in mind some demonic power which impedes his work[20] or even "the presence, beside him, of the angel of darkness, who has the power to get involved in his activities and thwart his intentions."[21] It seems very unlikely that the Apostle who lives in Christ would feel the presence of Satan in person so close to him. Also, by speaking of an angel of Satan and not Satan himself, he does not seem to have in mind such an immediate presence. But we must not reject the idea that Paul feels, behind the failures of his apostleship, the work of Satan, mediated at least. It is even possible to specify the nature of this obstacle. Paul's work is to preach the Gospel. The great adversary of the proclamation of the Gospel is Satan, who on one occasion in particular prevented Paul from going to Thessalonica (I Thess. 2. 18), but who, nevertheless, has not succeeded in making his calling in vain or his apostleship worthless, at least as far as the Gentiles are concerned. When Paul, a little later, writes the epistle to the Romans, he draws up this list of missionary victories: "beginning with Jerusalem and the surrounding districts, I have preached without restraint even as far as Illyricum the gospel of Christ" (Rom. 15. 19) so that it is necessary for him to go to the West to find new fields of endeavor (Rom. 15. 22-24). But his heart and his mind bear a wound which causes him pain and humiliation. He cannot win for the Gospel his "kinsfolk, the Israelites." This is psychological suffering, because Paul will always feel that he is one with his own people.[22] It is also theological suffering which humiliates his apostolic conscience. The negative attitude of the Jews is not only the rejection of their own salvation; it is a contradiction of the redemption prepared within Israel and intended primarily for Israel; it is the denial of the Gospel which Paul proclaims to the world; it is, of itself, a counter-mission. God will reveal to Paul this "mystery" that the unbelief of the Jews is temporary and that it plays a positive role in the history of salvation, in spite of appearances, since it permits the Gentiles to be grafted on to the stock of Israel. But while the Apostle was writing to the Corinthians he had not yet received the illumination given to him when he was writing to the Romans; he finds the unbelief of the Jews inexplicable. From the moment when he sees evil powers at work in the crucifixion of the Lord Jesus Christ, he must quite naturally think that an angel of Satan is at work to prevent the Jews from believing and to incite them to oppose the preaching of the Gospel. And Paul's opinion of his apostolic mission was too high for him not to think that this Satanic intervention was directed against him personally, and that it was, at the same time, the will of the Lord in order to keep him humble, a state from which his successes with the Gentiles might have removed him. In the idea that Paul must accept not being able to convince the Jews, that the Lord's grace must be sufficient for him and that he must pursue his ministry among the Gentiles in spite of "the thorn" and "the angel of Satan" - in this idea there is, as it were, a prologue to the "mystery" which will be revealed to the the Apostle when he writes the epistle to the Romans.[23]

It must also be emphasized that in attributing the blame to a superhuman power for the unbelief of the Jews and their opposition to the Gospel, Paul excuses his compatriots rather than accusing them, since it makes them victims rather than transgressors.

We can summarize Paul's attitude by saying that he expresses his resentment and grief at the unbelief of the Jews in stronger terms than Peter. He was exposed to the Jews' animosity more than Peter because he had a clearer vision of the uniqueness of the Gospel and he labored to make it independent of Judaism. We must return to this aspect of the problem later. However the Apostle to the Gentiles did not become the enemy of his own people, although they remained sceptical, and in him, as in Peter, love of Israel definitely triumphed over anti-Judaism.

Let us move on to the gospel of John. The anti-Jewish theme is more marked there than anywhere else in the New Testament, except perhaps in Stephen's speech.

According to John, a great majority of Jews - we might believe, from a rapid reading of the gospel, almost all of them - reject the "Light" which is sent to them, although those who have previously received God's revelations in Israel testify to it: Abraham (8. 56), Moses 1. 45; 5. 46), Isaiah (12. 41), the Scriptures generally (2. 22; 5. 39; 13. 18 etc.) and John the Baptist (1. 6-8, 15, 19f; 3. 29f). Moreover the Jews, or more precisely their leaders, intimidate believers or those who are tempted to believe by the fear they instill in them (7. 13; 9. 22) and the threats they hold over them (9. 22; 12. 42; cf. 16. 2).

Jesus declares that their sin "remains" (9. 41) and that it is "without excuse" (15. 22). By refusing "the truth" and "the life" which Jesus brings them from God, they show that they do not have God as their Father, as they claim (8. 41) but the Devil "a murderer from the beginning...there is no truth in him." (8. 44). It is this last verse in particular which places the fourth evangelist among the ranks of the avowed enemies of the Jewish people whose conversion he no longer expected and whom he considered definitely excluded from salvation[24] - an opinion which Paul did not share.

The pericope which brings to an end the public ministry of Jesus (John 12. 37-50) comprises two elements. First the evangelist explains (v. 37-43) the reason why the Jews do not believe: it is in order to fulfill the prophecy of Isaiah: "Lord, who has believed our preaching...?" The prophet not only attested the unbelief of the Jews in advance, he also proclaimed that it was part of the divine plan, by saying, "He has blinded their eyes and hardened their minds, lest they should see with their eyes and perceive with their minds, and should turn and I should heal them." The prophesied resistance did not reach all the people however, since "even from among the Rulers many believed in Him," albeit with a timid faith since they did not dare confess Jesus publicly for fear of the Pharisees.

It might be thought that the revelation of Jesus to the world was finished. But the evangelist does not think so. In the verses which follow (44-50) Jesus makes one more appeal to faith; this call is His last word to the Jews - not a condemnation nor even an acknowledgement of their unbelief. This arrangement fits the evangelist's general intention and there is no reason to change the order of the verses.[25]

John's aim is to bring his readers to the faith (20. 30-31) and although his gospel may not be "a missionary writing to win over the Jews,"[26] yet it is intended for the Jews also, not all of whom rejected Jesus; far from it (cf. 4. 45; 7. 43; 8. 30-31; 11. 45; 12. 11, 42). Nowhere does John's universalism seem to exclude the Jewish people (cf. 10. 16) and it cannot do so, since "salvation comes from the Jews" (4. 22).

The tone and purport of this statement are so completely different from that of verse 8. 44 ("the father whose sons you are is the devil") that several exegetes do not hesitate to consider it to be a comment by the editor of the evangelist's work to make it fit into the thought of the Church.[27] It is said that the evangelist could not have written these words seeing that he no longer considers that the Jews are the holders of the divine revelation. If John himself had written verse 4. 22, it is asserted, he would have expressed is as "salvation comes from Israel."[28] This argument is untenable. It presupposes that in the language of John the name "Jews" always means the unbelievers, which is not the case. In John, "the Jews" and "Israel" are not contrasted as the rebel people and the people who are loyal to their divine calling. Doubtless Nathanael is called "a true Israelite, in whom there is no guile" (John 1. 47), because he relinquishes his early scepticism, obeys Philip's invitation: "Come and see" and goes to meet the approaching Jesus.[29] But Nicodemus who remains ignorant of the mystery of birth from on high, yet merits the title of "the Teacher of Israel" (John 3. 10) although he should be called "the Teacher of the Jews" if the explanationwe are given is to be upheld.

The distinction between "Israel" and "the Jews" is not a matter of belief or unbelief in the presence of the Revelation. Jesus is "the King of Israel" (1. 49; cf. 12. 13), because He is the One sent from God who was proclaimed by Moses and the prophets; He is the sovereign Lord of the theocratic people, which also has its Teachers, since it is the people of the Law. "Israel" therefore is the people of God collectively, the depository of the divine revelation in history. "The Jews" are the contemporary members of this people: it is through them that Israel is present in the contemporary world. The sovereignty of Jesus over Israel is concretely expressed by His sovereignty over the Jews. If He were not also "the King of the Jews" then "the Jews" would be abandoned by God. The title of "King of the Jews" (John 18. 33; 19. 19) does not only show Pilate's scorn for those whom he governs.[30] The expression has two meanings, as is common with many Johannine expressions.[31] It means particularly that, in spite of Pilate's irony and the Jews' unbelief, Jesus reigns over all those who hear His voice because they are of the truth. And all men are destined for this since He will draw them all to Him (John 12. 32), including the Jews from whom salvation comes.

Therefore there is no reason to doubt that the evangelist himself wrote: "salvation comes from the Jews" and that he used the expression intentionally. It also has two aspects. First it shows that the divine line in history, which goes through Abraham and Moses, leaves the Samaritans aside; it is not from them that salvation comes. The history of salvation which starts in Israel with Abraham, passes through the Jewish people. Salvation is accomplished by Jesus (John 19. 30) who is a Jew (4. 9). The preaching of the disciples (17. 21), who are also Jews, will proclaim salvation to the world, so that all men, Jews, Samaritans (cf. 4. 41) and Gentiles (cf. 11. 52) should be united into one body (11. 52; cf. 10. 16).

Through Abraham and Moses salvation certainly comes from Israel. But, and this is the second aspect of the Johannine expression, salvation does not jump, so to speak, from the Israel of the past to the Church of the new covenant. Salvation passes, without missing a single stage, through the Jews of the first century, just as the Word lives in Jesus of Nazareth, the son of Joseph (1. 45; 6. 42). Although for the most part this people remained unbelieving they were none the less the intermediary of salvation, the universality of which Caiaphas, himself an unbeliever, unwittingly prophesies.

The theologian of the incarnation cannot forget that the Word "became flesh" in the midst of the Jews. The very manner in which he speaks of it shows that, in his view, Judaism is not irremediably and utterly condemned.[32] In John anti-Judaism is only severe disapproval of the unbelief of the Jews. Although this disapproval may sometimes be extremely harsh yet the call to believe resounds throughout the gospel.

From the preceding investigation it is clear that the attitude of the first generations of Christians towards the Jews and Judaism is an ambivalent one. The believers are anti-Jewish; they emphasize the distance between themselves, who believe in Jesus of Nazareth as the Lord and as the Christ sent by God, and the Jews who reject their Messiah. At the same time the believers do not lost sight of the fact that the Jews are the people of God's promises and they cannot be totally excluded from a salvation intended for all mankind.

In spite of appearances this ambivalent attitude is not contradictory. It would be so if it indicated an uncertainty, a wavering between two opposing sentiments; but the anti-Judaism of the Church, in contrast to the anti-Semitism of the Roman world, is not sentimental. It is a doctrine and not a feeling.[33] This point deserves emphasis. The behavior of the believers is not the result of personal resentment. Their persons, as such, are not the cause of the conflict. When the Apostles, released by the Sanhedrin, by whom they have been threatened and forbidden to speak or to teach in the name of Jesus, return to their friends and pray to God, as reported in Acts (4. 25-30), they do not intercede that the unbelievers should be punished and their personal security threatened. They ask only that they themselves should be given strength to proclaim the Gospel of Jesus Christ with fearless courage. Similarly, although the Apostle Paul recalls the ill-treatment he has suffered at the hands of the Jews (II Cor. 11. 24f), it is not to heap abuse upon his countrymen - he too is a Hebrew, an Israelite, a descendant of Abraham (II Cor. 11. 22) - it is to prove to the Christians who might doubt it that he is "a servant of Christ" (II Cor. 11. 23). Finally the Johannine Christ, who warns His followers that they will be excluded from the synagogues (John 16. 2) asks the Father that they might be protected from evil (John 17. 15), that is to say that they may continue in the witness they are to give to the world.

Like their anti-Judaism, the believers' love for Israel is the result of their faith. Their attachment to Christ, which distinguished them from the unbelieving Jews, does not detach them from the historic people of God, but on the contrary makes them see that Christ has already beaten down the wall which divides Jews and Gentiles (Eph. 2. 15), and will be the one Shepherd of one flock (John 10. 16). The believers' attitude has one single and identical foundation - faith in Christ, the Messiah of Israel and Savior of the world.

This ambivalent attitude is common to almost all the early Christians. Stephen is the only exception in the New Testament and he brings an accusation against the Jewish people which has no restraint and no hope. His speech, reported in Acts 7, is interrupted by the angry protests of his hearers so that we will never know what conclusion Stephen would have reached. Doubtless it was that the Jews have irretrievably fallen from their privileged position, since all God's interventions on their behalf have led to nothing but failure. Stephen, in fact, sees in the Jews' unbelief towards Jesus the final end of their secular oppositions to God's will. The children of Israel did not obey Moses who was sent to them as their deliverer and who handed on to them "the oracles of life;" they abandoned the Law and gave themselves up to idolatry in the desert; they tried to install in a Temple made by man the One for whom "the sky is the throne and earth is the footstool;" they persecuted all the prophets and killed the righteous One; in short they have always resisted the Holy Spirit (Acts 7. 35-53).

It must be emphasized that Stephen does not simply go further or more deeply along the lines which Paul and John follow after him. His thought goes in another direction. Paul and John it is true, also recall that the Jews killed the Lord Jesus and the prophets (I Thess. 2. 15), that they are of the Devil who is a murderer (John 8. 44); but, for the Apostle and for the evangelist, the rebellion of the Jews really only begins with their rejection of Jesus. According to Saint Paul, it is in relation to the knowledge of Jesus Christ that the theocratic privileges granted to Israel lose all value (Phil. 3. 3f); for the time when they were given, they were the means of grace (cf. Rom. 9. 4; 7. 14, 16). In the fourth gospel, if Moses becomes the accuser of the Jews (John 5. 45), it is only because the Jews do not believe in the Jesus proclaimed by Moses: the evangelist has so little thought for any Jewish opposition to the divine plan before the advent of Jesus, that the Johannine Christ declares: "If I had not come and spoken to them, they would have had no sin" (John 15. 22; cf. 9. 41).

In Stephen's opinion the sin of the Jews began in the time of Moses and continued in the building of the Temple.[34] The same charge of sin is brought against all generations of the chosen people up to the time of the present generation which rejects Christ and the Christian Gospel. Doubtless Stephen would conclude that God, by bringing together all those who confessed the Son of Man, would gather a new people without any connection to the unbelieving people. In this perspective the problem of the relationship between Christianity and Judaism would have apparently had a very simple and radical solution. Christianity would have been constituted as a religion quite independent from Judaism, in opposition to it or at least completely detached from its traditions.

Stephen found no followers in this line of thought. The infant Church does not break with the Israelite past, although it denounces the unbelief with which the Jews reject its preaching. In its view the old covenant remains of value as a temporary institution and the line of salvation continues unbroken despite the unbelief of the Jews. Even more, by virtue of the unity of the divine plan, the Church will claim the theocratic past for itself; it will affirm that it is the legitimate heir, since it believes that the promises contained in this tradition have been realized within itself. It will present itself before Judaism and before the Empire as the true Israel.

This attitude of the infant Church, based on its christological faith, will of necessity bring to its relationship with Judaism the character of a bitter conflict and a struggle for existence, both on the theological level and on the juridical level.

II. *The theological conflict*

From a rapid reading of the first chapters of the book of Acts, it might be concluded that the conflict between infant Christianity and Judaism had nothing fatal about it and that the Church could live in peace in Israel. This could happen if the Christians maintained the apparent conciliatory spirit of the first believers. The accusation lodged against Stephen and later against Paul of speaking "against the Law and the Temple" (Acts 6. 11, 13; 21. 28) is not leveled against Peter. The persecution undergone by the Greek Christians - after Stephen himself had been the victim of a popular uprising in which legal forms were obviously ignored - did not touch the believers grouped around the Twelve at Jerusalem (not just the

Apostles themselves) since we do not see the apostolic Christians return to the city after the dispersion mentioned in Acts 8. 1. This is an indication that the Jewish authorities could distinguish between, on the one hand, a Messianism which they did not like since it was a disavowal of their attitude towards Jesus of Nazareth, but which they could tolerate as it was in no way illegal in the Mosaic sense of the word, and, on the other hand, a much more radical movement, like that of Stephen, which attacked, or seemed to attack, the sacred institutions of Judaism: the Law and the Temple, and which seemed to challenge the right of the Jews to call themselves the people of God.

It also appears that the Judeo-Christian Church existed peacefully at Jerusalem and throughout Palestine while Paul pursued his missionary journeys. The persecution directed by Herod Agrippa against the leaders of the Church and in the course of which James, the brother of John, perished, was short-lived and limited in its scope.[35] The Christians in Jerusalem were not solidly behind Paul when he was arrested. They did not really approve of the freedom he showed with regard to the Law or at best they did so reluctantly. They preferred to align themselves with James, the Lord's brother, who, according to the testimony of Hegesippus, continued to attend the Temple and live like a Jew.[36]

Therefore, after Stephen, it would be the Apostle Paul who who would have provoked opposition and brought about a confrontation, by his own intransigence and by his flaunting of the Jewish Law. In other words, Christianity would not have been intolerable to Judaism had it not departed so far from the Law.

However attractive this explanation may be, it does not seem to be wholly tenable. It ignores the prime importance of christological preaching which was common to all primitive Christianity.

Our knowledge of early Christian preaching comes from Peter's sermons in Acts and the references made to them by Paul in his epistles. The message can be summarized as follows: the time for the fulfilling of the prophecies has come; Jesus of Nazareth has appeared as the One sent from God. He has taught with authority and has accomplished miracles, signs and wonders. He was crucified and He died. But God has raised Him from the dead; He has made Him Christ the Lord by raising Him to His right hand, from where He will come to bring about the reestablishment of all things. In the meantime, the Holy Spirit is given to men who accept the preaching in faith and who form the people of God, gathered together in the name of the Lord Jesus Christ.[37]

Paul and John, the theologians of the first century, will make this primitive message more specific and more profound. They will give to Jesus the title of Son of God; they will bring to light the expiatory and substitutionary value of His death; they will emphasize the personal relationship which exists in the present life between Christ and His believers and also Christ's office as the mediator between those who believe in Him and God.[38] These are developments of the primitive doctrine; they do not change it basically. The whole of Christianity is already present in the proclamation that the salvation expected in the future by Israel is now realized in Jesus Christ, the Lord.

Christian preaching finds its roots in Israelite theology. It is based on a concept of God, the world, man and his destiny, which is the Jewish concept. It is in its Messianism that the thought of the Church shows it originality. The question therefore is whether, from the Jewish point of view, Christian Messianism conforms to or is contrary to the Law and, therefore, whether it is permissible or not.

At first glance, Christian Messianism does not seem to go against any of the dogmas of Judaism. Undoubtedly the Christians confess the name of the One who has been rejected by the Sanhedrin as a false Messiah, and they preach that the ultimate drama has begun with the death and resurrection of Christ. But eschatology and Messianism were not rigorously defined doctrines of Judaism. One could hold very different opinions on these subjects while still belonging to the chosen people. The Sadducees denied the resurrection of the dead but without losing their position as religious leaders of the people. The Jews who lived by the Messianic hope had a choice of many different eschatological forms; they expected salvation either by the intervention of God Himself, the only Judge and King, or of a Messiah, the son of David, or of a prophet like Moses, or even of the Son of Man arriving from the sky on a cloud. In the second century, R. Akiba, who had hailed Bar Kochba as the Messiah, was still one of the most venerated scholars in Israel's memory.[39] The single dogma of Judaism is the affirmation that the only God revealed Himself to His people of Israel in the Law handed down by Moses. Christian preaching does not rise up against the God of Israel, who is its God, and, as Saint Paul will say, "the Father of our Lord Jesus Christ." Nor does it rise up against Moses, nor against the Law... On the contrary, in the view of the believers, Moses announced in advance the coming of Christ who is the prophet referred to in Deuteronomy (18. 15-18). This passage is quoted by Peter (Acts 3. 22) and by Stephen (7. 37);[40] John alludes to it on several occaions (John 1. 21 and 25; 6. 14; 7. 40; cf. 5. 45f). For his part Paul is quite sure that he is confirming the Law and not destroying it (Rom. 3. 31). In short, the early Christians had no feeling of ceasing to belong to Judaism because they believed in Jesus Christ.

At first it seems that the Jews agreed with this and there were no legal reasons to be found for condemning the new Christianity. The two accounts of the arrests of the Apostles (Acts 4. 1-22 and 5. 17-42) are significant in this respect. According to the first account, Peter and John are threatened for having caused disturbances in the Temple and not for committing any sin of heresy. Their arrest is merely a police matter intended to put an end to a public disturbance; it is not an act by which one religion starts a wave of persecution against another religion. The next day Peter explains to his judges that the lame man at the Temple was cured through the name of Jesus, the only name by which men can be saved. The account continues with this comment: "The members of the Sanhedrin had no reply to make" (4. 14). These words are not necessarily to be regarded as a comment by the writer of the Acts anxious to show that from the beginning Christianity triumphed over Judaism. If that were his motive he would not report the episode of Stephen which would contradict his hypothesis. On the other hand, the comment describes very well the real embarrassment the Sanhedrin must have felt in the face of Christian propaganda.

In connection with this chapter and the following one credit is due to Karl Bornhäuser and Joachim Jeremias for providing information about the details of Jewish criminal law.[41] According to Rabbinic law, already in use in the first century, four conditions had to be met for a defendant to be condemned, and particularly the two following: the Law must have a specific punishment for the crime committed and the accused must have been warned first about the criminal character of his action before he could be prosecuted. This is the situation in which Peter and John found themselves according to the fourth chapter of Acts. They could not be accused of having knowingly violated any article of the Law. Therefore they were warned not to speak any more in the name of Jesus and they were set free.

In the following chapter the Apostles are arrested again because they have continued to preach and thus have disobeyed a formal order of the Sanhedrin. The High Priest reminds them of the warning given to them previously; their punishment will be legal. But the flogging of the Apostles solves nothing, and Gamaliel's speech reveals the impotence of the Jewish authorities in the face of Messianic preaching. It cannot be opposed since Messianism has its roots in the Law, and it cannot be tolerated, for fear of political repercussions. The Jewish authorities view "Christian preaching with a certain mistrust, not as incompatible with Judaism, but as inopportune and capable of provoking a disturbance which might provide a pretext for the dreaded intervention of the power of Rome."[42]

Paul of Tarsus, it is true, seems to have had a clearer view of the originality of the Christian message even before his conversion. Otherwise it would be difficult to explain his persecuting activities. From the evidence in Acts it is difficult to see whether Paul is persecuting the Church at Jerusalem or the Greek Christians.[43] In any event it seems doubtful whether he ever had the power either to bring believers in custody from Damascus to Jerusalem (Acts 9. 2) or to put them to death (Acts 22. 4). The personal testimony of the Apostle, although very brief, gives us more information. Paul persecuted the Church and attempted to destroy it (Gal. 1. 13, 23; I Cor. 15. 9; Phil. 3. 6). "To ravage the Church" (Gal. 1. 13) and "to ravage the faith" (Gal. 1. 23) are synonymous expressions to him. He attributes his persecuting activity to what he calls his excessive zeal for the traditions of his forefathers (Gal. 1. 14), in other words, to theological passion. These passages suggest that his attacks were more verbal than physical. His persecution consisted of showing that Jesus of Nazareth could not be the Christ, since it is written: "Cursed is every one who hangs upon a tree" (Deut. 21. 23; Gal. 3. 13) and thereby destroying the Church which after his conversion he will work "to build up." However Paul undoubtedly held that the Christians he persecuted were his brethren who had strayed and not enemies of Judaism. The following fact seems to prove this.

Paul does not have the feeling that he can be or should be rejected by the Jewish community because he has become the Apostle of Jesus Christ and preaches to the Gentiles the Gospel of uncircumcision. Doubtless he is well aware that his Gospel evokes the mistrust of the Judeo-Christians and provokes the anger of the Jews. He knows that he is accused of destroying the Law, while in reality he confirms it. For, in his view, what he preaches is the true Judaism,[44] and his fellow Jews would understand this, if only faith would remove the veil that covers their minds when they read the Scripture (cf. II Cor. 3. 15). Also, in his epistles, the Apostle shows no fear of falling under the legal condemnation of the Sanhedrin. The travel plans he sets out in the epistle to the Romans (15. 22-37) reveal that the only risk in his view is that he should become the victim of "the unbelievers in Judea," presumably of an uprising provoked by his adversaries. Paul would not have announced his intention of going to Rome if he had thought that he could be legally arrested in Jerusalem and prosecuted for a crime against Judaism.

The perspective is a little different in the book of Acts where the Apostle Paul, in the view of the Jewish authorities, appears as "the ringleader in the sect of the Nazarenes" (Acts 24. 5). This is because years have passed between the time when the letter to the Romans was sent and when the second book to Theophilus was written. The Temple has now been destroyed.[45] The Christians and the Jews know that from now on they are completely separate. In reality that had been so for a long time, although neither of them had been aware of it.

If the Christian judges the destruction of the Temple quite differently from the Jews, it was because the Temple had already lost for the believers in Christ the significance it still had for the Jews. In fact the believers have, in the person of the Lord Jesus Christ, and in the communion they have with him, a different sign of the presence of God in their midst. Therefore they have, in the proper sense of the word, a different religion from that of the Temple. Undoubtedly they continue to attend the national sanctuary, as they continue to observe the Law, but because of an attachment which is more traditional and sentimental than theologically rationalized. But their minds and their hearts are elsewhere, and they do not hesitate when the time comes that they must choose between the Temple and Christ, even though, like James the Just, they seem outwardly very attached to Judaism.

This attitude of the believers shows that Christianity is something other and something more than a form of Jewish Messianism, and is so from the very beginning, although the ultimate consequences of the Christian affirmations about Jesus are not immediately apparent either to those who confess them or to those who challenge their validity. If it is true that the Christian faith, in the course of the first centuries, makes use of more and more aggrandizing expressions to describe Jesus, it is also quite certain that the Christian faith, during this evolution, does not change essentially. Christianity was born because the Apostles saw Jesus resurrected from the dead and believed, at least from that time on, that He was a unique being, bringing about, with God, a salvation which He Himself did not need, unlike the rest of mankind. Without this conviction which was present in the Apostles from the very beginning there would be no Church of Jesus Christ. There would only have been one more sect in Judaism. But the Church appears soon after the crucifixion, as a unique historical and theological reality, in spite of strong sociological links binding it to Judaism. It does not emerge gradually from within Judaism which could have carried it for a long time in its bosom, so to speak, before bringing it out into the light of day.

From the time when the Apostles preach that Jesus is risen from the dead and has been seen, clothed in celestial glory, and that the believers admit that this testimony is true, the Christian faith comes into existence with its fundamental propositions: Jesus Christ is the Lord who offers salvation; it is to Him that believers address their prayers.

There is no reason to take as anachronistic Peter's words in his first sermon after Pentecost: "Jesus - God has made Him both Lord and Christ" (Acts 2. 36). Peter would have nothing to say if he did not proclaim this message. It was not Paul who was the first to describe Jesus as *Kurios*, since he found the term in the hymn, probably of Aramaic origin, which he cites in the epistle to the Philippians (2. 5-11). The Apostle to the Gentiles is certain that, leaving aside the question of the observation of the Law by Christians who have come out of paganism, he preaches the same Gospel as the Apostles in Jerusalem (I Cor. 15. 11). The latter, for their part, would not have given "the right hand of fellowship" to Paul (Gal. 2. 9) if he had not been united with them in worshipping the same Lord. It is to the Lord Jesus that the prayers of the infant Church are addressed.[46] The first distinct title used by the believers - apart from the words "brethren" or "disciples" which have nothing original about them - is "those who call upon the name of the Lord" (Acts 9. 14), evidently the name of the Lord Jesus. If it was a question of Yahweh, the expression would lose its distinctive character. It is "the name of Jesus" which has redemptive power (Acts 4. 10).

It is difficult to know the exact meaning given by the first Christians to the word *Kurios*, which the Septuagint kept for God alone, with rare exceptions, and which was too great to be a common Messianic title.[47] The least that can be said is that, by calling the glorified Christ "Lord," the believers are placing Him in as close a relationship as possible with God. By calling on the Lord Jesus, they confess that they expect from Him the salvation which the Jews hope for from the Lord Yahweh. Thus they pave the way for the categorical statements by Paul and John: "God was in Christ, reconciling the world to Himself" (II Cor. 5. 19) and "He who has seen me has seen the Father" (John 14. 9).

To make Jesus of Nazareth the Lord and the Savior and the Son of God, in the sense that Paul and John give to that expression, is to come up against the touchy subject of Jewish monotheism. The breaking-point between Christians and Jews is the christology of the Church. It is teaching "in the name of Jesus" for which the Sanhedrin reproves the Apostles, as we have seen. From the end of the first century Jewish polemics reproaches Christian preaching for equating Jesus with God.[48] The great argument of the Talmud against Christianity is that it institutes the worship of a second God.[49]

It is not by chance that the dominant christologies connected to the first statements of faith (that is the christologies of the Son of God of Paul and John) are those which appear where the distance from Judaism is the greatest. Jesus is most exalted where the separation from Jewish thought is the clearest. The two facts are correlative, This connection also shows that the major reason for conflict between the Church and Judaism is christological faith. There is no conflict and the separation is hardly noticeable when the Church's christology keeps its avowals to a minimum and confines itself basically to the Jewish Messianic faith; that is, when urged to declare for or against Jesus, a believer reputed to be loyal to Judaism, can make a confession which reveals, at one and the same time, both his Christian faith and his detachment from the Jewish faith, to which he would appear to belong almost entirely.

The first Christian martyr, after Stephen and James the brother of John, is "by the irony of fate,"[50] James, the brother of Jesus. Hegesippus tells us, in the passage to which we referred above, that he was surnamed the Just, because many were called James and his fidelity in living the Jewish religious life made him earn that title. But the sympathy which James won for himself in this way with his fellow Jews was of no avail on the day when he testified to his Christian faith. Hegesippus, continuing his account, tells us that James believed that Jesus was the Savior and that those Jews who had faith held it from Him; the Scribes and the Pharisees were disturbed by this and, on the day of the Passover, they demanded of James a public denial in order to dissuade the crowd from believing in Jesus.[51] Then Hegesippus writes:

> The Scribes and Pharisees made James stand on the turret of the Temple and they cried out to him and said: 'O, just one, to whom we all owe obedience, since the people go astray after Jesus who was crucified, tell what is the door of Jesus.' And he answered with a loud voice: 'Why do you ask me about the Son of Man? He is sitting in heaven, on the right hand of the great Power, and he shall come upon the clouds of heaven.' Many were fully satisfied and glorified in the testimony of James and said: 'Hosanna to the Son of David.' But the same Scribes and Pharisees said to one another: 'We have done badly in furnishing Jesus with such testimony;

> let us go up and cast him down; they will be afraid and will no longer believe him.' They began to cry out: 'Oh, oh, even the Just one has erred...' They went up and cast down the Just.[52]

As an introduction to his long quotation from the *Memoirs* of Hegesippus, Eusebius himself briefly recalls the facts in these terms:

> The Jews brought James into their midst and demanded of him a denial of faith in Christ in the presence of all the people. To the surprise of everyone, he spoke up with courageous freedom and independence which went far beyond what they expected; he confessed that our Lord and Savior Jesus Christ was the Son of God. They could not endure such a testimony from such a man; because he was believed by all, on account of his wisdom and goodness of life, to be unequalled in righteousness. They put him to death, taking advantage of the absence of the governor; since Festus had just died in Judea. This attack was therefore committed without any authorization or control by a procurator.[53]

Even if "it is not certain that the profession of faith ascribed to James was as strictly orthodox as Eusebius would have it,"[54] the two passages we have quoted are important. They both show that the Jews did not expect from James a christological confession like the one he gave them. It is this confession which turned them against him and made them forget all his merits.

Why should there be this outburst of Jewish fury at that time, while several years previously, as we have mentioned, Paul, when he writes to the Romans, thinks that he can risk going to Jerusalem, in spite of "the unbelievers in Judea," and come away again safe and sound in order to proceed to Rome. Several explanations can be given which complement rather than contradict each other. It is possible that Paul underestimated the violence of the Jews' hatred for him. Also he may perhaps have felt that he was protected, if the necessity arose, both by his status as a Roman citizen and by the presence of the imperial power. But Eusebius specifically emphasizes that the execution of James was only made possible because there was no procurator present. In fact, "in the interval between the death of Festus and the arrival of his successor (in 62 A.D.) complete anarchy ruled in Jerusalem."[55] Eusebius also says, before describing the death of James, that the Jews directed their fury against him because they had been disappointed in their hope of laying hold of Paul.[56] So, in order for their anti-apostolic fury to achieve its ends, Roman control must have been temporarily suspended.

However that may be, the martyrdom of James was an event of great significance. The position taken by the different Apostles with regard to the Law is not what determines the Jews' attitude towards them. The dominant fact, the one which earns for James a condemnation as rigorous as that which the Jews might have already carried out against the Apostle to the Gentiles if they had been free to do so, is the confession of faith in the Lord Jesus Christ. Nothing shows more clearly the prime importance of the role of christological faith in the conflict between the Church and Judaism.

The christology of the Church divides and sets Christians and Jews against each other not only because of its own nature but also because of the consequences resulting from it. The christology of the Church was not formulated to exalt the person of Jesus without good reason. It is in order to express and to vouch for the value of the salvation offered to believers by the person and work of Christ. It has often been rightly emphasized that Christian christology is functional rather than ontological.

The desire not to separate the work of Christ from His person is already evident in Peter's speeches. The Apostle urges his hearers to "escape from this perverse generation" and be baptized in the name of Jesus (Acts 4. 41). "the only name given to men by which they are to be saved" (Acts 4. 12). After being baptized the believers join those who, while still belonging to Israel and still attending the Temple, come together with others who confess Christ, in order to devote themselves to the teaching of the Apostles and the fellowship, the breaking of bread and the prayers (Acts 2. 42).

Certainly Peter is far from thinking that in this way a new people of God is instituted, gathered by Jesus Christ instead of by Moses, saved by faith instead of by the Law, decked with the seal of the new covenant which is baptism, and thereby absolved from the seal of the old covenant which is circumcision. Yet the material with which Paul will assure his position is already there before he makes use of it. The Church precedes him since he persecuted it before he was called to extend it from Jerusalem to Illyria. Baptism precedes him; when he writes to the Romans, whose precise situation he does not know, he has no doubts about the fact of their baptism and he says to them, as if it were a matter of course for all Christians: "We have all been baptized." Similarly the eucharist precedes him, since, in the churches he establishes, he hands on the eucharistic tradition he has himself received and which goes back to the Lord Himself. (cf. I Cor. 11. 23).

Just as the faith of the believers in the Lord Jesus Christ is more than Jewish Messianism, so the implications of this faith go beyond the limits of Jewish religious thought and practice. The call to belief in Christ is addressed to all mankind, so that the new people will go beyond the old theocracy. As the Law of Moses is not imposed on the converted Gentiles the people called to Jesus Christ will soon not only be new in respect to the historic people of Israel - they will be quite distinct from them.

In short, by confessing that Jesus is the Lord, by preaching salvation through Him, by baptizing in His name, by communicating with Him through prayer and the eucharist, the believers create a new religion, quite different and distinct from Judaism.

If the only concern of Christianity had been to set up a new religion by gathering the Church together and separating it from Israel, by substituting the administration of baptism for the rite of circumcision, by expecting the return of the Lord rather than the coming of an unknown Messiah, then Christianity could have lived in peace alongside Judaism, or at least have existed without bitter conflict. The two religions could have gone their separate ways in mutual independence and indifference. But Christianity is not merely something new; it is just as much a tradition. It is the heir to a lengthy past, the past of Israel to be exact. It interprets this past quite differently from Israel. It understands it in the light of the new revelation which has just been granted and which is ignored by Israel and rejected as worthless. Herein lies the drama of the encounter between Christianity and Judaism.

The Lord of the Church is the Messiah of Israel. This is why Christianity is both new and old, without being destroyed by a contradiction within itself. In his preaching the Apostle Peter presents the whole Christian event as the accomplishment of what was foretold in Scripture. The rejection of Christ and His death conform to the eternal plan of God (Acts 2. 23); all the prophets foretold that He would be the instrument of salvation (Acts 10. 43); the pouring out of the Spirit and the new experiences of the believers happen according to the prophecies (Acts 2. 16f).

From the very beginning all the believers are quite sure that the Gospel is the realization of the hope of Israel. The history of salvation, which was begun in Israel, is continued in and by the Church which received the promised Messiah and believes in Him. The Church is the normal result of the old revelations. The great line of God's activity in mankind which has passed through Abraham, Moses, David and the prophets, is now going through the Church. By its refusal to believe, Judaism is placed outside the line of the promise.
In a word, it is Christianity which is "according to the Scriptures" (*kata tas graphas*) and it is unbelieving Judaism which loses the meaning of these same Scriptures (*para tas graphas*).

The Church does not break with the past, just because it is a new revelation of God, in order to be the fulfillment of the revelations made in Israel. Far from giving up the religious institutions of Judaism as one might have expected, the Church appropriates these institutions precisely because it is the final act of God, who has already been at work in Israel, and because continuity is the mark of divine activity. The Church judges the Jewish institutions by the norm of Christian faith. Judged in this way, these institutions, these sacred personages, these actions of God in history, can be divided into two categories. Some are found to have permanent significance: the Church incorporates them. Others appear of only temporal value: the Church regards them as historic institutions, devoid of any beneficial character. In any case, by the policy of the Church, Judaism finds itself robbed of its theocratic heritage and all its privileges, since the Church takes as its own those which are permanent, and those which are only temporary the Church now considers obsolete for Jews as well as for Christians.

These ideas are expressed in concrete terms in several

places in the New Testament. According to the Apostle Paul, the rule of faith, which is characteristic of the Gospel, is new in that it is made possible by the new event in the history of salvation, the sending of the Son "when the time was fully come" (Gal. 4. 4). But this is not a real innovation. God had already based His relationship with Abraham on faith. The Law came later "four hundred and thirty years after the promise" (Gal. 3. 17); it was imposed later (Gal. 3. 19; Rom. 5. 20); its role and its time were limited. By His death and resurrection Christ puts an end to the rule of the Law (Rom. 10. 4) in satisfying its demands once and for all. Thus he firmly re-opens the age of faith which had already flourished at the time of the patriarchs. The age of the Law is in parentheses in God's plan for mankind. Since Christ has closed the parentheses, to remain bound to the Law is to move backwards in the history of salvation, it is to misunderstand God's plan and the steps He is taking towards revelation. Undoubtedly the Law is holy and spiritual, in a word, divine. But it is temporary and its role has come to an end. Now that the promise made to Abraham has been realized in his "seed" which is Christ (Gal. 3. 16) - that is to say Christ in the inclusive sense of the Lord and His believers - the true sons of Abraham are the believers. All who believe, even if they were Gentiles, have Abraham as their father (Rom. 4. 1); they are the true sons of Abraham, who had faith (Gal. 3. 9). The Church is the Israel of God (Gal. 6. 16). The Apostle writes along the same lines in Philippians (3. 3): "For we are the true circumcision - we who render to God a spiritual worship and make our boast in Christ Jesus." So, in Paul's view, within the heritage of the old covenant, faith in Christ makes some necessary distinctions. Abraham is elevated to the rank of ancestor of all the believers, because he already represents the age of justification by faith, while the Law, on which the Jews base their rejection of the Gospel, is reduced to the state of a religious system made obsolete by the progress of salvation.

Ideas developed by Paul on the juridical level appear in the epistle to the Hebrews on the liturgical level which is characteristic of that epistle, but with striking parallels to Pauline thought. The outline is identical. Just as the age of faith, securely established in Christ, is joined through the temporary age of the Law to that first age of faith begun by God with Abraham, so, according to the writer to the Hebrews, the priesthood of Jesus Christ, High Priest in the order of Melchisedek, is joined through the priesthood of Aaron, which was also temporary and is now obsolete, to the priesthood of Melchisedek, which preceded that of Aaron and was superior to it, and which foretold the priesthood of Christ. The Levitic priesthood is thrust aside; it lacked the qualities of the priesthood of Christ. It only procured for the Israelites a "carnal," ceremonial purity and did not sanctify the very being of man (Heb. 9. 13), in a word, it did not lead to perfection (10. 1) while, on the other hand, the priesthood of Christ brings about a perfect expiation which "sets the people free from sin" (10. 14; 13. 12). The only effective sacrifice is the perfect one of Christ. This is why the patriarchs and the righteous men of the old covenant, although they won God's approval by their faith, "apart from us they were not to be perfected" (11. 40). According to the concept of salvation of the epistle to the Hebrews, like that of Saint Paul, Christianity does not appear as something new, but as the accomplishment of a very old design of God; Jewish priesthood, like the Law, is ranked as a historic institution limited both as to its capacity and its length of life.

The gospel of John reflects the same idea and to some extent presents a synthesis of the juridic line of Pauline thought and the priestly line of the theology in the epistle to the Hebrews. The Johannine Christ comes from God as the Revelation which was foretold by Moses (John 5. 46); He gives men grace and truth, while Moses only gave them the Law (1. 17). At the same time, Christ is the new Temple; the presence and glory of God are now revealed in His person and no longer in the Temple at Jerusalem; His death and His resurrection are the sacrifice through which the believers are brought into communion with the Father and receive life from Him (2. 19-22).[57] The life which the Word incarnate gives to the world both by His mission of revelation and by His sacrifice, is the same life which the Word had already offered to mankind, at the time of creation (1. 3). In this concept God shows in Jesus Christ the plan He had started at the very beginning before the temporary institutions of Judaism began to flourish.

In different but parallel modes of expression the Christians reveal their sure belief that the instruments of salvation of Judaism, although they are instituted by God, are now set aside by God Himself. He substitutes for them salvation in His Son, whose work was foreseen and foretold, in one way or another, before the Law and priesthood of Israel appeared on the scene.

There is no cause to see in these ideas later creations by Christian theology, processes to give the Church an ancient tradition. For the same trend of thought is already apparent in the preaching of Jesus. When asked about marriage and the legality of divorce, Jesus replies to the Pharisees that permission to divorce was given by Moses in consideration of their stubborn hearts, but it does not express the first or the final will of God, revealed at the time of creation and restored by the word of Jesus, that marriage is an indissoluble union and that "man should not put asunder what God has joined together" (Mark 10. 2-9; Matt. 19. 3-6). In a sense the whole teaching of Jesus appears as the definitive expression of God's will, the completion and perfection of the Mosaic Law which is regarded as a primary but inadequate stage in the revelation process. This is why Jesus declares: "You have heard it was said by Moses and the men of old,[58] but I say to you..." (Matt. 5. 21). The perfect revelation brought by Jesus, makes evident, or rather makes evident again, the primary intention of God, shown in the order and beauty of creation. This is precisely what John is saying when he affirms that the light shed by the Word incarnate is the same light which illuminated the world at the time of the creation.

In short, the revelations given in Israel during the course of its history are partial and temporary, and foretell the complete and definitive revelation which is in Christ.

The christological faith of the Church thus leads it to a christological interpretation of the whole history of salvation. All the benefits God has given to His people in the past now belong to the Church. "The God of Abraham, of Isaac and of Jacob" is "the Father of our Lord Jesus Christ;" the unbelieving Jews have the Devil as their father (John 8. 44). The Scripture, which proclaims Christ, becomes the Bible of the Church; it is the Church which understands it; but this Scripture remains hidden to the Jews; a veil lies upon their hearts when they read it without believing in Christ (II Cor. 3. 15). The believers are the people of God, already appearing in the old covenant in the person of Abraham, Melchisedek, Moses, David and all the prophets, those testimonies of Christ and forerunners of the believers. The believers are the descendants of Isaac, while the Jews are the descendants of Ishmael (cf. Gal. 4. 28-31) or even "a synagogue of Satan" (Rev. 2. 9; 3. 9).

Just as there is only one God and one Scripture, so there is only one people of God, only one true Israel. The true Israel is the one which now brings together all those who confess Christ, so that the Jewish race is deprived of its privilege of theocracy, which is in some respects the most essential, the one which is the basis for all the others. In short, the Church is universal, and everything belongs to the Church. For a time the Jews were the recipients of God's gifts and promises. As they do not believe that God's promises are fulfilled in Christ, they see His benefits slip away from them. They can only regain them, or rather these benefits will only be restored to them when, through faith, they will have a place in the new and final stage of the history of salvation which began with the coming of Jesus of Nazareth, Messiah of Israel and Lord of the Church.

The Church only leaves to Judaism those divine institutions which, as far as it is concerned, are no more than historic monuments, that is the Law and the sacrificial rites. As the priesthood disappears with the fall of the Temple, the Church of Christ only has before it the Synagogue of the Law. "The disagreement which sets the two religions against each other has two aspects: christology - 'the other God' of the Rabbis - and the Law."[59] The struggle does not start as soon as the Apostles begin to preach the Gospel, but the underlying reason for the conflict has been there from the very beginning. It is in the name of his christological faith that John sets the truth of Christ higher than the Law of Moses, that Paul contrasts "the ministry of the Spirit" with the covenant of the letter, that Peter disobeys the order of silence imposed on him by the Sanhedrin in order to follow Christ's commandment: "You shall be my witnesses."

For its part, in order to safeguard its existence, Judaism had to declare to be inadmissible the claims of the Church to be the people of God, to possess the key of the Scriptures and to benefit from a better revelation. Judaism also understood that, for the Christians, faith in Christ was pre-eminent. It was on this point that Judaism's main objection focussed, and it was the confession of Christ as Lord that Judaism could not forgive to those of the believers who otherwise lived strictly according to the Law.

III. *Political rivalry*

In principle the conflict which sets infant Christianity and Judaism against each other is a theological conflict. The reason for its existence is the single fact that the Christians see in Christ the Messiah of Jewish hope and even a being who actualizes and goes beyond this hope, and that the Jews deny that Jesus of Nazareth is what the Christians believe and preach. This theological conflict inevitably engenders a political rivalry, by virtue of the particular status given to Judaism by the Roman state and the measures used by the Emperors to control the propagation of Eastern religions.

"Judaism, in effect, occupied a unique position in the Empire. It had been granted considerable privileges by a series of public acts renewed and confirmed by Caesar and by Augustus. The Jewish communities were free to govern themselves, to come together and exercise discipline with regard to their members. The Jews were absolved from all participation in civil worship; they could take an oath without calling upon the gods. Their scruples with regard to the Sabbath were respected. They were not required to appear before a court of justice on that day, and when distributions were made to the populace on a Saturday, they were repeated the next day for their benefit. This may have been so because Judaism was considered as the national religion of a people who, before becoming the slave, had been the friend and ally of the Roman people."[60] In a word, within the Empire, Judaism was a *religio licita*.[61]

However, the practice does not always follow the precept. Even if those who succeeded Augustus did not intend to remove the privileges granted to Judaism, as opportunity arose they took measures intended to limit the advantages the Jews had as a result of their particular status and especially to restrict, and even forbid, propaganda and proselytism. They intervened in local conflicts between Jews and non-Jews, usually taking sides against the Jews, like Claudius in Alexandria and Nero at Caesarea.[62]

Nevertheless Judaism enjoyed to a large extent the hospitality and recognition granted by Rome to the national religions of the peoples incorporated into the Empire.[63] The situation of Judaism was much more assured than that of the Eastern religions. The latter seemed to have enjoyed only *de facto* tolerance, and their *collegia* might be forbidden when the Emperors were of a mind to preserve the old Roman religion and dignity, and put an end to the spread of new sects.[64]

In these circumstances it is clear that the Christians would be able to live in peace, if the State considered Christianity as a form of Judaism, or even the true Judaism, and granted to the Church the privileges and exceptions enjoyed by the Synagogue. On the other hand, if the powers were led to think the Christians had lost the quality of Jewry, the situation of infant Christianity would become rapidly more precarious than that of the Eastern religions. For the confession that Jesus is Lord and the refusal to give the Emperor divine honor would bring down upon the believers the charge of high treason. They would be pursued as atheists and enemies of the State.

As the people of Christ the Messiah of Israel, the Christians feel that they are the people of God, the true Israel. Strictly speaking they are neither a new people nor a new religion. What they are on the theological level they must be, just as concretely, on the juridical level. If the political reality did not agree exactly with the theological affirmations, the truth of their theology would be questioned. Heirs of the theocratic benefits of Israel, the Christians should consequently enjoy the juridical status granted to the Jews. The concern for theological truth, more than the prospect of material advantages, would be what would stir infant Christianity to present itself as the true Israel, not only to the Jews but also to the Roman Empire.[65]

This would be an intolerable claim in the eyes of the Jews. They can only see that the Christians are robbing them of their political privileges after they have already laid hold upon their theocratic title and inheritance. Judaism can only defend its own position by denying the quality of being Jews to the Christians and, to make the distinction between them even more clear, by accusing them of political disturbance and rebellion. In addition to this, Christian theology, in spite of itself, came to the assistance of its adversaries by the emphasis it placed on the Lordship of Christ. It was enough for anyone desiring to destroy the Christians to hear in a political sense their fundamental confession "Jesus is Lord." They could then be accused of preaching rebellion and of saying "one other than Caesar is Emperor, one called Jesus" (Acts 17. 7; cf. Luke 23. 14; 19. 12, 15). In the relationship between infant Christianity and Judaism, political rivalry is therefore the inevitable result of theological conflict.

Traces of this political rivalry can be found throughout the New Testament. They are particularly obvious in the book of Acts. The Writer to Theophilus shows that "Christianity is nothing more than a development of Judaism which keeps faith with the promises which were the basis of the religion of Israel and, consequently, it has the right to enjoy the privileged position granted to Judaism within the Roman Empire."[66] This is something Gallio is quick to recognize when he refuses to get involved in a Jewish dispute (Acts 18. 14-15). In the view of the writer of Acts Paul is innocent and the charges brought against him by the Jews to the Roman authorities have no legal basis. If the Apostle is not set free, it is because of the relentlessness with which the Jews pursue his downfall, because of the influence they have on Felix and because of the corruption of the procurator (cf. Acts 24. 26).

Exegetes and historians are often very hard on the writer of Acts. They would maintain that he was defending an apologetic thesis by asserting that the Christians did not cease to be Jews, and that he would allow himself to distort the facts in order to support his thesis.[67] This severity is not justified. That the Church is the true Israel is not an original idea of the writer of Acts, it is the profound conviction of the whole of Christianity in the first century. That a Jew does not cease to belong to Judaism when he becomes a Christian is the sincere belief of Saint Paul, to name but one. We have had the opportunity to emphasize these facts in the preceding sections of this study.

What is described as the thesis of the writer of Acts is the reality in which the Church lives. On the larger scale, the nature of Christian-Jewish relations, as it emerges from the account in Acts, corresponds to historical truth. According to the writer of Acts, the Roman authorities only intervene against the Christians as a result of intrigues and accusations in which the Jews take a large part. This is certainly what happened in the first century. The only Roman persecution which was aimed specifically against the Christians, was the one unleashed by Nero after the burning of Rome in A.D. 64, when he was looking for scapegoats. Historians are in agreement that Jewish influences were at work among the Emperor's advisers to accuse the Christians and absolve the Jews.[68]

Before Nero's persecution and after it until the end of the first century, Christians and Jews are not distinguished as far as the imperial powers are concerned.[69] The situation changes under Trajan. In his letter to the Emperor to request approval for the measures he has taken against the Christians in Bithynia, Pliny writes that he has released those who, accused of being Christians, have agreed to make sacrifices to the Emperor and to the gods and to call down curses upon Christ; among those who confess Christ and in particular two deaconesses whom he has had tortured, he found nothing more than "an immoderate, wicked superstition."[70]

If Pliny consults the Emperor it is obviously because Christianity no longer exists as a crime in itself. The crime which concerns Pliny with regard to those sent before him is their refusal to make sacrifices to the Emperor and their neglect of the gods, it is not their adherence to a new religion. If the new religion is a crime it is so because of its exclusivity and anti-Roman characteristics. For Pliny never gives the impression that he would allow to the Christians the dispensations granted to the Jews. At the beginning of the second century the Christians are no longer Jews in the opinion of the authorities. Consequently they are excluded from the special status and the toleration enjoyed by the adherents of Judaism. In the struggle in which Christianity and Judaism are engaged on the juridical level, Judaism is the victor; it will keep its privileges until Christianity triumphs under Constantine.

If infant Christianity was defeated by Judaism on the juridical level, the reason is still to be found in its christology. The Jews were driven, both by their concern to safeguard their own particular status and by the aversion the Church's teaching inspired in them, to separate their cause from that of the Christians. From the Jewish point of view it was good politics in all respects to denounce the Christians to the imperial authorities. For its part the Empire could not help but notice the differences which became more and more marked as time passed, between the old national people whose characteristics were familiar to it, and the newcomers who also claimed they were "Jews." But the latter were more disquieting because of the role they attributed to a certain *Christus* and because of the undivided worship they offered to Him alone.

Christology, which had already separated infant Christianity from Judaism, aligned the Jews and the Romans firmly together in their opposition to the Christians. This situation could only be changed when the Emperor himself confessed his faith in the Lord Jesus Christ.

Conclusion

At first glance it seems that the Christians and Jews are destined to live together in peace. They share the same faith in the same one God, creator and ruler of the world, the same respect for the same Scriptures, the same hope that God will put an end to this present wicked age and re-establish His reign over the whole universe. The Jews and the Christians are the only ones in the ancient world to live this theology which they share and which divides them both from Eastern, and Greek and Roman paganism. They are often bound together, expecially when they are threatened by the same misrepresentations and persecutions.

Yet they are separated by the very thing which seems as though it should unite them. They trace the history of salvation along different lines. Judaism lives in the expectation of a Messiah who will come at the end of time: Christianity is based on faith in the Christ who has already come and will come again. The Christ in whom the Church believes makes the promises of Scripture a reality. But Judaism relies on the same texts to refute the Church's christological interpretation. It is Jesus of Nazareth who separates the Christians and the Jews, or, more precisely, it is the attitude they both take when confronted with His person and His Gospel. All the other reasons for opposition stem from this one fundamental reason.

Accidental happenings have played their part in the development and the worsening of the conflict. However, they are not adequate enough to explain its origins, because this conflict is an essentially theological one.

It is true that the Christians were grievously concerned about the comparative lack of success of the apostolic preaching to the Jews.[71] It is also true that "the Christian missionaries, and particularly Paul, felt that the Jews were responsible for the obstacles they encountered in their path" and that "the development of the Gospel tradition...has tended to make the Jews more and more responsible for the death of Jesus."[72] But the infant Church places these facts which nourish its feelings of anti-Judaism in a perspective where love for Israel also asserts itself. If the New Testament recalls that the Jews caused the death of Jesus of Nazareth, it emphasizes equally forcefully that the death of Christ was necessary to bring about the redemption of mankind, that this death was part of God's plan, so that the Jews, in fact, were instruments of a providential God. Although the Apostles are constantly encountering obstacles placed by the Jews in their way, they assert, and Paul does so more than any other, that salvation is intended for the Jews also and it will reach them ultimately. Their unbelief, and consequently the Apostles' inability to convince them, is also part of the mystery of the divine plan of redemption. If the Jews had had no part in the trial of Jesus, if they had left the Apostles alone and only greeted their preaching with indifference, the separation between the infant Church and Judaism would still have taken place. Doubtless the circumstances would be different but nevertheless it would have happened.

For the conflict not to have happened certain conditions would have had to be realized: that no Jew had faith in Jesus Christ, or that no Jew rejected Him. But this was not the case. The new Israel was the same as the old Israel; in history there was only one Israel just as there is only one on the theological level. The conflict arose because of the separation which was established between the theological truth - God has but one people - and historical fact: the Church on the one hand, Judaism on the other, each claiming to be the one people of God. To give up this claim was for each of them to renounce their very existence.

It is its christology which separated the infant Church from Judaism and set them against each other, with no possibility of reconciliation, as is proved by the failure of Judeo-Christianity. The conflict begins as soon as the Church begins to confess its christological faith. It is there, in principle, from the very beginning of Christian preaching.

The conflict can only be brought to an end by the restoration of the unity of Israel, in other words, by the return of Christianity to Judaism by giving up faith in Christ, or by the conversion of Israel by giving up its lack of belief that Jesus is the Messiah. The latter solution is the one which the infant Church portends and which Saint Paul in particular accepts as a "mystery" from God. This is why, in the final analysis, the first Christians adopt an ambivalent attitude towards Judaism. By their anti-Judaism, they assert that God has perfected His revelation in Jesus Christ. By their love for Israel, they take care not to forget that the gifts and the calling of God are irrevocable.

NOTES

1. The present study reproduces and develops the address given at the convocation of the *Faculté libre de théologie protestante* at Montpellier on November 9, 1951. It appeared in *Etudes théologiques et religieuses* 1, 1952, Montpellier.

2. Ignatius, *Magn.* 10. 3.

3. *Magn.* 8. 1. (We should read this as *kata Ioudaismon,* with Lightfoot, Funk, Lelong and Bauer. The reading *kata nomon*, adopted notably by Camelot, seems to be an emendation.) Cf. also *Philad.* 6. 1.

4. *Magn.* 8. 2.

5. *Magn.* 9. 2.

6. M. Simon, *Verus Israël. Etude sur les relations entre Chrétiens et Juifs dans l'empire romain (135-425),* Paris, 1948 (Bibliothèque des écoles françaises d'Athènes et de Rome, fasc. 166).

7. Cf. *The Jewish Encyclopaedia*, New York, 1903, V, p. 286; Strack-Billerbeck, *Kommentar zum Neuen Testament aus Talmud und Midrash,* München, 1928, IV. I, p. 331; H. J. Schoeps, *Theologie und Geschichte des Judenchristentums,* Tübingen, 1949, p. 284-285; M. Simon, *op. cit.*, p. 235-236.

8. It is not quite correct to speak of the "anti-Semitic prejudices" of the New Testament (F. C. Grant, *An Introduction to New Testament Thought,* New York - Nashville, 1950, p. 94-96) and it is wrong to maintain that either the New Testament (G. Kittel), or the gospel of John (A. Merx) is the most anti-Jewish of all literature. The New Testament is no more the source of modern anti-Semitism (cf. J. Parkes, *The Conflict of the Church and the Synagogue. A Study in the Origins of Antisemitism,* London, 1934) than the communal life of the believers in Jerusalem is the source of communism (cf. G. Walter, *Les origines du communisme*, Paris, 1931).

9. M. Simon, *op. cit.*, p. 239-245.

10. *Op. cit.,* p. 242.

11. *Op. cit.,* p. 243 and 244.

12. *Op. cit.,* p. 248f.

13. The same motif reappears in Acts 13. 27: the inhabitants of Jerusalem and their leaders, "not recognizing Jesus," accomplished, by condemning Him, the words of the prophets. This is in the speech of Paul at Antioch of Pisidia, but the idea itself certainly preceded Paul and has been placed by the writer of Acts into the mouth of the Apostle to the Gentiles. The next part of the speech (verses 28-38) is full of elements which have already appeared in the speeches of Peter and particularly in that in chapter 2. But Paul himself, in spite of I Thessalonians 2. 15, seems to come to the conclusion that, in the final analysis, it is cosmic powers, hostile to the redemptive plan realized by Christ, who "crucified the Lord of glory." They acted out of ignorance, but out of an ignorance which no repentance seems to be able to redeem, since, according to the Apostle, these powers are doomed to destruction (I Cor. 15. 24; cf. Col. 2. 15).

14. On the attitude of the writer of Acts towards Judaism, cf. P. H. Menoud, "The Western Text and the Theology of Acts," *Studiorum Novi Testamenti Societas, Bulletin II,* Oxford, 1951, p. 28-29 and *supra* p. 61-93.

15. Cf. M. Dibelius, *Handbuch zum Neuen Testament*, 11. 3, Aufl., Tübingen, 1937, p. 12 and 34-36.

16. On the second part of the accusation, cf. H. J. Schoeps, *Die jüdischen Prophetenmorde,* a study which appeared first in *Symbolae Biblicae Upsalienses* II (1943) and then in the volume *Aus frühchristlicher Zeit. Religionsgeschichtliche Untersuchungen*, Tübingen, 1950, p. 126-143.

17. Paul's concern is to defend the faith of the Thessalonians rather than to attack the Jews, as the context shows (cf. Bo Reicke, *Diakonie, Festfreude und Zelos im Verbindung mit der altchristlichen Agapenfeier,* Uppsala-Wiesbaden, 1951 (Acta Universitatis Uppsaliensis, 1951, 5), p. 246.

18. Cf. Strack-Billerbeck, *op. cit.*, III, p. 575; H. Schlier, *Der Brief an die Galater (*Kritisch-exegetischer Kommentar über das N. T., begründet von H. A. W. Meyer, VII, 10 Aufl.), Göttingen, 1949, p. 161.

19. Cf. Lietzmann-Kuemmel, *An die Korinther I-II,* 4. Aufl. (Handbuch zum Neuen Testament, 9), Tübingen, 1949, p. 156-157 and 212; J. Klausner, *From Jesus to Paul,* 2. ed., London, 1946, p. 325; M. Goguel, *La naissance du christian-*

isme, Paris, 1946, p. 233; J. Baruzi, *Création religieuse et pensée contemplative*, Paris, 1951, p. 49. - Opinions differ, however, when it is a question of deciding the nature of Paul's illness.

20. K. Bornhauser, "Der Pfahl im Fleisch," *Die Furche*, 1937, p. 383f.

21. L. Cerfaux, "L'antinomie paulinienne de la vie apostolique," *Mélanges Jules Lebreton I, Recherches de science religieuse*, 1951, p. 229-230.

22. "Paul never felt himself a non-Jew," J. Klausner, *op. cit.*, p. 452.

23. A transposition of this theme must be seen in the strange passage in Acts (22. 17-21) where Paul, describing his conversion, says that the Lord appeared to him in the Temple, ordered him to leave Jerusalem, warning him that the Jews would not receive his testimony - while the Apostle seems to protest that he would be the one who could convince the Jews, since he was known as a persecutor of the infant Church - and calls him to evangelize the Gentiles.

It is difficult to see in these verses Paul's *ipsissima verba*. When he speaks of his vocation, he makes no distinction between his conversion and his call to apostleship, but we find this distinction in this passage in Acts. It is with apostleship to the Gentiles in view that God stopped him on the road to Damascus - but this did not exclude preaching to the Jews also.

But this passage in Acts suggests that those who knew Paul kept alive the idea that his failure with the Jews had been very hard for him to bear and yet that this failure was part of the divine plan. The vision of the Lord in the Temple is a manifestation of the "grace that suffices" rather than one or other of the christophanies that Paul mentions (Gal. 1. 15-16; I Cor. 9. 1; 15. 8).

24. Cf. for example, W. Bauer, *Das Johannesevangelium* (Handbuch zum Neuen Testament, 6), 3. Aufl., Tübingen, 1933, p. 31; C. R. Bowen, "Love in the Fourth Gospel," *Journal of Religion*, 1933, p. 47; E. C. Colwell, *John defends the Gospel*, Chicago, 1936, p. 150; H. Strathmann, *Das Evangelium nach Johannes* (Das Neue Testament Deutsch, 4, 6. Aufl.), Göttingen, 1951, p. 152.

25. Examples of this rearrangement will be found in the commentaries of J. H. Bernard and R. Bultmann.

26. K. Bornhauser, *Das Johannesevangelium, eine Missionschrift für Israël*, Gütersloh, 1928 (Sammlung wissenschaftlicher Monographien, 15).

27. E. Hirsch, *Studien zum vierten Evangelium* (Beiträge zur historischen Theologie, 4), Tübingen, 1936, p. 54; R. Bultmann, *Das Evangelium des Johannes*, (Kritisch-exegetischer Kommentar über das N. T., begründet von H. A. W. Meyer, II, 10 Aufl.), Göttingen, 1941, p. 139, n. 6; W. Grundmann, *Jesus der Galiläer und das Judentum*, 2 Aufl., Leipzig, 1941, p. 224f.

28. W. Grundmann, *ibid.*

29. It does not seem quite true to say: "In John it does not seem as though the name of Israel is applied by extension to the new people of God. One is already a true Israelite if one is a Jew who observes the Law and thereby one with God" (W. Gutbrod, *Theologisches Wörterbuch zum N. T.*, III, p. 388).

30. K. Bornhauser, *op. cit.*, p. 148.

31. Cf. O. Cullmann, "Der johanneische Gebrauch doppeldeutiger Ausdrücke als Schlüssel zum Verständnis des vierten Evangeliums," *Theologische Zeitschrift*, 1948, p. 360-372.

32. Cf. in this sense, with different approaches, K. Bornhauser, *op. cit.*, p. 140-152; P. Feine, *Theologie des Neuen Testaments*, 7 Aufl., Leipzig, 1936, p. 335-338; W. W. Sikes, "The Anti-Semitism of the Fourth Gospel," *Journal of Religion*, 1941, p. 23-30; G. Schrenk, *Der göttliche Sinn in Israëls Geschick*, Zollikon-Zürich, 1943, p. 30-31.

33. Cf. M. Simon, *op. cit.*, p. 244.

34. On the subject of Stephen, his opposition to the worship of the Temple, and the origins of his thought, see the recent researches, which are sometimes similar and at times divergent, of M. Simon, *Verus Israël*, p. 56 and 112; "Saint Stephen and the Jerusalem Temple," *Journal of Ecclesiastical History*, II, 1951, p. 127-142 and H. J. Schoeps, *Theologie und Geschichte des Judenchristentums*, p. 233-242 and 440-456.

35. Cf. M. Goguel, *op. cit.*, p. 503-505.

36. Eusebius, *Ecclesiastical History*, 2, 23, 4-7.

37. Cf. C. H. Dodd, *The Apostolic Preaching and its Developments*, 6th ed., London, 1950, p. 7f. and "Le Kerygma apostolique dans le quatrième évangile," *Revue d'histoire et de philosophie religieuses*, 1951, p. 265f.

38. Cf. C. H. Dodd, *The Apostolic Preaching*, p. 36f. and *RHPhR*, 1951, p. 267f.

39. Cf. M. Simon, *Verus Israël*, p. 303; M. Goguel, *op. cit.*, p. 488.

40. It is Stephen, the most anti-Jewish Christian in the book of Acts, who exalts Moses most, emphasizing that Moses was the chosen one of God (Acts 7. 20), that he was powerful in eloquence and achievements (7. 22), that he was sent as a leader and a deliverer (7. 33), and that God spoke to him (7. 44).

41. K. Bornhauser, *Studien zur Apostelgeschichte*, Gütersloh, 1934, p. 58; J. Jeremias, "Untersuchungen zum Quellenproblem der Apostelgeschichte," *Zeitschrift für die neutestamentliche Wissenschaft*, 1937, p. 209f. - Viewed in this light the accounts in Acts 4 and 5 do not appear "inconsistent" in spite of anachronisms on the part of Gamaliel (cf. M. Goguel, *op. cit.*, p. 491-495).

42. M. Goguel, *op. cit.*, p. 495.

43. On this controversial topic, cf. M. Goguel, *op. cit.*, p. 499-501.

44. "Paul considered his teaching as true Judaism, as the fulfillment of the promises and assurances of authentic Judaism" (J. Klausner, *op. cit.*, p. 591).

45. The event of the year 70 did not create a completely new situation for Christianity as it did for Judaism. This is why the destruction of the Temple has left, on the whole, little trace in Christian literature of the first century and even in the whole evangelical tradition. The importance of the event is that it inspired in Christians and Jews totally different judgments of its significance, and thus it revealed to them that for a long time they had been going their separate ways. - On the subject of the destruction of the Temple and its effects, cf. H. Windisch, "Der Untergang Jerusalems im Urteil der Christen und Juden," *Theologische Tijdschrift*, 1941, p. 519-550 and particularly 542f; M. Simon, *Verus Israël*, p. 12-14 and 87-90. On the Jewish view of it, cf. H. J. Schoeps, *Die Tempelzerstörung des Jahres 70 in der jüdischen*

Religionsgeschichte, a study published first in *Coniectanea Neotestamentica,* Uppsala, VI, 1942, and reprinted in the volume *Aus frühchristlicher Zeit. Religionsgeschichtliche Untersuchungen,* Tübingen, 1950, p. 144-183.

46. This appears to be the case in Acts 7. 59 and 9. 10f, and probably also in Acts 1. 24 and 8. 22 and 24. When the Church speaks to God, it makes use of the Jewish term *despotès* [Sovereign] (Acts 4. 24).

47. On this subject, cf. among others Strack-Billerbeck, *op. cit.,* IV, p. 452-460; J. Bonsirven, *Le judaïsme palestinien au temps de Jésus-Christ. Sa théologie,* Paris, 1934, I, p. 367-368; J. Daniélou, "Christos Kyrios. Une citation des Lamentations de Jérémie dans les Testimonia," *Mélanges Jules Lebreton I, Recherches de science religieuse,* 1951, p. 338-352.

48. A verse like John 5. 18, in particular, suggests that very early the Jews made the objection to Christian christology which R. Abahu (about the year 300) expresses as follows: "The Holy One, blessed be he, says 'I am the first' (Isaiah 44. 6), for I have no father, and 'I am the last,' because I have no brother, and 'besides me there is no God,' because I have no son" (Ex. Rabba 29. 5). - It is perhaps not too bold to suggest that Paul foresaw the objection and intentionally defined the Christian position with regard to Judaism as with regard to paganism, when he writes, in I Cor. 8. 6: "For us there is but one God, the Father...and but one Lord, Jesus Christ."

49. Cf. M. J. Lagrange, *Le messianisme chez les Juifs,* Paris, 1900, p. 226-228; Strack-Billerbeck, *op. cit.,* III, p. 20; G. F. Moore, *Judaism in the First Centuries of the Christian Era. The Age of the Tannaim,* Cambridge (Mass.), 1927, II, p. 105.

50. M. Simon, *Verus Israël*, p. 304.

51. Eusebius, *Ecclesiastical History,* 2, 23, 8-11.

52. *Ibid.* 2, 23, 12-15.

53. *Ibid.* 2, 23. 2.

54. M. Simon, *Verus Israël*, p. 304.

55. E. Schuerer, *Geschichte des jüdischen Volkes im Zeitalter Jesu Christi,* 4 Aufl., Leipzig, 1901, I, p. 581.

56. Eusebius, *ibid.,* 2, 23, 1.

57. Cf. C. Spicq, "L'origine johannique de la conception du Christ-prêtre dans l'Epître aux Hébreux," *Aux sources de la tradition chrétienne. Mélanges Goguel,* Neuchâtel-Paris, 1950, p. 259-260; O Cullmann, *Les sacrements dans l'évangile johannique. La vie de Jésus et le culte de l'Eglise primitive,* Paris, 1951, p. 42-43.

58. On this interpretation which is to be preferred, cf. C. Jaeger, "A propos de deux passages du sermon sur la montagne, 2, Matthieu 5. 21 and 33," *Revue d'histoire et de philosophie religieuses,* 1938, p. 417-418; J. Héring, "Dieu, Moïse et les Anciens," *ibid.*, 1941, p. 200-203.

59. M. Simon, *Verus Israël,* p. 437.

60. M. Goguel, *op. cit.*, p. 507-508, which refers to the classic works on the subject: E. Schuerer, *op. cit.,* 4 Aufl., III, p. 108-121; J. Juster, *Les Juifs dans l'Empire romain. Leur condition juridique, économique et sociale,* Paris, 1914, I, p. 213-242.

61. The expression is Tertullian's, *Apol.* 21 (*insignissima religio certe licita*). It is not a technical term in Roman law, which speaks rather of *collegia licita* (Digest 47, 22), thereby emphasizing that the members of a sect have permission to organize themselves as a group and to come together for worship. Hence the expressions *coire licet* and *convenire licet,* which appear often in the edicts of tolerance granted to the Jews (E. Schuerer, *op. cit.,* 4 Aufl., III, p. 111, n. 40).

62. Cf. E. Schuerer, *ibid.,* p. 116f; J. Juster, *op. cit.,* I, p. 254f; V. M. Scramuzza, *The Policy of the Early Roman Emperors towards Judaism* in Jackson-Lake, *The Beginnings of Christianity, The Acts of the Apostles,* V, London, 1933, p. 277-297 and particularly 296.

63. Cf. A. von Harnack, *Die Mission und Ausbreitung des Christentums in den ersten drei Jahrhunderten,* 3. Aufl., Leipzig, 1915, I, p. 23.

64. Cf. V. M. Scramuzza, *op. cit.,* p. 293 and 296. Cf. also J. Carcopino, *Aspects mystiques de la Rome païenne,* 6ème éd., Paris, 1942, p. 49f. - Cicero (*De leg.* 2, 8) cites a law thought to go back to Numa, which prohibits the propagation of foreign religions not sanctioned by the Senate (M. Goguel, *op. cit.,* p. 517-518). Was the situation the same under the Empire? Our knowledge of the Roman laws is too limited for us to make a definite statement on this point (cf. H. J. Cadbury,

Roman Laws and the Trial of Paul, in Jackson-Lake, *op. cit.*, V, p. 299).

65. The objection is not valid that their feeling that the second coming was at hand should prevent the believers from being preoccupied with the current position of the Church in the world. First the Church must have its place in the world in order to preach the Gospel until the parousia, and secondly, it must itself continue to exist until that time so that, when the Lord appears, He will have a people over whom He can reign. Whether the parousia is imminent or not makes no difference to the situation.

66. M. Goguel, *op. cit.*, p. 515.

67. This is the theme which A. Loisy developed particularly in his two commentaries on the book of Acts and which he summarized in *La naissance du christianisme*, Paris, 1936, p. 206. - Cf. also M. Goguel, *op. cit.*, p. 515, 533 and *passim*.

68. Cf. for example V. M. Scramuzza, *op. cit.*, p. 296-297; M. Goguel, *op. cit.*, p. 544 and 546-547; M. Simon, *Verus Israël*, p. 127-128 and 146.

69. Cf. M. Goguel, *op. cit.*, p. 581, n. 4.

70. Cf. M. Goguel, *op. cit.*, p. 585f.

71. "Christian anti-Semitism is above all the expression of the resentment caused by the resistance of Israel. It goes along with the claims of the infant Church to take the place of the chosen people. Moveover it expresses the need to explain the refusal of the Jews to listen to the message which was intended for them ," M. Simon, *Verus Israël*, p. 245. Cf. also p. 274: "The distorted picture which the gospels present of the Pharisees expresses, at a time when the legal profession is responsible for the failure of the mission in Israel, the disappointment and resentment of infant Christianity."

72. M. Goguel, *Revue d'histoire et de philosophie religieuses*, 1950, p. 241, Cf. also *La naissance du christianisme*, p. 474f, *passim*.

The Christian Meaning of Death[1]

In his first epistle to the Corinthians, in chapter 15, Saint Paul sketches in broad outline the history of salvation. He recalls its beginning: the fall of Adam, by which death came upon all men; the central part of the story: the resurrection of Christ, the second Adam, the second beginning for mankind, by which life is given to all who believe; finally the end: the establishment of the kingdom of God by the destruction of all evil powers. And the Apostle concludes: "the final enemy conquered is death."

The whole of Christian teaching about life and death is contained in this concise statement. According to the New Testament death is not a natural phenomenon; it is not the normal end of human existence; it is not by itself a release. It is the ultimate expression of evil; it is evil which has become a demonic force and which extends its power over all divine creation, over mankind and over the whole world. It is, in a word, that which should not exist and which will not exist for ever.

This power will be destroyed. The proof of this is that it has already been conquered. The resurrection of Jesus Christ is the first decisive victory of divine life over death. Already the quickening effects of the victory of Christ are being felt on the mystical level, by henceforth giving life to the believers. On the final day this victory will be complete on the physical level by the resurrection of the believers, the restoration of the world and the destruction of death.

According to Christianity, the dominant factor is the living Christ; it is not death. For Christ is more powerful than death; He is "longer" than death; for He is eternal and death is temporary.

It is within this perspective that we intend to look at the two aspects of the problem in these two studies: death is the enemy; but this enemy has already been conquered.

Since the time of Origen, theologians have been accustomed to distinguish between three different meanings of the word: death.

1. Physical death, or the state in which biological life no longer exists. It is the most common meaning and needs no explanation.

2. Spiritual death, or the state in which spiritual life and particularly Christian life no longer exists. This is the condition of mankind apart from Christ.

3. Mystical death, that is the participation in the divine life offered by Christ, even in this present life and in spite of physical death which is always at hand. This is the state of the believers, as Saint Paul describes it: "You have already died, and your life is hid with Christ in God" (Col. 3. 3). Mystical death is by definition the complete antithesis of spiritual death. Mystical death is the victory over physical death since it is "life hid with Christ in God," life which is hidden now, but which will be revealed at the time of the resurrection of the believers. We shall return to this in our second study.

What must be emphasized now is this: this mystical death and resurrection - two parts of the same event - is the only concept of life after death which is known to Christianity. There is no eternal life apart from the life given to the world by Christ. That must be our starting-point if we are to understand the Christian meaning of death.

I

When we read the Holy Scripture we cannot help noticing that it always presents immortality as a gift of God in Jesus Christ. This contradicts our tendency to consider the immortality of the soul as a characteristic which belongs to it by nature. In fact there are two different problems here, or, more precisely, two different ways of looking at man, life and death.

The idea of immortality of the soul developed particularly in Hellenic mysticism and philosophy. It is bound up with a dualist conception of man and the world. According to this idea a superior world, which is divine and unsubstantial, rules over an inferior, material world. Man who is matter and spirit, body and soul, has a place in both worlds. A purely spiritual essence, the human soul belongs to the superior world; it is, in principle, immortal. Through necessity, or through a fall, temporarily it enters a body. But death comes as a deliverance; through it the soul, set free from the prison of the body, returns to the heavenly regions.

The New Testament makes not the slightest reference to this philosophical explanation, which passed from the Greeks into modern deism and through deism into certain degenerate forms of Christianity. But the New Testament ignores this idea. In the few passages where it mentions immortality or incorruptability,[2] it applies the term to God, "who alone possesses immortality,"[3] or to the salvation brought by Jesus Christ, who "has brought life and immortality to light through the Gospel."[4] If the human soul were immortal by nature, the work of Christ, which is to bring life to the world, would lose its reason for existence.

The objection will be made that the texts quoted are all from Saint Paul and that the theology of Paul is not the Gospel of Jesus, that Jesus sends His "straight and simple" message to the human soul, of which He affirms the absolute value and therefore the immortality.

This is where serious misunderstandings arise. Undoubtedly the word "soul" appears frequently in the gospels and in the New Testament as a whole. But the question is whether the word has the same meaning in the New Testament as it has in Greek thought. Obviously not.

In the gospels, the word *psychè*, soul, means the breath of life which inspires a human being, and, by extension: the living being, existence, life. This is the meaning which fits the words of Jesus:

> Whoever would save his life (*psyche*) will lose it; and whoever loses his life for my sake and the gospel's will save it. or what does it profit a man, to gain the whole world and forfeit his life? For what can a man give in return for his life? For whoever is ashamed of me and of my words in this adulterous and sinful generation, of him will the Son of man also be ashamed, when he comes in the glory of his Father with the holy angels.[5]

It is not a question here of the "soul" as an indestructible and very precious part of the human being. Jesus wants to justify the two-fold demand, negative and positive, made of those who want to follow Him: to abnegate one's self and to bear one's cross, in other words: to lose one's life in the eyes of the world, but to save it in the eyes of Jesus and the Gospel. To establish a relationship between the renunciation He demands and the promise which He brings, Jesus uses the double meaning of the word "life" which represents the principle of existence on this earth and also the prospect of salvation offered to those who believe in Him.

The one who, by denying Jesus "saves his life" and perhaps escapes persecution and martyrdom, will in reality, "lose his life" in the deeper sense of the term, because he will be robbed of true life, which is the life to come. Conversely, the one who "loses his life," either in the sense in which the world understands this expression, or in the proper sense of accepting death for the sake of the Gospel, will truly "save his life" because he will inherit the life of the world which is to come.

The words of Jesus certainly imply an antithesis. But it is not between a perishable body and an immortal soul, it is between two "lives," each of which has its own scale of values; this present life and the life to come, or salvation. It is not a matter of "the infinite worth of the human soul" as has been suggested but of the infinite worth of the salvation which Jesus brings to men. In order to "save one's life," to receive salvation and the life to come, man has to do nothing but believe in Jesus, to give nothing but obedience to Jesus. In short, man has no possibility of surviving unless he links himself, here and now, to "the One who speaks of eternal life," the one who is "the resurrection and the life." These concise expressions from the gospel of John state in precise terms the more elaborate explanations given in the first three gospels.

It is in the same sense that we must understand the warning given by Jesus: "Do not fear those who kill the body but cannot kill the soul; rather fear him who can destroy both soul and body in hell."[6] Here again there is not a contrast between a perishable body and a soul which lives for ever, but between what men can do: kill another man and nothing else, and what God can do: destroy the "soul" (or "life") as well as the body; which means: to leave in a state of death those whom the Son will deny before His Father in heaven, because they have denied Him before men.[7]

We could cite many more examples. We cannot avoid the conclusion that always and everywhere in the New Testament, the life to come depends on belief in the person of Jesus Christ.

Christian theology does not add to the affirmation of the immortality of the soul any proof or guarantee. Nor is the idea of the immortality of the soul an expression of Christian faith in the resurrection of the believers which is deemed more scholarly or more spiritual. The idea of the immortality of the soul, as we have seen, is linked to a certain concept of the world and of man: a divine world thought to be immaterial, and distinct from the world of matter which is identified with evil; and a man made up of earthly matter, the body, and of an immortal soul, death being but the event and the time when each of these two elements finds its autonomy.

II

The biblical doctrine of God and of man is quite different. According to Scripture, God is the creator of the whole universe. There is no cosmic dualism at the beginning of the world. God has created everything, including matter and this is why, according to biblical thought, evil is elsewhere than in matter, as we shall see shortly. God is the creator and the sole creator of everything which exists. Because God is love and because the attribute of love is to desire something on which its affection can be bestowed, God creates mankind to respond to His love and reflect His glory.

According to Scripture, man created by God is also made up of two elements, the body or the flesh on one hand, and on the other, the vital spirit, the soul. But man, according to biblical thought, is a unity, in spite of the two elements which combine to make a living being. In the totality of his physical and psychological being, man is the creature of God. The book of Genesis declares that everything which makes a man: the life which moves him, and the material flesh and blood in which he exists, come from God. "The Lord God formed man of dust from the ground, and breathed into his nostrils the breath of life; and man became a living being." (Gen. 2. 7). The object of this early account is to emphasize that a human being, body and soul, is in entirety a creation of God, destined to live on the earth which God has prepared for it. The writer of the Book of Wisdom - supposedly Solomon - as he reflects on the work of creation and the purpose of it, writes: "God created all things that they might have being," which is a way of emphasizing that the prospect of death does not enter into the work of creation. In other words, death does not come from God; it comes from elsewhere.

Mankind, created by God for His glory, has been created free, so that it can freely worship and obey God. In His almighty power God could have created people who would have been forced to worship and obey Him; but that would have been like worshipping Himself, and that kind of worship would have added nothing to His glory. Worship and love are meaningless and worthless unless they are freely given.

It is the evil use man has made of his freedom which brought death into the divine creation where it had no place originally. In other words, it is not because of his nature that man does not live for ever; if he dies, it is not because he is made of matter, it is because he has disobeyed.

When Saint Paul writes to the Romans: "The wages of sin is death" (Rom. 6. 23), he recalls a commonplace of biblical thought, already expressed in the sentence pronounced on the first man and the first sinner: "You shall die" (Gen. 2. 17).

But God only pronounces a sentence of death by virtue of His holiness and His justice. It is not God the creator who is the one behind the power which kills. In so far as man himself is not responsible for his misfortune, it is "an enemy who has done that," an inimical power anxious to introduce disorder and destruction into the Creator's good work.

Death appears here in its true colors. It does not appear as a natural phenomenon - on the contrary it is the very denial of creation, that is to say of nature itself. Nor does it appear as the normal end of human existence - once again, "God created all things that they might have being," - nor as the door which must be entered to have access to a higher form of life. As man is entirely a creation of God, death overtakes the whole man, body and soul. Death is the breaking of the life-line between the creature and his creator; it is not only physical - the end of existence - it is also spiritual: it is the loss of divine love.

According to Scripture, if God and man are separated, it is not because God is infinite and man is finite, or because God is insubstantial and man is material; it is because God is holy and man is a sinner; it is because God is a living God and man is reaping the wages of sin, which is death.

To bring an end to death and to give back life to the creation - in other words, to make "life after death" possible - man must be set free not from matter but from sin. Therefore, first of all, sin must be expiated and forgiven - this is a negative condition - and then - the positive condition - the living God must intervene a second time to give back life to His creation, which He has recreated, body and soul, by a supreme action comparable only to that of creation itself. In short, sin must be expiated and there must be a second creation, which is the resurrection.

This is why, according to biblical thought, the possibility of life after death does not depend on a physical and mechanical event, as in Greek thought, but on God's accomplishment of a redemptive work.

III

We have two proofs in Scripture that redemption and the future life are organically linked in this way; a negative proof, so to speak, in the Old Testament, and a positive proof in the New Testament.

Let us look first at the negative proof. The old covenant is the covenant of the promise. When speaking of the time before the coming of Christ, Saint John writes: "The Spirit was not yet" because Christ had not yet been glorified (John 7. 39). This statement does not mean that God had been missing from the history of salvation between the fall and the incarnation, nor that the prophets He raised up did not speak with the help of His Spirit. John's words mean that the Spirit only revealed itself in the world as a power for regeneration and new life after the time when the redemptive work was made real in Christ. The old covenant existed only with the hope and in the expectancy of this regeneration.

This explains a fact which is at first glance disconcerting. It is clear that the Old Testament is poorer in its hopes for the future life than most of the religious traditions of mankind. This is surprising, even shocking, but such a reaction is quite wrong. It is not for want of faith or for lack of imagination that Israelite thought has not developed the theme of life after death. It is because it has taken seriously the holiness of God and the wretchedness of man. If, for the Greeks, man is really a fallen god who remembers the heavens and returns there almost automatically, for the Israelites, God alone is God, the living God, and man is a sinful creature, condemned to death, unless redemption intervenes. Man's punishment can be to some extent postponed through God's mercy; but he still moves inexorably towards a grave in which he will be entombed. Because the whole man is God's creation, death overtakes the whole being, body and soul. These statements may seem somewhat theoretical but they will become clearer if we refer to several passages in the Old Testament.

Let us look first of all at one of the best known passages, the famous words in Ecclesiastes: "The dust returns to the earth, as it was, and the spirit returns of God who gave it" (12. 7). The body was made of dust and to dust it returns. Life was given by a breath of the spirit of God and when this spirit is removed by its source, life disappears. The spirit only belongs to man in so far as it is given to him; for the spirit of man is in reality the spirit of God. The spirit and the dust from which the body was made have both been borrowed. "Dust was of the earth before it became the body of man, and it is not said of the spirit that God created it but only that He gave it. It will not be surprising then that one day, when the dust returns to the earth, which it was before, the spirit returns to God who gave it, or more precisely, lent it."[8] In short, life is not the inamissible property of man; life belongs only to God. When a man dies, not only does he lose his body, but at the same time he loses what is commonly called his soul or his spirit. He gives back the soul, he gives back the spirit to the God who had lent it for the time of man's earthly existence. The one who has died no longer lives as a person either in this world or in another world. He has utterly ceased to exist. If anything of him continues to exist it can only be an impression, a shadow without form and substance.

This is why, according to the Old Testament, the abode of the dead (Sheol) is a place of darkness, silence and oblivion. "For he who is joined with the living has hope," we read in Ecclesiastes, "for the living dog is better than a dead lion. For the living know that they will die, but the dead know nothing, and they have no more reward, for the memory of them is lost. Their love and their hate and their envy have already perished, and they have no more, for ever, any share in all that is done under the sun" (9. 4-6).

Ecclesiastes is not the lone cry of a sceptic. It is the common belief of Israel that the dead are forgotten not only by men but by God Himself. If the lot of the dead is tragic, it is not because they are dead, it is rather because by ceasing to live, they have no share in God's benefits in the land of the living. The dead are for ever separated from God. Undoubtedly the Eternal Being reigns over the abode of the dead as He reigns over the whole universe.[10] But the dead can no longer enter into communion with Him nor receive His blessings; they can no longer praise Him. To express the distress of believers thus deprived of God's love, the Old Testament has elements which would be sought in vain in Greek literature:

> For Sheol cannot thank thee,
>   death cannot praise thee,
>   those who go down to the pit
>   cannot hope for thy faithfulness.
> The living, the living, he thanks thee,
>   as I do this day.[11]
> I am like one forsaken among the dead,
>   like the slain that lie in the grave,
>   like those whom thou dost remember no more,
>   for they are cut off from thy hand...
> Dost thou work wonders for the dead?
>   Do the shades rise up to praise thee?
> Is thy steadfast love declared in the grave,
>   or thy faithfulness in Abaddon?
> Are thy wonders known in the darkness,
>   of thy saving help in the land of forgetfulness?[12]

This woeful concept of life after death is common to the Israelites throughout the whole period covered by the Old Testament. It is the concept of the prophets, who reveal no prospect of life to come in the promises or threats they address to the people to urge them to serve the Eternal One. When they describe future blessings, they always place them within the limits of this earthly life. They do not proclaim that in another world the righteous will be rewarded for their belief, but that they will be divinely blessed in this world. This is eloquently proved by two examples. First the ever present affirmation that a longer life under the sun is the greatest reward that God can bestow: to die "full of days" is the sign of divine blessing, since the present existence is the absolute limit of possible happiness. The second is that the Israelite puts his hopes for the future in his descendants and not in his own survival; it is through his sons that he will continue to live. Many sons are also one of the great blessings. This explains institutions like the law of levirate, which allowed a dead man to have descendants and thus survive in some way, and also the harsh curses which were heaped on a barren woman.

And the hope of the resurrection? This hope only appeared quite late in Judaism, barely two centuries before the Christian era. In the Old Testament, only the book of Daniel (c. 165) speaks unequivocally of the resurrection of the dead. This hope remained a more or less optional opinion; it did not become an article of faith to which one had to subscribe on pain of being condemned as a heretic. The well-known anathema in the Talmud against those who denied the resurrection is not earlier than the third century A.D. At the time of the New Testament the Sadducees did not believe in the resurrection of the dead, and they were not regarded as unorthodox; on the contrary, they held firmly to the single dogma of Judaism: God is revealed in the Law, and they were opposed to all new ideas. There was no definitive text in the Law to remove the curse written into the Law: "You shall die." No event had yet taken place to break the hereditary line of death.

The resurrection of the dead remained a very vague hope without any real connection to the faith. We have proof of this in the well-known passage in the gospel of John which recounts the conversation between Martha and Jesus, after the death of Lazarus. Martha, the Jewess, says to Jesus - and her words barely conceal the despair of a too-distant hope: "I know that my brother will rise again on the last day." And Jesus says to her: "I am the Resurrection and the Life," which means: in me eternal life and the resurrection are already present realities.

IV

We now reach what we called a short time back the positive proof that, according to Christianity, redemption and the future life are organically linked to each other. The intervention of Jesus Christ is the new fact which entirely changes the destiny of man.

"Now," writes Saint Paul to the Corinthians - and by "now" he means that the time of the promise has come to an end and the time of salvation has begun - "now Christ has been raised from the dead, the first fruits of those who have fallen asleep. For as by a man came death, by a man has come also the resurrection of the dead. For as in Adam all die, so also in Christ shall all be made alive" (I Cor. 15. 20-22).

In other words, instead of the interdependence of sin and death which have ruled since the beginning of mankind, the risen Christ substitutes an interdependence of redemption and life; and He does this by virtue of what He is. What He is: a new beginning for mankind, a being untouched by the sin of the race. The New Testament is unanimous in its affirmation that the life of Jesus was without sin, and this testimony is of considerable theological importance. It is by His life without sin that Jesus Christ breaks the line: law - sin - death. He is the only being who has lived according to the law of God and has not sinned, therefore He has nothing to do with the wages of sin which is death. His death has an entirely different meaning from the death of man. His death is an expiatory death, which once and for all pays the wages of sin for all men; at the same time His death is a substitutive death, that is to say He accepts the death which should strike down all men. In short, he dies in order to give life to those who, because they are united to Him by faith, becoming part of His body, are, as Saint Paul says, "crucified with Him" and "raised with Him" and consequently inherit eternal life with Him. God Himself affirms that he recognizes this expiatory and substitutionary death of Christ by raising Him from among the dead and making Him "the first-born of the dead," that is to say the first of a new humanity which no longer lives according to the flesh but according to the Spirit.

Mankind before Christ - and without Christ - is heading for the grave, but the new race of men, linked to Christ through faith, receives the revivifying effects of the Spirit of regeneration and resurrection.

We say advisedly that the Spirit of Christ is at work to regenerate and resuscitate the believers. The reconstruction of mankind by the Spirit comes in two stages. At the moment, the Spirit regenerates those who believe in Christ and starts them off again "in newness of life." For the present this action of the Spirit is only partial, since the believer, the man "in Christ," remains a man "in the flesh," and since the man who is made by Christ "a citizen of heaven" is still "in the world." But this action is none the less real. In Paul's view baptism, which transmits the Spirit, is a death and resurrection with Christ,[13] so that the Spirit creates a new man. John says, in the same vein, that baptism by water and the Spirit makes a creature "born of the flesh" a creature "born of God."[14] This new-born creature of the Spirit must grow and become a child and then a man. As he believes in Jesus he must "dwell" in Him. The present incorporation into Christ makes a new point of departure. "If anyone is in Christ, he is a new creature;"[15] he has passed out of death into life.[16]

We said above that this regeneration is only partial at this time. It is impeded, even endangered, by the influence exerted by "the flesh" or "the world" to keep or to regain the believer. For the appearance of the powers of the Spirit within a man does not break the connections between him and the world in which he lives. The gift of the Spirit does not materially change the Christian. Although saved by faith in Christ, the believer remains tied to his natural environment: the present world, only suitable for this present existence and tainted by sin; in a word, he is still in a "body of death."[17] He is only saved by "hope."[18] He awaits the "redemption of the body."[19] But he awaits it in faith and hope, because the new birth and the gift of the Spirit qualify him to enter through resurrection into the world to come, when this present world disappears, and consequently to be truly saved. "If the Spirit of Him who raised up Jesus from the dead is dwelling in you, He who raised up Christ from the dead will give life also to your mortal bodies through His Spirit dwelling in you,"[20] writes Saint Paul, specifically emphasizing that the resurrection is the final end of the regeneration begun in this world. John expresses the same idea, keeping the promises of resurrection only for those who believe in Christ now: "'Everyone who believes in me,' says Jesus, 'I will raise him to life on the last day.'"[21]

Thus the resurrection appears as the second and final state in this reconstruction of mankind effected by the Spirit. At that time, the believers will be in full possession of the salvation of which they have only had "tokens" in this present world. Regenerated throughout, they will live in a form suitable for the new world, in a bodily form which defies all description and which Saint Paul calls "the spiritual body" as opposed to the present physical body: "the body is sown perishable, and it rises imperishable; it is sown in dishonour, it rises in glory; it is sown in weakness, it rises in power; it is sown an animal body, it is raised a spiritual body."[22]

The New Testament idea of the resurrection is the accomplishment, on the last day, of the work of the Spirit started among the believers in this world. It is an act which, at the dawn of the new world, unites with Christ those who in this present world, and despite all the tribulations of flesh and blood, were already His followers, "waiting for a Saviour, the Lord Jesus Christ, who...will transform this body of our humiliation until it resembles the body of His glory."[23] There is no doubt that those who "stand firm in the Lord"[24] in this expectation will still pass through death. But for them death will have a completely different meaning from the one it had for mankind before the resurrection of Christ and which it still has for the unbelievers. For the believers, death is no longer a curse and a punishment; it is the necessary prologue to resurrection; it is, in the words of Father Daniélou, "a crisis in our growth."

Now we must describe this "crisis in growth" and show that the believer should look at death and at his own death in this perspective of life. This we shall do in our second lecture.

NOTES

1. *L'homme face à la mort*, Delachaux & Niestlé, Neuchâtel-Paris, 1952, p. 155-169.

2. Cf. I Cor. 15. 33f; I Tim. 6. 16; I Cor. 15. 42; II Tim. 1. 10; Rom 2. 7.

3. I Tim. 6. 16.

4. II Tim. 1. 10.

5. Mark 8. 35-38; cf. Matt. 16. 25-27; Luke 9. 24-26.

6. Matt. 10. 28. We should note that the parallel passage in Luke 12. 4-9 ("Do not fear those who kill the body and after that have no more that they can do...fear him who, after he has killed, has power to cast into hell") has dropped the term *psychè* while keeping the sense of the passage. If the antithesis *body* and *soul* (in the Hellenic sense) was the motif of this passage it would also appear in Luke.

7. Matt. 10. 32-33.

8. E. Podechard, *L'Ecclésiaste*, Paris, 1912, p. 470-471. - In this well-known passage it is not a matter of the individual soul and even less of its survival.

9. Cf. Ps. 31. 12; 41. 6 etc.

10. Ps. 139. 8; Job 26. 5-6.

11. Isaiah 38. 18-19.

12. Ps. 88. 5, 10-12.

13. Cf. Rom. 6. 3-11.

14. Cf. John 3. 3-7.

15. II Cor. 5. 17.

16. John 5. 24; I John 3. 14.

17. Rom. 7. 24.

18. Rom. 8. 24.

19. Rom. 8. 23.

20. Rom. 8. 11.

21. John 6. 39, 40, 44.

22. I Cor. 15. 42-44.

23. Phil. 3. 21.

24. Phil. 4. 1.

The Christian Victory over Death[1]

In our preceding lecture we concerned ourselves with the specific question of the meaning of death, in the light of the norms of Christianity, the texts of Scripture. We saw that according to Christianity death is not a natural phenomenon; it is not the normal end of human existence. May is a creature of God and, as such, he is destined to live, and to live for ever, in the company of his Father in heaven, and not return to the dust from whence he came.

That no human being escapes death, in spite of the fact that he is destined by God for life, is the simplest and most obvious proof that man is not in a normal situation. This is expressed by Scripture when it says that man is a sinner: a being oriented naturally towards evil and who marches inexorably towards death, since death is the wages of sin, as Saint Paul reminds us.

If man is separated from God and cannot share in the life divine, it is because he is a sinner and God is holy. Eternal life can only be assured for mankind if the obstacle of sin is removed. This obstacle can only be removed if two conditions are fulfilled: the first is an objective condition - God Himself must effect a redemption. The believers maintain that God has done this through the earthly life, the death and the resurrection of Jesus Christ. But this divine fulfillment of one condition is not enough for man to achieve salvation. Nobody ever has been or ever will be saved automatically, without any decision on his own part. To the objective condition already fulfilled by God, must be added a subjective, personal condition which is as follows: through an act of my own free will, my own mind and my own heart, I believe in the salvation that God has realized in Jesus Christ, I believe that it is for me too that Jesus Christ died and rose again and that I myself died with Christ and rose with Him. The fulfillment of this condition will make the work of redemption real for me; it will be my redemption and my salvation; living in this way the life of Christ, I will pass victoriously through death; Christ's victory over the final Enemy will be my victory.

So it appears quite clear that, according to Christianity, life after death is only possible for those who join themselves to Jesus Christ in faith and who henceforth share His destiny. Life after death is not automatic. According to the Gospel the human soul is not by nature immortal; future life is promised only to those who believe in Christ.

I recalled these fundamental points of Christian doctrine in my previous lecture. I have been told that they provoked not strictly speaking a disagreement, but surprise and a desire for clarification, in the minds of some listeners. The two following questions, in particular, have been asked:

1. The affirmation of the immortality of the soul and belief in the resurrection, are these really two truths in opposition to each other?
2. What does "to believe" mean? Is it to agree to the dogmatic statements of the Church about Jesus? Is it not, more simply, to put Christian love into practice, to live the life which Jesus lived, following His example?

Before proceeding further I should like to answer these two questions and, if possible, remove any misunderstandings. Also it is by taking note of the concerns of our listeners that we shall most easily get to the heart of the subject we must deal with this evening.

I

Our culture goes back to the Greeks, and the Greek philosophers tended to consider the immortality of the soul as a characteristic which belonged to it by nature. They affirmed that man was made up of matter - his body - which was by definition perishable, or at least unsuited to the higher life, and of an insubstantial element, the soul, by definition immortal. But this is nothing more than a metaphysical statement, as has often been pointed out. The clearest and most succinct demonstration of this was made by the philosopher Henri Bergson, in some noteworthy passages in his book, *Les deux sources de la morale et de la religion.*[2] He writes:

> It is possible, with Plato, to lay down *a priori* a definition of the soul as a thing incapable of decomposition because it is simple, incorruptible because it is indivisible, immortal by virtue of its essence. This leads, by a process of deduction, to the idea of souls falling into Time, and thence to that of a return into Eternity. But what is to be the answer to those who deny the existence of the soul thus defined? And how could the problems touching a real soul, its real origin, its real fate, be resolved in accordance with reality, or even posited in terms of reality, when one has merely been speculating upon a possibly baseless conception of the soul, or, at the very best, defining conventionally the meaning of the word which society has inscribed on a slice of reality set apart for the convenience of conversation? The affirmation remains as sterile as the definition was arbitrary. The Platonic conception has not helped our knowledge of the soul by a single step, for all that it has been meditated upon for two thousand years. It was as complete and final as that of the triangle, and for the same reasons. How can we help seeing, however, that, if there really is a problem of the soul, it must be posited in

> terms of experience, and in terms of experience it must be progressively, and always partially, solved?
>
> Society doubtless follows certain suggestions of inner experience when it talks of the soul; but it has made up this work, like all others, for its own convenience. It has applied it to something distinct from the body. The more radical the distinction, the better the word answers its purpose: now it cannot be more radical than when the qualities of the soul are taken to be purely and simply the negations of those of matter. Such is the idea that the philosopher has received only too often, ready made, from society through language. It appears to represent the acme of spirituality, just because it goes to the very end of something. But this something is only negation.

We should like to pick out one particular sentence from this passage: "How can we help seeing...if there is a problem of the soul, it must be posited in terms of experience."

It is precisely in these terms that Christianity poses and solves the problem of man and his eternal destiny. The Gospel at the beginning does not define it arbitrarily. It establishes between Christ, who is the Living One, and man who is condemned to death, bonds of personal love and fellowship, by virtue of which the life of Christ is communicated to those who are joined to Him in faith. For a man to have knowledge of victory over death he must believe in Jesus Christ and not speculate about the nature of the human soul.

So we reach the second of our two preliminary questions: what is Christian faith?

To believe means to accept as true the testimony to Jesus Christ given by the believers in the New Testament.
This testimony, in outline, can be presented as follows. In order to save mankind, which is unable of itself to escape from the influence of sin and from the power of death, God sends His Son into the world. Jesus of Nazareth appears unique

in the midst of mortal men. He is truly man and yet He has no part of the sin of man; so He does not deserve to die like all the sons of Adam. He indicates a new beginning of the history of man; He is the second Adam, who leads all the believers towards life. He dies on the cross, but His death is an expiation and a substitution. He does not have to pay the wages of a sin He has not committed; therefore He pays on behalf of others and instead of them. God accepts this sacrifice. He proves it by raising Him up from among the dead. The living Christ is henceforth a power of new life for all men who understand the meaning of His death and His resurrection. This meaning is as follows: Christ has taken the sin of men upon Himself; therefore they are freed from it. Freed from their sin, they are at the same time freed from the sentence of death which sin pronounced on them. In a word they have died with Christ and have risen with Him; henceforth they live a new life with Him. Christ gives them a part in His own destiny. This is why He is "the only name under heaven given among men by which we must be saved" (Acts 4. 12). To believe is to admit that this firm bond exists between Christ and His believers and that it is strong and effective. In Christ the believers pass from death to life. They now live by the Spirit - that is by the power of God which gives life to Christ and now gives life to them - a life of communion with Christ which nothing can cut short or destroy.

But I can see an objection looming up. You will say to me: what you are telling us are the ideas inspired in the Church by the death and resurrection of Christ; it is the theology of Saint Paul, Saint John, the writer of the epistle to the Hebrews. It is a development - and some will say a regrettable development - of the simple Gospel of Jesus, illustrated by His parables which are so easy to understand and which speak directly to the human heart, like the parable of the prodigal son. Let us take our inspiration simply from this perfect Gospel, and let us leave the theologians to their theological subtleties.

It is a weak objection. The contrast one tries to make between the "simple Gospel" of Jesus and the "theology of blood" formulated by the Apostles, does not in fact exist. Look at the gospels. From the very first page you will come up against the mystery of the person of Jesus. Jesus comes to Galilee and begins to preach: "Repent, and believe in the Gospel," which means: stop being ordinary men living for your own selfish ends and accept as being true for you the good message of salvation which I bring. This good message, this Gospel, consists of the words: "Come unto me!" This means: "you are saved or you are lost according to whether you answer 'yes' or 'no' to the question I put to you, to the question that I myself am for you, as I am present in your midst." And the answer is already 'no', that is you lose salvation, if you do not answer. For Jesus speaks with divine authority. Moses in earlier times handed over God's commandments, but Jesus knows God's will better than Moses, and he says: "You have heard that it was said...but I say to you..." (Matt. 5. 21-22).

In truth the One who speaks in this way is a living mystery, and every reader of the Gospel is brought up short by the question on the lips and in the minds of the disciples after Jesus had stilled the tempest which threatened them: "Who then is this, that even wind and sea obey him?" (Mark 4. 41). The answer is to be found on the last page of the gospels: "He is risen, he is alive, he is the Lord." What is called the theology of the Apostles is only the commentary on this answer.

But what about the parable of the prodigal son? The prodigal son is one simple. particular case. For all men, alas, are not prodigal sons, that is, men who, in the very depths of their wretchedness, can still look at themselves and confess: "I have sinned against heaven, against God," and can find the way back to the Father's house. Mankind, alas, is made up of more elder sons than prodigal sons; there are more men as incapable of doing good as of admitting that they are doing wrong, and of offering to the Father the honor due to Him. In the parable, the problem of the elder son is not solved, because the solution is elsewhere. It is in the cross silhouetted on the horizon, when Jesus reveals the condition necessary for the kingdom of God to come, and at the same time shows the final reason for His mission as He says: "The Son of man came to give his life as a ransom for many" (Mark 10. 45).

But what is the significance of the expression "the Son of man" used by Jesus to describe Himself, in preference to the term "Messiah" which is more common but loaded with political expectation.[9] "The Son of man" is not the antitheses of "the Son of God" and is not used in conjunction with the latter to affirm that Jesus was both perfectly human and perfectly divine. On the contrary, "the Son of man" is a greater attribute than "Son of God" and also more specific. All men are called to become the sons of their Father in heaven, through redemption. There is only one "Son of man" - just as there is only one God - and by this title the Jewish writers from the time of the second century before Christ mean that heavenly being who lives with God and who will come into history as the Savior of the human race. The Son of man is the heavenly man who will wipe out the mistake made by the first earthly man, and all its consequences. He is the one whom Saint Paul calls by the quite unequivocal name of "the second Adam." By describing Himself as "the Son of man", by calling men to come to Him, by declaring that He dies to save them and that His death is not the end of His ministry of redemption, Jesus Himself already proclaims the Gospel which the Apostles will preach. There is only one Gospel; there are not two. This is the only one: the Gospel which the Apostles preach, after the resurrection of Jesus takes place as an act of God of which they are witnesses, sheds definitive light on the mystery of the person of Jesus and gives His message its integral resonance.

In short, the Gospel is a person - Jesus Christ, who came into the world, who was crucified, who died, who rose again, who is alive and who gives divine life to His followers. To believe is to give complete adherence to this testimony, an adherence which can never be merely verbal. One adheres verbally to a doctrine; but Christianity is a person before it is a doctrine. To confess the Gospel witness is to agree to live with Jesus in personal communion and thereby die with Him, be raised with Him and live eternally with Him.

II

Believers are those who live in communion with Christ and share His destiny. This means they die with Christ and are raised with Him. Their real death has already taken place in the past, when Christ died for them and instead of them on the cross. Their real life has already started with Christ's resurrection. In short, they have already passed from death to life. With Christ they have already conquered death. Death, in the Christian sense of the word, means separation from God, the loss of divine love. Life, in the Christian sense of the word, means communion with God through the Lord Jesus Christ. In these circumstances, to believe is to die in order to start living the real life of eternity.

This verification of faith finds its physical expression in baptism. Christian baptism is the outward and visible sign of the death of the believer with Christ and of his new life with Him. This is what Saint Paul explains, when he writes to the Romans:

> Do you not know that all of us who have been baptized into Christ Jesus were baptized into his death? We were buried therefore with him by baptism into death, so that as Christ was raised from the dead by the glory of the Father, we too might walk in newness of life. For if we have been united with him in a death like his, we shall certainly be united with him in a resurrection like his. We know that our old self was crucified with him so that the sinful body might be destroyed... But if we have died with Ch ist, we believe t at we shall also live with him. For we know that Christ being raised from the dead will never die again; death no longer has dominion over him. The death he died he died to sin, once for all, but the life he lives he lives to God. So you also must consider yourselves dead to sin and alive to God in Christ Jesus. (Rom. 6. 3-11)

This passage is clear enough and well enough known that there is no need of lengthy explanations. We should like to emphasize just two points. First this: death, in so far as it is the wages of sin, has already been suffered by the believer, at the time of his baptism, which refers to Christ's death on the cross and which takes its efficacy from that: the baptized believer therefore lives with the risen Christ. Secondly, take note that the Apostles' explanation ends with an exhortation. The work of death and resurrection effected by baptism on the mystical level of union with the living Christ, must be realized on the practical level in the new life of the believer from this time forward. Already dead in principle, he must now die in fact; living with Christ in principle, he must make it abundantly clear that he is living a new life by walking, as Saint Paul says, "in obedience to the faith." In other words, the believer puts an end to the former man within him, by putting him to death day after day, and he searches out everything which can bring him closer to Christ and keep him in communion with Him. The Christian life thus appears as a life of death and resurrection, of putting to death and bringing to life, the death of sin and everything which might turn the believer away from Christ, and new life - an ever more real and closer communion with the person of Christ.

This Christian life is described by Saint Paul in his epistle to the Colossians in these terms:

> Put to death therefore what is earthly in you: immorality, impunity, passion, evil desire, and covetousness, which is idolatry. (Col. 3. 5)

That is the life of the Christian, in so far as it is a daily putting to death of the former man, who, in principle, died at the time of baptism. There is also the life of the Christian, in so far as it is a daily participation in the life of Christ. Saint Paul describes this too, in the same epistle to the Colossians:

> You have been raised with Christ; so seek the things that are above, where Christ is, seated at the right hand of God. Set your minds on things that are above, not on things that are on earth. For you have died, and your life is hid with Christ in God. (Col. 3. 1-3)

These words would strike us more forcibly if familiarity with them did not hide their impact. There is no description more exact or more astonishing in its brevity of the present state of the Christian. His new life is real, yet it does not appear in its full reality. The believer lives in communion with Christ yet remains prone to all the miseries of flesh and blood. Now he only has tokens of redemption; he is not yet glorified with Christ; he is still subject to illness, old age and physical death. His life is hidden. This hidden life of the believers, which will be made clear one day, appears like a water-mark on a paper held up to a window, when the light of Christ scatters the darkness of this world. Christ reveals His presence and His power in two ways: through the eucharist and by miracles.

The Church comes together in the name of Christ when it comes together for worship. It enters into communion with the Lord through prayer and through the preaching and exposition of the word. This communion takes on a very concrete form when the believers repeat the ritual of the last meal Jesus took with His disciples, and when, breaking the bread and drinking the cup, they "proclaim the Lord's death until he comes" (I Cor. 11. 26). The death of Christ, proclaimed by the celebration of the eucharist, is the death of one who is now alive, since the believers live in the expectation of His coming in person. The eucharist is a reminder that Christ was present in their midst at the time of the incarnation; it expresses the believers' conviction that Christ will be in their midst when His kingdom comes. The eucharist is the means by which Christ is present now among His believers, by the visible signs of His person which He Himself chose: the bread and the wine. He is there, and it is He who, through the officiating minister, gives the elements of eternal life to His believers.

Nobody has understood the mystery of the eucharist more profoundly than John, nor has anyone been able to express better than John that the life of Christ is handed on to the believers when they receive, as if from the very hand of their Lord, this lowly piece of bread, which remains bread, just as the paper which bears the Holy Scripture is the same as that of the daily newspaper. But, just as the paper bears the effective word of God, so the bread which the Lord gives to His followers is "the living bread which came down from heaven" to which Christ added this promise: "If anyone eats of this bread, he will live for ever" (John 6. 51). This bread is His body, given to His believers so that they may live henceforth His life, while awaiting the fulfillment of His prayer to God: "Father, I desire that they also, whom thou has given me, may be with me where I am" (John 17. 24). The eucharist is the personal meeting to which Christ calls His followers to renew divine life in them for their pilgrimage on earth; it is the anticipation and the guarantee of the eternal resting-place that Christ has prepared for His believers in the house of His Father.

There is an even more obvious way in which Christ reveals how His life touches the lives of His followers. This is when He intervenes miraculously and powerfully to drive back the forces of illness and even of death, and to make one of His followers participate, in anticipation, in His own victory over death. It is true that while all the believers take part in the eucharist, miracles are uncommon and not many believers share in them, and, moreover, this has always been the case. During the time of His ministry Jesus cured only a few of the sick and only raised a few from the dead. Nobody has the right to a miracle just because he has faith; and nobody should be an unbeliever because he has not benefited from a miracle. But by the miracles He has effected, and by those He still effects, Christ shows all the believers that deliverance is promised to them; He gives them all the assurance that the communion started between Him and them in this present life will be completed in total redemption.

This is what Saint Paul reminds the Colossians in the passage we started to cite earlier:

> Your life is hid with Christ in God.
> When Christ who is your life appears, then
> you also will appear with him in glory.
> (Col. 3. 3-4)

This is the ultimate prospect which is opening up for all the believers.

For them, the dominant fact is not death, for they are moving towards death just as inevitably as the unbelievers. The dominant fact is the living Christ, with whom they entered into communion during their earthly lives, who has already created true life in them, who, through death, will reveal their life which is now hidden, and who, finally, will join them to Him in glory.

Faith in God does not absolve the believer from common, biological laws; it does not allow him to escape physical death. But it completely transforms death. Death is not the ultimate end of human existence. It is "a crisis in growth which leads to a greater dimension of life". It is the flowering of that life in Christ which now is at its feeble beginning.

As the believer goes along in life, as the years pass and gradually the shadows lengthen on the horizon, he realizes, like the unbeliever, and even more so, that time is short. He also feels the powers of death approaching; he senses their presence within him in the guise of tiredness, old age and illness. But even more he senses the powers of the real life at work within him.

The divine life of which the Gospel speaks is dynamic and not static. The new life begins with a birth, as does all physical life, and every creature is born in order to grow. This is as true on the spiritual level as on the biological level. The newborn of the Spirit, the believers, are at first, says Saint Paul, "babes in Christ" (I Cor. 3. 1). They must grow in order to become "mature men" (I Cor. 2. 6) and to attain to "the measure of the stature of the fullness of Christ" (Eph. 4. 13; cf. Col. 1. 28).

In a normal Christian life, nurtured by Christ who is present in His word and in the eucharist, the forces of death and the forces of life are not evenly balanced. The divine powers of life, slowly perhaps, but surely, triumph over the powers of death, and the believer experiences what Saint Paul expresses so concisely: "Though our outer nature is wasting away, our inner nature is being renewed every day" (II Cor. 4. 16). In truth what the believer sees before him is victory over death, victory made real.

In this perspective, the purely physical death of the believer is nothing. It puts an end to nothing, it impairs nothing; it is no longer death. The believer has put real death behind him; he did that on the day when, joining himself to Christ in faith and through baptism, he died with Him and was raised with Him. True life started when communion with Christ began. The believer is not on his way to the grave; he is on his way to Christ who knows him and whom he knows. Physical death only serves ultimately to disclose the true life in its fullness, just as the sightlessness of the man born blind, of whom Saint John speaks, only served to reveal the light to him.

III

You will have noticed that everything we have said about victory over death and eternal life only applies to the believers. Then what is the fate of the unbeliever? We should say a few words about that.

All the promises in the New Testament concerning life after death are intended for the believers. This is why the doctrinal message of the Gospel: the proclamation of the Lord who died and rose from the dead and who comes again, is always accompanied by an urgent exhortation to believe. There is no salvation outside faith. Those who do not believe cannot rise again. They do not possess the Spirit; they are only "flesh"; and "flesh and blood cannot inherit the Kingdom of God" (I Cor. 15. 50).

When the New Testament mentions resurrection in connection with unbelievers it is always in a particular sense. It is a case of resurrection to "judgment" (John 5. 29; cf. Rev. 20. 12-15), that is, a resurrection which reveals a state of condemnation, in contrast to a "resurrection to life" which affirms that the believer receives full possession of divine life. The resurrection of unbelievers is quite the opposite to resurrection in the proper sense of the word. Also, in contrast to the promises of eternal life which are made to the believers, the New Testament enumerates warnings to those who scorn the gift of God in His Son. The reproachful words of Jesus to "those who have not known him," the troubles in store for those who, because they do not believe, will go "into outermost darkness, where there is wailing and gnashing of teeth," "into the fiery furnace," "into the consuming fire of judgment," "far from the Lord's presence," - all these descriptions, depicted so vividly in Christian art, are in all the accounts.

However, God Himself does not take "those who are lost" as being irretrievably lost. The New Testament often contrasts "those for whom salvation begins" now and "those who are on the way to perdition" at the present time (I Cor. 1. 18; II Cor. 2. 15). It sometimes mentions believers who have gone through the first stage and are "saved" (Eph. 2. 5, 8). But the opposite term, which here would be "lost," those whose ruin is certain and who are, as it were, already destroyed, this term never appears. When it is a case of "lost sheep"

(Matt. 10. 6; 15. 24; Luke 15. 4, 6) or a "son which was lost" (Luke 15. 24, 32) mention is always made immediately that salvation came to deliver them from destruction. "For the Son of man has come to seek and to save that which was lost" (Luke 19. 10).

This contrast between the state of the unbelievers on the strictly religious level - they are condemned by their refusal to believe - and the demands of theological thinking: God must establish His Kingdom over the whole world to reveal His glory in its fullness; this contrast explains God's policy of intervening untiringly, both with His grace and in anger, on behalf of those who do not seek Him. If, on the historical level, His will is revealed in His censure of the ungodly (Rom. 9-11), this historical will is ordered by His eschatological will, and the latter claims that redemption can reach all those who have fallen into sin (Rom. 3. 23-24; 5. 18; 11. 32).

This is why the New Testament suggests that, just as God's intentions for the believers go beyond the limits of this present life, so God continues to draw to Him, by ways which go beyond the limits of the present time, those who have not yet confessed the name of Jesus Christ. The love of God still seeks out those condemned by divine justice. Even for those who, as sinners, have already died, there still remains a possibility of divine life (cf. I Pet. 4. 6). For God can save "as through fire" (I Cor. 3. 15; cf. 5. 5). So representations of "hell" and "purgatory" are at the service of universal redemption.

As for those ever-present sectarians, who produce theories implying that there can only be a few who are "chosen," as if God were not powerful enough to save more, they add the odious to the ridiculous. The Christian faith recognizes a God who "wishes all mankind to be saved and to come to a knowledge of the truth" (I Tim. 2. 4; cf. 4. 10). This is why neither the New Testament nor the confessions of the Church make damnation an article of faith.

Unless faith which is the condition for salvation becomes optional, unless the risks of redemption endanger divine love and justice, the history of salvation will reach the only end which is compatible with divine majesty: all creatures will ultimately, one day or another, agree to reflect voluntarily the glory of God. It is this perspective which gives their full and proper meaning to the proclamations of the disappearance of death (I Cor. 15. 26; Rev. 21. 4), of the submission to Christ of all powers "in heaven and on earth and under the earth" (Phil. 2. 10), of reconciliation and peace for the whole universe through the blood of the cross (Col. 1. 20), so that "God may be all in all" (I Cor. 15. 28).

There will perhaps be some surprise that we seem to be reaching the end of our lectures without describing life after death. We have only searched the thought of the New Testament and the biblical writers are very reserved on this subject. We look in vain to find in them the equivalent of those descriptions of heaven and hell which so many believers have felt impelled to write throughout the ages.

In speaking of life in the new world, the gospel writers make use of images like that of a feast given by an important person for his guests, that of a banquet presided over by the Messiah, that of the wedding feast of the Lamb. These pictures reveal one important fact. Life in heaven will be a joyful communion with the divinities, known "partially" in this world, and seen, as Saint Paul says, "in a mirror, dimly, but then face to face," communion also with all those who have been redeemed by Christ and gathered into the many mansions of His Father's house.

From now on the life of the believer is oriented in this perspective - a perspective which is continuous and unbroken since, for the believer, there is no death in the religious - and the only decisive - sense of the word, since there is no longer any separation from God. Christ has revealed God to each of His followers and has opened before them the way which leads to the Father. In Jesus Christ, the victor over death, death takes an essentially positive meaning for the believer. It is growth and not destruction; it is gain and not loss. From now on the believer is associated, through faith, with the victory of Christ; he is destined for eternal life and resurrection.

He will live henceforth in peace, without boastful confidence if this earthly life opens up many possibilities before him, and without being discouraged if age or illness or the various troubles which beset a man enfeeble him in body and spirit. For the believer knows that "nothing can separate him from the love of God which is in Jesus Christ" (Rom. 8. 38-39), who has delivered him from the vanities of this world, from the anguish of death and from the uncertainty of what comes after death. The believer will simply say with Blaise Pascal:

> I hold out my arms to the one who sets me free,
> who was foretold for four thousand years,
> who came to earth to suffer and die for me,
> at a time and in a place which had been foretold.
> And through His grace I await death in peace
> in the hope of being eternally one with Him,
> and yet I live this present life with joy,
> either in the benefits He is pleased to give me,
> or in the misfortunes He sends me for my good
> and which, by His example, He has taught me to endure.

NOTES

1. *L'homme face à la mort*, Delachaux & Niestlé, Neuchâtel-Paris, 1952, p. 171-186.

2. Pages 251 and 253 taken from the English translation by R. Ashley Audra and Cloudesley Brereton: *The Two Sources of Morality and Religion*, New York, 1935, and used with the agreement of the reprint publisher, Greenwood Press.

The People of God in Early Christianity[1]

According to the New Testament the expression "the people of God" is used to describe two different religious and sociological realities. The people of God is Israel, and it is also the Church.

The people of God, first, as in the Old Testament, is the people set apart by God from the time of the patriarchs, through whom, in the course of the ages, He has made His revelations (cf. Rom. 9. 4-5). He delivered them from bondage in Egypt (cf. Acts 7. 34; Hebr. 11. 25), and He visited them with His salvation by sending Jesus the Messiah as He had promised (Luke 1. 68-79; 2. 32; 7. 16). The great majority of Israel did not welcome the One God sent to them but that in no way changes their place in God's eyes. To the question "Has God rejected his people?" Saint Paul replies: "By no means; God has not rejected his people whom he foreknew" (Rom. 11. 1-2), "the gifts and the call of God are irrevocable" (Rom. 11. 29). According to the New Testament, it is not God who rejects His people; it is Israel who always rejects the calls of God, formerly delivered by Moses (Acts 7. 27-39), now brought by the Apostles (Acts 13. 46). Although the deafness of Israel to the preaching of the Gospel gives Christ's witnesses the right to carry their message to the Gentiles, it does not bring about the fall from grace of God's chosen people. In spite of its temporary lack of obedience to the Gospel Israel keeps its privileges of being for ever the people of God.

The people of God, in the New Testament, is also the Church, bringing together in unity the Jews and the Gentiles who believe in the Messiah Jesus (cf. Eph. 2. 11-13). Saint Paul writes to the Christians in Corinth: "We are the temple of the living God; as God said, 'I will live in them and move among them; I will be their God and they shall be my people'" (II Cor. 6. 16; cf. Lev. 26. 12; Ezek. 36. 28; 37. 27). In the epistle to the Romans, it is to the Church of the Jews and Gentiles that he applies the prophecy of Hosea: "Those who were not my people, I will call 'my people,' they will be called 'sons of the living God'" (Rom. 9. 25-26; cf. 2. 21; 2. 1). The first epistle of Peter honors those who believe in Christ with the titles given to Israel: "You are a chosen race, a royal priesthood, a holy nation, God's own people..., once you were no people but now you are God's people" (I Pet. 2. 9-10; cf. Ex. 19. 3-6; Isaiah 43. 21; Hosea 2. 25). This list could be even longer. These examples will suffice to show that the Church is the people of God because it is heir to the promises of the old covenant. By its faith in the Messiah Jesus, it is in continuity with Israel's past. This idea, shown so clearly in our examples, is explicit or implicit on every page of the New Testament. The story of God and His people, which begins in Israel, continues in and through the Church which received the promised Messiah and believes in Him. The Church is the people of God which lives out the fulfillment of the promises.

The assurance of Christ's followers that they are the people of God is expressed nowhere more clearly than in the word "Church" which they have kept, in preference to any other, to describe themselves. The idea never entered their heads that they might be one sect among many. It is those outside who call them "a sect of the Nazarenes" (Acts 24. 5), more or less comparable to "the party of the Sadducees" or "the Pharisees" (Acts 5. 17; 15. 5). As for the Christians, they did not appropriate for themselves any of the names held by those Jews who, in the Christian era, were more concerned with living in conformity to the will of God. Christ's followers are not "a synagogue of pious men [Hasidaeans]" (I Macc. 2. 42), nor even a "congregation of the new covenant" (Damascus Fragments 6. 19) - the Christians, as we shall see later, are very sparing in their use of the adjectives "old" and "new" - they are the Church of God, that is the Messianic people, and not a fragment or a remnant of that people, and still less a new formation without any roots in Israel's past.

The old expression "the Church of God" means to the Jews the solemn assembly of the whole of Israel brought together by God in the desert to receive His law and His covenant (Deut. 4. 10 etc.; cf. Acts 7. 38). Now that God has fulfilled His promises and the hope of Israel is realized in the coming of the Messiah Jesus, it is around Him that all Israel and even the Gentile nations should gather.

By divine right first place belongs to the Jews. For the fact of Christianity is the fulfillment of the Scriptures. The ministry and death of Jesus happened in conformity to God's plan (Acts 2. 23); the resurrection of the Messiah was foretold by David (Acts 2. 31); all the prophets predicted that He would be the instrument of salvation (Acts 10. 43); the pouring-out of the Spirit and the new life which inspires the believers fulfill the earlier prophecies (Acts 2. 16f). "Let all the house of Israel therefore know asuredly," declares the Apostle Peter, "that God has made him both Lord and Christ, this Jesus whom you crucified" (Acts 2. 36). Therefore let Israel repent of its sin (Acts 2. 38), that is to say of its lack of belief in Jesus of Nazareth and let it accept the salvation which has been foretold for it and which is now presented in Jesus Christ.

The people God brings together in His Son includes the Gentiles also. For Scripture did not only announce the coming of the Messiah of Israel; it foretold that the salvation He would bring would be for all nations (Luke 24. 46-47). The idea that the promise made to the chosen people is intended for all humanity is a dominant theme in the book of Acts; it determines the plan of the book. The command given by the Risen Christ to the Twelve (Acts 1. 8): "You shall be my witnesses in Jerusalem, in all Judea and Samaria and to the uttermost parts of the earth" fixes a point of departure, followed by three stages which are more theological than geographical. Christ's witnesses must testify before Jews, before those half-Jews, the Samaritans, and before the Gentiles, thus fulfilling the words of the prophet (Isaiah 49. 6) that, through the intervention of the servant of God, "salvation may reach to the end of the earth." And it is Paul, "the chosen vessel," who is particularly charged with the mission foretold by Isaiah; Paul who stands before the Roman governor and King Agrippa, "testifying...saying nothing but what the prophets said would come to pass: that the Christ must suffer, and that, by being the first to rise from the dead, he would proclaim light both to the people of Israel and to the Gentiles" (Acts 26. 22-23). What is affirmed here by the Apostle under the pen of Luke, he himself shows in his epistles, where he continually develops this theme that the Gentile believers are also part of the people of God. For the promise which is now fulfilled in Christ is as old as the election of Israel and this ancient promise, from the very beginning, has had a universal application. God said to Abraham: "in your descendants shall all the nations of the earth be blessed" (Gen. 22. 18; Gal. 3. 8; Acts 3. 25). And the posterity of Abraham is Christ (Gal. 3. 16), that is to say the nation of believers who, following the example of their father

Abraham, walk in faith and obedience. Through faith in Christ these "Gentile sinners" become part of the chosen people; they are wild olive branches grafted on to the pure olive tree which is Israel (Rom. 11. 17-18). They are no longer "excluded from the commonwealth of Israel, strangers to the covenants of promise, having no hope and without God in the world" (Eph. 2. 12). They are now joined to their brothers, who have come from Judaism, into the Church of Christ.

So the New Testament offers us two different pictures of the people of God; this people is not the same in both periods of the history of salvation defined by the coming of Christ. Before the incarnation the picture is a simple one. The people of God is the Jewish nation. After the incarnation the people of God is a complex phenomenon. On the one hand it is the Jews and the Gentiles who are bound together in a common faith in Jesus Christ. It is also Israel in the flesh which as yet does not walk in obedience to the faith and so is not within the Church, but which does not lose its quality of being the people of God by virtue of the irrevocable nature of divine election. After the coming of Christ 'the people of God' goes beyond the limits of the Church, since it still includes the whole of Israel. The Jews who cannot be within the Church as believers in the Messiah Jesus still remain the people of God as the sons of Abraham. Moreover the Church, by virtue of its basic christological faith, gathers together believers "of every race, nation, people and tongue" and goes beyond the narrow confines of the Jewish race.

However, to show the difference between the people of God who are the physical descendants of Abraham and the believers who follow Christ, the New Testament never mentions the "old people of God" or the "new people of God" or an "old" or a "new" Israel. Although the Apostle Paul on one occasion describes the Israelites as "Israel by the flesh" (I Cor. 10.

18), he never uses the opposite expression "by the spirit" to describe the Church. It was the Fathers of the second century who introduced the terms "new people of God," "true Israel," "spiritual Israel" into the Christian vocabulary. This manner of expression became so common and customary in the Church that it is now hardly recognized as being traditional and not biblical.[2]

The writers of the New Testament were wont to weigh their words carefully. If they do not speak of two peoples of God while they distinguish between the old and the new covenant, and while they realize that Jesus Christ is a sign of contradiction in Israel, it is because in their view God has only one people, just as Christ has only one Church. Neither the unbelief of the Jews, nor the Gentiles' accession to the rank of spiritual sons and heirs of Abraham, puts into question the one-ness of the people of God.

II

Why does the Church which believes in Jesus the Messiah who is rejected by the Jews, the Church in which the divine Spirit works its regenerative power, why do these believers who live "in the new life of the Spirit" (Rom. 7. 6) not form a new people of God, a spiritual Israel? To try to answer this question we must broaden the debate and see the force of "old" and "new" in the thought of the biblical writers.

Newness is the characteristic of the creations or re-creations brought about by God to save His first work which was spoiled by sin and to raise mankind from the natural level, as Saint Paul describes it, to the spiritual level. As soon as new realities appear they cause the disappearance of the corresponding elements in the first creation, now considered old and obsolete.

The first Christians inherited from Judaism faith in the sovereign intervention of God who will put an end to the present system and who will create a new universe. But their certainty that God has intervened in Christ to save the world changed their view of history. While for the Jews the whole drama of salvation is eschatalogical, in the sense that the Messiah will only arrive at the end of time to preside over the reestablishment of all things, for the Christians, salvation takes place in two stages defined by the coming of Christ into history and again at the end of history. The second coming of Christ on the last day will be the sign of the advent of the world which is to come. At that time the believers, raised up and clothed in glory in their spiritual bodies, will reach the fulfillment of their redemption (I Cor. 15. 23-57). Then God will make all things new, for the former things will have passed away (Rev. 21. 4-5).

Christian redemption, which will be completed at the Parousia, begins with the coming of Christ in history. The incarnation is the beginning of the reign of the Holy Spirit, "the powers of the age to come" (Hebr. 6. 5), and brings about three new things: the new covenant, the new man and the new commandment.

The new covenant which Jesus establishes in the eucharist and which He seals with His blood on the cross, is substituted for the old covenant which is now useless, since the believers are now saved by faith in Christ and no longer by Mosaic Law (cf. II Cor. 3. 6) and sacrifices in the Temple (cf. Hebr. 8). The Holy Spirit, which rested on Jesus during His ministry, after His glorification is given to all who are one with Him through faith. "If anyone is in Christ, he is a new creation; the old has passed away, behold, the new has come."[3] The believer walks "in newness of life" (Rom. 6. 4). But all things are not yet made new; far from it. Although it is real, this renewal of the being remains partial at the present time because the old man still exists in the new man. Paul in no way conceives this coexistence as being static. On the contrary he sees it as vital and dynamic. Here also the rule which characterizes all God's re-creations in view of salvation prevails: the new can only be established to the destruction of the old. Divine power works on the believer who has received the Spirit and urges him to put to death the old man within him (Col. 3. 5), so that the new creation can grow in him and he can develop from being a babe in Christ to a mature man (I Cor. 3. 1; 2. 6). From now on the believer, in the Spirit which dwells within him, has "the first fruit" (Rom. 8. 23) or "the guarantee" (II Cor. 1. 22; 5. 5; Eph. 1. 14) of salvation; the gift of the Spirit is the pledge of ultimate resurrection.[4] In its own way, the gospel of John develops Pauline ideas in speaking of the divine birth or the birth of the Spirit - that is to say of a new birth through which the believer must go (John 3. 3-5) in order to possess from this point on eternal life and the certainty that Jesus will raise him up on the last day (6. 40, 54). John adds that it is the believers born to divine life who are called to practice the "new commandment" of true love of which Jesus has set the example (13. 34). Though not speaking specifically of the new law, the Apostle Paul teaches that the new man lives under the law of Christ (I Cor. 9. 21) and no longer under the law of Moses.

The Gospel introduces three new aspects of salvation into history: a new covenant, which means that the redemption accomplished by Christ makes the old institutions valid for salvation under the old covenant null and void; a new man, regenerated by the Spirit, which puts to death the old man within him; and a new commandment so that from now on the believer serves His Lord "not under the old written code but in the new life of the Spirit" (Rom. 7. 6). In short, these three facts, a new covenant, a new man, and a new commandment, exhaust the list of new items necessary for the people of God, chosen in Abraham and redeemed in Christ, to realize their calling.

It is impossible to add a fourth to this list of new creations of the Spirit which have taken the place of the outdated institutions, that of a new people of God taking the place of the old people of God. The people of God of the old covenant is not destined to disappear, and the people of God of the new covenant is not a new creation. To describe the Jews as the old Israel is to take away their privilege of being the chosen people which God still keeps for them, although the majority of them have not yet turned to the Messiah Jesus; it is to deny the "mystery," that important element in God's plan, that all Israel will ultimately be saved (Rom. 11. 25-26). To describe the Church as the new Israel is to imagine that God has made a new tree spring up, but this is not so - the Gentile believers are branches grafted on to the root of Israel and borne by it (Rom. 11. 17-18). The everlastingness of the privilege of Israel on one hand and the continuity of the divine work on the other, do not permit us to apply to the people of God the adjectives "old" and "new". God has only one people.

The basis of the Apostles' preaching of the Gospel to the Jews and the Gentiles is the divine promise made to Abraham, that in his posterity all the nations of the earth shall be blessed (Acts 3. 25; Gal. 3. 8-16). In the design of God, the election of the patriarch has universal import. Abraham is the stock of a people which will spread from Israel to all mankind. God therefore announces in advance that He will never have more than one people. The arrival of the Messiah will not result in the uprising of a new people - that would be a denial of God's promise - but in the bringing about, according to God's promises, of a new and everlasting covenant (cf. Jer. 31. 31; Isaiah 55. 3) and of the pouring out of the Holy Spirit so that God will be served by new creatures, living the law of Christ.

God has only one people, but, in so far as the whole of Israel does not confess that Jesus of Nazareth is the Messiah foretold by the prophets, this people includes some who do not yet live "in obedience of the faith" as Saint Paul says. The Apostle's expression emphasizes that the only line of division between the two parts of the people of God, between the Church and the still unbelieving Israel, is the person of Jesus Christ. This is doubtless the reason why the first Christians chose to describe themselves with the word "Church" which is more or less equivalent to the expression "people of God" and which leaves a door open to Israel still called to salvation in the Messiah. If they had called themselves the "New Covenant" they would have emphasized that they were cutting themselves off from the people of the old covenant.

If we give a sociological significance to this designation of "new covenant," if we make this the characteristic name for a group of believers, we cut off these believers from the people as a whole and make them a sect. In this respect the example of the community of Qumrân is a striking one. "The New Covenant" is one of the many titles of the community, and in the writings which have come from it, the contrast between the two covenants and the developments of the new covenant are much more marked than in the New Testament. According to the *Damascus Document*, the covenant made by God with Abraham, Isaac and Jacob which is valid for ever (3. 2-4), is only renewed with the Community (3. 12-19). In Qumrân itself there are many texts which make the "sons of light" "the survivors of the covenant" of God (I QM 13. 8), while the "ungodly in the covenant" that is, the unbelieving Jews, are ranked with the Gentiles among "the sons of darkness" (*ibid.* 1. 1-2). This is a complete contradiction of the Pauline concept that God has not rejected His people and that all Israel will be saved. If there is one point at which the infant Church differs from the Qumrân community it is in the idea of the Covenant and the People of God. In Qumrân, there is no hesitation in saying that salvation is reserved for the members of the group and reflections on the new covenant result in a narrowing of the people of God. In the Church few parallels between the two covenants are made, as if there was an attempt to keep away from sectarian theology, and in the few instances where there is effective mention of the new covenant in Christ, the inclusive nature of this covenant is always emphasized. It is a covenant made "for many" (Mark 14. 24), that is to say, for all; it is a covenant in which the children of Israel will have their place by right when they turn to the Lord (cf. II Cor. 3. 6 and 16), and the same broad spirit pervades the texts in Hebrews on the new covenant (8, 9. 15; 12. 24). In short, in the Christian texts, the new covenant is the instrument of a salvation newly realized by Jesus Christ and intended for all the people of God.

III

Beginning in the second century a new vocabulary is gradually introduced into the Church. Emphasis is placed on the originality of the Christian people who are distinct from the Jews and the Gentiles. "There are in this world," explains the apologist Aristides to the Emperor, "three kinds of men, those whom you call god-worshippers, the Jews and the Christians."[5] This implies that the Christians constitute a third nation in opposition to both the Jews and the Greeks. The expression which was to become quite well-known in the early centuries, appears for the first time in the *Predigt des Petrus*: "We find in the Scriptures that the Lord speaks as follows: 'Behold, I establish a new covenant for you, not like the covenant I established with your ancestors on mount Horeb.' He has established a new covenant for you; Hellenism and Judaism are out-dated and you are a new people who offer new worship, the Christians."[6] The three kinds of people are mentioned in Paul's exhortation to the Corinthians: "Give no offense to Jews or to Greeks or to the Church of God" (I Cor. 10. 32) but the Apostle regards the three groups as a whole, like the vast public audience which watches the Christians flourish and before whom the believers must honor the Gospel. Basically the Apostle simply means: give offense to no-one. He enumerates them to give a better comprehension of the whole world. Moreover, to make the Christians a third nation would be to separate them from the Jews as much as from the Greeks; that would make them a third people. The expression "new people" can be found in the Epistle of Barnabas. He declares that Christ suffered "to prepare the new people for himself" and that He gave His body as a sacrifice "for the sins of his new people." (5. 7; 7. 5). It is "this people" who inherit salvation and not the people "who appeared first in history" (13. 1f).

Justin Martyr calls the Christians "a different people" from the Jews (Dial. 119. 3) and he is the first, if we are not mistaken, to describe the Church as the spiritual Israel. He writes: "The true, spiritual, Israelite race, that of Judah, of Jacob, of Isaac and of Abraham, who in uncircumcision received testimony for its faith from God, who has been blessed and called the father of many peoples, it is we, whom Christ crucified has brought to God" (Dial. 11. 5).

Although the early Fathers make the Church the new people of God and the spiritual Israel, they by no means intend to break with the old covenant. There is no sign of Marcionism in them. It is on the past of Israel, which is their past, that they rely when replying to the Gentiles' accusation that they preach a new, and therefore suspect, religion in an era when there is little respect for institutions not hallowed by time. Already, before the Christian era, the great argument of Jewish propaganda among educated Gentiles was the great antiquity of the traditions of Israel in which the writers of the Greek world found inspiration. The same argument is used unhesitatingly by the Christian apologists who claim as their own the writings of the Old Testament. "It is from our teachers, that is, from the teaching of the prophets, that Plato borrows his theory, when he teaches that God created the world out of unformed matter," writes Justin Martyr (Apol. 76) and Tertullian shows that the coming of Christ was the fulfillment of very early prophecies when he says to the Romans: "for you also the credibility of something is proved by its antiquity" (Apol. 19).

The ecclesiastical writers do not lost sight of the fact that Christianity's roots are to be found deep in the revelations granted in earlier times to Israel. However, they no longer have the apostolic concept of the one-ness of the people of God and they give to the Church the attributes of "new people" and "spiritual Israel" which will be preserved in Christian tradition. There are three reasons for this change of attitude.

A psychological reason: in the very beginnings of Christianity the firm tie binding the Church to Judaism could not help but be felt. The Apostles were Jews and Paul himself did not feel that he ceased to belong to his people because he preached Jesus the Messiah. In the second century the bearers of the Gospel are Greeks, more sensitive to the originality of the Gospel and to the ever greater distance between the Church and Israel.

A historical reason: events brought out the difference. The destruction of the Temple in A.D. 70 - and the war, in a certain sense the Messianic war, which preceded it - did not arouse the same reactions among the Christians and Jews, and thus made it clear to both of them that they were going their separate ways.[7] Moreover, the imperial power did not mete out the same treatment to the Christians and the Jews. Nero's persecution was aimed only at the Christians. Later, under Trajan, Pliny the governor of Bithynia was not inclined to allow to the Christians denounced in his court the dispensation granted to the Jews; the latter were not required to make sacrifices to the Emperor and to the gods.[8]

A theological reason: the facts of history make the theological affirmation that God has only one people more difficult. The Apostles still lived in the hope that the Jewish people would turn to the Messiah. Their anti-Judaism is little more than disapproval of the Jews' unbelief, and if this disapproval is sometimes expressed in violent terms, it is nevertheless dominated by love of Israel and by the appeals addressed to Israel to believe.[9] Let Israel accept the Gospel, let the whole of Israel come into the Church; the theological affirmation will express a reality, God will have only one people, *de facto, de iure*. From the second century, this view becomes blurred. Reality inspires theology with a more realistic point of view. From now on the Church is called the new people of God, the true, spiritual Israel.

Let us conclude briefly. It is not too bold to suppose that if Saint Paul had read the Fathers, he would have expressed the same surprise as at Corinth when he learned of the divisions separating the believers. And in the same tone as he said: "Is Christ divided?" he would have added: "Has God two peoples?" He would have set the eternal plan of God against the accidental events of reality. He would have recalled that God did not reject the Jews in spite of their lack of belief in the Messiah and that the Gentile believers were grafted on to the stock of Israel, so that the unity of the people of God was maintained. He would perhaps have said particularly: "Have you not read that salvation has come to the Gentiles, so as to make Israel jealous?" (Rom. 11. 11). And he would have urged the Gentile believers to fulfill the law of Christ with an ardor capable of inciting the jealousy of Israel.

NOTES

1. *Foi et vie,* 63, 1964, p. 386-400.

2. M. Carrez was well aware of the problem; he examined it shrewdly but unfortunately too briefly in "Le Nouvel Israel. Réflexions sur l'absence de cette désignation de l'Eglise dans le Nouveau Testament," *Foi et vie,* 1959, 6, p. 30-34.

3. II Cor. 5. 17. Cf. also Gal. 6. 15; Col. 3. 10; Eph. 4. 24. In connection with II Corinthians 5. 17 let us note that the current translation "all is new" is based on a later and obviously faulty text ("all" is not to be found in the earliest and most authentic texts). The transcriber has forgotten that according to the Apostle, and, for that matter, the whole of the New Testament, Christian redemption is brought about in two stages: the regeneration of man by the Spirit here and now and, at the end of time, the reestablishment of all things. Also, how could the Apostle who has just said in the same epistle that "we groan in our earthly home longing for a building from God in heaven" (II Cor. 5. 1-2) and who writes to the Romans (8. 8) that "the sufferings of this present time are not worth comparing with the glory that is to come;" how could the Apostle, who lives with a thorn in his flesh which is not taken away from him (II Cor. 12. 7-8) say that *all* is made new *now*? All will be made new at the second coming of Christ.

4. We should note that the expression "old World" and "new world" which appear more often, if that is possible, than the expressions "old Israel" and "new Israel" under the pen of contemporary writers, are not to be found in the New Testament. The biblical writers speak of the present world and the world to come, and they always place the transition from one world to another - the changing of *eons* - at the end of history, at the time of the parousia. What coexists between the resurrection of Christ and His second coming is not two *eons* outdoing each other; temporal splendors come one after another and are not concomitant. What do coexist, and only within the believer, are two contrary forces: the flesh - in the inclusive sense of Paul - a nature which holds the believer back (the old man who does not wish to die) and the Holy Spirit which urges the believer forward (the new man called to grow and develop). It is only through the Spirit given to the believer that the power of the world to come can

be already at work here and now. This is why, in the overall view, the present age is still evil (Gal. 1. 4). - Cf., among others, W. Michaëlis, "Zur Frage der Aeonenwende," *Theol. Blätter*, 1939, col. 113-118; "Reich Gottes und Aeonenwende in der Verkündigung Jesu," *Festschrift J. Schmid*, 1963, p. 161-166.

5. *Apol.* 2. Cf. also M. Simon, *Verus Israël. Etude sur les relations entre Chrêtiens et Juif dans l'empire romain (135-425)*, 1948, p. 17. A. Puech (*Les apologistes grecs du IIe siècle de notre ère*, 1912, p. 38) stands with those who, on the concordant depositions of the Syriac and Armenian versions, maintain that the quadripartite division "Barbarians and Greeks, Jews and Christians" is more probable. In this case the Christians and Jews form a single group which is in contrast to that of the Gentiles.

6. E. Preuschen, *Antilegomena*, 1901, p. 53 and 144.

7. Cf. P. H. Menoud, "L'Eglise naissante et le Judaïsme," *Etudes théol. et. relig.*, 1952, 1, p. 30f and n. 44, translated *supra* p. 436-496.

8. *Ibid.* p. 47f.

9. *Ibid.* p. 6-22. What is said about the attitude of Stephen (p. 23-24) goes too far. Cf. the shrewd observations of P. Benoit, *Revue biblique*, 1954, p. 136.

The Preaching of the Gospel and the Celebration of the Sacraments in the Infant Church[1]

At the present time, almost everywhere, Church law and discipline, or even customary habits, do not place the preaching of the Gospel and the celebration of the sacraments on the same level. The ability to preach the word of God is not necessarily always accompanied by an ability to perform the rites of baptism or celebrate the eucharist. The stricter requirements when the sacraments, and particularly communion, are concerned, are to be found not only within almost all Christian communities but even in ecumenical relationships.

Let us cite a few examples. In the Roman Catholic Church the tendency is to entrust to the deacons all the functions of the ministry of the word, but to reserve the celebration of the eucharist for the priests. In most Protestant churches there is no difficulty in a layman mounting the pulpit on occasion, or even regularly, while baptism and the communion are the province of the clergy. In the Reformed Church particularly, there must be some exceptional circumstances for laymen, already authorized to preach, to be able to celebrate the sacraments also. If this power is conferred on them it takes the name of "pastoral delegation." Nothing indicates better that, for those of the Reformed faith, in principle only the pastor, because of his ordination or his consecration - both terms are in use - has proper liturgical qualifications.

The same distinction appears in inter-church relationships. On the one hand, almost all churches admit that, in the present state of affairs, the practice of intercommunion is not possible, even among the confessions who are joined to each other in the World Council of Churches. On the other hand, they are much less exclusive where preaching is concerned. During the week of prayer for Christian unity in January, 1968, the Anglican Archbishop of Canterbury preached in the Roman Catholic Cathedral at Westminster, and in Neuchâtel the Roman Catholic priest of the town occupied the pulpit of the old collegiate church devoted since 1530 to Reformed worship. We must beware of giving to these events an importance they do not possess. It is a matter here of exceptional exchanges of preachers, taking place in the course of special worship services which are on the periphery of the current life of the believers. Nevertheless these events remain significant. Neither in London, nor in Neuchâtel could the preacher, when his sermon was finished, gather together round the Lord's table the congregation which had come together beneath his pulpit; nor could the preachers have received communion from those who had invited them to preach the Gospel in their sanctuary.

It is obvious. Whether it is a matter of ecumenical relationships or the exercise of ministerial functions within a particular confession, the kerygmatic ministry and the sacramental ministry are not on the same level. In the eyes of our contemporaries, the pulpit, theologically and juridically, is lower than the altar. Why this difference of level? Is preaching deemed at this point so ineffective and innocuous that kerygmatic communion seems quite natural when eucharistic communion is forbidden, or does the believer, already deemed worthy and capable of preaching, not also have the ability to celebrate baptism and communion? In every confession, it is the same doctrine which nourishes the preaching and which upholds the sacramental liturgy. By the very freedom which it leaves to the speaker, the sermon entails more risk than the liturgy, which only needs to be read with dignity and devotion. Then why so much latitude when it is a matter of the ministry of the word and so much restriction where the sacraments are concerned?

These questions are all the more legitimate in that the infant Church presents us with a quite different picture. There the primary importance of the ministry of the word is universally evident. Although baptism and the eucharist are practiced everywhere, we do not see that the celebration is restricted to privileged ministries. It must be concluded that anyone who is recognized as worthy and able to preach and teach, by the same fact is qualified to baptize and to conduct the service of the eucharist. Let us look at this more closely.

Apostleship appears in Christian tradition as an essential kerygmatic ministry. It is as preachers that the Risen Christ sends His disciples into the world, according to Luke (24. 47f). In the corresponding passage in Matthew (28. 19-20: "Go therefore and make disciples of all nations, baptizing them...and teaching them to observe all that I have commanded you.") the practice of baptism is inserted between the charge to preach and that to teach, without which baptism would be only an unspecified rite. On this point the Gospel tradition is a faithful reproduction of reality. Paul declares that preaching is indeed his most important charge: he writes: "Christ did not send me to baptize but to preach the gospel" (I Cor. 1. 17), but these words, we repeat, do not denigrate baptism itself; they merely emphasize that the specific task of those who have seen the glorified Christ is to carry salvation to parts where it is still unknown. This is why Paul says: "Woe to me if I do not preach the gospel!" (I Cor. 9. 16). When the Apostle, faithful to his own vocation, leaves a newly established church to pursue his pioneering work further afield, he leaves behind him believers who are capable of continuing the work of preaching and teaching which he started.

The book of Acts (14. 23) shows us Paul and Barnabas installing elders in each of the churches they have founded. The scene is repeated everywhere. It is historically inaccurate in that Paul does not seem to have intended to create in His churches a Christian priesthood such as was doubtless already in existence in Jerusalem, like that of the Jewish priesthood. The word "elder" is not to be found in Paul's epistles, except in the partoral epistles. It is later, at the time of Luke and of the epistles to Timothy and Titus, that the word "elder" becomes one of the most common terms to describe the ministers of local churches. But the pictures in Acts make it quite clear that the Apostle to the Gentiles, without having the slightest intention of endowing his churches with a uniform organization, was nevertheless concerned not to leave behind him flocks without a shepherd.

This is why we encounter "prophets" and "teachers" at Corinth (I Cor. 12. 28), and elsewhere (Eph. 4. 11), as there had been at Antioch (Acts 13. 1). At work in Rome are "the prophet," "one who teaches," "one who exhorts," (Rom. 12. 6-7) and "one who presides" (Rom. 12. 8), which can mean either one who presides over a gathering, or a spiritual leader. These "leaders" are to be found again in Thessalonica; they are also charged with "admonishing" the believers, unless this is a distinct function, entrusted to another group (I Thess. 5. 12). The church at Philippi has the benefit of both "bishops" and "deacons" (Phil. 1. 1); if the deacons are charged with the work of aiding and helping, the bishops apparently fulfill the same office as the instructors at Antioch and Corinth, as the "teacher" or "exhorter" at Rome, or as those charged with "admonishing" the Thessalonians; in short, their function is one of teaching and preaching. The epistle to the Galatians (6. 6) where the Apostle writes: "let him who is taught the word share all good things with him who teaches," suggests that there was a ministry of the word, under different name, throughout almost all the Pauline churches.

The same applies to other areas apart from those won over to the Gospel by the Apostle to the Gentiles. In Jerusalem "elders" keep an eye on the community in the absence of the Apostles (Acts 11. 30). We shall come across these elders elsewhere also. They are charged to tend the flock, according to Peter (5. 1-4) and to pray for the sick, according to the epistle of James (5. 14). There is no room for doubt that these elders carry out the same duties of leading and teaching as the other different ministers at work in the Pauline churches. The leaders of the church at Ephesus called together at Miletus so that Paul can urge them to fulfill their ministry faithfully, are called at one time "elders," following the vocabulary in Jerusalem (Acts 20. 17) and at another time "bishops" (Acts 20. 28) like the ministers in Philippi. The duty of the "elder/bishops" is to "tend the flock of God," that is to say to nurture it with apostolic teaching and thus arm it against the dangers of heresy which are foretold (Acts 20. 28-31). In short, the emphasis here is on a kerygmatic ministry.

Towards the end of the first century the pastoral epistles sound the same note. They too, in the picture they draw of the different charges (deacons, elders, bishop, and apostolic delegates like Timothy and Titus) put the functions of instruction on the highest level. We read in I Timothy 5. 17:

"Let the elders who rule well be considered worthy of double honor, especially those who labor in preaching and teaching." We find once again here the pre-eminence always given to ministries of the word because the basis of the Church is the apostolic message, by which it is edified and urged to remain faithful to tradition. The function of the bishop is not limited to teaching (I Tim. 3. 2) like that of the elders; he must also be able to confute heresy (Titus 1. 9) which presupposes he has wider knowledge and is more skilled in argument. Finally, the apostolic delegates, Timothy and Titus, like the Apostle, not only have to watch over a much broader territory than one local church, but also must ensure the continuity of the kerygmatic ministry. Titus has to appoint elders in each church (Titus 1. 5), that is to say he has to carry out the task reserved for the Apostles according to the book of Acts. Timothy must be for the elders the leader which Paul was for the bishop/elders at Ephesus (I Tim. 5. 17f). Moreover, Timothy must entrust what he has learned from the Apostle "to faithful men who will be able to teach others also" (II Tim. 2. 2), which shows that the charge laid on him by the Apostle is to be perpetuated in the Church. Here it is on the level of preaching and teaching that apostolic successions is exercised.

Now let us look at the other aspect of the problem: what is the place of the sacraments in the infant Church and who is charged with performing the rites of baptism and with celebrating Holy Communion?

The reply to the first question is simple. There is absolutely no doubt of the existence of the two sacraments in the Church from the very beginning. Paul's testimony is clear. The Apostle does not know a Christian who has not been baptized, either in the churches which the Apostle himself has established (cf. I Cor. 12. 13) or in a church even older than his own mission, that of Rome (Rom. 6. 3). This latter testimony is even more important since it has often been asserted that Paul was ignorant of the exact situation in the Roman church. One thing is quite clear in his view, however: from the very moment when the Romans become believers, they are the recipients of Christ's baptism. Similarly, in the Apostle's view, there is no church which does not celebrate the eucharist. When he reminds the Corinthians that "the Lord's Supper" must not be taken "in an unworthy manner" he makes use of an expression (I Cor. 11. 23) which places it among the traditions going back to the very beginning which are universally accepted (cf. I Cor. 11. 16; 14. 33; 15. 3). Therefore there is no reason to question Luke's assertions that baptism and "the breaking of bread" were practiced from the very early days in the church in Jerusalem (Acts 2. 38; 2. 42). Moreover, the proof that the two sacraments always accompany the preaching of the Gospel is provided by the following fact. It was the question of the sacraments which provoked the first disagreements within the Church: can Gentiles who have not first become Jews be baptized (cf. Acts 10. 47) and can former Jews and former Gentiles gather at the same eucharistic table (cf. Gal. 2. 12)? We do find numerous references to baptism in early Christian writings, although it must be admitted that the traces of baptismal hymns are less obvious than it is currently fashionable to declare. If the celebration of the eucharist is more rarely confirmed, if we must wait for the testimony of Justin Martyr to have a brief description of it, this can be explained, if not be the discipline of the arcana, at least by the reluctance of the first generations of Christians to reveal to public view the very heart of their worship, which can only be understood through faith.

The Church of the first century does not only practice baptism and the celebration of the eucharist, but it also considers the two sacraments as necessary for salvation. If preaching is of prime importance because it is preaching which which brings faith to birth (Rom. 10. 17), it is through baptism that the believers become one with the crucified and resurrected Christ and live the new life of the Spirit (Rom. 6. 3f). What Paul states so explicitly is outlined implicity in the traditions gathered together by Luke. The Apostle Peter invites his hearers to go from repentance to baptism, in order to receive, along with forgiveness of sins, the gift of the Holy Spirit (Acts 2. 38); the evangelist Philip preaches the Gospel to the Ethiopian eunuch and then baptizes him (Acts 8. 35f); when the Holy Spirit descends on Cornelius and his household after Peter has preached to them, the Apostle concludes that there is now no obstacle in the way of their baptism, and not that they are absolved from being baptized (Acts 10. 44f). If the new life begins with faith and baptism, it is maintained and strengthened by participation in the eucharist. It is through the eucharist that the believers life in communion with Christ and with one another (I Cor. 10. 17). This is why Paul is so severe in his rebuke of the Corinthians who partake of the Lord's Supper "in an unworthy manner" (I Cor. 11. 27f). According to Johannine Christianity also, particpation in Holy Communion is a necessity and it is through that particpation that the believer receives divine life in its fullness (John 6. 53).

To whom is the celebration of the two sacraments which are indispensable to the life of the Church entrusted? If is more difficult to answer this second question. Undoubtedly the Apostles were the first to baptize and to celebrate the eucharist. It would be hard to believe that the Twelve, who were the only ones present at the first communion, did not preside over the service of eucharist for the believers. Yet it is noticeable that the traditions about the Apostle Peter which have been preserved in the book of Acts never show the Apostle himself performing a baptism or breaking the bread. During the visit to Caesarea is seems likely that it was the brethren from Joppa who accompanied Peter (Acts 10. 23) who baptized Cornelius and his household (Acts 10. 48). For his part, Paul is thankful that he only baptized a few believers at Corinth (I Cor. 1. 14), perhaps the first converts, "the first-fruits" (I Cor. 1. 16; 16. 15). It was these first believers to be baptized or Paul's companions who performed the other baptisms. In fact, we see that an evangelist like Philip (Acts 8. 12f; 8. 38) or a simple believer like Ananias at Damascus (Acts 9. 18) can baptize. Therefore it is clear that the Apostles did not keep the celebration of baptism to themselves nor have they instituted a purely baptismal ministry.

We have even less information about the celebration of the eucharist. The tradition about Paul tells us that he undoubtedly celebrated communion at Troas (Acts 20. 7, 11) and perhaps at Philippi (Acts 16. 34) and that is all. No text specifically states who presided over the services of the eucharist at Jerusalem when the Twelve were absent or in the Pauline churches after the departure of the Apostle. In the many lists of charges and functions which Paul gives on several occasions (I Cor. 12; Rom. 12. 6-8), there is no sign of a specifically eucharistic office, comparable to the kerygmatic ministry which is to be found wherever the Apostle established a church.

But, as the Church, from the very beginning, has a sacramental life which continues despite the absence of the Apostles, we are forced to ask ourselves of what other form of ministry or function is the charge of celebrating the eucharist a part? If we read the passages in this perspective we will see that their testimony is more positive than it seems at first glance. The "leaders" or "directors" who are at work in the churches in Thessalonica and Rome (I Thess. 5. 12; Rom. 12. 8) doubtless also preside over the service of the eucharist. Moreove, it seems certain that the bishop/ elders in Acts (20. 17) and the elders in I Peter (5. 1-4) who were charged with "tending the flock" of God, actually fulfilled a two-fold mission: preaching the Gospel and celebrating the sacraments, because the believers are nourished both by the word of God and by the eucharist. When the epistle of James (5. 14) recounts that the elders should pray for the sick and anoint them with oil, it is describing just one particular task; here again the elders apparently have the double charge of preaching and celebrating the sacraments.

So, if the Church of the first century does not designate a particular ministry of the sacraments, it is because it only recognizes ministries which are also ministries of the word. In other words, in the view of the infant Church, it goes without saying that anyone who is qualified to preach and teach by the call of God or of the Holy Spirit (I Cor. 12. 28; Acts 20. 28, etc.) and by appointment by the Apostles or their disciples (Acts 14. 23; II Tim. 22, etc.) is also qualified to celebrate the sacraments. The kerygmatic ability brings with it sacramental ability. To proclaim the word of God and to perform the eucharist are but two complementary aspects of one and the same ministry: to maintain the spiritual life of the people of God.

Christian writings in the first half of the second century follow the same line as the New Testament but become more specific. Clement of Rome makes it quite clear that the bishop/elders have the two-fold task of preaching the Gospel and conducting Holy Communion. On the one hand he declares that the Apostles, whom he presents as the preachers of salvation, "tested their first-fruits in the Spirit and installed them as bishops and deacons of the later believers" (I Cor. 42. 4). In other words these bishops and deacons, and particularly the bishops, are ministers of the word as the Apostles were. On the other hand, Clement writes that these same bishops are also "those who present the offerings in an irreproachably pious manner." (I Cor. 44. 4). These offerings presented so solemnly would appear to be the elements of the eucharist and the eucharist itself and not simply communal prayers.

Ignatius of Antioch is not merely the first to testify to the only bishopric in Asia; he also affirms the unity of the ministry of word and sacrament. He declares that the bishop preaches the Gospel (*Philad.* 11. 1) and presides over the eucharist (*Smyr.* 8. 1) and that, in these two functions, he is supported by others. These are the deacons who assist him in the ministry of the word of God (*Philad.* 11. 1; *Smyr.* 10. 1). As for the eucharist, he writes that, when it is not presided over by the bishop, it is presided over by "the one whom he has put in charge" (*Smyr.* 8. 1). Who is this replacement for the bishop? Quite naturally we would think it would be one of the elders who, in the hierarchy of Ignatius, came between the bishop and the deacons. On second thought we have doubts about this. For although the bishop of Antioch enumerates many honorable designations when he speaks of the elders, he says not one word about their duties except this: he urges the elders of Trallia as well as all the believers in this church to "support their bishop" (*Trall.* 12. 2). That is a great deal for the bishop but very little for the elders. On the other hand, Ignatius gives a very prominent place to the deacons. He keeps for them the title of *syndouloi*,

"fellow-servants" (*Eph,* 2. 1; *Magn.* 2. 1; *Philad.* 4. 1; *Smyr.* 12. 2) sometimes bestowed upon the companions of the Apostle Paul (Col. 1. 7; 4. 7). These deacons who, he says, "are so dear to me" (*Magn.* 6. 1) he places higher than the elders; as when he writes: "The deacons should be as revered as Jesus Christ, the bishop as the image of God and the elders as the council of God and the group of Apostles" (*Trall.* 3. 1). It is a deacon and not an elder who is sent as a missionary from Philadelphia to Antioch (*Philad.* 10. 1). If we take these passages into account, if moreover we think that Ignatius only recognized as tradition the practice of entrusting presiding over the eucharist to whomever was already authorized to preach, we would be inclined to think that the companion to whom the bishop of Antioch turned to celebrate the eucharist is one of the deacons who also help him in the ministry of the word. So we would find once more at Antioch the old Christian practice according to which whoever is recognized as being able to preach, can also celebrate the service of the eucharist.

Through the explicit testimony of Justin Martyr we know that Christian worship includes first the reading of the commentaries of the Apostles and the writings of the Prophets (*First Apol.* 87); then "the one who presides over the gathering of the brethren" (85) preaches the sermon, and, after all have prayed, presides over the eucharist (85; 87). The deacons distribute the bread and the wine with water to those who are present and take it also to those who cannot attend (85; 87). What is important to emphasize here is that "the one who presides" (cf. I Thess. 5. 12; Rom. 12. 8) is at one and the same time minister of word and of sacrament, like the bishop (and the deacons) at Antioch and like the bishop/elders in the time of Clement of Rome. In short, we can see the perpetuation of the original tradition according to which the one

who has been deemed worthy and able to preach and teach the Gospel is thereby also authorized to celebrate the sacraments.

To describe the later history of ministry would be beyond the scope of this work. It is time to conclude. Neither the New Testament nor the early Fathers give us an explanation of why the celebration of baptism and particularly of Holy Communion was entrusted to those who preached the Gospel. It is perhaps because it was felt instinctively that the Church lives on the word of God and the eucharist, together forming a unity which cannot be broken. This unity is shown in the fact that the infant Church did not know a eucharist which was not preceded by preaching, nor a service of the word which was not concluded in that further expression of the word - the communion of the eucharist. The balance of worship is threatened if these two constitutive elements are entrusted to officiants whose kerygmatic and liturgical capabilities are unequal. This is proved in history. Either the service of the word will be clothed in greater dignity and eminence, but then the eucharist tends to become insignificant and even disappear; or, on the other hand, there will be a tendency to become more demanding where the sacraments are concerned and their celebration will not be put into the hands of just anyone who can preach. Then preaching will be nothing more than a complement to the reading of the Scriptures, and soon an optional complement. So preaching becomes devalued. It also becomes devalued if it takes place in circumstances where the eucharistic communion, which should follow it, is forbidden. In the wisdom of the early Church we can find many great and useful lessons for our present situation.

NOTE

1. *L'Evangile hier et aujourd'hui. Mélanges offerts au Professeur Franz-J. Leenhardt*, Geneva, 1968, p. 99-108, by kind permission of éditions Labor et Fides, Geneva.